Teaching
Holocaust and Human Behavior

Facing History & Ourselves is an international educational and professional development organization whose mission is to use lessons of history to challenge teachers and their students to stand up to racism, antisemitism, and other forms of bigotry and hate. For more information about Facing History & Ourselves, please visit our website at www.facinghistory.org.

Copyright © 2018 by Facing History & Ourselves, Inc. All rights reserved.

Facing History & Ourselves® is a trademark registered in the US Patent & Trademark Office.

Last updated August 2025.

Cover art: iStock.com / Claudiad; iStock.com / monkywrenched

ISBN: 978-1-940457-33-8

Contents

Get Started	1
Lesson 1: Introducing the Unit	4
Lesson 2: Exploring Identity	13
Lesson 3: Stereotypes and "Single Stories"	30
Lesson 4: Universe of Obligation	42
Unit Assessment Step 1: Introducing the Writing Prompt	50
Lesson 5: The Concept of Race	54
Lesson 6: The Roots and Impact of Antisemitism	65
Lesson 7: World War I and Its Aftermath in Germany	76
Lesson 8: The Weimar Republic	87
Unit Assessment Step 2: Introducing Evidence Logs	113
Lesson 9: The Rise of the Nazi Party	115
Lesson 10: European Jewish Life before World War II	128
Lesson 11: Dismantling Democracy	144
Lesson 12: Do You Take the Oath?	161
Lesson 13: Laws and the National Community	173
Unit Assessment Step 3: Adding to Evidence Logs, 1 of 3	185
Lesson 14: The Power of Propaganda	187
Lesson 15: Youth and the National Community	200
Lesson 16: Kristallnacht	218
Lesson 17: Responding to a Refugee Crisis	242
Lesson 18: Race and Space	253
Unit Assessment Step 4: Adding to Evidence Logs, 2 of 3	263

Lesson 19: The Holocaust: Bearing Witness — 265

Lesson 20: The Holocaust: The Range of Responses — 286

Lesson 21: Justice and Judgment after the Holocaust — 310

Unit Assessment Step 5: Adding to Evidence Logs, 3 of 3 — 324

Lesson 22: How Should We Remember? — 326

Lesson 23: Choosing to Participate — 340

Unit Assessment Step 6: Refining the Thesis and Finalizing Evidence Logs — 365

Get Started

Using This Unit to Help Us Understand Ourselves and Our World

Teaching "Holocaust and Human Behavior" leads students through a unit of study that examines the catastrophic period in the twentieth century when Nazi Germany murdered six million Jews and millions of other civilians, in the midst of the most destructive war in human history. Following our unique methodology, students take a parallel journey through an exploration of the universal themes inherent in a study of the Holocaust that raise profound questions about human behavior.

Throughout the unit, students will pay special attention to the choices of individuals who experienced this history as victims, witnesses, collaborators, rescuers, and perpetrators. This approach to teaching about the Holocaust helps students make connections between history and the consequences of our actions and beliefs today—between history and how we as individuals make distinctions between right and wrong, good and evil. As students examine the steps that led to the Holocaust, they discover that history is not inevitable; it is the result of our individual and collective decisions.

This unit draws upon and adapts resources from the resource book *Holocaust and Human Behavior* and its related media collection, and it follows our scope and sequence. Students begin with an examination of the relationship between the individual and society, reflect on the way humans divide themselves into "in" groups and "out" groups, and dive deep into a case study of the Weimar Republic and the Nazi Party's rise to power in Germany. Students then bear witness to the human suffering of the Holocaust and examine the range of responses from individuals and nations to the genocidal mass murder perpetrated by the Nazi regime. In the unit's later lessons, students draw connections between this history and the present day, weighing such questions as how to achieve justice and reconciliation in the aftermath of atrocities, how painful histories should be remembered, and how this history educates us about our responsibilities in the world today.

While this unit is designed to be used across a range of grade levels, in both middle and high school, we trust that teachers will adapt activities and resources to best meet the needs of their students.

Teaching Emotionally Challenging Content

Many teachers want their students to achieve emotional engagement with the history of the Holocaust and therefore teach this history with the goal of fostering empathy. However, like any examination of the Holocaust, *Teaching "Holocaust and Human Behavior"* includes historical descriptions and firsthand accounts that some students may find emotionally disturbing. We can't emphasize enough the importance of previewing the readings and videos in this curriculum to make sure they are appropriate for the intellectual and emotional needs of your students.

It is difficult to predict how students will respond to such challenging readings, documents, and films. One student may respond with emotion to a particular reading, while others may not find it powerful in the same way. In addition, different people demonstrate emotion in different ways. Some students will be silent. Some may laugh. Some may not want to talk. Some may take days to process difficult stories. For some, a particular firsthand account may be incomprehensible; for others, it may be familiar.

Our experience tells us that it is often problematic to use graphic images and films or to attempt to use simulations to help students understand aspects of this history. Such resources and activities can traumatize some students, desensitize others, or trivialize the history.

We urge teachers to create space for students to have a range of reactions and emotions. This might include time for silent reflection or writing in journals, as well as structured discussions to help students process content together. Some students will not want to share their reactions to emotionally disturbing content in class, and teachers should respect that in class discussions. For their learning and emotional growth, it is crucial to allow for a variety of responses, or none at all, from students to emotionally challenging content.

Activities and resources that we believe may be especially challenging for younger students can be found in the Extensions section. We expect teachers to incorporate such activities into their instruction as appropriate.

Fostering a Reflective Classroom Community

We believe that a classroom in which a Facing History & Ourselves unit is taught ought to be a microcosm of democracy—a place where explicit rules and implicit norms protect everyone's right to speak; where different perspectives can be heard and valued; where members take responsibility for themselves, each other, and the group as a whole; and where each member has a stake and a voice in collective decisions. You may have already established rules and guidelines with your students to help bring about these characteristics in your classroom. If not, it is essential at the beginning of this unit to facilitate a supportive, reflective classroom community.

Two ways in which you can create a strong foundation for a reflective classroom are through the use of classroom contracts and student journals. Even if you already incorporate both of these elements into your classroom, we recommend taking a moment to review both teaching strategies at facinghistory.org/thhb.

Unit Essential Question

The following essential question provides a framework for exploring this unit's main ideas and themes:

> *What does learning about the choices people made during the Weimar Republic, the rise of the Nazi Party, and the Holocaust teach us about the power and impact of our choices today?*

This essential question challenges students to make important connections between history and the power of the choices and decisions they make today. We do not expect students to determine a single, "correct" answer. Essential questions are rich and open-ended; they are designed to be revisited over time, and as students explore the content in greater depth, they may find themselves emerging with new ideas, understandings, and questions.

Guiding Questions

Each lesson includes one or more guiding questions. Unlike the unit's essential question, which is broad and open-ended, guiding questions help to direct student inquiry at the lesson level and are aligned with its specific learning objectives. Answering guiding questions requires deep thinking and textual interpretation. Unlike essential questions, guiding questions might have a clear answer, which students should be able to support with specific evidence from the lesson to demonstrate their understanding of the content.

Unit Assessment

Teaching "Holocaust and Human Behavior" includes a unit assessment that asks students to write a response to the unit's essential question in an argumentative essay. Six activities are interspersed throughout the unit to introduce students to the assessment and guide them as they gather evidence and develop their ideas, develop their theses, and begin to write their essays. The activities can be skipped if you opt not to use the unit assessment.

Please consult *Common Core Writing Prompts and Strategies*, available at facinghistory.org/thhb, for alternative prompts and additional writing strategies and graphic organizers.

Developing Student Vocabulary

The readings and videos in this unit introduce some vocabulary and concepts that may pose a challenge for your students, especially for struggling readers, so you may want to consider using a word wall strategy to keep a running list of critical vocabulary posted in your classroom that you and your students can refer to over the course of the unit. Students might have a corresponding list in a section of their journals or notebooks, and you could also challenge them to incorporate word wall terms into their writing and discussions to help them internalize and understand these challenging terms and concepts.

Accessing Online Materials

To help with your preparations for teaching these lessons and administering the unit assessment, we have conveniently organized all materials associated with this unit on our website. Visit facinghistory.org/thhb for all videos, teaching strategies, handouts, readings, and images that will help you implement this unit.

Unit Essential Question

What does learning about the choices people made during the Weimar Republic, the rise of the Nazi Party, and the Holocaust teach us about the power and impact of our choices today?

Lesson

Introducing the Unit

Duration

One 50-minute class period

Materials

 Reading
Letter to Students

 Handouts
Classroom Experience Checklist

Sample Facing History Classroom Expectations

 Teaching Strategies
Read Aloud

Journals in a Facing History Classroom

Find all materials referenced in this lesson at facinghistory.org/thhb.

Guiding Question

- How can we create a class that is both safe and challenging? How can we create an environment in which everyone is willing to take risks, test ideas, and ask questions?

Learning Objective

- Students will come together as a community of learners to develop a contract that establishes a safe but challenging environment in their classroom.

Overview

The purpose of this first lesson is to help the class develop an environment that is conducive to learning and sharing: a reflective classroom community.

Throughout this unit, students will be talking about sensitive topics, such as prejudice and discrimination, and how those concepts have impacted historical events and students' own lives. When students feel empowered to contribute honestly and wrestle with multiple perspectives besides their own, such discussions can be positive and even life-changing.

Prior to exploring the historical case study of this unit—the collapse of democracy in Germany and the steps leading up to the Holocaust—it is important that students and teachers spend some time establishing and nurturing classroom rules and expectations of respect and open-mindedness. These "habits of behavior" will equip students with the skills to engage with each other in important and sometimes uncomfortable conversations.

In this lesson you will review the classroom rules you may have already established, as well as create new norms and expectations generated by the students themselves. While we urge you to consider the language and expectations that are most appropriate for your classroom context, the handout "Sample Facing History Classroom Expectations" provides examples of the kinds of classroom norms Facing History teachers have used to support a reflective classroom community.

Context

Facing History & Ourselves conceives of its program as a journey—a journey that provides a unique and engaging way for students to study history and the world around them. As one student remarked,

> Something about our Facing History class felt different. We were studying the very things I was afraid of: being singled out, teased, and bullied; stereotyping; neighbors against neighbors in Nazi Germany. Students couldn't react angrily to how people treated each other in history and then turn around and do these very things to me.

By helping students develop as moral philosophers, critical consumers of information, and civic agents, we hope to change the way they see themselves as individuals in a larger society.

It takes a particular kind of learning environment to help students achieve these objectives.

A reflective classroom community is a place where students are encouraged to voice their own opinions—even when their ideas are unpopular—and to actively listen to others; to treat different perspectives with patience and respect; and to recognize that there are always more perspectives and there is always more to learn. Psychologist John Amaechi explains:

> Teachers have to create this emotional space where it is safe but challenging, where people can be themselves, where people can take chances and fail, where people can tell stories about themselves and reveal things about themselves without risk of derision, without fear of being marginalized. Without safety, there is nothing, there is no learning.[1]

Journal writing is also an integral part of the unit. See the teaching strategy Journals in a Facing History Classroom for important suggestions about how to incorporate journals.

The habits of behavior found in a reflective classroom community—attentive listening to diverse viewpoints, voicing clear ideas, and raising relevant questions—not only help students deeply understand historical content but also require them to practice skills essential for their role as engaged citizens. Philosopher John Dewey believed that classrooms are not the training grounds for future democratic action, but rather places where democracy is already enacted. Professor Diane Moore has argued that "encouraging students to take themselves seriously and inspiring in them the confidence to do so are two of the most important roles of an educator in a multicultural democracy."[2]

These characteristics may be helpful in teaching many different units of study, but they are essential to teaching in a Facing History & Ourselves classroom.

---

[1] See https://www.facinghistory.org/resource-library/video/john-amaechi-discusses-identity.
[2] Diane Moore, *Overcoming Religious Illiteracy: A Cultural Approach to the Study of Religion in Secondary Education* (New York: Palgrave, 2006), 11.

Notes to Teacher

1. Facing History Journals

Journals are an integral means of participation in the unit for each student. See the teaching strategy Journals in a Facing History Classroom for important suggestions about how to incorporate them into the unit.

Typically, student journals are not considered public for the entire class to read. However, informally reviewing students' journal entries can help you know the questions that are on students' minds about this unit and can be a place for individual conversations between you and each student. Doing this can also help you correct any misconceptions about what students are learning. If you choose to periodically review students' journals, it is important to inform them (and remind them throughout the unit) that you plan to do so.

2. The Facing History Classroom Contract

Facing History teachers have found that useful class contracts typically include several clearly defined expectations as well as logical consequences for those who do not fulfill their obligations as members of the classroom community.

There are many ways to facilitate the development of a classroom contract, and we suggest one method in the Activities section of this lesson. You also might revisit your current classroom contract, if the class has already created one, to determine whether the group wants to make changes to the existing contract after finishing the Letter to Students and participating in the journal activity.

The contract should be considered a living document that can be returned to or altered at any time. For this reason, you may want to structure time to return to the contract at strategic points throughout the unit—for instance, to preface a particularly emotionally charged reading or in-class activity.

3. Previewing Vocabulary

The following are key vocabulary terms used in this lesson:
- Norms
- Contract
- Community

Add these words to your word wall, if you are using one for this unit, and provide necessary support to help students learn these words as you teach the lesson.

Activities

1. Introduce the Unit

Begin by explaining to students that they are about to begin a unit called Holocaust and Human Behavior. Write this title on the board.

Pass out the reading Letter to Students. You might choose to adapt this letter to become your own version instead of using the one we have provided. Either way, read aloud the letter as a group, as students highlight any words or phrases that stand out to them.

Pass out a journal to each student. This is an appropriate time to establish the expectation that journal responses do not have to be shared publicly. Ask students to react to the Letter to Students (or your own letter) in their journals. Specific questions you can use to prompt students' writing and prepare them for the contracting activity include:

- What does it mean to have to use both your head and your heart while learning?
- What does it mean for a classroom to be a "community of learners"? In what ways does your classroom feel like a community of learners? What might help it feel more like a community of learners?

Debrief the journal prompts. To help students understand the idea of using both head and heart while learning, draw a blank head and blank heart on the board. Ask students to brainstorm what words might fill the diagram for "head learning" and the one for "heart learning." For example, students might suggest words like *events, facts,* or *vocabulary* for head learning and *relationships, morals,* or *connections* for heart learning.

Transition to the class contract by explaining that in this class, you will ask students to think about history both from an intellectual ("head") angle and from a more emotional or ethical ("heart") angle.

2. Create a Class Contract

Explain that before students begin exploring new material, the class needs to agree on some *rules, norms,* or *expectations.* You can strengthen students' vocabulary by spending a few moments asking them to define one or more of these terms. Students can record definitions in their journals.

When a community agrees on norms or expectations for behavior, these are often articulated in a *contract.* Students can define the term *contract* in their journals. A contract implies that all parties have a responsibility in upholding the agreement.

To prepare students to develop a class contract, ask them to reflect on their experiences as students in a classroom community. Pass out the handout Classroom Experience Checklist, and ask students to complete it individually.

Ask small groups of students to work together to write rules or expectations for the classroom community. Distribute handout Sample Facing History Classroom Expectations to help them get started. Students will discuss each of the sample items on the handout and decide whether they should adopt it in their class contract, modify it, or omit it. Have each group select three items from the list (or create their own) to share with the class.

We suggest keeping the final list brief (e.g., three to five items) so that the norms can be easily published in a visible place in the classroom and remembered. As groups present, organize their ideas by theme. If there are any tensions or contradictions in the expectations that have been suggested, discuss them as a class. While the process is inclusive of students' ideas, ultimately it is the teacher's responsibility to ensure that the ideas that make it into the final contract are those that will best nurture a safe learning environment.

Finally, discuss with students what they think should happen when someone violates one of the norms in the contract. It may be useful to help students distinguish between school and classroom rules and the community norms outlined in the class contract. When rules are broken, adults will often need to respond. But the students themselves should outline potential responses for rebuilding the community after an individual breaks with the norms in the class contract.

After the class has completed its contract, reaching consensus about rules, norms, and expectations, it is important for each student to signal their agreement. Students can do so by copying the contract into their journals and signing the page. If there is no time, the teacher can create printed contracts or a poster to be signed in the next class period.

Assessment

- Creating a final class contract that can be recorded in the students' journals and posted on the wall keeps everyone accountable for the learning from this lesson. The real measurement of understanding, however, resides in students' efforts to abide by the contract throughout this unit.

- Other possible formative assessments can include the handout Classroom Experience Checklist and the classroom expectations developed during the small-group activity.

Extensions

1. Letter to Parents and Guardians

Because this unit is different from many other units students experience in school, some Facing History teachers like to provide an overview of the unit to parents and guardians. One way to do this is to send a letter home. The reading "Letter to Parents and Guardians" provides a sample that you can use or adapt to inform parents about what students will experience in the weeks to come.

2. Personalizing the Journals

Since students will be invited to explore aspects of their identities throughout this unit, you might invite students to personalize their journals with images or words that represent who they are. Journals can be decorated with markers or by pasting on pictures from magazines. We suggest setting some limits for what may not be appropriate to put on a journal.

 Reading

Letter to Students

Dear students,

Welcome. You are about to begin a unit titled *Teaching "Holocaust and Human Behavior"* that was created by our organization, Facing History & Ourselves. You are joining a community of tens of thousands of students from around the world who have explored the same questions you are about to explore—questions such as: Who am I? What shapes my identity? Why do people form groups? What does it mean to belong? What happens when people are excluded from membership?

After taking part in a unit similar to the one you are about to study, one student said, "I've had 13 math classes, 20 English classes, 6 or 7 science classes, art, P.E., Spanish . . . but in all the time I've been in school, I've had only one class about being more human." In the next few weeks, you will be learning a lot about the choices made by people living in Germany before and during the Holocaust, a tragic event in which millions of children, women, and men were murdered. At the same time, you will also be learning about yourselves and the world around you. That is what we mean by "Facing History & Ourselves." As another former Facing History student explained, "When I took the Facing History course back in eighth grade, it helped me understand that history was a part of me and that I was a part of history. If I understood why people made the choices they did, I could better understand how I make choices and hopefully make the right ones."

This unit may be different from others you have experienced. In this unit, you will be asked to share your own ideas and questions, in discussions and through writing in a journal. You will be asked to listen carefully to the voices of others—the voices of people in your classroom community as well as the voices of people in the history you are studying. In this unit, you may hear things that spark powerful emotions, such as anger or sadness. You will be asked to use both your head and your heart to make sense of the choices people have made in the past and the choices people continue to make today.

At Facing History, we like to think of a unit as a journey. When taking this journey, you need to bring your journal, your curiosity, an open mind, and a willingness to share. As you embark on and continue this journey with the students and adults in your classroom, it is important for you to support each other so that everyone can do their best learning. We wish you a meaningful journey during which you learn about the past and the present, about yourself and about others. You may even find that you have changed as a result of this experience.

Thank you for participating in this journey with us.

Facing History & Ourselves

Handout

Classroom Experience Checklist

Directions: Check the box that best matches your experience as a student.

Part 1

As a student in a classroom, have you ever . . .

1. Shared an idea or question out loud? ☐ Yes ☐ No

2. Shared an idea or question that you thought might be unpopular or "stupid"? ☐ Yes ☐ No

3. Had an idea or answer to a question but decided not to share it? ☐ Yes ☐ No

4. Felt "put down" after sharing an idea or asking a question? ☐ Yes ☐ No

5. Felt smart or appreciated after sharing an idea or asking a question? ☐ Yes ☐ No

6. Asked for help in understanding something? ☐ Yes ☐ No

7. Been confused but have not asked for help? ☐ Yes ☐ No

8. Interrupted others when they have been speaking? ☐ Yes ☐ No

9. Been interrupted by others when you have been speaking? ☐ Yes ☐ No

10. Said something that you thought might have hurt someone's feelings? ☐ Yes ☐ No

11. Thought of your classroom as a community? ☐ Yes ☐ No

Part 2

1. What do you think should happen in a classroom in order for the best learning to take place?

2. What can students do to support your learning and each other's learning?

3. What can teachers do to support your learning?

 Handout

Sample Facing History Classroom Expectations

- Listen with respect. Try to understand what someone is saying before rushing to judgment.

- Make comments using "I" statements.

- This class needs to be a place where we can take risks in the questions we ask, perspectives we share, and connections we make. If you do not feel safe making a comment or asking a question, write the thought in your journal. You can share the idea with your teacher first and together come up with a safe way to share the idea with the class.

- If someone says something that hurts or offends you, do not attack the person. Acknowledge that the comment—not the person—hurt your feelings and explain why.

- Share the talking time—provide room for others to speak.

- We all have a role in creating a space where people can share their ideas, their questions, and their confusion honestly.

 Reading

Letter to Parents and Guardians

Dear parents and guardians:

It is my pleasure to welcome you as your child embarks on a Facing History & Ourselves unit of study. Facing History is an international educational and professional development organization with over 40 years of experience. For more information, please visit our website, www.facinghistory.org.

Facing History is committed to helping students make the essential connections between history and the moral choices they face as adolescents. We know that students are grappling with key questions such as: Who am I? How do I fit into my community as well as the larger world? How can I make a difference? All of these questions will be explored by looking deeply at a historical moment when individuals made decisions about their own lives and the lives of their neighbors. Your student will begin their Facing History journey by examining issues of identity and community. This introduction prepares them for a study of the events that led up to the Holocaust. Years of research have shown that a study of this history helps students understand how their decisions influence others and strengthens their ability to take multiple perspectives and consider the ethical implications of their choices.

In the creation of this material, you can be assured that great care has been taken to consider the age appropriateness of the content and the pedagogical tools teachers will need to ensure that adequate time is given for discussion and reflection. Facing History provides ongoing support for educators who are implementing the curriculum. We hope that your child's participation in this unit invites many meaningful conversations between you and him or her. A parent of a past Facing History student sums it up best:

> In no other course was [my daughter] exposed to real dilemmas as complex and challenging [as in the Facing History class]. In no other course has she been inspired to use the whole of her spiritual, moral, and intellectual resources to solve a problem. In no other course has she been so sure that the materials mattered so seriously for her development as a responsible person.

Sincerely,

Roger Brooks
President and Chief Executive Officer
Facing History & Ourselves

Unit Essential Question What does learning about the choices people made during the Weimar Republic, the rise of the Nazi Party, and the Holocaust teach us about the power and impact of our choices today?

Lesson 2

Exploring Identity

Duration

One 50-minute class period

Materials

 Readings
Words Matter
Finding Confidence
Finding One's Voice
Gender and Identity

 Teaching Strategies
Identity Charts
Jigsaw

Find all materials referenced in this lesson at facinghistory.org/thhb.

Guiding Questions

- What factors shape our identities? What dilemmas arise when others view us differently than we view ourselves?
- How do our identities influence our choices?

Learning Objective

- Students will identify social and cultural factors that help shape our identities by analyzing firsthand reflections and creating their own personal identity charts.

Overview

The question "Who am I?" is especially critical for students during adolescence. The goal of this lesson is to prompt students to consider how the answer to this question arises from the relationship between the individual and society, the topic explored in the first stage of Facing History & Ourselves' scope and sequence.

Understanding identity is not only valuable for students' own social, moral, and intellectual development, it also serves as a foundation for examining the choices made by individuals and groups in the historical case study later in the unit. In this lesson, students will learn to create visual representations of their own identities, and then they will repeat the process for the identities of several individuals they read about. In the process, they will analyze the variety of ways we define ourselves and are defined by others.

The factors that influence our identities are too numerous to capture in a single class period. The resources suggested in this lesson include some of these influences—such as race, sexual orientation, and personal interests—but not others. Chapter 1 of *Holocaust and Human Behavior* includes resources that address a larger variety of factors that influence identity, most of which can easily be added or swapped into the activities of this lesson.

In some environments, it might be especially important to address one specific identity: Jewish identity. Because Jews were a primary target of malicious stereotyping, discrimination, and horrible violence in the historical period explored later in this unit, it is important for students to have a basic understanding of the faith, culture, diversity, and dignity inherent in Jewish identity. In some schools and communities, students may not know anyone who identifies as Jewish, or they might not have had any exposure to Jewish faith, culture, and diversity. This lesson's first extension is designed to help students start to recognize that identifying as Jewish implies membership in a rich and diverse set of beliefs and cultural practices.

Context

"Who am I?" is a question all of us ask at some time in our lives. It is an especially critical question for adolescents. As we search for the answer, we begin to define ourselves and to notice how we are defined by others. Our exploration of identity includes questions such as:

- To what extent are we defined by our talents, tastes, and interests? By our membership in a particular ethnic group? By our social and economic class? By our religion? By the nation in which we live?
- How do we label and define ourselves, and how are we labeled and defined by others?
- How do our identities inform our values, ideas, and actions?

Answers to these questions help us understand ourselves and each other, as well as history.

Our society—through its particular culture, customs, institutions, and more—provides us with the language and labels we use to describe ourselves and others. These labels are based on beliefs about race, ethnicity, religion, gender, sexual orientation, economic class, and so on. Sometimes our beliefs about these categories are so strong that they prevent us from seeing the unique identities of others. Sometimes these beliefs also make us feel suspicion, fear, or hatred toward some members of our society. Other times, especially when we are able to get to know a person, we are able to see past labels and, perhaps, find common ground even as we appreciate each person as unique.

This lesson explores how individuals and society influence each of our identities. It also begins to explore some of the dilemmas people face as they establish themselves both as individuals and as members of a group—as they define themselves and are defined by others.

Notes to Teacher

1. ### Using Identity Charts as a Teaching Strategy

   Identity charts are a graphic tool that can help students consider the many factors that shape the identities of both individuals and communities. In this lesson, students will use identity charts to analyze the ways they define themselves and the labels that others use to describe them. Sharing their own identity charts with peers can help students build relationships and break down stereotypes. In this way, identity charts can be used as an effective classroom community-building tool. A sample identity chart is included below.

2. ### Addressing Different Reading Levels in the Class

   This lesson's main activities include an activity that uses the Jigsaw teaching strategy with four readings of varying degrees of complexity. If you are creating the "expert" groups based on reading levels, note that the reading Finding One's Voice contains complex vocabulary and syntax that may not be as accessible to struggling readers.

3. ### Previewing Vocabulary

   The following are key vocabulary terms used in this lesson:
   - Identity
   - Dilemma

   Add these words to your word wall, if you are using one for this unit, and provide necessary support to help students learn these words as you teach the lesson.

4. ### Exploring Jewish Identity

   If your school or community does not have a large Jewish population, or your students have not had exposure to Jewish faith and culture through their friends, families, or curriculum, it is important to include the extension "Explore the Complexity of Jewish Identity" and the reading "Being Jewish in the United States" when you teach this lesson. The extension is designed to help students start to recognize that identifying as Jewish implies membership in a rich and diverse set of beliefs and cultural practices. You might devote extra time to this reading and its subsequent questions or include the reading in the activity "Explore the Complexity of Identity."

Activities

1. Introduce Identity

Explain to students that today they will be thinking about what makes up their identities and reading firsthand accounts of how various individuals grapple with the different ways they define themselves and are defined by others.

Tell students to write a response to the question "Who am I?" in a quick journal entry. They might list, or write in complete sentences, the first five to seven ideas that come to mind when they think about this question.

Now ask students to use the information from their journals to create an identity chart. You might start an identity chart for yourself on the board to help your students understand the format. Make sure that students create their identity charts on a new page in their journals, because they will be adding to them throughout the lesson and later in the unit.

2. Explore the Complexity of Identity

Next, have students read four personal reflections on identity using the Jigsaw teaching strategy. Begin by dividing the class into four "expert" groups, and pass out one of the following readings to each group:

- Words Matter
- Finding Confidence
- Finding One's Voice
- Gender and Identity

Explain to students that each "expert" group will read together the group's assigned reading, briefly discuss the connection questions on the handout, and then create an identity chart representing the person featured in that reading.

Then divide the class into new "teaching" groups. The members of each "teaching" group should have read a different reading in their "expert" groups.

Instruct each student to summarize their "expert" group's reading for the new "teaching" group and share the identity chart they created. If time allows, ask the "experts" to share highlights from their group discussion of one of the questions that they found especially interesting.

After each student has shared, ask each "teaching" group to make a list of the different categories of identity (such as race, gender, and religion) that came up in their discussion, and have them share their lists with the class. You might record this list on the board or on chart paper.

Ask students to add information to their personal identity charts if new categories emerged through the Jigsaw activity that they hadn't previously considered.

3. Identity Chart Journal Reflection

Ask students to reflect on their own identity charts in their journals by selecting from the following questions:

- What parts of your identity do you choose for yourself? What parts of your identity do you think are determined by others, by society, or by chance?
- Whose opinions and beliefs have the greatest effect on how you think about your own identity?
- What dilemmas arise when others view you differently than you view yourself?
- What aspects of your identity do you keep private in order to be accepted? What aspects of your identity are you willing to change to fit in?

You might ask a few students to volunteer to share from their responses. Because students are writing about a personal topic in this reflection, it is important that they not be required to share.

Assessment

- Observe the group discussions during the Jigsaw activity to assess students' understanding of the readings and the factors that shape our identities. You might tell students in advance that they will be assessed on these conversations in order to ensure that everyone contributes.
- Collect the identity charts that students created based on the readings in the Jigsaw activity, as well as the lists they have compiled of factors that shape identity, in order to check for understanding and ensure that students have completed their work.

Extensions

1. Explore the Complexity of Jewish Identity

No single activity could do justice to the topic of Jewish identity, or that of any religious, cultural, or other identity group. Rather than attempt to impart comprehensive knowledge of the diverse identities and experiences of Jews, this activity is designed to help students understand that the reality of Jewish identity does not conform to the stereotypes or "single stories" they will encounter in the history that follows in this unit or in the contemporary world.

Pass out the reading "Being Jewish in the United States." Applying the Read Aloud teaching strategy, ask students to answer the connection questions. You might ask students to first respond to the questions on their own or with a partner before opening a larger class discussion.

After discussing the reading, begin an identity chart on the board with the words *Jewish identity* at the center. Lead the class in adding characteristics to the identity chart. Guide this activity carefully to avoid including inaccurate stereotypes or generalizations that students may have heard from outside of class. Instruct students to use evidence from the reading in order to support their suggestions for the identity chart.

Make sure that at the end of the activity, the identity chart clearly reflects the following ideas:

- Jewish identity is complex and varied.
- It cannot be defined by a "single story" or stereotype.
- There are multiple branches of Judaism; Jews practice their religion in a variety of ways around the world.
- Jews around the world define what it means to be Jewish in a variety of ways, just as the members of other groups often debate what makes one part of the group.
- Some Jews are not religious but identify as Jewish because of their connection to a culture.

2. Read *The Bear That Wasn't*

If you have an additional class period, consider reading and discussing with students the children's book *The Bear That Wasn't*. The book explores the relationship between the individual and society, and between how we define ourselves and the ways that others try to define us. While written for younger children, *The Bear That Wasn't* often prompts sophisticated discussion among adolescents and becomes a touchstone throughout the unit.

After reading, students can discuss how the bear responds to the way others define his identity, including both the ways he accepts others' definitions of him and the ways he resists. Students might then create an identity chart for the bear in the story. Give students a few minutes to share their identity charts with each other, and encourage them to add words and phrases from others' charts to their own.

Visit **facinghistory.org/thhb** to access these additional resources.

 Reading

Words Matter

How does it feel to be called by a name you did not choose for yourself? Over time, people have used a long list of names for the Indigenous Peoples of the Americas, but those words have rarely been what they would call themselves.

The power and meaning of labels comes not only from the choice of words but also from how those words are said. Niin, an Anishinaabe woman of both Cree and Ojibway descent, talked in an interview about the first time in her childhood when someone called her an "Indian."

> I'm not sure whether I was in grade one or in grade two; actually I think it was in kindergarten, because my Mom was home at that time. I remember being outside for recess. You know, everyone was running around, playing in the middle of the field. All of a sudden I stopped because I realized that a few of the kids who were in my classroom had formed a circle around me. They were going around and around the circle and I realized I was in the middle of this circle. I was trying to figure out what the heck is going on here? They were saying something and I started listening to them. They were saying "Indian, Indian, Indian." And I was like what? I really didn't understand myself, first and foremost, as an "Indian." Right in the middle of when they were doing that, the bell rang and everybody just turned toward the door and started walking in. I remember looking down on the ground wondering, what are they talking about Indian, Indian, Indian? I don't even know how that circle formed in the first place. I didn't catch it. It just seemed all of a sudden they were all around me and I just stopped, looking at them all. The bell rang right away. I just remember putting my head down, walking, looking at the grass, I was really thinking about, what was that all about? I didn't even remember it by the time we got to the door. Except for when I got home I asked my Mom.
>
> I remember when I went home, my mother was standing at the counter. She was baking something or other but she was working at the counter and I just walked up to her and I was watching what she was doing. I remember my chin barely touched the counter and I was watching her. I said, "Mom, what am I?" And she looked down at me and said really fast, "Were people asking you what you were?" I said, "Yes, they were calling me Indian." She said, "Tell them you're Canadian." I couldn't really figure out why she was sounding so stern and kind of angry. I just thought okay and I turned around but I remember that afternoon really clearly. I think why it stuck in my mind so much is because they were in a circle ridiculing me. And I don't even know. I didn't even take offence because I didn't know what they were doing. Even though they were calling me Indian, I was still going yeah, so what? So it always puzzled me about why, why they were calling me Indian. And because I didn't really feel any different from them, even though I knew my skin was darker, my hair was brown, and I had a shinier face. I really didn't feel any different from them or feel I was different from them.

I just felt we were all just kids. I think that's when I started learning that there were different kinds of people. I knew that there were different kinds of people by just looking and seeing like different looking people but not people who are different from one another.[1]

Connection Questions

1. What do you think the word *Indian* meant to the kids in Niin's class? What factors might have shaped her classmates' understanding of the word?

2. Why do you think Niin's mother told Niin she was Canadian? What did she want Niin to understand about herself?

3. Considering the rest of the story, what might Niin's mother have wanted Niin's classmates to learn?

4. Do you have a memory of becoming aware of differences? If so, what was it?

---

1 Mary Young, *Pimatisiwin: Walking in a Good Way, a Narrative Inquiry into Language as Identity* (Manitoba: The Prolific Group, 2005), 47–48. Reproduced by permission from Pemmican Publishers.

 Reading

Finding Confidence

In the following passage, Cameron Tuttle explains how her need for acceptance shaped her experience when she was in high school and came to understand that she was gay.

No one bullied me in high school because absolutely no one knew I was gay. Definitely not me. It took me years to figure that out.

I was one of those squeaky-clean, annoyingly mainstream, overachiever types. I got good grades, did student government, sang in musicals, played team sports, and joined lots of clubs to fatten up my college applications. But even though I was popular and friends with lots of different people, I felt alone, really alone, like no one knew the real me.

How could they? I was trying so hard to be perfect.

On the outside, I was a thriving, active, make-my-family-proud, successful teenager. But on the inside, I was emotionally numb, comatose, flat-lining. My mom had died of breast cancer two weeks before the beginning of ninth grade. She was an amazing mom, loving and supportive, and she gave me enough freedom to explore who I was so I could succeed or fail with my own personal style. After she died, I was devastated. But I was determined to prove to the world and to myself that I was okay.

I found myself working really, really hard to be the best because I was scared. Scared of being different. Scared of being defective. Scared of feeling my feelings. So for years, I didn't let myself feel.

I got a lot done in high school but I didn't have a lot of fun. And even though I wasn't ever bullied by other people, I was relentlessly bullied by my own thoughts and fears about who I was, how I was supposed to behave, and what would happen if I didn't.

I actually had this pathetic idea that I would somehow let down my community—people I barely knew in the conservative, snooty neighborhood where I grew up—if I ended up being a lesbian. How ridiculous is that?

Bullying isn't just what real people in real time say to you or try to do to you. Bullying is everywhere—it's in the words of fearful, judgmental parents who are trying to control you. (BTW: it's also in the words of well-meaning but misguided parents who are trying "to protect you from being hurt.") Bullying is in the news and in government policy. It's in the imagery of pop culture. It's in religion. And as a result, it gets into your head.

How did it get better for me? Slowly. It helped that I went to college across the country, as far away as I possibly could go from my hometown without needing a passport.

I eventually found the guts to stand up to my inner bully, the judgmental, fearful, bossy voice in my head that kept telling me, You can't . . . You shouldn't . . . Don't you dare! And then I finally found the confidence to listen to my body and to my heart and to be honest with myself.

And then I moved to New York.

When I was living there, I met tons of people who were a lot like me—squeaky-clean, annoyingly mainstream overachievers who just happened to be gay: former high-school cheerleaders, homecoming kings, class officers, student leaders, star athletes. And I realized . . . yeah, I can do this. Yeah, I can be this. And now, I love being different—in my squeaky-clean, annoyingly mainstream way.[1]

Connection Questions

1. How do you define "bullying"? How does Cameron Tuttle's story add to your thinking?

2. Create an identity chart for Tuttle. How might the identity chart you made for her be different from the one she would make for herself? What might be some differences between the way others see her and the way she sees herself?

3. What did it mean for Tuttle to find her own voice?

---

1 Cameron Tuttle, "Too Good to Be True," in *It Gets Better: Coming Out, Overcoming Bullying, and Creating a Life Worth Living*, ed. Dan Savage and Terry Miller (New York: Plume, 2012), 130–32. Reproduced by permission from Cameron Tuttle.

Reading

Finding One's Voice

How much of our identities can we define for ourselves, and how much is determined by other influences, such as our families, our culture, and the circumstances of our lives? Writer Julius Lester defied other people's expectations on his journey toward understanding and defining his identity. Here, he reflects on the way violence and humiliation affected his childhood:

> I grew up in the forties and fifties in Kansas City, Kansas, and Nashville, Tennessee, with summers spent in Arkansas. The forties and fifties were not pleasant times for blacks and I am offended by white people who get nostalgic for the fifties. I have no nostalgia for segregation, for the "No Colored Allowed" signs covering the landscape like litter on the smooth, green grass of a park, I have no nostalgia for a time when I endangered my life if, while downtown shopping with my parents, I raised my eyes and accidentally met the eyes of a white woman. Black men and boys were lynched for this during my childhood and adolescence.[1]

Lester describes the way he survived those years as follows:

> I grew up in a violent world. Segregation was a deathly spiritual violence, not only in its many restrictions on where we could live, eat, go to school, and go after dark. There was also the constant threat of physical death if you looked at a white man in what he considered the wrong way or if he didn't like your attitude. There was also the physical violence of my community . . . What I have realized is that on those nights I lay in bed reading westerns and detective novels, I was attempting to neutralize and withstand the violence that was so much a part of my dailiness. In westerns and mysteries I found a kind of mirror in which one element of my world—violence—was isolated and made less harmful to me.[2]

Not surprisingly, Lester found his voice in a book. He explains:

> One of the pivotal experiences of my life came when I was eighteen. I wandered into a bookstore in downtown Nashville one frosted, gray day in late autumn aware that I was looking for something: I was looking for myself, and I generally find myself while wandering through a bookstore, looking at books until I find the one that is calling me. On this particular day I wandered for quite a while until I picked up a paperback with the word *Haiku* on the cover. What is that? I wondered. I opened the book and read,
>
>> On a withered branch
>> a crow has settled —
>> autumn nightfall.

---

1 Julius Lester, *Falling Pieces of the Broken Sky* (New York: Arcade, 1990), 69. Reproduced by permission of Menza-Barron Literary Agency.
2 Lester, *Falling Pieces of the Broken Sky*, 71–73. Reproduced by permission of Menza-Barron Literary Agency.

I trembled and turned the pages hastily until my eyes stopped on these words:

> A giant firefly;
> that way, this way, that way, this —
> and it passes by.

I read more of the brief poems, these voices from seventeenth-century Japan, and I knew: This is my voice. This simplicity, this directness, this way of using words to direct the soul to silence and beyond. This is my voice! I exulted inside. Then I stopped. How could I, a little colored kid from Nashville, Tennessee—and that is all I knew myself to be in those days like perpetual death knells—how could I be feeling that something written in seventeenth-century Japan could be my voice?

I almost put the book back, but that inner prompting which had led me to it would not allow such an act of self-betrayal. I bought the book and began writing haiku, and the study of haiku led to the study of Zen Buddhism, which led to the study of flower arranging, and I suspect I am still following the path that opened to me on that day when I was eighteen, though I no longer write haiku . . .[3]

I eventually understood that it made perfect sense for a little colored kid from Nashville, Tennessee, to recognize his voice in seventeenth-century Japanese poetry. Who we are by the sociological and political definitions of society has little to do with who we are.

In the quiet and stillness that surrounds us when we read a book, we are known to ourselves in ways we are not when we are with people. We enter a relationship of intimacy with the writer, and if the writer has written truly and if we give ourselves over to what is written, we are given the gift of ourselves in ways that surprise and catch the soul off guard.[4]

Connection Questions

1. What barriers did society place in the way of Julius Lester's becoming the kind of person he wanted to be? How did he overcome these barriers?

2. When Lester found a book of haiku in the bookstore, why did he almost put it back?

3. Lester writes that when he found the book of haiku, "I knew: This is my voice." Have you ever found your voice in a work of art, music, literature, or film?

---

[3] Lester, *Falling Pieces of the Broken Sky*, 71–73. Reproduced by permission of Menza-Barron Literary Agency.
[4] Lester, *Falling Pieces of the Broken Sky*, 71–73. Reproduced by permission of Menza-Barron Literary Agency.

Reading

Gender and Identity

Sometimes our assumptions and expectations about others prevent us from seeing who they really are as individuals. Some of the most powerful expectations about people that we learn from our culture are about gender. A person's sex often leads us to make assumptions about that person's identity. Martha Minow, a legal scholar, explains:

> Of course, there are "real differences" in the world; each person differs in countless ways from each other person. But when we simplify and sort, we focus on some traits rather than others, and we assign consequences to the presence and absence of the traits we make significant. We ask, "What's the new baby?"—and we expect as an answer, boy or girl. That answer, for most of history, has spelled consequences for the roles and opportunities available to that individual.[1]

American author Lori Duron and her husband, Matt, have two children, both boys. She writes about what happened the first time her younger son, C.J., got a Barbie doll.

> For days after C.J. discovered her, Barbie never left his side. When I'd do a final bed check at night before I retired for the evening to watch reality television and sneak chocolate when no one was looking, I'd see his full head of auburn hair sticking out above his covers. Next to him there would be a tiny tuft of blonde hair sticking out as well.
>
> The next time we were at Target near the toy aisle—which I've always tried to pass at warp speed so the kids don't notice and beg me to buy them something—C.J. wanted to see "Barbie stuff." I led him to the appropriate aisle and he stood there transfixed, not touching a thing, just taking it all in. He was so overwhelmed that he didn't ask to buy a single thing. He finally walked away from the aisle speechless, as if he had just seen something so magical and majestic that he needed time to process it.
>
> He had, that day, discovered the pink aisles of the toy department. We had never been down those aisles; we had only frequented the blue aisles, when we ventured down the toy aisles at all. As far as C.J. was concerned, I had been hiding half the world from him.
>
> I felt bad about that, like I had deprived him because of my assumptions and expectations that he was a boy and boys liked boy things. Matt and I noticed that C.J. didn't really like any of the toys we provided for him, which were all handed down from his brother. We noticed that C.J. didn't go through the normal boy toy addictions that Chase [C.J.'s older brother] had gone through: he couldn't care less about balls, cars, dinosaurs, superheroes, The Wiggles, Bob the Builder, or Thomas the Tank Engine. What did he like to play with? We didn't worry ourselves much about finding the answer (a case of the second-born child not getting fussed over quite like the first-born); we trusted that in time something would draw him in. Which it did. It just wasn't at all what we were expecting.

---

1 Martha Minow, *Making All the Difference: Inclusion, Exclusion, and American Law* (Ithaca, NY: Cornell University Press, 1990), 3.

At about the eighteen- to twenty-four-month mark of a child's life, the gender-neutral toys disappear and toys that are marketed specifically to boys or to girls take over. We didn't realize it until later, but that divide in the toy world and our house being filled with only boy toys left C.J. a little lost at playtime. We and the rest of society had been pushing masculine stuff on him and enforcing traditional gender norms, when all he wanted was to brush long blonde hair and dress, undress, and re-dress Barbie . . . [2]

Reflecting on C.J.'s identity, Duron concludes:

On the gender-variation spectrum of super-macho-masculine on the left all the way to super-girly-feminine on the right, C.J. slides fluidly in the middle; he's neither all pink nor all blue. He's a muddled mess or a rainbow creation, depending on how you look at it. Matt and I have decided to see the rainbow, not the muddle. But we didn't always see it that way.

Initially, the sight of our son playing with girl toys or wearing girl clothes made our chests tighten, forged a lump in our throats, and, at times, made us want to hide him. There was anger, anxiety, and fear. We've evolved as parents as our younger son has evolved into a fascinating, vibrant person who is creative with gender. Sometimes, when I think of how we behaved as parents . . . I'm ashamed and embarrassed.[3]

Connection Questions

1. What are the differences between the toys in the pink aisle and the toys in the blue aisle? What assumptions do the toys in these aisles reflect about what it means to be a boy or a girl?

2. How do you explain the anxiety, anger, and fear that Duron felt when C.J. started playing with the "girl toys"? How did her feelings change?

3. What are some other stereotypes about gender in your world? How do you respond to the assumptions people make about you because of your gender? To what extent do you accept or reject those assumptions?

---

2 Lori Duron, *Raising My Rainbow: Adventures in Raising a Fabulous, Gender Creative Son* (New York: Broadway Books, 2013), 9–10. Reproduced by permission of Penguin Random House.

3 Duron, *Raising My Rainbow*, 4. Reproduced by permission of Penguin Random House

 Reading

Being Jewish in the United States

Judaism, a religious faith that began in the Middle East over 3,500 years ago, is the world's oldest monotheistic religion. Today, more than 14 million Jews live in dozens of countries around the world, the majority in Israel and the United States. (In the United States, there were about 7 million Jews, comprising about 2% of the population, in 2016.[1])

There are several branches within Judaism—including but not limited to Reform, Orthodox, and Conservative—in the United States and elsewhere. According to scholar Stephen Prothero, "The simplest way to describe these three groups [Reform, Orthodox, and Conservative] is to say that each focuses on one key element in Judaism: the Reform on ethics, the Orthodox on law, and the Conservative on tradition."[2] But these simple descriptions do not fully express the richness of the various branches of Judaism or the ideas and beliefs that unite them. A Jewish house of worship is called a synagogue, and the most important religious text in Judaism is the Torah. The Torah includes five books that also appear as the first five books in the Christian Old Testament.

Like the members of any religion or culture, Jews think about and express their identities in a variety of ways, prioritizing their Jewish identity differently within the mix of other factors that make them who they are. In the following three reflections, Rebecca, then age 17, Sara, then age 18, and Angela, an adult, explain the influence that Judaism has on their lives. These are only three examples from the numerous ways that Jews around the world relate to the faith and culture of Judaism. Rebecca writes:

> [I]n the Torah, there are 613 commandments. They involve everything from how you treat other people, to Jewish holidays and how we observe them, and the Sabbath, which is every week, and how we observe that. It's like a guide how to live.
>
> There are also a lot of dietary laws. The dietary laws say we can only eat certain kinds of meat that are killed and prepared in a certain way. We can't eat meat at nonkosher restaurants. My parents like to remind me of this funny story. One time when I was two, we were driving past a Burger King. I saw the sign, and I yelled out, "That sign says Burger King. No burgers for Jewish people." I picked up on those observances. It was always something that was part of me. I recognized that it was important.
>
> We set the Sabbath aside as a day of rest because God rested on the seventh day after creating the world. Because of this, there are lots of rules for things you can and can't do . . . It's supposed to be a day of rest—you're not supposed to do any type of work, or watch television, use the computer, use electricity, any of that stuff . . . For me it's very spiritual. It really separates the day out from the rest of the week.

---

1. Brandeis University, "American Jewish Population Project," Steinhardt Social Research Institute, accessed May 30, 2017, http://ajpp.brandeis.edu/.
2. Stephen Prothero, *God Is Not One: The Eight Rival Religions That Run the World* (New York: HarperOne, 2010), 267.

I spend a lot of time with my family—from Friday night at sundown until Saturday night. I go to prayers at my synagogue in the morning and sometimes in the afternoon. It's just a really spiritual experience. It makes it more of an important day . . .

I haven't gone to see a movie on a Saturday or Friday night ever.

It's weird being in a public high school because you're faced with being in a school where there's lots of activities on Friday nights and things to miss out on. Like all the school plays are on Friday nights. I have to give up trying out for school plays. And sports—I used to play softball. But there are games every Saturday, so I couldn't play those.

A lot of people look at it like, "How can you give up all of this stuff because of your religion?" It's just a matter of how you look at it. You can look at it as being a burden—that you have these religious obligations, so you're not able to do your school activities. But I look at it as a more positive experience. It's something that I choose to do.[3]

Sara, age 18, feels differently about the rituals and worship practices of Judaism:

I feel really connected with my Jewish community, but a little less connected to the observance factor of my religion. I don't keep kosher. I don't really feel that's necessary. When I was little, my whole family would sit down every Friday night and light the Shabbat candles and say the blessings. We don't do that anymore. Now it's like, "It's Friday night. I'm going to go out with my friends."

I don't like organized prayer. Every once in a while I go to services, but I appreciate it a lot more when I do my own thing and say my own prayers . . .

When I was younger, I never really thought I was different 'cause I was Jewish. It didn't occur to me until high school when I started getting really involved with stuff. It's kind of weird when I really think about it. It's like I'm just like everyone else, except there's that little part of me that's going to be Jewish forever, and that makes me different.[4]

Born in Seoul, Korea, to a Korean Buddhist mother and an American Jewish father, Angela explains how she grew to understand herself within the diversity of Jewish life around the world and throughout history:

Growing up, I knew my family was atypical, yet we were made to feel quite at home in our synagogue and community . . .

As a child, I believed that my sister and I were the "only ones" in the Jewish community—the only ones with Asian faces, the only ones whose family trees didn't have roots in Eastern Europe, the only ones with kimchee on the seder plate. But as I grew older, I began to see myself reflected in the Jewish community. I was the only multiracial Jew at my Jewish summer camp in 1985; when I was a song-leader there a decade later, there were a dozen. I have met hundreds of people in multiracial Jewish families in the Northeast through the Multiracial Jewish Network. Social scientist Gary Tobin numbers interracial Jewish families in the hundreds of thousands in North America.

---

3 "How Can You Give Up All of This Stuff Because of Your Religion?," in Pearl Gaskins, *I Believe In . . . : Christian, Jewish, and Muslim Young People Speak About Their Faith* (Chicago: Cricket Books, 2004), 58–59. Reproduced by permission from Carus Publishing Company.

4 "I Wear Two Stars of David," in Gaskins, *I Believe In . . .* , 33.

As I learned more about Jewish history and culture, I found it very powerful to learn that being of mixed race in the Jewish community was not just a modern phenomenon. We were a mixed multitude when we left Egypt and entered Israel, and the Hebrews continued to acquire different cultures and races throughout our Diaspora history. Walking through the streets of modern-day Israel, one sees the multicolored faces of Ethiopian, Russian, Yemenite, Iraqi, Moroccan, Polish, and countless other races of Jews—many facial particularities, but all Jewish . . .

What does it mean to be a "normal" Jewish family today? As we learn each other's stories we hear the challenges and joys of reconciling our sometimes competing identities of being Jewish while also feminist, Arab, gay, African-American, or Korean. We were a mixed multitude in ancient times, and we still are . . . [5]

Connection Questions

1 Create identity Charts for Rebecca, Sara, and Angela in your journal. Use evidence from the text to support your ideas about each young woman's identity. What do they have common? What differences do you notice?

2 What role does religious belief and practice seem to play in the identities of Rebecca, Sara, and Angela?

3 How do the information and reflections in this reading connect to, extend, or challenge your understanding of what it means to be Jewish? What new questions does this reading raise for you?

---

[5] Angela Warnick Buchdahl, "My Personal Story: Kimchee on the Seder Plate," Sh'ma: A *Journal of Jewish Responsibility* (June 2003). Reproduced with permission from *Sh'ma* as part of a larger issue on inclusivity.

Unit Essential Question: What does learning about the choices people made during the Weimar Republic, the rise of the Nazi Party, and the Holocaust teach us about the power and impact of our choices today?

Lesson

Stereotypes and "Single Stories"

Duration
Two 50-minute class periods

Materials

 Image
Street Calculus

 Video
The Danger of a Single Story

 Reading
The Danger of a Single Story

 Handout
The Danger of a Single Story Viewing/Reading Guide

 Teaching Strategies
Concept Map
Think, Pair, Share
Identity Charts
Concentric Circles
Wraparound

Find all materials referenced in this lesson at facinghistory.org/thhb.

Guiding Question

- In what ways do "single stories" impact our own identities, how we view others, and the choices we make?

Learning Objectives

- Students will recognize that it is a natural and common human behavior to group the people and things we encounter in the world into categories, but that sometimes these categories become "single stories" that give us incomplete and simplistic understandings of the identities of others.

- Students will construct a "working definition" of *stereotype* and recognize how stereotypes can lead to prejudice and discrimination.

Overview

In the previous lesson, students began the first stage of the Facing History scope and sequence, "The Individual and Society," by considering the complexity of answering the question "Who am I?" In this lesson, students will continue to explore the relationship between individual and society by examining how we so often believe "single stories" and stereotypes about groups of people. The activities that follow ask students to reflect on the basic human behavior of applying categories to the people and things we meet and to think about the circumstances in which "single stories" about others can be harmful or even dangerous.

Context

We know that every person is different from any other in countless ways, yet when we encounter others, we often rely on generalizations to describe them. "It's a natural tendency," says psychologist Deborah Tannen.

> We must see the world in patterns in order to make sense of it; we wouldn't be able to deal with the daily onslaught of people and objects if we couldn't predict a lot about them and feel that we know who and what they are. But this natural and useful ability to see patterns of similarity has unfortunate consequences. It is offensive to reduce an individual to a category, and it is also misleading.[1]

Author Chimamanda Ngozi Adichie uses the phrase "single stories" to describe the overly simplistic and sometimes false perceptions we form about individuals, groups, or countries. Her novels and short stories complicate the single stories many people believe about Nigeria, the country where she is from.

In a speech excerpted in this lesson, Adichie recounts her experiences as the subject of the "single stories" others have created about groups to which she belongs, as well as times when she herself has created single stories about others. She says:

> I've always felt that it is impossible to engage properly with a place or a person without engaging with all of the stories of that place and that person. The consequence of the single story is this: It robs people of dignity. It makes our recognition of our equal humanity difficult. It emphasizes how we are different rather than how we are similar . . .
>
> The single story creates stereotypes, and the problem with stereotypes is not that they are untrue, but that they are incomplete. They make one story become the only story.[2]

Adichie's speech provides a framework for discussing stereotypes, prejudice, and discrimination with your students. A *stereotype* is a belief about an individual based on the real or imagined characteristics of a group to which that individual belongs. Stereotypes can lead us to judge an individual or group negatively. Even stereotypes that seem to portray a group positively reduce individuals to categories and tell an incomplete or inaccurate "single story." *Prejudice* occurs when we form an opinion about an individual or a group based on a negative stereotype. When a prejudice leads us to treat an individual or group negatively, *discrimination* occurs.

It is important to reflect on the relationship explored in this lesson between the ways that we *think* about others and the ways that we *treat* others. Investigating the connections between stereotyping, prejudice, and discrimination will provide an important framework for exploring in future lessons the ways that people create "in" groups and "out" groups, both in our everyday lives and throughout history.

Notes to Teacher

1. Working Definitions and Concept Maps

Before introducing the reading The Danger of a Single Story, it is important for students to first consider the word *stereotype*—a word they have likely heard often but may not have explored in depth. To do so, students will each create a concept map that will help them define *stereotype* as well as establish the

---

[1] Deborah Tannen, *You Just Don't Understand: Men and Women in Conversation* (New York: Morrow, 1990), 16.
[2] Chimamanda Adichie, "The Danger of a Single Story," TED video (filmed July 2009, posted October 2009), 18:49, accessed March 28, 2016, https://www.ted.com/talks/chimamanda_adichie_the_danger_of_a_single_story/transcript?language=en.

relationship between stereotypes, prejudice, and discrimination. We recommend that you create a "durable" class concept map for *stereotype* on chart paper, which can be saved and posted in the classroom for reference in later lessons.

Students will use their concept maps to help them construct a "working definition," which is a less formal way of explaining what a word means. Unlike dictionary definitions, working definitions are often multi-layered, using less formal language and examples.

2. Previewing Vocabulary

In addition to *stereotype,* the following are key vocabulary terms used in this lesson:

- Assumption
- Prejudice
- Discrimination

Add these words to your word wall, if you are using one for this unit, and provide necessary support to help students learn these words as you teach the lesson.

3. Choosing a Discussion Strategy

Discussions can happen in many formats, ranging from whole-class to small-group conversations. When beginning a unit, or when prompts involve personal reflection, we recommend using smaller, paired conversation strategies rather than whole-group discussions, as they allow for each student to share and be heard and for students to share more openly than when in front of a larger audience. For this reason, in this lesson we suggest using the Concentric Circles teaching strategy to debrief the content of The Danger of a Single Story.

4. Exit Tickets: Capturing Student Understanding

This lesson introduces the Exit Tickets teaching strategy. This formative assessment allows teachers to capture each student's understanding at the end of a lesson and provides valuable feedback about content and skills that might need to be revisited in future lessons. Teachers can also redistribute completed exit tickets later in the unit and ask students to discuss or write about how their thinking on the topic has been changed, challenged, or confirmed over time.

5. Video or Reading: Choosing the Right Medium

Because Chimamanda Ngozi Adichie's TED Talk The Danger of a Single Story, is so compelling, we recommend that you show the entire 19-minute video to the class to explore the relationship between stories and stereotypes. If you prefer a reading over a video for your class, use the excerpt of Adichie's talk provided here.

Activities

Day 1

1. **Journal Response: Responding to Assumptions**

   Begin the lesson by giving students a few minutes to write in their journals in response to the following question:

   > Has someone else ever made an assumption about you because of some aspect of your identity? Was it a positive assumption or a negative one? How did you find out about the assumption? How did you respond?

2. **Create a Concept Map for *Stereotype***

   Tell students that the assumptions we make about each other are sometimes based on stereotypes. Most middle- and high-school students have heard the word *stereotype,* but they might struggle to articulate a definition. Tell students that to help them reflect on their understanding of *stereotype,* they will create a concept map, a visual representation of the word, using words, phrases, questions, the space on the page, lines, and arrows. Later in the lesson, they will use their concept maps as a launching point to help them explore the relationship between stereotypes, prejudice, and discrimination.

   Lead students through the steps of the Concept Map teaching strategy, first brainstorming words, phrases, and ideas that they associate with stereotypes and then organizing these around the word *stereotype* on a page of their journals.

   Have students share their concept maps using the Think, Pair, Share strategy. Invite them to revise their maps by adding new information they learned from their conversations that extends or challenges their thinking.

   You might then facilitate a discussion in which students share ideas from their maps for you to add to a class concept map that you hang in the room, refer back to, and modify over the course of the unit as their thinking about stereotyping develops.

3. **Create a Working Definition for *Stereotype***

   Using the information on their concept maps and from their discussions, ask students to write a "working definition" of *stereotype* underneath their concept map. They will have the opportunity to share these working definitions with the class. Explain that a working definition is a less formal way of explaining what a word means—a definition that can change over time and might use less formal language. Tell students that they might expand, focus, or revise their working definitions as they learn more about the topic over the course of the unit.

   After students have drafted their own working definitions, ask volunteers to share their ideas to create a class working definition of *stereotype,* which you can then add to the class concept map.

Explain the relationship between *stereotype, prejudice,* and *discrimination,* and ask students to add these terms to their concept maps. Then ask students to share their ideas about where they placed *prejudice* and *discrimination* and how they connected these to other concepts on their maps.

4. Reflect on the Role of Stereotypes in Daily Life and Society

Project or pass out Garry Trudeau's cartoon Street Calculus and discuss students' first impressions of the image by asking the following questions:

- What's happening in this image?
- What do you notice about what each person is thinking in his thought bubble?
- How are each of their thoughts similar? How are they different?

Next, analyze the cartoon more deeply by having students discuss the following questions:

- Do you think the situation depicted here is realistic? Do people use "lists" like these to make judgments about each other?
- How aware do you think people are of the lists they make? When someone sees you walking down the street, what lists might they make about you? What lists do you sometimes make about others?
- How might these lists shape choices people make (beyond greeting each other)? What would it take to change the lists people make about each other?

Next, connect the discussion of Street Calculus to stereotyping by asking students to reflect in a class discussion or in their journals on the role that stereotypes play in our society and in their own experiences. Depending on time, one or more of the following questions can be used to guide this reflection and debrief:

- Where do stereotypes come from?
- What stereotypes do the two men in the cartoon have about the groups the other one belongs to?
- When, if ever, can stereotypes be harmless or even helpful? When do stereotypes become harmful?
- What does the cartoon suggest about how stereotypes might impact the way we see ourselves and the way we see others? How might stereotypes impact the choices we make?

Day 2

1. Watch a Video that Explains the Danger of "Single Stories"

If it was not part of the Day 1 discussion, introduce students to the idea that stereotypes are a type of story that we tell about individuals based on our beliefs (erroneous or accurate) about a group to which they belong. You might ask students to review their concept maps and journal responses in preparation for today's lesson.

Tell students that today they will be exploring the relationship between storytelling and stereotyping, as well as what it means to have a "single story" of a person or group of people.

Pass out the handout The Danger of a Single Story Viewing/Reading Guide. Then show the video The Danger of a Single Story (18:43) at facinghistory.org/thhb or pass out and read aloud the reading The Danger of a Single Story. While viewing or reading, students should record their thoughts about the three questions posed on the guide.

Ask students to work with a partner to create an identity chart for Adichie. If your class watched the video, you might consider passing out the reading version for students to reference during this activity. Students can refer to the identity charts they created in the previous lesson and the three viewing/reading questions to guide their thinking.

2. Discuss "Single Stories" in Concentric Circles

To debrief Adichie's TED Talk, use the Concentric Circles strategy. Have students stand in two concentric circles, facing a partner in the opposite circle, and use the prompts below to begin the discussion. Rotate to a new partner for each new prompt.

- What does Adichie mean by a "single story"? What examples does she give?
- How did Adichie learn single stories about others? How did these stories impact her understanding of herself and of others? How did these single stories impact the choices she made at home and in her travels?
- What enabled Adichie to change her single story? What are other ways for these types of stories to change?
- According to Adichie, why can "single stories" be dangerous? What is the relationship between "single stories" and stereotypes?
- Why is it that people sometimes make the same mistakes that they so easily see others making?

3. Write about the Connection between "Single Stories" and Stereotypes

After the concentric circle discussion, use the quotation below or one or more of the subsequent questions as a prompt to allow for individual student reflections in their journals. Encourage students to use their resources, such as their concept maps, working definitions, notes from today's lesson, and identity charts, to help them make connections between "single stories" and stereotyping.

- "The single story creates stereotypes, and the problem with stereotypes is not that they are untrue, but that they are incomplete. They make one story become the only story." (Adichie)
- What single stories have you noticed that others have about you? What dilemmas have you experienced when others view you differently than you view yourself?

- What single stories have you noticed that you hold about others? What dilemmas have you seen arise when we view others differently than they view themselves?
- What steps can you take, or have you taken, to challenge these single stories?

Lead the class in a discussion that allows students to share their ideas about the concentric circle questions and journal responses with the whole group.

4. Close the Discussion with a Wraparound Activity

If time allows, tell the class that they will be sharing a concluding idea in a Wraparound activity. As you go around the room, students can share a memorable word or short phrase from the lesson. It could be something they wrote or something they heard from a classmate (or from The Danger of a Single Story).

Assessment

- Evaluate students' concept maps for *stereotype* to gauge their understanding of the concept.

- Instruct students to make text-to-text, text-to-self, and text-to-world connections with The Danger of a Single Story. Use or adapt the "Text-to-Text, Text-to-Self, Text-to-World" handout, available on the teaching strategy page on Facing History's website, to help guide their work.

Extension

Explore Why "Little Things Are Big"

The reading "Little Things Are Big" (visit facinghistory.org/thhb) provides students with the opportunity to examine how the stereotypes we believe about each other can affect our choices. The author of this piece describes a dilemma he faced over whether or not to help a woman late at night on the New York City subway. The dilemma he describes, and his own evaluation of the choice he made, can provide the basis for a meaningful and engaging class discussion. Consider sharing the reading with students and using the connection questions that follow for discussion and reflection.

Street Calculus

Garry Trudeau's cartoon from the *Doonesbury* comic strip comments on the calculations we make about one another.

 Reading

The Danger of a Single Story

Chimamanda Ngozi Adichie is a writer who has won several awards for her novels, short stories, and essays. She was born in Nigeria, and she attended universities in both Nigeria and the United States. She continues to live in both countries. In her TED Talk "The Danger of a Single Story," Adichie describes the effects that labels can have on how we think about ourselves and others.

> I come from a conventional, middle-class Nigerian family. My father was a professor. My mother was an administrator. And so we had, as was the norm, live-in domestic help, who would often come from nearby rural villages. So, the year I turned eight, we got a new house boy. His name was Fide. The only thing my mother told us about him was that his family was very poor. My mother sent yams and rice, and our old clothes, to his family. And when I didn't finish my dinner, my mother would say, "Finish your food! Don't you know? People like Fide's family have nothing." So I felt enormous pity for Fide's family.

Then one Saturday, we went to his village to visit, and his mother showed us a beautifully patterned basket made of dyed raffia that his brother had made. I was startled. It had not occurred to me that anybody in his family could actually make something. All I had heard about them was how poor they were, so that it had become impossible for me to see them as anything else but poor. Their poverty was my single story of them.

Years later, I thought about this when I left Nigeria to go to university in the United States. I was 19. My American roommate was shocked by me. She asked where I had learned to speak English so well, and was confused when I said that Nigeria happened to have English as its official language. She asked if she could listen to what she called my "tribal music," and was consequently very disappointed when I produced my tape of Mariah Carey [an American pop singer]. She assumed that I did not know how to use a stove.

What struck me was this: She had felt sorry for me even before she saw me. Her default position toward me, as an African, was a kind of patronizing, well-meaning pity. My roommate had a single story of Africa: a single story of catastrophe. In this single story, there was no possibility of Africans being similar to her in any way, no possibility of feelings more complex than pity, no possibility of a connection as human equals.

I must say that before I went to the U.S., I didn't consciously identify as African. But in the U.S., whenever Africa came up, people turned to me. Never mind that I knew nothing about places like Namibia. But I did come to embrace this new identity, and in many ways I think of myself now as African . . .

So, after I had spent some years in the U.S. as an African, I began to understand my roommate's response to me. If I had not grown up in Nigeria, and if all I knew about Africa were from popular images, I too would think that Africa was a place of beautiful landscapes, beautiful animals, and incomprehensible people, fighting senseless wars, dying of poverty and AIDS, unable to speak for themselves and waiting to be saved by a kind, white foreigner. I would see Africans in the same way that I, as a child, had seen Fide's family . . .

And so, I began to realize that my American roommate must have throughout her life seen and heard different versions of this single story . . .

But I must quickly add that I too am just as guilty in the question of the single story. A few years ago, I visited Mexico from the U.S. The political climate in the U.S. at the time was tense, and there were debates going on about immigration. And, as often happens in America, immigration became synonymous with Mexicans. There were endless stories of Mexicans as people who were fleecing the healthcare system, sneaking across the border, being arrested at the border, that sort of thing.

I remember walking around on my first day in Guadalajara, watching the people going to work, rolling up tortillas in the marketplace, smoking, laughing. I remember first feeling slight surprise. And then, I was overwhelmed with shame. I realized that I had been so immersed in the media coverage of Mexicans that they had become one thing in my mind, the abject immigrant. I had bought into the single story of Mexicans and I could not have been more ashamed of myself. So that is how to create a single story, show a people as one thing, as only one thing, over and over again, and that is what they become.

It is impossible to talk about the single story without talking about power. There is a word, an Igbo [a language spoken in Nigeria] word, that I think about whenever I think about the power structures of the world, and it is "nkali." It's a noun that loosely translates to "to be greater than another." Like our economic and political worlds, stories too are defined by the principle of nkali: How they are told, who tells them, when they're told, how many stories are told, are really dependent on power.

Power is the ability not just to tell the story of another person, but to make it the definitive story of that person . . .

[T]he truth is that I had a very happy childhood, full of laughter and love, in a very close-knit family.

But I also had grandfathers who died in refugee camps. My cousin Polle died because he could not get adequate healthcare. One of my closest friends, Okoloma, died in a plane crash because our fire trucks did not have water. I grew up under repressive military governments that devalued education, so that sometimes, my parents were not paid their salaries. And so, as a child, I saw jam disappear from the breakfast table, then margarine disappeared, then bread became too expensive, then milk became rationed. And most of all, a kind of normalized political fear invaded our lives.

All of these stories make me who I am. But to insist on only these negative stories is to flatten my experience and to overlook the many other stories that formed me. The single story creates stereotypes, and the problem with stereotypes is not that they are untrue, but that they are incomplete. They make one story become the only story.

Of course, Africa is a continent full of catastrophes: There are immense ones, such as the horrific rapes in Congo, and depressing ones, such as the fact that 5,000 people apply for one job vacancy in Nigeria. But there are other stories that are not about catastrophe, and it is very important, it is just as important, to talk about them.

I've always felt that it is impossible to engage properly with a place or a person without engaging with all of the stories of that place and that person. The consequence of the single story is this: It robs people of dignity. It makes our recognition of our equal humanity difficult. It emphasizes how we are different rather than how we are similar.

So what if before my Mexican trip, I had followed the immigration debate from both sides, the U.S. and the Mexican? What if my mother had told us that Fide's family was poor and hardworking? What if we had an African television network that broadcast diverse African stories all over the world? . . .

. . . What if my roommate knew about the female lawyer who recently went to court in Nigeria to challenge a ridiculous law that required women to get their husband's consent before renewing their passports? What if my roommate knew about Nollywood, full of innovative people making films despite great technical odds, films so popular that they really are the best example of Nigerians consuming what they produce? What if my roommate knew about my wonderfully ambitious hair braider, who has just started her own business selling hair extensions? Or about the millions of other Nigerians who start businesses and sometimes fail, but continue to nurse ambition?

Every time I am home I am confronted with the usual sources of irritation for most Nigerians: our failed infrastructure, our failed government, but also by the incredible resilience of people who thrive despite the government, rather than because of it. I teach writing workshops in Lagos every summer, and it is amazing to me how many people apply, how many people are eager to write, to tell stories . . .

Stories matter. Many stories matter. Stories have been used to dispossess and to malign, but stories can also be used to empower and to humanize. Stories can break the dignity of a people, but stories can also repair that broken dignity.

The American writer Alice Walker wrote this about her Southern relatives who had moved to the North. She introduced them to a book about the Southern life that they had left behind. "They sat around, reading the book themselves, listening to me read the book, and a kind of paradise was regained." I would like to end with this thought: That when we reject the single story, when we realize that there is never a single story about any place, we regain a kind of paradise.[1]

---

1 Chimamanda Adichie, "The Danger of a Single Story," TED video (filmed July 2009, posted October 2009), 18:49, accessed March 28, 2016, https://www.ted.com/talks/chimamanda_adichie_the_danger_of_a_single_story/transcript?language=en.

 **Handout**

The Danger of a Single Story Viewing/Reading Guide

Directions: As you watch the video or read aloud the text with your class, respond to the following questions:

1. How does Adichie describe herself at the beginning of her talk? What words and phrases might she put on her own identity chart?

2. Later in the story, we learn how other people view her. How do those views differ from how she describes herself?

3. According to Adichie, what dilemmas can arise when others view us differently than we view ourselves?

Unit Essential Question What does learning about the choices people made during the Weimar Republic, the rise of the Nazi Party, and the Holocaust teach us about the power and impact of our choices today?

Lesson

Universe of Obligation

Duration
One 50-minute class period

Materials

 Reading
Universe of Obligation

 Handout
Universe of Obligation Graphic Organizer

 Teaching Strategy
Think, Pair, Share

Find all materials referenced in this lesson at facinghistory.org/thhb.

Guiding Question

- What factors influence the extent to which we feel an obligation to help others? How does the way we view others influence our feelings of responsibility toward them?

Learning Objectives

- Students will apply a new concept of human behavior—universe of obligation—to analyze how individuals and societies determine who is deserving of respect and whose rights are worthy of protection.
- Students will recognize that a society's universe of obligation often changes, expanding or shrinking depending on circumstances such as peace and prosperity or war and economic depression.

Overview

In this lesson, students build on their previous discussion about stereotypes by examining why humans form groups and what it means to belong. This examination begins the second stage of the Facing History scope and sequence, "We and They." Students will learn a new concept, *universe of obligation*—the term sociologist Helen Fein coined to describe the circle of individuals and groups within a society "toward whom obligations are owed, to whom rules apply, and whose injuries call for amends."[1]

Understanding the concept of universe of obligation provides important insights into the behavior of individuals, groups, and nations throughout history. It also helps students think more deeply about the benefits of being part of a society's "in" group and the consequences of being part of an "out" group.

---

1 Helen Fein, *Accounting for Genocide* (New York: Free Press, 1979), 4.

The activities in this lesson ask students to think about the people for whom they feel responsible. The activities also help students analyze the ways that their society designates who is worthy of respect and caring and who is not.

Context

Collecting ourselves into groups is a natural behavior. Being part of a group helps to meet our most basic needs: we share culture, values, and beliefs, and we satisfy our yearning to belong.

Like individuals, groups have identities. How a group defines itself determines who is entitled to its benefits and who is not. Sometimes the consequences of being excluded from a group are minor or harmless. For example, someone who does not enjoy running is unlikely to be affected by not being a member of a track club. But sometimes the consequences can be substantial, even dire. If someone is denied citizenship by a country, their freedom, livelihood, or safety may be at risk. Moreover, a society's universe of obligation can change. Individuals and groups that are respected and protected members of a society at one time may find themselves outside the universe of obligation when circumstances are different.

Societies with governments dedicated to democratic values and human rights tend to define their universes of obligation in a more expansive and inclusive manner than other societies do. Yet, even within democratic countries, political movements and ideologies such as nationalism, racism, or antisemitism can take hold and lead to a more narrow definition of whose rights and privileges deserve protection and whose do not. In times of crisis—such as war or economic depression—societies also tend to define more narrowly who is "one of us" and whose loyalty is now under suspicion, making them undeserving of protection and respect. Individuals or groups who fall outside a nation's universe of obligation become vulnerable not only to being deprived of the rights, privileges, and economic benefits afforded to citizens but also to expulsion, physical harm, and, in the most extreme cases, genocide (as Helen Fein warned when she articulated this concept in the 1970s).

Although Fein conceived of the term to describe the way nations determine membership, we can also recognize that individuals have a universe of obligation—the circle of other individuals a person feels a responsibility to care for and protect. This concept helps us recognize the internalized hierarchies that influence how we think about and respond to the needs of others. While it is neither practical nor possible that one's universe of obligation could include everyone in its center (the position of most importance), acknowledging the way we think about and prioritize our obligations toward others can help us act in a more thoughtful, compassionate manner.

During this lesson, students will examine their universe of obligation, as well as those of groups and nations to which they belong. By investigating the "us and them" dynamic that so often plays out in all of our lives and throughout history, students will be better prepared to analyze and understand the case study of Nazi Germany and the Holocaust.

Notes to Teacher

1. Previewing Vocabulary

The following are key vocabulary terms used in this lesson:

- Universe of obligation
- Responsibility
- Membership

Add these words to your word wall, if you are using one for this unit, and provide necessary support to help students learn these words as you teach the lesson.

2. Student Privacy

Some of the activities in this lesson require students to record what may be sensitive or personal information. Note that students may feel uncomfortable sharing their completed handouts for Activity 3, and we do not recommend requiring them to do so. Instead, we encourage asking students to share their thought processes as they completed the exercise, rather than divulging the personal reflections they made about who is included (or excluded) in their universes of obligation.

3. The Unit Assessment

If your students are writing the final essay assessment for this unit, after you complete this lesson, proceed to Introducing the Writing Prompt.

Activities

1. Journal Responses: Groups and Belonging

Ask students to respond in their journals to the following prompt:

> Think about a group you belong to. It might be your family, a team, a faith community, a club, a classroom, an online community, or some other type of group. How did you become a member of that group? Did you choose to be a member, or are you one automatically? What do you gain by belonging to that group? What, if anything, do you have to give up or hide about yourself to be a member?

Briefly debrief the prompt by asking students to share some of the things they gain by belonging to groups and some of the things they give up in order to belong. Honor student privacy and refrain from requiring all students to share their responses in detail.

Then pose a new question to students:

> Why do humans so often divide themselves into groups? When is this a good thing? When is it harmful?

Give students a few minutes to respond in their journals, and then discuss the question using the Think, Pair, Share strategy.

2. Introduce the Concept of "Universe of Obligation"

Introduce the concept of *universe of obligation* to students, and explain that it is one way to consider the benefits of belonging to groups and the consequences of being excluded. An individual's or group's universe of obligation represents the extent to which they feel responsible for others. We often feel a greater sense of responsibility for those who belong to the same groups that we do.

Pass out the reading Universe of Obligation and read it aloud.

This reading includes quotations that feature the perspectives of three people: David Hume, Chuck Collins, and William Graham Sumner (connection question 4). Re-read the quotations from each of these people to the class, and then discuss with students the following questions:

- In what ways do these three people agree? In what ways do they disagree?
- Which of these people seems to have the most inclusive universe of obligation? Which seems to have the most exclusive?
- Is it possible for everyone in the world to be included in a person's or country's universe of obligation? If not, how should we prioritize?

3. Illustrate Individual Universes of Obligation

Finally, ask students to illustrate their own universes of obligation using the graphic organizer in the Universe of Obligation Graphic Organizer. The concentric circles on this handout can help students visualize and diagram what an individual, group, or country's universe of obligation might look like.

Give students time to follow the instructions and complete the activity on the handout. It might be helpful first to quickly brainstorm a variety of types of individuals and groups that might appear on one's graphic organizer, including family, friends, neighbors, classmates, strangers in one's town, and others.

Have students meet in groups of two or three to discuss their experience of trying to illustrate their universes of obligation. In their discussions, students should address some of the following questions:

- What was the experience of diagramming your universe of obligation like?
- What did you think about when deciding where to place certain groups in your universe of obligation? Which decisions were difficult? Which were easy?
- Under what conditions might your universe of obligation shift? What might cause you to move some groups to the center and others to the outside?
- What is the difference between an individual's universe of obligation and that of a school, community, or country?

Assessment

- Due to their personal nature, we do not recommend using students' individual Universe of Obligation Graphic Organizer handouts for assessment. Instead, gauge their understanding of the concept by asking each student to complete a separate universe of obligation handout, this time illustrating a group to which they belong—such as a school, neighborhood, or country.

- Observe the group discussions at the end of the lesson to understand how students are responding to the moral and ethical dilemmas inherent in attempting to define explicitly one's universe of obligation.

Extension

Supplement with Additional Readings

You might deepen the discussion of groups and belonging in this lesson by introducing additional readings from Chapter 2 of *Holocaust and Human Behavior* for student discussion and reflection. The reading "What Do We Do with a Difference?" includes a poem that raises important questions about the ways we respond to differences. In the reading "Understanding Strangers," journalist Ryszard Kapuscinski discusses the ways the earliest humans likely responded to "the Other" and suggests models for how we can constructively respond to unfamiliar groups of people today. Both readings and their related connection questions can help support a larger class discussion about the human behavior of dividing ourselves into groups. You might use the following question to guide the discussion:

> Why do humans so often divide themselves into "we" and "they"? When does it become a problem? What historical examples help you answer this question? What examples from the world today help you answer it?

Visit facinghistory.org/thhb to access these additional resources.

 Reading

Universe of Obligation

What does it mean to be a member of a group? In groups we meet our most basic needs; in groups we learn a language and a culture or way of life. In groups we also satisfy our yearning to belong, receive comfort in times of trouble, and find companions who share our dreams, values, and beliefs. Groups also provide security and protection from those who might wish to do us harm. Therefore, how a group defines its membership matters. Belonging can have significant advantages; being excluded can leave a person vulnerable.

How the members of a group, a nation, or a community define who belongs and who does not has a lot to do with how they define their universe of obligation. Sociologist Helen Fein coined this phrase to describe the group of individuals within a society "toward whom obligations are owed, to whom rules apply, and whose injuries call for amends."[1] In other words, a society's universe of obligation includes those people who that society believes deserve respect and whose rights it believes are worthy of protection.

A society's universe of obligation can change. Individuals and groups that are respected and protected members of a society at one time may find themselves outside of the universe of obligation when circumstances are different—such as during a war or economic depression. Beliefs and attitudes that are widely shared among members of a society may also affect the way that society defines its universe of obligation. For instance, throughout history, beliefs and attitudes about religion, gender, and race have helped to determine which people a society protects and which people it does not.

Although Fein uses the term to describe the way nations determine membership, we might also refer to an individual's universe of obligation to describe the circle of other individuals that person feels a responsibility to care for and protect. Rabbi Jonathan Sacks describes how individuals often define those for whom they feel responsible: "[Eighteenth-century philosopher] David Hume noted that our sense of empathy diminishes as we move outward from the members of our family to our neighbors, our society, and the world. Traditionally, our sense of involvement with the fate of others has been in inverse proportion to the distance separating us and them."[2]

Scholar and social activist Chuck Collins defines his universe of obligation differently from the example Sacks offers. In the 1980s, Collins gave the half-million dollars that he inherited from his family to charity. Collins told journalist Ian Parker:

> Of course, we have to respond to our immediate family, but, once they're O.K., we need to expand the circle. A larger sense of family is a radical idea, but we get into trouble as a society when we don't see that we're in the same boat.[3]

---

1 Helen Fein, *Accounting for Genocide* (New York: Free Press, 1979), 4.
2 Jonathan Sacks, *The Dignity of Difference: How to Avoid the Clash of Civilizations* (London: Continuum, 2002), 30.
3 Ian Parker, "The Gift," *New Yorker*, August 2, 2004, 60.

Connection Questions

1. What factors influence the way a society defines its universe of obligation? In what ways might a nation or community signal who is part of its universe of obligation and who is not?

2. What do you think might be some of the consequences for those who are not within a society's universe of obligation?

3. What factors influence how an individual defines their universe of obligation? In what ways might an individual show others who is part of their universe of obligation and who is not?

4. In the 1800s, sociologist William Graham Sumner wrote, "Every man and woman in society has one big duty. That is, to take care of his or her own self." Do you agree with Sumner? Why or why not? Is it wrong to prioritize caring for those closest to you over others? How does Sumner's suggestion about how we define our universe of obligation differ from Chuck Collins's view?

5. How would you describe your nation's universe of obligation? Your school's? Your own?

Handout

Universe of Obligation Graphic Organizer

In **Circle 1,** write your name.

In **Circle 2,** write the names of people to whom you feel the greatest obligation—for example, people for whom you'd be willing to take a great risk or put yourself in peril (you don't have to write actual names).

In **Circle 3,** write the names of people to whom you have some obligation, but not as great as for those in circle 2.

In **Circle 4,** write the names of those to whom you have some obligation, but not as great as for those in circle 3.

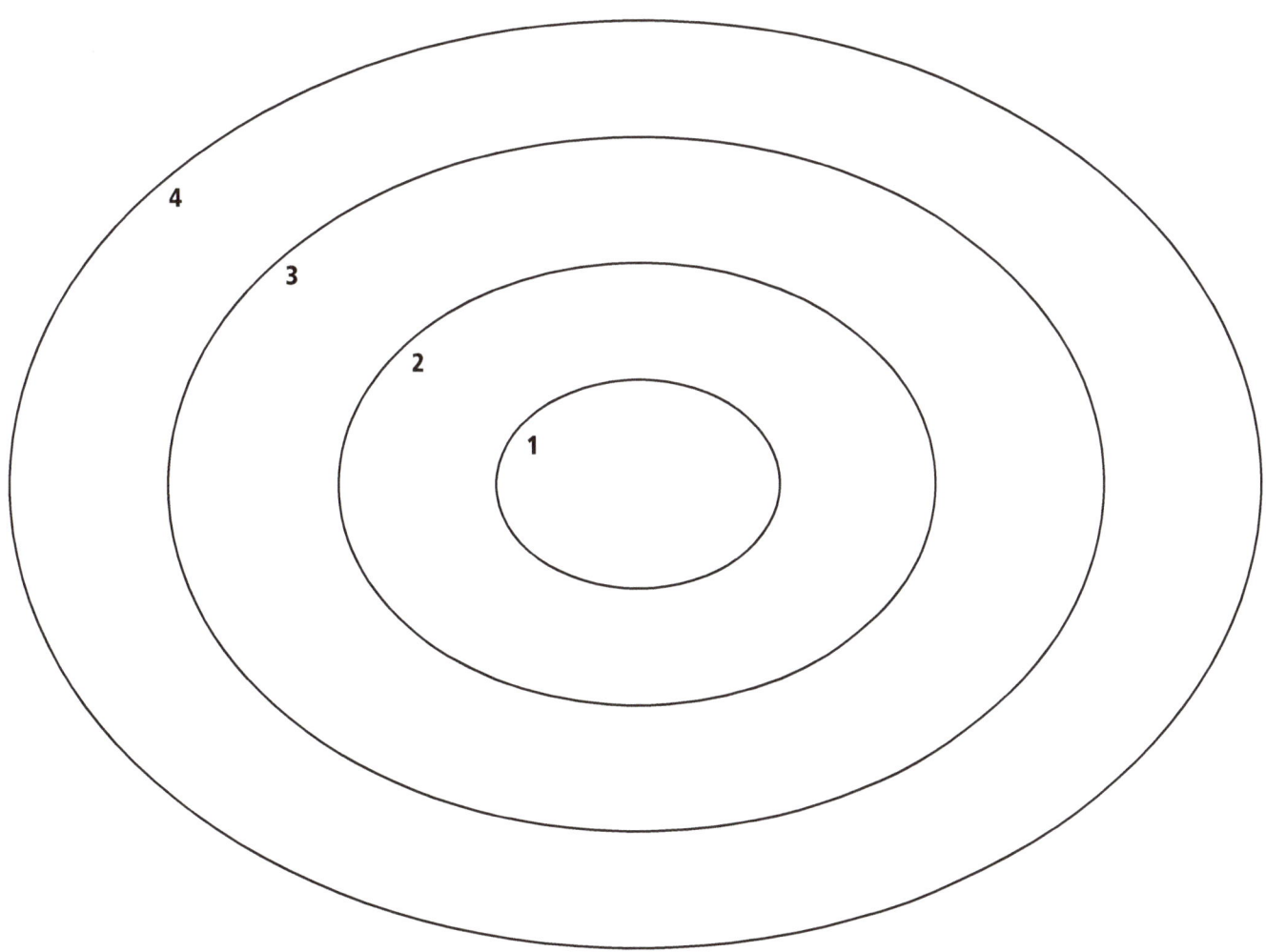

STEP 1

Introducing the Writing Prompt

Unit Essential Question

- What does learning about the choices people made during the Weimar Republic, the rise of the Nazi Party, and the Holocaust teach us about the power and impact of our choices today?

Guiding Question

- Why study history?

Learning Objective

- Students will develop an initial position for an argumentative essay in response to a question about the importance and impact of choices in history.

Overview

In the first four lessons of the unit, students explore questions about identity, stereotyping, and group membership. This assessment step introduces students to a writing prompt that builds on these important themes and connects them to the history students explore later in this unit. The prompt is designed to serve as both a thematic frame for the unit and a final writing assignment at the unit's end.

Unit Writing Prompt:
What does learning about the choices people made during the Weimar Republic, the rise of the Nazi Party, and the Holocaust teach us about the power and impact of our choices today?

Because the students have not yet been introduced to the Weimar era, the rise of the Nazi Party, and the Holocaust, this lesson begins with a modified version of the prompt:

Modified Writing Prompt for Lesson 5:
How does learning about the choices people made throughout history help us understand the power and impact of our choices in the world today?

This modified prompt enables students to think through larger themes about history and decision making before delving into the specific history in later lessons. This lesson's activities provide suggestions to help students start to understand the meaning of the prompt and to stake out a preliminary position in response

Duration
One 50-minute class period

Materials

 Handout
Why Study History?

 Teaching Strategies
Anticipation Guides
Four Corners
Think, Pair, Share
Exit Tickets

Find all materials referenced in this lesson at facinghistory.org/thhb.

to it. At key points later in this unit (after Lessons 8, 13, 18, 21, and 23), you will be prompted to give students the opportunity to revisit the prompt and consider stories, documents, and other evidence from history that may influence their thinking about it. At these times, students will also have the opportunity to reflect back on, and potentially modify, the initial position they articulate in this lesson.

There are two additional writing prompts that can be used as summative assessments for this unit included in Facing History's *Common Core Writing Prompts and Strategies: Holocaust and Human Behavior*, available at facinghistory.org/thhb. This resource includes lesson plans and writing strategies to help guide students through all phases of the writing process.

Notes to Teacher

Anticipation Guide Activity

This lesson introduces the Anticipation Guides teaching strategy. You might return to the handout Why Study History? later in the unit to see if students' ideas about the study of history have changed.

Activities

Visit facinghistory.org/thhb to access all materials referenced in these activities.

1. **Warm Up with an Anticipation Guide**

    Before the activity begins, hang four signs in the corners of the classroom that read "Strongly Agree," "Agree," "Disagree," and "Strongly Disagree."

    Pass out the handout Why Study History? and ask students to read the statements and decide if they strongly agree, agree, disagree, or strongly disagree with each one. They should circle their responses and then write a brief explanation for each choice.

    Use the Four Corners strategy to debrief the anticipation guide. Read each statement aloud and ask students to stand near one of the signs in the classroom to indicate their response. After students find their positions, ask them to explain their thinking to others in their corner.

    Next, ask students in each corner to share their ideas with the rest of the class. As one corner disagrees with another, encourage students to respond directly to each other's statements and have a mini-debate about the prompt. If students' ideas change due to the debate, tell them that they are free to switch corners.

2. **Generate Initial Responses to a Modified Essay Prompt**

    Next, ask students to return to their seats and take out their journals so they can reflect on the Four Corners activity and start to think about a new and related question.

    Write the modified essay topic on the board and ask students to respond to it in their journals. Students might also reference their ideas about one or more of the quotations on the handout Why Study History? when formulating their responses.

> How does learning about the choices people made throughout history help us understand the power and impact of our choices in the world today?

Next, ask students to debrief the journal prompt in a Think, Pair, Share discussion. Ask students to try to support their thinking with an example from the history they have studied or their own lives. Finally, ask students to share a few opinions or ideas with the larger group.

Tell students that they will build on these ideas in the upcoming weeks as they learn about the history of Nazi Germany and the Holocaust. They can keep all their notes about these ideas in their journals and use them later to help them think about their essays.

3. Exit Tickets

Give each student an exit ticket with the following question:

> Did today's class affect your thinking about why we should study history? Did it affect how you think about the connection between the choices people made in history and the choices you make in your own life? If so, explain how. If not, explain why not.

Collect the exit tickets as students leave the classroom. You might share some interesting ideas or patterns at the start of the next lesson. Unless you have permission from the student, we recommend that you keep these anonymous.

Assessment

- Observe carefully the discussion that occurs during the Four Corners activity in order to check students' understanding of the themes embedded in the writing prompt. It is important that every student has the opportunity to talk, either in the small groups in their corners or when sharing with the whole group.

- Evaluate students' responses on the exit tickets. While their thinking about the writing prompt will evolve over time, check now for evidence that they have a basic understanding of the question itself.

Extension

Dissect the Essay Writing Prompt

If your class is ready, you might introduce the full unit writing prompt, rather than the one modified for this lesson. Using the Dissecting the Prompt strategy, students can take apart and analyze the prompt, identifying the historical topics they need to learn more about in the rest of the unit to be able to fully answer the question. This will establish several inquiry questions for the class that are related to students' broader thinking about the purpose of studying history in this lesson.

 Handout

Why Study History?

Read the statement in the left column. Decide if you strongly agree (SA), agree (A), disagree (D), or strongly disagree (SD) with the statement. Circle your response and provide a one- to two-sentence explanation of your opinion. Use separate paper if needed.

Statement	Your Opinion
1. "Those who fail to learn from history are doomed to repeat it." – George Santayana, philosopher	SA A D SD **Explain:**
2. Every situation is different. There's nothing to learn from the choices people made in history.	SA A D SD **Explain:**
3. "The past is never dead. It's not even past." – William Faulkner, author	SA A D SD **Explain:**
4. What happened in history has nothing to do with me.	SA A D SD **Explain:**
5. History never has to unfold the way it does, because the choices each of us make shape history.	SA A D SD **Explain:**
6. "History is not the past. It is the present. We carry our history with us. We are our history." – James Baldwin, author	SA A D SD **Explain:**

| **Unit Essential Question** | What does learning about the choices people made during the Weimar Republic, the rise of the Nazi Party, and the Holocaust teach us about the power and impact of our choices today? |

Lesson

The Concept of Race

Duration

One 50-minute class period

Materials

Handouts

Which of These Things Is Not Like the Others?

Race: The Power of an Illusion Viewing Guide

Race and Racism

Video

Race: The Power of an Illusion (The Difference Between Us)

Reading

Growing Up with Racism

Teaching Strategy

Think, Pair, Share

Find all materials referenced in this lesson at facinghistory.org/thhb.

Guiding Questions

- What is *race*? What is *racism*? How do ideas about race affect how we see others and ourselves?
- How have race and racism been used by societies to define their universes of obligation?

Learning Objective

- Students will define and analyze the socially constructed meaning of race, examining how that concept has been used to justify exclusion, inequality, and violence throughout history.

Overview

In the previous lesson, students began the "We and They" stage of the Facing History scope and sequence by examining the human behavior of creating and considering the concept of *universe of obligation*. This lesson continues the study of "We and They," as students turn their attention to an idea—the concept of *race*—that has been used for more than 400 years by many societies to define their universes of obligation. Contrary to the beliefs of many people, past and present, race has never been scientifically proven to be a significant genetic or biological difference in humans. The concept of race was in fact invented by society to fulfill its need to justify disparities in power and status among different groups. The lack of scientific evidence about race undermines the very concept of the superiority of some "races" and the inferiority of other "races."

Race is an especially crucial concept in any study of Nazi Germany and the Holocaust, because it was central to Nazi ideology. However, the Nazis weren't the only ones who had notions about race. This lesson also examines the history and development of the idea of "race" in England and the United States.

Context

For at least 400 years, a theory of "race" has been a lens through which many individuals, leaders, and nations have determined who belongs and who does not. Theories about "race" include the notion that human beings can be classified into different races according to certain physical characteristics, such as skin color, eye shape, and hair form. The theory has led to the common, but false, belief that some "races" have intellectual and physical abilities that are superior to those of other "races." Biologists and geneticists today have not only disproved this claim, they have also declared that there is no genetic or biological basis for categorizing people by race. According to microbiologist Pilar Ossorio:

> Are the people who we call Black more like each other than they are like people who we call white, genetically speaking? The answer is no. There's as much or more diversity and genetic difference within any racial group as there is between people of different racial groups.[1]

As professor Evelynn Hammonds states in the film *Race: The Power of an Illusion*: "Race is a human invention. We created it, and we have used it in ways that have been in many, many respects quite negative and quite harmful."[2]

When the scientific and intellectual ideals of the Enlightenment came to dominate the thinking of most Europeans in the 1700s, they exposed a basic contradiction between principle and practice: the enslavement of human beings. Despite the fact that Enlightenment ideals of human freedom and equality inspired revolutions in the United States and France, the practice of slavery persisted throughout the United States and European empires. In the late 1700s and early 1800s, American and European scientists tried to explain this contradiction through the study of "race science," which advanced the idea that humankind is divided into separate and unequal races. If it could be scientifically proven that Europeans were biologically superior to those from other places, especially Africa, then Europeans could justify slavery and other imperialistic practices.

Prominent scientists from many countries, including Sweden, the Netherlands, England, Germany, and the United States, used "race science" to give legitimacy to the race-based divisions in their societies. Journalists, teachers, and preachers popularized their ideas. Historian Reginald Horsman, who studied the leading publications of the time, describes the false messages about race that were pervasive throughout the nineteenth century:

> One did not have to read obscure books to know that the Caucasians were innately superior, and that they were responsible for civilization in the world, or to know that inferior races were destined to be overwhelmed or even to disappear.[3]

Some scientists and public figures challenged race science. In an 1854 speech, Frederick Douglass, the formerly enslaved American political activist, argued:

---

1 Pilar Ossorio, *Race: The Power of an Illusion,* Episode 1: "The Difference Between Us" (California Newsreel, 2003), transcript accessed May 2, 2016, http://newsreel.org/transcripts/race1.htm.

2 Evelynn Hammonds, interview, *Race: The Power of an Illusion,* Episode 1: "The Difference Between Us" (California Newsreel, 2003), transcript accessed April 12, 2017, http://newsreel.org/transcripts/race1.htm.

3 Reginald Horsman, *Race and Manifest Destiny: The Origins of American Racial Anglo-Saxonism* (Cambridge, MA: Harvard University Press, 1981), 157.

> The whole argument in defense of slavery becomes utterly worthless the moment the African is proved to be equally a man with the Anglo-Saxon. The temptation, therefore, to read the Negro out of the human family is exceedingly strong.[4]

Douglass and others who spoke out against race science were generally ignored or marginalized.

By the late 1800s, the practice of eugenics emerged out of race science in England, the United States, and Germany. Eugenics is the use of so-called science to improve the human race, both by breeding "society's best with the best" and by preventing "society's worst" from breeding at all. Eugenicists believed that a nation is a biological community that must be protected from "threat," which they often defined as mixing with allegedly inferior "races."

In the early twentieth century, influential German biologist Ernst Haeckel divided humankind into races and ranked them. In his view, "Aryans"—a mythical race from whom many northern Europeans believed they had descended—were at the top of the rankings and Jews and Africans were at the bottom. Ideas of race and eugenics would become central to Nazi ideology in the 1920s, 1930s, and 1940s.

Despite the fact that one's race predicts almost nothing else about an individual's physical or intellectual capacities, people still commonly believe in a connection between race and certain biological abilities or deficiencies. The belief in this connection leads to racism. As scholar George Fredrickson explains, racism has two components: difference and power.

> It originates from a mindset that regards "them" as different from "us" in ways that are permanent and unbridgeable. This sense of difference provides a motive or rationale for using our power advantage to treat the . . . Other in ways that we would regard as cruel or unjust if applied to members of our own group.[5]

The idea that there is an underlying biological link between race and intellectual or physical abilities (or deficiencies) has persisted for hundreds of years. Learning that race is a social concept, not a scientific fact, may be challenging for students. They may need time to absorb the reality behind the history of race because it conflicts with the way many in our society understand it.

Notes to Teacher

1. Navigating Race

Race and racism are often difficult subjects for teachers and students to navigate. For this reason, you may want to briefly return to the class contract and to the agreed-upon norms of classroom discussion at the beginning of this lesson. You may also want to explore the lesson "Preparing Students for Difficult Conversations" (specifically Activities 2 and 3) for additional strategies and guidance.

That the meaning of race is socially, rather than scientifically, constructed is a new and complex idea for many students and adults that can challenge long-held assumptions. Therefore, we recommend providing opportunities for stu-

---

4 Frederick Douglass, *The Claims of the Negro Ethnologically Considered: An Address Before the Literary Societies of Western Reserve College, at Commencement, July 12, 1854* (Rochester, NY: Lee, Mann & Co., 1854), 8–9.

5 George M. Fredrickson, *Racism: A Short History* (Princeton, NJ: Princeton University Press, 2002), 9.

dents to process, reflect, and ask questions about what they've learned in this lesson. The Exit Tickets teaching strategy used in the Assessment section is one way to achieve this, but you could also use the 3-2-1 strategy to elicit reflections and feedback from students.

2. Previewing Vocabulary

The following are key vocabulary terms used in this lesson:

- Race
- Racism

Add these words to your word wall, if you are using one for this unit, and provide necessary support to help students learn these words as you teach the lesson.

Activities

1. Opener: One of These Things Is Not Like the Others

Race is one of the concepts that societies have created to sort and categorize their members. Before discussing race, this brief opening activity introduces students to the idea that when we sort and categorize the things and people around us, we make judgments about which characteristics are more meaningful than others. Students will be asked to look at four shapes and decide which is not like the others, but in doing so they must also choose the category on which they will base their decision.

Share with students the handout Which of These Things Is Not Like the Others? If possible, you might simply project the image in the classroom.

Ask students to answer the question by identifying the object in the image that is not like the others.

Prompt students to share their answers and explain their thinking behind the answer to a classmate, using the Think, Pair, Share strategy. What criterion did they use to identify one item as different? Why? Did their partner use the same criterion?

Explain that while students' choices in this exercise are relatively inconsequential, we make similar choices with great consequence in the ways that we define and categorize people in society. While there are many categories we might use to describe differences between people, society has given more meaning to some types of difference (such as skin color and gender) and less meaning to others (such as eye and hair color). You might ask students to brainstorm some of the categories of difference that are meaningful in our society.

2. Reflect on the Meaning of Race

Tell students that in this lesson, they will look more closely at a concept that has been used throughout history by groups and countries to shape their universes of obligation: the concept of race. Race is a concept that continues to significantly influence the way that society is structured and the way that individuals think about and act toward one another.

Before asking students to examine the concept closely in this lesson, it is worth giving them a few minutes to write down their own thoughts and assumptions about what race is and what it means. Share the following questions with students, and give them a few minutes to privately record their responses in their journals. Let them know that they will not be asked to share their responses.

What is race? What, if anything, can one's race tell you about a person? How might this concept impact how you think about others or how others think about you?

3. Learn about the History of "Race"

Show students a short clip (07:55 to 13:10) from the film **Race: The Power of an Illusion (The Difference Between Us)**, available at **facinghistory.org/thhb**. Before you start the clip, pass out the *Race: The Power of an Illusion* Viewing Guide and preview the questions with students.

Instruct students to take notes in response to the viewing guide questions as they watch the clip. If time permits, consider showing the clip a second time to help students gather additional details and answer the questions more thoroughly.

Debrief the video and the viewing guide responses with students. Be sure that students understand the following ideas:

- Race is not meaningful in a biological sense.
- It was created rather than discovered by scientists and has been used to justify existing divisions in society.

4. Explore the Meaning of *Racism*

Pass out the **Race and Racism** handout. Alternatively, you might project the handout in the classroom and instruct students to copy down Frederickson's definition of *racism* into their journals.

Read the handout aloud to students and ask them to complete the following tasks:

- Circle any words that you do not understand in the definition.
- Underline three to four words that you think are crucial to understanding the meaning of *racism*.
- Below the definition, rewrite it in your own words.
- At the bottom of the page, write at least one synonym (or other word closely related to *racism*) and one antonym.

Allow a few minutes after this activity to discuss students' answers and clear up any words they did not understand.

5. Consider the Impact of Racism

Now pass out the reading **Growing Up with Racism**. Read Lisa Delpit's letter together, and then lead a discussion about the following questions using the **Think, Pair, Share** strategy:

- What has been the impact of racism on Delpit? How has racism influenced the ways that people think and act toward her?

- How has racism affected how Delpit thinks about herself? According to her observations, how has racism affected how other African Americans think about themselves?
- How does racism affect how a society defines its universe of obligation?

6. Reflect on the Impact of Categorizing People

Finish the lesson by asking students to respond to the following prompt:

> When is it harmful to point out the differences between people? When is it natural or necessary? Is it possible to divide people into groups without privileging one group over another?

If you would like to use this response as an assessment, consider asking students to complete it on a separate sheet of paper for you to collect. You might also ask students to complete the reflection for homework.

Assessment

- Use the handouts in this lesson to help you gauge students' understanding of the concept of race. The viewing guide to provides a window into the evolution of students' understanding in the middle of the lesson, while the student-annotated Race and Racism handout can help you see their ability to articulate their understanding of these concepts.

- Read students' written reflection from the end of the lesson to help you see how they are thinking about the broader patterns of human behavior—categorizing ourselves and collecting ourselves into groups—discussed in this lesson.

Extensions

1. View *A Class Divided*

The streaming video *A Class Divided* (53:53) provides a powerful example of how dividing people by seemingly arbitrary characteristics can affect how they think about and act toward themselves and others. It tells the story of teacher Jane Elliott's second-grade classroom experiment in which she temporarily separated her students by eye color. Consider showing this compelling video to deepen your class discussion of why people create groups and why that behavior matters.

2. Go Deeper in *Holocaust and Human Behavior*

Another way to deepen the discussion of groups and belonging in this lesson is to introduce additional readings from Chapter 2 of *Holocaust and Human Behavior* for student discussion and reflection. The reading "What Do We Do with a Difference?" includes a poem that raises important questions about the ways we respond to differences. Other readings in the chapter trace the evolution of the concept of race during the Enlightenment and the emergence of "race science" in the eighteenth and nineteenth centuries.

Visit facinghistory.org/thhb to access these additional resources.

Handout

Which of These Things Is Not Like the Others?

 **Handout**

Race: The Power of an Illusion Viewing Guide

Directions: As you view the clip from the film *Race: The Power of an Illusion,* record notes that help you answer the questions on this handout.

How do the experts in the film define *race*?

How did people in the past use the idea of race to explain their society? Why was the idea of race portrayed as natural?

Respond to the following question after viewing the film:

What did you learn from the video that supports your journal reflection about the meaning and impact of race? What did you learn from the video that challenges what you wrote? Go back and revise or continue your journal reflection based on what you learned from the video.

 Handout

Race and Racism

By knowing one's race, scientists can predict almost nothing else about an individual's physical or intellectual abilities. Despite this fact, it remains common for people to believe falsely in a connection between race and particular and permanent biological abilities or deficiencies. The belief in this connection leads to *racism*. According to scholar George Fredrickson, racism has two components: *difference and power.*

Directions: After reading Fredrickson's definition of *racism* below, complete the following tasks:

- Circle any words that you do not understand in the definition.
- Underline three to four words that you think are crucial to understanding the meaning of *racism*.

> [Racism] originates from a mindset that regards "them" as different from "us" in ways that are permanent and unbridgeable. This sense of difference provides a motive or rationale for using our power advantage to treat the . . . Other in ways that we would regard as cruel or unjust if applied to members of our own group.[1]

Now rewrite the definition in your own words:

Write at least one synonym (or other word closely related to *racism*) and one antonym:

---

1 George M. Fredrickson, *Racism: A Short History* (Princeton, NJ: Princeton University Press, 2002), 9.

 Reading

Growing Up with Racism

Lisa Delpit is an educator who grew up in Baton Rouge, Louisiana, at a time when police officers patrolled the street that separated the city's Black and white residents. Although that time in history has passed, her experiences continue to shape Delpit's views, including her hopes and fears for her child. In a letter to her daughter, Maya, Delpit writes:

> As much as I think of you as my gift to the world, I am constantly made aware that there are those who see you otherwise.
>
> Although you don't realize it yet, it is solely because of your color that the police officers in our predominantly white neighborhood stop you to "talk" when you walk our dog. You think they're being friendly, but when you tell me that one of their first questions is always, "Do you live around here?" I know that they question your right to be here, that somehow your being here threatens their sense of security. . . .
>
> I did not have to be told much when I was your age. When I was growing up in Louisiana in the 1950s and 1960s, the color lines were very clearly drawn. I followed my mother to the back entrance of the doctor's office, marked "colored." I knew which water fountain I was supposed to drink from. On the bus ride to my all-black school, I watched white children walk to schools just two or three blocks from my house.
>
> In large part, my childhood years were wrapped in the warm cocoon of family and community who all knew each other and looked out for one another. However, I remember clearly my racing heart, my sweaty-palmed fear of the white policemen who entered my father's small restaurant one night and hit him with nightsticks, the helpless terror when there were rumors in our school yard that the Ku Klux Klan would be riding, the anxiety of knowing my college-aged foster sister had joined the civil-rights marchers in a face-off against the white policemen and their dogs. And, I remember, my Maya, the death of your grandfather when I was seven, who died of kidney failure because the "colored" ward wasn't yet allowed the use of the brand-new dialysis machine.
>
> Your world is very different, at least on its surface. In many ways now is a more confusing time to live. . . .
>
> As any mother would, I have a great need to protect you, but it is hard to know how. My childhood experience was different from yours. As was the case in many African-American Louisiana families, our family was a rainbow of colors from chocolate-brown brunettes to peach-colored blondes . . . I was the light-skinned, freckled, red-headed child, who always got the sunburn whenever we went to the beach. Because of my coloring, I had another role, too. When traveling by car, African Americans were not allowed to use the restrooms or other facilities white travelers took for granted. Black families had to develop all sorts of strategies to make a road trip workable. When it was time for a rest stop, one of our ruses was to pull around to the side of the service station and send in the one who looked most like white to get the key. Then, outside of the attendant's view, everyone would use the facility.

Decades later, when you were an infant, your aunt and I drove to Mississippi. I had not made that trip for many years, and although segregation was officially over, I still felt uneasy at the rest stops. Any African American would. There were Confederate flags printed on every possible souvenir in the gift shops, and restaurants and gas stations were filled with burly, white, cigarette-smoking men with gun racks mounted in their rear windows. Heart racing, cradling my beautiful brown baby, I suddenly realized I did not know how to protect you from the vicious hatred in some of the eyes that stared at us. Or, for that matter, from a society whose very structure privileges some and marginalizes you.

. . . When I was in my segregated, all-black elementary school, we were told by teachers and parents that we had to excel, that we had to "do better than" any white kids because the world was already on their side. When your cousin Joey was in high school, I remember berating him for getting a "D" in chemistry. His response was, "What do you expect of me? The white kids get C's." Recently a colleague tried to help an African-American middle-schooler to learn multiplication. The student looked up at the teacher and said, "Why are you trying to teach me this? Black people don't multiply. Multiplication is for white people." You know, Maya, I think that may be the biggest challenge you and other brown children will face—not believing the limits that others place upon you.[1]

---

[1] Lisa Delpit, "Explaining Racism," *The Magazine of the Harvard Graduate School of Education* (Spring 2000), 15–17.

Unit Essential Question

What does learning about the choices people made during the Weimar Republic, the rise of the Nazi Party, and the Holocaust teach us about the power and impact of our choices today?

Lesson

The Roots and Impact of Antisemitism

Duration

One 50-minute class period

Materials

Handout

Overview of Anti-Judaism and Antisemitism

Readings

"We Don't Control America" and Other Myths, Part 1

"We Don't Control America" and Other Myths, Part 2

"We Don't Control America" and Other Myths, Part 3

Find all materials referenced in this lesson at facinghistory.org/thhb.

Guiding Questions

- What is antisemitism, and how has it impacted Jews in the past and today?
- What are the consequences when a "single story" is used to exclude a group of people from a society's universe of obligation?

Learning Objectives

- Students will be able to explain how anti-Judaism developed into antisemitism in the nineteenth century.
- Students will consider the present-day implications of longstanding patterns of discrimination and violence against Jews.

Overview

In the previous lesson, students examined the concept of race and learned how it was created by society in order to justify unequal power and status between different groups. This lesson continues the study of "We and They" in the Facing History scope and sequence by introducing *antisemitism*, another historical example of how humans have created "in" groups and "out" groups. Students will explore the long history of hatred and discrimination against Jews, and they will see how anti-Judaism, a religious prejudice, was transformed in the nineteenth century into antisemitism, a form of racism. Learning about the development of antisemitism will provide students with important context for the worldview of the Nazis. It will also help students recognize and understand the impact of stereotypes and myths about Jews that persist today.

A note on terms:

- The term *anti-Judaism* refers to religious prejudice against Jews before the historical emergence of the concept of race.

- The word *Semitic* does not actually refer to a group of people. It is not a "race" but rather a linguistic term that refers to a group of languages traditionally spoken in the Middle East and parts of Africa, including Amharic, a language spoken in Ethiopia, as well as Hebrew and Arabic. Because there is no such thing as a Semitic race, Facing History & Ourselves uses the alternate spelling *antisemitism*.

Context

Although antisemitism—a central component of the Nazi worldview—is based on the belief that Jews are members of a distinct race, the history of hatred, prejudice, and discrimination targeting Jews extends back in time more than two millennia, long before the idea of race emerged during the Enlightenment.

In the late 1800s, many European and American scientists continued to divide humankind into smaller and smaller "races." One of these was the "Semitic race," which they used to categorize Jews. The term *antisemitism* was coined by German Wilhelm Marr, who published a pamphlet in 1878 titled "The Victory of Judaism over Germandom." Filled with lies and myths about Jews, Marr's pamphlet argued that Jews were more than a distinct "race." They were dangerous and alien, intent on maliciously destroying German society. Marr founded the League of Anti-Semites in Berlin in 1879 to combat the threat he imagined that Jews posed. Although his political organization did not gain much support, the racist beliefs of antisemitism spread across Europe, providing justification for discrimination and violence against Jews in the twentieth century.

Antisemitism relies on the idea that certain physical and intellectual differences exist between groups and that these differences are biological, permanent, and irreversible. Because they believed, falsely, that differences between so-called races were justified by modern science, antisemites were convinced that science also justified discrimination against Jews.

Historian Deborah Dwork explains:

> The move from anti-Judaism—against the religion—to antisemitism with this notion of "race" was only possible when Europeans *conceived* of the idea of race. And once they had conceived of the idea of race in the 19th century, Wilhelm Marr had the notion that *Jews* constituted a "race." And thus, antisemitism can be seen as a form of racism.[1]

Notes to Teacher

1. Teaching about the History and Impact of Antisemitism

As with the topic of race in the previous lesson, students may begin this lesson with misconceptions about Judaism. Antisemitic beliefs and stereotypes persist today. Students may encounter facts and information in this lesson that conflict with things they learned at home or in church and that they did not realize were rooted in the history of anti-Judaism and antisemitism. Therefore, it is important to be ready to respond to "single stories" about Jews that may arise

---

1 "Antisemitism from the Enlightenment to World War I," Facing History & Ourselves video, https://www.facinghistory.org/resource-library/video/antisemitism-enlightenment-world-war-i.

in class, help students consider where such stories came from, and ground the discussion in what we know from history about the origins of antisemitic ideas.

If, in the course of teaching this lesson, you become concerned that your students have a limited understanding of what it means to be Jewish and are relying on stereotypes and single stories instead, consider returning to the Lesson 2 extension "Explore the Complexity of Jewish Identity."

If you taught the extension about Jewish identity in Lesson 2, you might review the identity chart for "Jewish identity" that the class created in order to remind students of the variety of ways that individuals define their relationship to Jewish culture and religion and the idea that there is no single story that explains what it means to be Jewish.

2. **Previewing Vocabulary**

    The following are key vocabulary terms used in this lesson:
    - Antisemitism
    - Anti-Judaism
    - Aryan
    - Marginalize

    Add these words to your word wall, if you are using one for this unit, and provide necessary support to help students learn these words as you teach the lesson.

Activities

1. **Reflect on the Persistence of Rumors, Lies, and Myths**

    The history of anti-Judaism and antisemitism is in part a story of rumors, lies, and myths that have persisted over the course of centuries. Begin this lesson by asking students to record their observations about rumors, lies, and myths from their own experiences. Ask students to respond to the following question in their journals:

    > How do rumors get started? Why might lies and myths about people persist even after they have been proven wrong? Have you ever helped to spread a rumor that you doubted or knew wasn't true? Why?

    While students should be allowed to keep their own stories of spreading rumors private, you can ask for a volunteers to share their more general observations about why rumors and lies can be so persistent.

2. **Explore the History of Antisemitism**

    Inform students that in this lesson, they are going to learn about *antisemitism*. Tell them that its most basic definition is "hatred of or hostility toward Jews," but it is also a form of racism. In this lesson, they will look at history to understand how religious prejudice against Jews evolved into racism.

    Give students the handout Overview of Anti-Judaism and Antisemitism.

    Instruct students to read the handout with a partner, stopping at each box to annotate the section and answer the text-based questions.

Debrief the reading with students by asking them to share their answers to the questions. Take this opportunity to correct any misunderstandings regarding the history of anti-Judaism and antisemitism.

In the same pairs, ask students to discuss the following questions:

- What do students notice about the history of hatred, discrimination, and violence toward Jews?
- How is antisemitism, which emerged in the 1870s, different from the anti-Judaism that existed before the 1870s? Why is that difference significant?
- How were "single stories" used to exclude Jews from the universe of obligation of individuals and societies? What were the consequences?

Ask the student pairs to share their answers to these questions in a brief class discussion.

3. Explore the Impact of Antisemitic Myths and Attitudes Today

Have students work in pairs to read and respond to Part 1, 2, or 3 of "We Don't Control America" and Other Myths. Roughly a third of the groups should work with each of the three excerpts from the reading set.

Each group's task is to read the assigned excerpt and discuss the following questions:

- How does the myth described affect the writer? How does she respond when confronted with the fact that another person believes a false myth or stereotype about Jews?
- How do you explain why people might believe such myths and stereotypes about Jews? What might it take to overcome these false antisemitic beliefs?

Finish the lesson with a brief whole-group discussion in which each group has the opportunity to share their observations.

Assessment

- Gauge students' understanding of and response to the history and impact of antisemitism by asking them to complete a one-page writing assignment in which they list three takeaways from this lesson. You might use the following prompt:

  What did you learn in this lesson about the history and impact of antisemitism that you think everyone should know? In a one-page writing assignment, list three facts, ideas, or events you learned about in this lesson, and for each one, explain why you think it is important for others to know about it.

- Collect the handout Overview of Anti-Judaism and Antisemitism and examine students' responses to the embedded questions for evidence of their comprehension of the reading and the history of antisemitism.

Extension

Further Reading

For a deeper and more detailed exploration of the history of anti-Judaism and antisemitism, you can substitute the resources below for the handout "Overview of Anti-Judaism and Antisemitism." The readings in *Holocaust and Human Behavior* and videos listed below also include connection questions for additional discussion and reflection:

- Readings: "Anti-Judaism before the Enlightenment" and "From Religious Prejudice to Antisemitism" in *Holocaust and Human Behavior*
- Videos: *The Ancient Roots of Anti-Judaism* and *Antisemitism from the Enlightenment to World War I*

Visit **facinghistory.org/thhb** to access these additional resources.

 Handout

Overview of Anti-Judaism and Antisemitism

Directions: As you are reading, annotate the text by completing the following steps:

1. Circle words that are unfamiliar.
2. Put a question mark (?) in the margin in places where you feel confused.
3. Stop and answer the questions in the boxes. Underline the place(s) in the text where you found the answer to a question.

Judaism is the oldest monotheistic religion. Throughout much of the faith's history, Jews lived in territories ruled by other groups. They were often treated as outsiders and blamed for disasters suffered by the societies in which they lived. Continuous rumors, lies, myths, and misinformation about Jews have existed throughout history. Many of them persist in the contemporary world. Often this hatred has led to violence.

In 63 BCE, the Romans conquered Jerusalem, the center of Jewish life. They incorporated ancient Israel, the land where the Jews lived, into the Roman Empire. The Romans were brutal rulers who demanded that those they ruled worship their numerous gods. Jews worshipped only one god. The Romans responded with persecution and violence. They destroyed the center of Jewish life, the temple in Jerusalem, in 70 CE. In 130 CE, the Romans attacked Jerusalem again. They displaced much of the Jewish population from the region that the Jews considered their homeland.

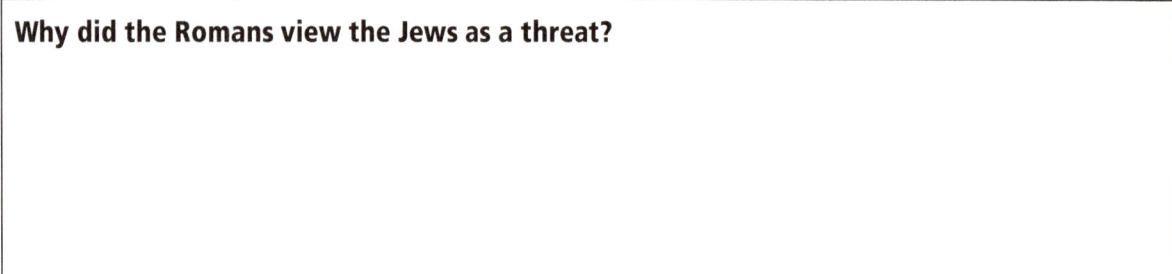

> **Why did the Romans view the Jews as a threat?**

During this period of Roman rule, a new faith, Christianity, emerged from Judaism. Jesus and his early followers were Jews. But as Christianity spread after the Romans executed Jesus, early Christians distanced themselves from Jews. This was partly to avoid being persecuted by the Romans. Christianity and Judaism eventually became separate and competing religions. By the 300s, Christianity became the official religion of the Roman Empire. Jews remained a minority.

Over time, lies and myths developed about Jews. Christian Roman society increasingly portrayed them as "Other." They were also blamed for various social ills. Among these myths was the false charge that Jews, not Romans, were responsible for the death of Christ. Another powerful lie charged Jews with associating with the devil.

Throughout the Middle Ages, European Christian armies attacked Jewish communities. Jews were also falsely blamed for causing the Black Death. They were forced in some places in Europe to live in ghettos and wear identifying badges. In other places, they were driven away entirely. This happened in 1492. King Ferdinand and Queen Isabella forced Jews to leave the Iberian Peninsula unless they converted. But in the 1500s, not even conversion was enough to save Jews in Spain. The claim emerged among many Christians that those born as Jews had "Jewish blood." This claim stated that conversion to Christianity did not change Jews' fundamental identity.

> **For what events did Christians blame Jews during the Middle Ages? What were the consequences for many Jewish communities?**

Later in the 1500s, Christians known as Protestants broke away from the Church of Rome. Many Protestants thought that Jews would convert to their new Christian faith. When that did not happen, Protestant leader Martin Luther turned on Jews. He called for synagogues and Jewish homes to be set on fire.

The ideas of the Enlightenment had spread across Europe by the 1700s. Among those ideas was that society could be improved through the use of human reason and science and through the ideals of equality. Between the late 1700s and early 1900s, laws and restrictions that discriminated against Jews were lifted in many European societies. In many places, Jews were allowed to participate more fully in the politics, economy, and social life of the places they lived.

As restrictions on Jews loosened across Europe in the 1800s, Jews became more integrated into European society. Some Jews became successful and visible leaders in a variety of professions, and a few became high-ranking government officials. This sparked a backlash from those who continued to be prejudiced against Jews or felt threatened by their increasing success (even though most European Jews remained poor). False conspiracy theories spread across Europe that Jews secretly controlled powerful governments. The theories also stated that Jews controlled financial institutions and sought to enrich themselves at the expense of non-Jewish Europeans.

How did the Enlightenment ideas impact the treatment of Jews in Europe?

During the same period, the field of "race science" emerged in Europe and North America. This happened in part to portray slavery and other divisions in society as "natural."

Race scientists who divided humans into separate races began to count Jews as a race. In 1878, German Wilhelm Marr popularized the idea that Jews are a distinct and dangerous race. He called them the "Semitic" race. He believed that this race was assaulting Germany and decreasing the fortunes of true "Aryan" Germans. "Aryans" were a mythical, supposedly superior race. Many northern Europeans believed they had descended from the "Aryan" race. Marr coined the term "antisemitism" to describe his belief that Jews were dangerous and should not be allowed to participate in German society.

How did Wilhelm Marr apply ideas of "race" to Jews? How did "race science" support his views?

Antisemitism became common across Europe in the early 1900s. Jews were falsely blamed for the destruction and defeat suffered by Germany and its allies in World War I. They were also blamed for the communist revolution that overthrew the tsar in Russia. Thus, they inspired fear in capitalist societies across Europe. These myths and lies were used to justify increasing discrimination and violence against Jews in the twentieth century.

 Reading

"We Don't Control America" and Other Myths, Part 1

Miriam observes:

> Last year I tutored at this nursing school. This woman was from Guatemala. I'm sure she's educated, but she didn't speak English. My job was to teach her enough English so she could pass the test to get in. One day she said, "Miriam, are you Jewish?" I said, "Yeah." She said, "You know how I knew? Because you're very smart and you dress modestly." Then she said, "The Jews are the people of God— it says so in the Bible. That's why they're very smart and wealthy."
>
> I didn't know what to say. If you're Jewish, there is definitely an emphasis on being smart and succeeding in school. If people think that, then OK. But it's a problem to think that all Jews are wealthy when they're not. I was in Argentina last quarter. They have this huge economic crisis and a lot of extreme poverty. Synagogues are feeding lots and lots of hungry people who are Jews. No one can pay tuition anymore at the Jewish schools. Anti-Semitism is more of an issue there. A woman from Uruguay told a friend of mine that Jews run everything in Argentina.
>
> People's willingness to believe things like that is weird. That's where I think stereotypes become a problem. It's not OK to say, "All Jews are wealthier," or "The Jews run things," or "There's something about the Jews."[1]

---

1 "There's Something About the Jews," in Pearl Gaskins, *I Believe In . . . : Christian, Jewish, and Muslim Young People Speak About Their Faith* (Chicago: Cricket Books, 2004), 92.

 Reading

"We Don't Control America" and Other Myths, Part 2

Darcy notes:

Sometimes it's just innocent questions: people don't know better. A Jewish girlfriend of mine was asked if it's true that Jews freeze the placentas of their babies and then eat them. No. But there are definitely versions of the blood libel still around—[the lie] that Jews use the blood of Christian children to make their matzo for Passover. . . .

I have a classmate who is Egyptian. She came with me to synagogue once and was looking through the prayer book, which is in Hebrew and English. She was looking for the part where it says we should kill all the Arabs, because that's what she was always taught. But there isn't anything in the prayer book or anything else about that because Jews don't believe that. We don't teach our children to hate Arabs or that they or any other non-Jews must die.

She also thinks that Jews rule the U.S., which a lot of people think. We don't control America. In fact, until very recently, in many ways we were similar to blacks. It was fashionable to dislike Jews. We got blackballed from country clubs. If you look at charters for covenant-controlled communities, the old charters will actually list in their rules: "No blacks, no Jews. Mow your lawn once a week." They just put it in like it was a normal thing.[1]

---

1 "There's Something About the Jews," in Pearl Gaskins, *I Believe In . . . : Christian, Jewish, and Muslim Young People Speak About Their Faith* (Chicago: Cricket Books, 2004), 92.

 Reading

"We Don't Control America" and Other Myths, Part 3

Olympic gymnast Kerri Strug writes:

> I have heard the same question over and over since I received my gold medal in gymnastics on the Olympic podium. "You're Jewish?" people ask in a surprised tone. Perhaps it is my appearance or the stereotype that Jews and sports don't mix that makes my Jewish heritage so unexpected. I think about the attributes that helped me reach that podium: perseverance when faced with pain, years of patience and hope in an uncertain future, and a belief and devotion to something greater than myself. It makes it hard for me to believe that I did not look Jewish up on the podium. In my mind, those are attributes that have defined Jews throughout history.[1]

---

1 Kerri Strug, "You're Jewish?" in *I Am Jewish: Personal Reflections Inspired by the Last Words of Daniel Pearl,* ed. Judea and Ruth Pearl (Woodstock, VT: Jewish Lights, 2004), 98.

Unit Essential Question

What does learning about the choices people made during the Weimar Republic, the rise of the Nazi Party, and the Holocaust teach us about the power and impact of our choices today?

Lesson

World War I and Its Aftermath in Germany

Duration
Two 50-minute class periods

Materials

Map
World War I in Europe and the Middle East

Readings
The Brutal Realities of World War I
Negotiating Peace

Teaching Strategies
Think, Pair, Share
K-W-L Charts
3-2-1
Wraparound

Find all materials referenced in this lesson at facinghistory.org/thhb.

Guiding Questions

- How was the reality of World War I different from what many people and nations expected?
- How did World War I end for Germany, and how did Germans respond to the war's aftermath?

Learning Objectives

- Students will be able to explain how the brutal realities of World War I conflicted with the expectations of quick victory shared by many nations.
- Students will be able to explain why the Treaty of Versailles shocked and upset many Germans.

Overview

In this lesson, students will begin to examine how the facets of human behavior they have learned about in previous lessons—including stereotypes, prejudice, racism, and antisemitism—influenced people and events in this unit's historical case study: Nazi Germany and the Holocaust. They will begin the case study by exploring some of the brutal realities of World War I, unexpected to most nations when they joined the war. They will also learn about Germany's surrender in 1919 and the terms imposed on it by the Treaty of Versailles, both of which shocked Germans and contributed to conditions that would provide fertile ground for the rise of the Nazi Party in the decade that followed.

Context

The history of World War I shows how the ways in which societies define "we" and "they" can help to precipitate war. To understand how this dynamic played out in the buildup to World War I, one must consider the ideology of nationalism and the theory of Social Darwinism. In the 1800s, the biological view of race shaped how many Europeans and Americans defined the word *nation*. Members of a nation shared not only a common history, culture, and language but also common ancestors, character traits, and physical characteristics. Many believed, therefore, that a nation was a biological community. Nationalists believed that their biological communities—their nations—were inherently superior to others. Through the practice of eugenics, nations sought to promote the health of their biological communities and protect them from "threat," which they often defined as mixing with other, allegedly inferior, "races."

How could a nation demonstrate its superiority to other nations? In the late 1800s, the answer to that question was increasingly demonstrated through competition and conflict. After Charles Darwin published his theory of evolution in 1859, many Europeans and Americans began to apply his ideas about natural selection to human society. The result was the theory of Social Darwinism and its belief in the "survival of the fittest." Social Darwinists believed that people who were at the top of the social and economic pyramid were society's fittest. People at the bottom must be "unfit," they reasoned, because competition rewards "the strong."

Inspired by the desire to prove that their societies were the "fittest" and enrich themselves in the process, European nations set out to extend their empires around the turn of the twentieth century throughout Africa and Asia. To sustain this imperialism, nations devoted more and more men and resources to their armies and navies. As militaries became more powerful and competition increased between European nations, they began to form military alliances to ensure that they had the necessary support to fend off rival nations in case war broke out.

It was in this context that the 1914 assassination of the Austrian archduke Franz Ferdinand in Sarajevo, by a Serbian nationalist, set off the series of events that engulfed the world in war. In response to the assassination, Austria-Hungary invaded Serbia. Soon after, Russia (Serbia's ally) and Germany (Austria-Hungary's ally) declared war on each other. Other nations, including France, England, and the Ottoman Empire, entered the hostilities soon after that.

World War I would eventually involve 30 nations and 65 million soldiers. It was a war with incredible loss of human life on every battlefront and huge damage to the land wherever fighting occurred—a conflict marked by genocide, civil wars, famines, and revolutions. By its end, more than 9 million soldiers and more than 5 million civilians had been killed. As a result of the war, three European empires fell (the German, Austro-Hungarian, and Ottoman), causing panic and displacement for millions of people.

This lesson explores the effect of World War I on Germany and how its aftermath created conditions that helped give rise to the Nazis in the years that followed.

Historian Doris Bergen writes that while World War I did not cause Nazism or the Holocaust, its aftermath left in place fertile ground for the history that followed in at least three ways:

1. The destruction and brutality of World War I "seemed to many Europeans to prove that human life was cheap and expendable."

2. The trauma of World War I created in Europeans and their leaders a "deep fear of ever risking another war."

3. The war's resolution left in place across Europe lingering resentments about the war and the terms of the peace. These resentments would later prove useful to leaders such as Adolf Hitler who sought to create "a politics of resentment that promoted a bitter sense of humiliation."[1]

Notes to Teacher

1. K-W-L Charts

The activities in this lesson introduce students to the effects of World War I, a pivotal event in world history and one that was instrumental in creating some of the conditions for the Holocaust. To access students' prior knowledge about World War I and encourage active reading, this lesson utilizes the K-W-L literacy strategy. In the first activity, you'll create a K-W-L chart for World War I on chart paper, and over the course of this lesson the class will likely generate more questions in the "W" column than they will be able to answer in this lesson and unit. Consider posting the chart in a prominent place in your classroom and advising students to return to it as questions (or answers) arise. You may also want to encourage students to explore the activities in the Extensions section if they would like to research the topic further.

If, in your planning, you decide that you need to abbreviate this lesson, you can meet the lesson's learning objectives by creating only a class K-W-L chart (rather than having each student complete one), or by adjusting the lesson to omit the chart entirely.

2. Previewing Vocabulary

The following are key vocabulary terms used in this lesson:

- Patriotism
- Nationalism
- Armistice
- Treaty

Add these words to your word wall, if you are using one for this unit, and provide necessary support to help students learn these words as you teach the lesson.

3. Going Deeper into World War I

World War I is a substantial historical topic, one to which an entire unit could be devoted. The extensions to this lesson can be used to help review the causes and outcome of the war with older students, or to introduce them to these topics

---

1 Doris L. Bergen, *War and Genocide: A Concise History of the Holocaust,* 3rd ed. (Lanham: Rowman & Littlefield, 2016), 42–43. Reproduced by permission from Rowman & Littlefield Publishing Group.

if they have not learned about the war before. Chapter 3 of *Holocaust and Human Behavior* includes additional resources about World War I, its impact on the home fronts, and its aftermath.

Activities

Day 1

1. Reflect on Patriotism and National Pride

Begin the lesson by asking students to respond to the following prompt in their journals:

> What are some ways that people express pride in their country? What are the benefits of patriotism? Can feelings of national pride ever go too far? If so, how?

Have students discuss their responses using the Think, Pair, Share strategy.

Explain to students that the countries that fought in World War I were motivated by a belief that the people of their nations were superior to the people of the nations they fought. This is a more extreme form of patriotism called *nationalism*, and, like racism, it involves the belief that one group of people is distinct from and superior to another.

Before delving into more detail about the war, briefly discuss the following question with students: How does war affect people's feelings of pride in and loyalty toward their country? Make sure students understand that war almost always amplifies people's feelings of loyalty toward their country.

2. Introduce World War I

Students may or may not know much about World War I at the beginning of this lesson. By examining a map of Europe and the Middle East during World War I, students can learn some basic facts about the war.

Have students draw a blank, three-column K-W-L chart in their journals. Also create a blank class K-W-L chart on the board or a piece of chart paper. Add "World War I: 1914–1918" to the class chart, and have students copy the same into their journals.

Pass out the map World War I in Europe and the Middle East. Lead students through an analysis of the map to gather some basic facts, using the questions below. While you record basic facts in the "Know" column on the class K-W-L chart, students can record them in the same column in their journals:

- What information does the map provide about the two sides that fought the war? What was each side called? What countries and empires were part of each side?
- What does the map suggest about where most of the fighting in the war took place in Europe?
- What else does the map suggest about the story of World War I?

After gleaning basic facts about the war from the map, have students take a few minutes to add questions to the "<u>W</u>ant to Know" column of their K-W-L charts.

Use the Think, Pair, Share strategy to have students share their questions, first with a partner and then with the entire class.

Tell students that since World War I is such a pivotal event in world history, over the course of this lesson the class will likely generate more questions in the "W" column of the K-W-L chart than they will be able to answer in this lesson and unit.

3. **Examine Statistics about the Brutal Realities of World War I**
One of the reasons World War I had such a profound impact on the history that followed was because victory was far more difficult to achieve and the fighting was far more brutal than most leaders and people of the nations involved (who all believed in their own superiority) expected. The reading The Brutal Realities of World War I includes data about the military deaths and casualties suffered by each country in the war, offering one way to get a sense of the profound impact the war had on the world.

Pass out the reading The Brutal Realities of World War I. Also project it at the front of the room, if possible. Read aloud the introductory paragraphs.

If necessary, take a few minutes to practice with students how to read the chart and extract data. To do so, you might ask students to answer specific questions (for example: How many French soldiers were wounded in the war?). After each question, choose a student to walk up to the screen, if you are projecting the chart for the class, and show how they found the answer. You might also ask students to use the map World War I in Europe and the Middle East to locate countries listed in the chart (note that some countries are not included on the map).

Next, give students time to look closely at the casualty chart and complete a 3-2-1 exercise using the following guidelines:

- Write down **3** numbers from the chart that seem significant to you, and explain why.
- Write down **2** questions about World War I that the data in this chart raise for you.
- Come up with **1** hypothesis, based on the chart, about how World War I affected people in Germany and other European nations in the decade that followed.

Have students share their 3-2-1 responses with a partner before debriefing with the entire class.

Return to the K-W-L chart. Ask students to contribute any new conclusions about World War I that they can add to the "L" column. Also, ask students to suggest new questions for the "W" column that this activity raised for them. As you add new items to the class chart, students should copy them into their journals.

Day 2

1. Evaluate the Treaty of Versailles

Explain to students that even though an armistice (truce) ended fighting on November 11, 1918, the war was not officially over until a treaty was signed. The Allies determined the terms of the treaty in negotiations in 1919, and Germany and other Central powers had no choice but to sign the treaty in 1920.

Before looking at some details about the Treaty of Versailles, pause to ask students to reflect on the purposes of a treaty to end a war. Have students respond to the following question in their journals and then discuss their responses with a partner:

> To what are the victors entitled at the end of a war? How should the countries that surrendered and lost a war be treated?

Pass out the reading Negotiating Peace, containing excerpts from the Treaty of Versailles. Read the excerpts from the treaty either individually or as a class. Next, have students respond to the following questions in their journals and then discuss their answers with the same partner from the previous journal exercise:

- Based on the information you have about the Treaty of Versailles, what do you think its goals were?
- Who benefited from the treaty? How? Who was harmed by the treaty? How?
- Do you think the treaty was fair?

Have each student re-read the reading and write a newspaper headline, in 15 words or less, that summarizes the impact of the Treaty of Versailles on Germany. Invite students to share and discuss their headlines using the Wraparound teaching strategy.

Return one final time to the K-W-L chart. Ask students to contribute any new conclusions about World War I that they can add to the "L" column. Also, ask students to suggest new questions for the "W" column that this activity raised for them. As you add new items to the class chart, students should copy them into their journals.

2. Discuss the Impact of the War on National Pride

End the lesson with another brief discussion about patriotism, national pride, and nationalism. In particular, ask students to respond to the following question in their journals:

> How do you think the outcome of World War I and the Treaty of Versailles might have affected Germans' feelings about their nation? How might people respond to evidence that their belief in their nation's superiority is wrong?

Assessment

- Examine students' K-W-L charts to see how their thinking and understanding evolved over the course of the lesson.

- Evaluate students' headlines about the Treaty of Versailles to look for evidence of their understanding of the war, the treaty, and the impact on Germany. You can either listen to the headlines as students share them in the Wraparound activity or you can ask students to turn them in on a notecard.

Extensions

To deepen students' understanding of the world-historical scope of this conflict, consider selecting one or more of the following activities to add to this lesson or assign as homework.

1. Explore the Beginning of World War I

The reading "The Beginning of World War I" introduces some important factors that helped lead to the war (and continued to affect Europe and the rest of the world after the war), and it describes the event that ignited the fighting.

Consider reading the overview aloud with the class, pausing so that students can locate the following places on the map World War I in Europe and the Middle East: Great Britain, Germany, Austria-Hungary, Russia, France, Serbia, and Sarajevo.

After you finish the reading, ask students to use the information in it to write working definitions of *militarism*, *nation*, and *military alliance* in their journals. Then discuss how each of those factors (militarism, nations, and alliances) contributed to the outbreak of World War I.

2. Analyze Eyewitness Accounts, Art, and Literature

Activity 2 (Day 1) in this lesson provides one way to get a sense of the brutality of World War I—through statistics. Firsthand accounts of the battlefield, paintings by soldiers and observers, and literary responses to the war provide other avenues for learning about the profound impact of the war on the bodies and minds of those who experienced it. The following resources provide a sampling of these kinds of responses to the war:

- Image: "John Singer Sargent, *Gassed*, 1917"
- Image: "Otto Dix, *Wounded Soldier*, 1924"
- Reading: "Disillusion on the Battlefield"

You can have students analyze and discuss these resources using the Jigsaw strategy. Use the following question to focus their analysis: What does this text or image suggest about the impact, physical and emotional, that World War I had on its creator and on the world in general?

3. Explore the Signing of the Armistice and the "Stab in the Back" Myth

The signing of the armistice shocked many Germans. It gave rise to the dangerous assertion that Germany's new leaders, as well as socialists and Jews, had "stabbed Germany in the back" when they signed the armistice. The reading Signing the Armistice explores the terms of the agreement and the vicious rumors that swirled in its wake.

Visit facinghistory.org/thhb to access these additional resources.

 Map

World War I in Europe and the Middle East

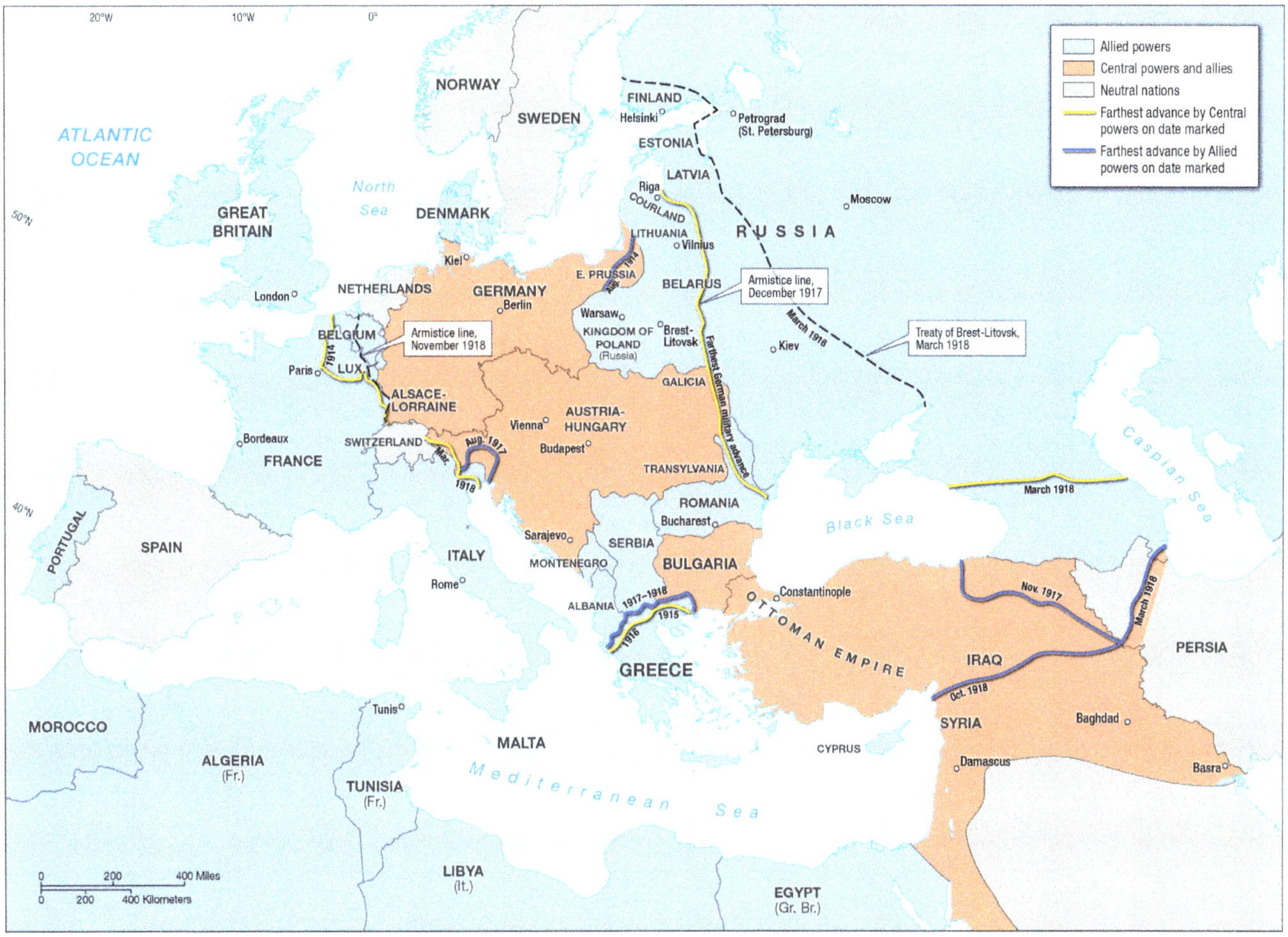

World War I was fought between the Central powers and the Allied powers simultaneously on several fronts in western Europe, eastern Europe, and the Middle East.

 Reading

The Brutal Realities of World War I

When World War I began in August 1914, both sides expected a quick victory. Neither leaders nor civilians from warring nations were prepared for the length and brutality of the war, which took the lives of millions by its end in 1918. The loss of life was greater than in any previous war in history. The carnage from World War I was incomprehensible to everyone, as millions of soldiers and civilians alike died.

The chart below provides estimates of the number of soldiers killed, wounded, and reported missing during World War I. Exact numbers are often disputed and are nearly impossible to determine for a variety of reasons. Different countries used different methods to count their dead and injured, and some methods were more reliable than others. Records of some countries were destroyed during the war and its aftermath. Also, some countries may have changed the number of casualties in their official records for political reasons. The numbers of civilians from each country killed during the war are even more difficult to determine, though historians estimate civilian deaths at about 5 million.[1] The numbers in the chart reflect the estimates made by most historians today.

World War I Casualties

Country	Total Mobilized Forces	Killed or Died*	Wounded	Prisoners or Missing	Total Casualties
Allied Powers					
Russia	12,000,000	1,700,000	4,950,000	2,500,000	9,150,000
France**	8,410,000	1,357,800	4,266,000	537,000	6,160,800
British Empire**	8,904,467	908,371	2,090,212	191,652	3,190,235
Italy	5,615,000	650,000	947,000	600,000	2,197,000
United States	4,734,991	116,516	204,002	—	320,518
Japan	800,000	300	907	3	1,210
Romania	750,000	335,706	120,000	80,000	535,706
Serbia	707,34	45,000	133,148	152,958	331,106
Belgium	267,000	13,716	44,686	34,659	93,061
Greece	230,000	5,000	21,000	1,000	27,000
Portugal	100,000	7,222	13,751	12,318	33,291
Montenegro	50,000	3,000	10,000	7,000	20,000
TOTALS	**42,188,810**	**5,152,115**	**12,831,004**	**4,121,090**	**22,104,209**

1 Martin Gilbert, *The First World War: A Complete History* (New York: Henry Holt and Company, 1994), xv.

Central Powers					
Germany	11,000,000	1,773,700	4,216,058	1,152,800	7,142,558
Austria-Hungary	7,800,000	1,200,000	3,620,000	2,200,000	7,020,000
Turkey	2,850,000	325,000	400,000	250,000	975,000
Bulgaria	1,200,000	87,500	152,390	27,029	266,919
TOTALS	**22,850,000**	**3,386,200**	**8,388,448**	**3,629,829**	**15,404,477**
GRAND TOTALS	**65,038,810**	**8,538,315**	**21,219,452**	**7,750,919**	**37,508,686**

Source: WWI Casualty and Death Tables, "The Great War and the Shaping of the 20th Century," WGBH website.

* **Includes deaths from all causes.**
** **Official figures.**

 Reading

Negotiating Peace

The Allied countries—including the United States, Britain, France, Italy, and Japan—negotiated the peace treaty at the Palace of Versailles in France from January 1919 to January 1920. The final Treaty of Versailles contained 440 articles, and the Germans had no choice but to accept it.

Article 231 of the treaty explained who would pay for the enormous cost of the war and the damage in the war-torn Allied countries:

> **Article 231**
>
> The Allied and Associated Governments affirm and Germany accepts the responsibility of Germany and her allies for causing all the loss and damage to which the Allied and Associated Governments and their nationals have been subjected as a consequence of the war imposed upon them by the aggression of Germany and her allies.

Other portions of the treaty stated the following:

- Germany would limit the size of its military to fewer than 100,000 soldiers.
- Germany would have new borders in Europe, losing about 13% of its area.
- Germany would lose all colonies and other overseas territories.

Germans grew more angry when the terms of the Treaty of Versailles were made public in May 1919. Many Germans felt that their nation had been humiliated by the further loss of territory and military power imposed by the treaty.

| **Unit Essential Question** | What does learning about the choices people made during the Weimar Republic, the rise of the Nazi Party, and the Holocaust teach us about the power and impact of our choices today? |

Lesson

The Weimar Republic

Duration

Two 50-minute class periods

Materials

Handouts

Introduction to the Weimar Republic

Weimar Republic Images

Education in the Weimar Republic

Voices in the Dark

Hyperinflation and the Great Depression

Women in the Weimar Republic

The Bubbling Cauldron

Teaching Strategy

Stations Activity

Find all materials referenced in this lesson at facinghistory.org/thhb.

Guiding Question

- Which aspects of German government and society during the years of the Weimar Republic helped to strengthen democracy, and which aspects weakened it?

Learning Objective

- Students will construct a working definition of *democracy* and then use it to analyze the politics, economics, and culture of Germany during the period of the Weimar Republic. They will then use a graphic organizer to represent the tensions and conflicts that existed for individuals and groups during that period.

Overview

In the previous lesson, students explored the brutal realities of World War I and the impact of the armistice and the Treaty of Versailles on Germany and its citizens. In this two-day lesson, students will continue this unit's historical case study by learning about the 14 years of the Weimar Republic, the democratic government that replaced monarchy in Germany after the war. While exploring the politics, culture, economics, and social trends of Germany during this era, students will also reflect on the idea of democracy itself, as well as the choices made by citizens and leaders that can strengthen or weaken it.

Context

After World War I ended in 1918, Kaiser Wilhelm fled to the Netherlands, and Germany became a republic, a government that is accountable to its people. The Weimar Republic was characterized by contrasts and conflicts. The new constitution granted significant new rights and freedoms to individuals and groups, beginning an era in which creativity and experimentation flourished. At the same time, the republic struggled to convince many Germans, accustomed to monarchy, to accept and trust its authority. The people's confidence in the republic was especially damaged as the country faced economic crises as well as challenges from political parties that were hostile to democracy.

Two very different moods characterized Weimar politics and society. On the one hand, there was a sense of excitement and creativity. In the early 1920s, Germany had a new constitution that established separate branches of government, and many groups vied for political power through an electoral process. Women took on new roles in Weimar society. They constituted about a third of the German workforce after World War I, exercised their newly acquired right to vote, and held political office for the first time. Freedom of expression in art, music, dance, and architecture flourished in Weimar culture and left a lasting legacy in the modern world.

On the other hand, many Germans felt anxious and fearful. The pace of change, especially in expanding political rights and social freedoms, made many Germans uneasy and sparked backlash against the changes. Many also feared the impact of communism, which had succeeded in Russia and threatened to spread its abolition of private wealth and property to Germany, by violence if necessary. This fear was heightened by two economic crises that tested the leadership of the Weimar government: the hyperinflation that beset the republic in its early years and the Great Depression in its final years. Parties from across the political spectrum clashed violently in the streets throughout the Weimar era, leaving citizens on edge. Meanwhile, interest in and enthusiasm for the message of ultra-conservative forces—in particular, the growing Nazi Party, with its message of racial hatred and its demand for a return to an autocratic government—continued to grow.

In his autobiography, artist George Grosz recalls how these moods shaped life in Germany during the 1920s (see also the handout The Bubbling Cauldron):

> Even the capital of our new German Republic was like a bubbling cauldron. You could not see who was heating the cauldron; you could merely see it merrily bubbling, and you could feel that heat increasing. There were speakers on every street corner and songs of hatred everywhere. Everybody was hated: the Jews, the capitalists, the gentry, the communists, the military, the landlords, the workers, the unemployed . . . the politicians, the department stores, and again the Jews.[1]

Learning about the Weimar Republic not only helps students understand the society in which a dictatorship ultimately took root but also serves as a lesson on the fragility of democracy. Democracy is a system of government that depends on the resilience of both its institutions and its citizens. For example, constitutional rights are solidified by a judicial system that actively protects those rights and an atmosphere in which citizens can safely express dissent. In a healthy democracy, leaders are held accountable by citizens who are critical consumers of information, especially political propaganda, and who are active participants who speak up against injustice rather than passively watching it unfold. Studying the Weimar Republic not only helps students recognize these essential ingredients of democracy; it serves as a warning for today.

---

1 George Grosz, *An Autobiography,* trans. Nora Hodges (Berkeley: University of California Press, 1998), 149–50.

Notes to Teacher

1. The Weimar Republic and the Nazi Party

The Nazi Party was formed during the Weimar era and rose to prominence in the republic's final years, but the Nazis are mentioned sparingly in this lesson. The lesson is designed this way because it is important for students to understand that the Nazis' rise to power was not inevitable; it was, rather, the result of choices made by many individuals and groups within the context of a vibrant society characterized by both creativity and anxiety. While a subsequent lesson will focus on the rise of the Nazi Party, this one digs deep into the society that faltered during that rise.

2. Constructing a Mini-Lecture

Activity 1 for Day 1 includes a mini-lecture that covers both historical context and information about the structure of the Weimar government. The handout **Introduction to the Weimar Republic** is designed to help students follow along with the lecture. You may choose to transfer the information from the handout to a PowerPoint presentation. If you would like to add images and other multimedia resources, "The Weimar Republic: The Fragility of Democracy," available at facinghistory.org/thhb can help you get started. This featured collection on the Facing History website provides a variety of additional primary sources, visual and print essays, and a timeline of the Weimar era.

3. Station Work

To prepare for the station activity on Day 2, we recommend that you set up desk groups or tables in advance. Each station will focus on one of four different readings. In order to keep group size manageable (we recommend four to five students per group), you may need to create multiple stations for each reading. The goal is for each group to have the opportunity to work with each of the four readings.

4. Previewing Vocabulary

The following are key vocabulary terms used in this lesson:

- Democracy
- Republic
- Paramilitary
- Inflation
- Constitution
- Suffrage
- Chancellor
- Reichstag

Add these words to your word wall, if you are using one for this unit, and provide necessary support to help students learn these words as you teach the lesson.

5. The Unit Assessment

If your students are writing the final essay assessment for this unit, after teaching this lesson, instruct your students to start gathering evidence in an evidence log. For suggested activities and resources, see Introducing Evidence Logs.

Activities

Day 1

1. Discuss the Meaning of Democracy

Ask students to briefly reflect in their journals on the meaning of the term *democracy*, using the following questions to spark their thinking:

> What is democracy? How would you define it? What words or phrases do you associate with it? If you live in a democracy, what might you be able to do that you might not under other forms of government?

Ask students to share ideas, words, and phrases from their journal entries and record them on the board or a piece of chart paper for later reference. Make sure that by the end of the discussion, the map includes the following topics: free and fair elections, the rule of law, equality before the law, free expression, free press, and freedom of religion.

2. Introduce the Weimar Republic

Tell students that to better understand the concept of democracy, they are going to spend the next two days learning about the Weimar Republic, the democratic government created in Germany after World War I.

Present a brief mini-lecture to introduce Weimar Germany using the information on the handout Introduction to the Weimar Republic. Pass out the handout before you begin the mini-lecture, and as you walk students through the information on the handout, have them annotate it by writing a *D* next to information about the Weimar Republic that represents an important characteristic of democracy and an *X* next to information that describes a problem or challenge for democracy.

3. Explore Free Expression in the Weimar Republic

Remind students that one of the hallmarks of democratic societies is that the government protects the free expression of ideas by its citizens. In the Weimar Republic, this protection allowed creativity to flourish in Germany and spawned artistic movements that challenged traditional forms of art. In this activity, students will examine examples of modern art from the Weimar Republic.

Divide the class into groups of four or five, and assign one of the five images in the Weimar Republic Images handout to each group.

Walk the class as a whole through the following steps to analyze their assigned images:

- Step 1: Ask students to look deeply at the picture for two or three minutes. Have them observe shapes, colors, textures, and the position of people and objects. Have them write down simple observations, not interpretations.

- Step 2: Ask students to brainstorm together questions they have about the image. In order to understand it, what questions might they want to ask the artist or the subject of the image?
- Step 3: Ask students to discuss possible interpretations of the image. What is the artist trying to communicate? What does this image or work of art suggest about life and culture in the Weimar Republic?

Briefly have each group share their assigned image and their ideas about what it suggests about life in the Weimar Republic.

To end the activity, share the titles and captions for each of the images with students. You could give students the key at the end of the Weimar Republic Images handout, project the information, or simply read it to students. If time permits, you might ask students to comment on how the titles and captions either support or change their interpretations of each image.

4. Record Impressions of the Weimar Republic

Either as a final activity or as a homework assignment, ask students to write a short paragraph about their impressions of the Weimar Republic so far. What has surprised them? What has interested them? How has what they learned so far supported or challenged their ideas about democracy?

Day 2

1. Explore Life in the Weimar Republic

Begin the class by asking students to review the short paragraphs they wrote at the end of the previous day. Ask a few students to share: What are their thoughts and impressions about democracy in the Weimar Republic so far?

Tell students that in this activity, they will explore several additional aspects of life in the Weimar Republic, including education, women's rights, antisemitism, and economics.

Set up the classroom for a Stations Activity with four stations, one for each of the handouts below. (Depending on class size, you might create multiple copies of each station.)

- Education in the Weimar Republic
- Voices in the Dark
- Hyperinflation and the Great Depression
- Women in the Weimar Republic

Divide the class into groups so that they are evenly distributed between the stations at all times. Then begin the activity by assigning each group a station at which to begin. Provide groups with ten minutes to read and answer the questions that accompany each reading on a separate sheet of paper before having them rotate to the next station.

Once the groups have finished visiting all of the stations, have the students discuss in their groups the following questions:

- What was most surprising about what you learned about the Weimar Republic in this activity? What was most interesting? What was most disturbing?
- Which aspects of Weimar society explored in this activity were good for democracy? Which created challenges for democracy?

2. Introduce the "Bubbling Cauldron" Metaphor

To close this lesson, ask students to consider the metaphor of the "bubbling cauldron" that artist George Grosz used to describe life in the Weimar Republic.

Pass out The Bubbling Cauldron handout. Read the quotation by Grosz with students, and then ask them to fill out the cauldron-shaped graphic organizer to represent life in the Weimar Republic. They should label the ingredients being heated in the cauldron, the fuel for the fire, and the names of the individuals and groups lighting the fire. The handout includes a bank of words and phrases students can use to label the graphic, but they will not be able to use all of the words in the bank and they may determine that some are not relevant. While part of the value of this activity is in thinking through the metaphorical relationship between ingredients, fuel, and those feeding the fire, some students may need assistance from the teacher in getting started filling in the graphic.

It is important to note for students that in this lesson, one key part of this history of the Weimar Republic has intentionally been left out: the rise of the Nazi Party. Students will examine the Nazi Party in a subsequent lesson, and they will revisit this handout to incorporate Adolf Hitler and the Nazi Party into the metaphor.

Assessment

- Evaluate the completed student versions of The Bubbling Cauldron handout to see how students are understanding the conflicts and tensions within German society during the years of the Weimar Republic. If you collect the handouts, make sure you return them so that students can add to them during the lesson on the rise of the Nazi Party.

- Assign students to write their own working definition of *democracy* on a notecard to turn in. Look for characteristics such as accountability to the people, free and fair elections, the rule of law, equality before the law, free expression, free press, and freedom of religion.

Extension

Investigate the Meaning of Democracy Further

For additional activities to help students explore the meaning of *democracy*, see the lesson "Defining Democracy."

The resources in "The Weimar Republic: The Fragility of Democracy" (mentioned above in the Notes to Teacher section) can be used to extend and deepen the class's investigation of the Weimar Republic beyond the materials in this lesson. Many teachers use this online collection to support inquiry-based lessons about the Weimar Republic, in which students gather information to help them respond to a set of guiding questions. You might use the guiding questions for this lesson to frame such an inquiry.

Visit facinghistory.org/thhb to access these additional resources.

 Handout

Introduction to the Weimar Republic

Directions: Write a **D** next to information about the Weimar Republic that represents characteristics of a democracy and an **X** next to information that describes problems or challenges for a democracy.

From Monarchy to Democracy

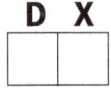 After World War I, Germany's political leaders sought to transform Germany from a monarchy to a democracy, called the Weimar Republic (1918–1933). The Weimar Constitution divided power into three branches of government. Elections were held for the president and the Reichstag (the legislature), while the judicial branch was appointed.

The Weimar Constitution

 Adopted on August 11, 1919, the new Weimar Constitution spelled out the "basic rights and obligations" of government officials and the citizens they served. Most of those rights and obligations had not existed in Germany under the kaiser, including equality before the law, freedom of religion, and privacy. Despite the inclusion of these rights in the Weimar Constitution, individual freedom was not fully protected. Old laws that denied freedoms continued, including laws that discriminated against homosexual men and "Gypsies" (the name, considered derogatory today, used to describe two groups of people called the Sinti and Roma).

The Reichstag

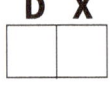 Germans voted for a party, rather than a candidate, to fill the Reichstag (the German legislature). The elections determined the percentage of seats each party received in the Reichstag, but the parties themselves selected the individuals who filled each allotted seat. For example, if a party received 36% of the vote, they would get 36% of the seats in the Reichstag.

The Roles of President and Chancellor

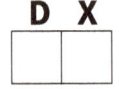 As head of the government, the president controlled the nation's armed forces and had the power to dismiss the Reichstag, triggering new elections. The president also appointed the nation's chancellor. In a parliamentary system, the chancellor (or prime minister, in some countries) is in charge of the day-to-day operations of government. During the first ten years of the Weimar Republic, the president usually appointed a chancellor from the party that had the most seats in the Reichstag.

Forming a Majority

No single party ever held a majority in the Reichstag during the Weimar period. Thus, two or more parties often banded together to form a majority to run the legislature. But almost any disagreement between parties might break up such a coalition. When that occurred, a new election would be held, which happened 20 times during the Weimar period.

Article 48

Article 48 of the Weimar Constitution gave the president special emergency powers. If "public order and security are seriously disturbed or threatened," the president was empowered to suspend civil liberties and enact laws without the consent of the Reichstag.

Article 48 was intended to be a safety valve to protect Germany during state emergencies by enabling leaders to act quickly. But the president alone was to decide whether an emergency existed, and the first president of the Weimar Republic, Friedrich Ebert, invoked Article 48 to issue decrees 136 times, only occasionally in times of actual emergency.

Violence in the Weimar Government

Dozens of political parties competed for the support of German citizens. In some elections, ballots listed more than 30 parties to choose from. Many political parties had their own private armies, or paramilitaries. As a result, political disagreements and arguments on the streets often turned violent.

Handout

Weimar Republic Images

Weimar Republic Image 1

Weimar Republic Image 2

Weimar Republic Image 3

Weimar Republic Image 4

Weimar Republic Image 5

Weimar Republic Images Key

1. *Metropolis* by Otto Dix (1928)
In addition to his depictions of World War I (see *Wounded Soldier* in Lesson 7), Otto Dix was also known for his ruthless criticism of German society during the Weimar years.

Credit: akg-images

2. *The Agitator* by George Grosz (1928)
Grosz is one of the most important artists associated with the New Objectivity movement. New Objectivists believed that they were challenging the public to see the world as it really was, rather than as they would like it to be. Grosz's paintings and sketches often offered critical judgments of German society during the Weimar Republic.

Credit: Collection Stedelijk Museum Amsterdam

3. Marlene Dietrich in the film *Blue Angel* (1930)
Blue Angel, directed by Josef von Sternberg, was Germany's first full-length "talkie," a motion picture with sound as opposed to a silent film. The film follows the story of a college professor who is undone by his attraction to Lola-Lola, a cabaret dancer played by German American Marlene Dietrich. The film made Dietrich an international star, and she continued her acting career in the United States.

Credit: MARKA / Alamy

4. *Kitchen Knife* by Hannah Höch (1919)
Höch's work consisted primarily of collages, often made from photographs. Höch was part of the Dada movement, which formed in part as a reaction to the death and destruction from World War I. Dada artists prized irrationality and considered their work "anti-art."

Credit: bpk, Berlin / Staatliche Museen / Jörg P. Anders / Art Resource, NY

5. *The Triadic Ballet* (1926)
The Triadic Ballet was created by Oskar Schlemmer, a painter, sculptor, designer, and choreographer who taught at the Bauhaus art school in Germany during the Weimar Republic. Schlemmer's ballet represented the Bauhaus style: uncluttered, modern, and geometric.

Credit: The J. Paul Getty Museum, Los Angeles

 Handout

Education in the Weimar Republic

Directions: As you are reading, annotate the text by completing the following steps:

1. Circle words that are unfamiliar.
2. Put a question mark (?) in the margin in places where you feel confused.
3. Answer the questions that follow the text.

In the Weimar Republic, Germany's schools remained centers of tradition. Most teachers were conservative, both in their way of teaching and in their politics, and many were anti-socialist and antisemitic. A young man known as Klaus describes his schooling in the 1920s:

> We were taught history as a series of facts. We had to learn dates, names, places of battles. Periods during which Germany won wars were emphasized. Periods during which Germany lost wars were sloughed over. We heard very little about World War I, except that the Versailles peace treaty was a disgrace, which someday, in some vague way, would be rectified. In my school, one of the best in Berlin, there were three courses in Greek and Roman history, four in medieval history, and not one in government. If we tried to relate ideas we got from literature or history to current events, our teachers changed the subject.
>
> I really don't believe that anyone was deliberately trying to evade politics. Those teachers really seemed to think that what went on in the Greek and Roman Empires was more important than what was happening on the streets of Berlin and Munich. They considered any attempt to bring up current political questions a distraction . . . because we hadn't done our homework.
>
> And there was always a great deal of homework in a school like mine, which prepared students for the university. At the end of our senior year, we were expected to take a detailed and exceedingly tough exam called the Abitur. How we did on the exam could determine our whole future. Again, the Abitur concentrated on our knowledge of facts, not on interpretation or on the expression of personal ideas.[1]

1. Record the title, and write a brief summary (three or four sentences) of this reading.

---

1 Ellen Switzer, *How Democracy Failed* (New York: Atheneum, 1977), 62–63. Reproduced by permission from Curtis Brown, Ltd.

2. What kind of education do you think would best prepare students to be citizens in a democracy? Do you think the education Klaus describes would prepare students for participation in a democracy? Explain your thinking.

Handout

Voices in the Dark

Directions: As you are reading, annotate the text by completing the following steps:
1. Circle words that are unfamiliar.
2. Put a question mark (?) in the margin in places where you feel confused.
3. Answer the questions that follow the text.

Life in Weimar Germany was often unpredictable, as a former soldier, Henry Buxbaum, discovered one evening in the early 1920s:

> The train was pitch-dark. The lights were out, nothing uncommon after the war when the German railroads were in utter disrepair and very few things functioned orderly. . . . That night, we were seven or eight people in the dark, fourth-class compartment, sitting in utter silence till one of the men started the usual refrain: "Those God-damned Jews, they are at the root of all our troubles." Quickly, some of the others joined in. I couldn't see them and had no idea who they were, but from their voices they sounded like younger men. They sang the same litany over and over again, blaming the Jews for everything that has gone wrong with Germany and for anything else wrong in this world. It went on and on, a cacophony of obscenities, becoming more vicious and at the same time more unbearable with each new sentence echoing in my ears. Finally, I couldn't stand it any longer. I knew very well that to start up with them would get me into trouble, and that to answer them wasn't exactly the height of wisdom, but I couldn't help it. . . . I began naturally with the announcement: "Well, I am a Jew and etc., etc." That was the signal they needed. Now they really went after me, threatening me physically. I didn't hold my tongue as the argument went back and forth. They began jostling me till one of them . . . probably more encouraged by the darkness than by his own valor, suggested: "Let's throw the Jew out of the train." Now, I didn't dare ignore this signal, and from then on I kept quiet. I knew that silence for the moment was better than falling under the wheels of a moving train. One of the men in our compartment, more vicious in his attacks than the others, got off the train with me in Friedburg. When I saw him under the dim light of the platform, I recognized him as a fellow I knew well from our soccer club. . . . I would never have suspected this man of harboring such rabid, antisemitic feelings.[1]

Buxbaum's experience would not have been uncommon in Germany in the 1920s. Antisemitic conspiracy theories abounded in post-war Germany, permeating all the way to the highest levels of government. In 1919, Erich Ludendorff, one of Germany's top military leaders, falsely claimed that Jews were one of several groups responsible for the nation's defeat. As proof, he cited the *Protocols of the Elders of Zion,* a document supposedly containing the minutes of a secret meeting of Jewish leaders. At that supposed meeting, the "Elders" allegedly plotted to take over the world. In fact, the *Protocols of the*

---

1 Henry Buxbaum, "Recollections," in *Jewish Life in Germany: Memoirs from Three Centuries,* ed. Monika Richarz, trans. Stella P. Rosenfeld and Sidney Rosenfeld (Bloomington: Indiana University Press, 1991), 303–04.

Elders of Zion is a forgery; Russian secret police wrote it in the early 1900s to incite hatred against Jews.

In the 1920s, Germany's 500,000 Jews accounted for less than 1% of the total population of about 61 million. Yet by focusing on Jews as "the enemy," antisemites made it seem as if Jews were everywhere and were responsible for everything that went wrong in the nation.

1. Record the title, and write a brief summary (three or four sentences) of this reading.

2. What role did the darkness play in the incident described in this reading? What role did the presence of a group of people who shared similar attitudes play?

3. What claims about Jews did the *Protocols of the Elders of Zion* make? What accounted for the popularity of the *Protocols* in Germany?

Handout

Hyperinflation and the Great Depression

A woman takes a basket of banknotes to buy cabbage at a market during the 1923 hyperinflation in Weimar Germany.

Directions: As you are reading, annotate the text by completing the following steps:

1. Circle words that are unfamiliar.
2. Put a question mark (?) in the margin in places where you feel confused.
3. Answer the questions that follow the text.

Value of German Currency, 1919–1923

Date	Marks	US Dollars
1918	4.2	1
1921	75	1
1922	400	1
January 1923	7,000	1
July 1923	160,000	1
August 1923	1,000,000	1
November 1, 1923	1300,000,000	1
November 15, 1923	1300,000,000,000	1
November 16, 1923	4200,000,000,000	1

Beginning in the fall of 1922, an extreme inflation, or hyperinflation, took hold of the German economy. During periods of inflation, prices rise continuously as the value of a currency drops sharply.

Many European countries experienced inflation after the war, but nowhere did prices rise as rapidly as they did in Germany. On some days, the value of the mark (the unit of German currency) fell almost hourly.

As a result of the inflation, Germans who had their savings in banks or were living on pensions or disability checks found themselves virtually bankrupt. Workers increasingly discovered that no matter how high their wages rose, they could not keep up with rapidly soaring prices.

Artist George Grosz described what shopping was like in those days:

> Lingering at the [shop] window was a luxury because shopping had to be done immediately. Even an additional minute meant an increase in price. One had to buy quickly because a rabbit, for example, might cost two million marks more by the time it took to walk into the store. A few million marks meant nothing, really. It was just that it meant more lugging. The packages of money needed to buy the smallest item had long since become too heavy for trouser pockets. They weighed many pounds. . . . People had to start carting their money around in wagons and knapsacks. I used a knapsack.[1]

In October of 1929, a worldwide depression began, one that exacerbated the economic problems Germany had faced with hyperinflation. A depression is a severe economic downturn that forces businesses to decrease production and lay off workers. Germany felt the effects of the depression almost immediately. By 1932, 6 million Germans were unemployed in a nation of about 60 million people. Among them were Lea Langer Grundig, who was a Communist, and her husband, Hans. Like other job seekers, they stood in long lines at labor exchanges day after day:

> Unemployment became a tragedy for many. Not only because of the poverty that mutely sat at their table at all times. Not working, doing nothing, producing nothing—work that not only provided food, but also, despite all the harassment and drudgery, was satisfying, developed skills, and stimulated thinking; work, a human need—it was not available; and wherever it was lacking, decay, malaise, and despair set in. . . .
>
> The grim poverty, the hopelessness, the laws governing the crisis that were incomprehensible for many, all these made people ripe for "miracles." Sects shot out of the ground. Diviners of the stars or coffee grounds, palm readers, graphologists, speculators and swindlers, clairvoyants and miracle workers had a great time; they reaped rich harvests among the poor, who along with their poverty and idleness fell prey to foolishness.[2]

1. Record the title, and write a brief summary (three or four sentences) of this reading.

2. How did inflation change daily life in Germany?

3. How might a depression change attitudes about "we" and "they"? How might it affect a country's universe of obligation?

---

1 George Grosz, *A Little Yes and a Big No: The Autobiography of George Grosz*, trans. L. S. Dorin (New York: Dial, 1946), 63.

2 From Lea Grundig, "Visions and History," in *The Nazi Germany Sourcebook: An Anthology of Texts,* ed. Roderick Stackelberg and Sally A. Winkle (London: Routledge, 2002), 97.

Handout

Women in the Weimar Republic

A crowd of women wait in line at a polling station in the Weimar Republic in 1919, the first year women were allowed to vote.

Directions: As you are reading, annotate the text by completing the following steps:

1. Circle words that are unfamiliar.
2. Put a question mark (?) in the margin in places where you feel confused.
3. Answer the questions that follow the text.

At the turn of the twentieth century, women throughout Europe and North America were demanding that their governments give them the right to vote. Germany was no exception; women began to hold demonstrations for women's suffrage there as early as 1910. They succeeded in 1919, when Article 109 of the Weimar Constitution stated that men and women have the same fundamental rights and duties as citizens, including the right to vote and to hold office:

> Article 109: All Germans are equal in front of the law. In principle, men and women have the same rights and obligations.

During the years of the Weimar Republic, a majority of the electorate was female, in part because so many men had died in the war or were so physically or psychologically wounded that they were unlikely to vote. In 1919, the first year women could vote in Germany, they held 10% of the seats in the Reichstag, and their numbers continued to rise throughout the next decade.

During and after the war, the position of women in the workforce also began to change. While the proportion of women who had jobs remained about the same as before the war, women began to take new kinds of jobs that had previously been dominated by men. For instance, they began to fill more jobs that were visible throughout society, such as tram conductor and department store clerk, as well as (in smaller numbers) factory worker, lawyer, and doctor. While many of these positions would return to men after the war, women also moved into professions that many would continue to associate with women in the years that followed, such as teaching, social work, and secretarial work. All in all, more than 11 million women were employed in Germany in 1918, accounting for 36% of the workforce.[3]

1. Record the title, and write a brief summary (three or four sentences) of this reading.

2. Why do you think women won the right to vote in Germany in 1919? What is significant about that date?

3. What were some of the reasons women were more represented in the German government after World War I than they had been before the war?

4. How might the changes discussed in this reading have affected Germany's universe of obligation?

---

3 Detlev Peukert, *The Weimar Republic: The Crisis of Classical Modernity* (New York: Hill and Wang, 1992), 96–97; Richard J. Evans, *The Coming of the Third Reich* (New York: Penguin, 2003), 127.

 Handout

The Bubbling Cauldron

Artist George Grosz said that the Weimar Republic was like a "bubbling cauldron." He wrote: "You could not see who was heating the cauldron; you could merely see it merrily bubbling, and you could feel that heat increasing."[1]

Directions: In this activity, you will use a graphic organizer based on Grosz's image to show your understanding of the Weimar Republic. Label the image of the cauldron as follows:

- **Who or what added fuel to the fire?** Outside of the cauldron, write the names of people, groups, events, and circumstances that caused tension and conflict in German society during the Weimar Republic (e.g., paramilitary groups).
- **What was the fuel for the fire?** In each log beneath the cauldron, write words and phrases describing human behaviors, feelings, and emotions in German society during the Weimar Republic (e.g., violence). Draw additional logs if you need them.
- **What was in the cauldron?** In the cauldron, write the aspects of German society that were affected by the behaviors and feelings you labeled in the logs (e.g., freedom of speech).

For instance, you might say that "paramilitary groups" added the "violence" log beneath the fire that created enough heat to affect the "freedom of speech" ingredient in the cauldron.

You can use words and phrases from the bank below as you label the image. You do not have to use all of the words provided. You may also add words and phrases that you think of on your own.

When you are finished, write your answers to the questions on the last page.

Anger	World War I	Weimar Constitution
Humiliation	Treaty of Versailles	Civil Rights
Alienation	Hyperinflation	Freedom of Speech
Anxiety	Great Depression	Women's Rights
Fear	Unemployment	Frequent Elections
Creativity	Leaders	Article 48
Violence	Artists	Trust in Democracy
Uncertainty	Teachers	Germany's Universe of Obligation
Education	Paramilitary Groups	Trust in Neighbors
Values	Political Parties	
Hatred	Voting	
Antisemitism	Intimidation	

1 George Grosz, *An Autobiography*, trans. Nora Hodges (Berkeley: University of California Press, 1998), 149–50.

1. What do you think Grosz's metaphor means? What does it suggest about what it felt like to live in Germany during that time? What might be the result of the increasing "heat"?

2. What was the process like of labeling the cauldron graphic? What challenges did you encounter? What new conclusions did you draw about the Weimar Republic from this activity?

STEP 2

Introducing Evidence Logs

After students have completed Lesson 8, it is an appropriate time to revisit and revise the working thesis statements they drafted in the initial assessment step Introducing the Writing Prompt. At that time, students were introduced to the first part of the writing prompt, which did not include the specific historical events they are studying in this unit, and they developed an initial position for an argumentative essay in response to a question about the importance and impact of choices in history. Now that students have learned about the Weimar Republic, they will reflect on the writing prompt a second time by adding this historical lens. It is important that students keep the materials for the essay (journal reflections, evidence logs, writing handouts) in a safe place, because they will refer back to them over the course of the unit in preparation to write the essay assessment.

Suggested Activities

Visit facinghistory.org/thhb to access all teaching strategies referenced in these activities.

1. **Journal Reflection**

   Ask students to reread their journal responses from the previous assessment step, Introducing the Writing Prompt, and then respond to the following question:

   > What does learning about the choices people made during the Weimar Republic teach us about the power and impact of our choices in the world today?

   Have students share their ideas with a partner or small group, or you might use the Two-Minute Interview strategy and encourage students to add new ideas to their journal responses that expand or challenge their thinking about the prompt.

2. **Annotate and Paraphrase Sources**

   If you have not yet taught students how to annotate or paraphrase sources, you might want to devote a class period to modeling and practicing this skill. You could select a reading from Lesson 8 to reread with the class, modeling the Annotating and Paraphrasing Sources strategy, or you might select a new reading about the Weimar Republic from Chapter 4 of *Holocaust and Human Behavior* that they didn't already read.

3. Gather Evidence in an Evidence Log

We recommend that students start to gather evidence that supports or challenges their initial thinking about the writing prompt at this point in the unit. Evidence logs provide a place where students can centralize and organize evidence they collect over the course of a unit. There are two templates on the Evidence Logs teaching strategy page on our website and an additional index card format in the *Common Core Writing Prompts and Strategies: Holocaust and Human Behavior* supplement.

Before students start to collect their own evidence, it is helpful if you model the process by doing a "think-aloud" where you complete the first row of an evidence log on the board. In your think-aloud, you might first select a piece of evidence that is irrelevant to the topic and then explain to the class why you are not going to use it. Then select a relevant piece of evidence and enter it into the chart.

Students should work individually, in pairs, or in small groups to gather evidence from their readings and class notes about the Weimar Republic that helps them answer the essay topic question.

After students have gathered their evidence, have them share their findings and add more evidence to their logs using the Give One, Get One strategy.

4. Final Reflection

In a final journal response or on exit tickets, ask students to respond to the following questions:

- Has any evidence that you recorded confirmed your initial thinking about the topic question?
- Has any evidence that you recorded conflicted with or challenged your initial thinking about the topic question?
- Which choices by individuals, groups, and nations in the history that you have learned about so far in this unit seemed most significant? What made those choices powerful or impactful?

| Unit Essential Question | What does learning about the choices people made during the Weimar Republic, the rise of the Nazi Party, and the Holocaust teach us about the power and impact of our choices today? |

Lesson

The Rise of the Nazi Party

Duration

One 50-minute class period

Materials

Video

Hitler's Rise to Power, 1918–1933

Handouts

Hitler's Rise to Power, 1918–1933 Viewing Guide

What Did the Nazis Believe?

Readings

National Socialist German Workers' Party Platform

Hitler in Power

Teaching Strategies

Think, Pair, Share

Read Aloud

Find all materials referenced in this lesson at facinghistory.org/thhb.

Guiding Question

- How did the Nazi Party, a small and unpopular political group in 1920, become the most powerful political party in Germany by 1933?

Learning Objectives

- Through class discussion and a written response, students will examine how choices made by individuals and groups contributed to the rise of the Nazi Party in the 1920s and 1930s.
- Students will label the 1920 Nazi Party platform and use it to draw conclusions about the party's universe of obligation and core values.

Overview

In a previous lesson, students explored the politics, culture, economics, and social trends in Germany during the years of the Weimar Republic (1919 to 1933), and they analyzed the strength of democracy in Germany during those years. In this lesson, students will continue the unit's historical case study by reexamining politics in the Weimar Republic and tracing the development of the National Socialist German Workers' (Nazi) Party throughout the 1920s and early 1930s.

Students will review events that they learned about in the previous lesson and see how the popularity of the Nazis changed during times of stability and times of crisis. They will also analyze the Nazi Party platform and, in an extension about the 1932 election, compare it to the platforms of the Social Democratic and Communist Parties. By tracing the progression of the Nazis from an unpopular fringe group to the most powerful political party in Germany, students will extend and deepen their thinking from the previous lesson about the choices that individuals can make to strengthen democracy and those that can weaken it.

This lesson includes multiple, rich extension activities if you would like to devote two days to a closer examination of the rise of the Nazi Party.

Context

Adolf Hitler, an Austrian-born corporal in the German army during World War I, capitalized on the anger and resentment felt by many Germans after the war as he entered politics in 1919, joined the small German Workers' Party, and quickly became the party's leader. By February 1920, Hitler had given it a new name: the National Socialist German Workers' Party (*Nationalsozialistische Deutsche Arbeiterpartei*), or Nazi, for short.

Originally drafted in 1920, the Nazi Party platform (see the reading National Socialist German Workers' Party Platform) reflects a cornerstone of Nazi ideology: the belief in race science and the superiority of the so-called Aryan race (or "German blood"). For the Nazis, so-called "German blood" determined whether one was considered a citizen. The Nazis believed that citizenship should not only bestow on a person certain rights (such as voting, running for office, or owning a newspaper); it also came with the guarantee of a job, food, and land on which to live. Those without "German blood" were not citizens and therefore should be deprived of these rights and benefits.

Fueled by post-war unrest and Hitler's charismatic leadership, thousands joined the Nazis in the early 1920s. In an attempt to capitalize on the chaos caused by runaway hyperinflation, Hitler attempted to stage a coup (known as the Beer Hall Putsch) in Munich to overthrow the government of the German state of Bavaria on November 23, 1923. The attempt failed and resulted in several deaths. Hitler and several of his followers were arrested, but rather than diminish his popularity, Hitler's subsequent trial for treason and imprisonment made him a national figure.

At the trial, a judge sympathetic to the Nazis' nationalist message allowed Hitler and his followers to show open contempt for the Weimar Republic, which they referred to as a "Jew government." Hitler and his followers were found guilty. Although they should have been deported because they were not German citizens (they were Austrian citizens), the judge dispensed with the law and gave them the minimum sentence—five years in prison. Hitler only served nine months, and the rest of his term was suspended.

During his time in prison, Hitler wrote *Mein Kampf* (My Struggle). In the book, published in 1925, he maintained that conflict between the races was the catalyst of history. Because he believed that the "Aryan" race was superior to all others, he insisted that "Aryan" Germany had the right to incorporate all of eastern Europe into a new empire that would provide much-needed *Lebensraum*, or living space, for it. That new empire would also represent a victory over the Communists, who controlled much of the territory Hitler sought. Hitler, like many conservative Germans, regarded both Communists and Jews as enemies of the German people. He linked the Communists to the Jews, using the phrase "Jewish Bolshevism" and claiming that the Jews were behind the teachings of the Communist Party. (The Bolsheviks were the communist group that gained power in Russia in 1917 and established the Soviet Union.) The Jews, according to Hitler, were everywhere, controlled everything, and acted so secretly and deviously that few could detect their influence.

By 1925, Hitler was out of prison and once again in control of the Nazi Party. The attempted coup had taught him an important lesson. Never again would he attempt an armed uprising. Instead, the Nazis would use the rights guaranteed by the Weimar Constitution—freedom of the press, the right to assemble, and freedom of speech—to win control of Germany.

However, in 1924 the German economy had begun to improve. By 1928, the country had recovered from the war and business was booming. As a result, fewer Germans seemed interested in the hatred that Hitler and his Nazi Party promoted. The same was true for other extreme nationalist groups. In the 1928 elections, the Nazis received only about 2% of the vote.

Then, in 1929, the stock market crashed and the worldwide Great Depression began. Leaders around the world could not stop the economic collapse. To an increasing number of Germans, democracy appeared unable to rescue the economy, and only the most extreme political parties seemed to offer clear solutions to the crisis.

The Communist Party in Germany argued that to end the depression, Germany needed a government like the Soviet Union's: the government should take over all German land and industry from capitalists, who were only interested in profits for themselves. Communists promised to distribute German wealth according to the common good. The Nazis blamed the Jews, Communists, liberals, and pacifists for the German economic crisis. They promised to restore Germany's standing in the world and Germans' pride in their nation as well as end the depression, campaigning with slogans such as "Work, Freedom, and Bread!"

Many saw the Nazis as an attractive alternative to democracy and communism. Among them were wealthy industrialists who were alarmed by the growth of the Communist Party and did not want to be forced to give up what they owned. Both the Communists and the Nazis made significant gains in the Reichstag (German parliament) elections in 1930.

In 1932, Hitler became a German citizen so that he could run for president in that year's spring election. His opponents were Ernst Thälmann, the Communist candidate, and Paul von Hindenburg, the independent, conservative incumbent. In the election, 84% of all eligible voters cast ballots, and the people re-elected President Hindenburg. Hitler finished second. But in elections for the Reichstag held four months later, the Nazis' popularity increased further. They won 37% of the seats in the legislature, more than any other party, and 75 seats more than their closest competitor, the Social Democrats.

1932 Presidential Election

Candidate	Party	Votes	Percentage
Paul von Hindenburg	Independent	19,359,983	53.0%
Adolf Hitler	Nazi	13,418,517	36.8%
Ernst Thälmann	Communist	3,706,759	10.2%

Number of Deputies in the Reichstag, 1928–1932

Party	1928	1930	July 1932	Nov. 1932
Social Democrat	153	143	133	121
Catholic Center	78	87	98	90
Communist	54	77	89	100
Nazi	12	107	230	196
German National	73	41	37	52

President Hindenburg and his chancellors could not lift Germany out of the depression. Their popular support began to shrink. In January 1933, Hindenburg and his advisors decided to make a deal with Hitler. He had the popularity they lacked, and they had the power he needed. Hindenburg's advisors believed that the responsibility of being in power would make Hitler moderate his views. They convinced themselves that they were wise enough and powerful enough to "control" Hitler. They were also certain that he, too, would fail to end the depression. When he failed, they would step in to save the nation. But they were tragically mistaken.

Notes to Teacher

1. The Power of Individual and Collective Choices

As in the past two lessons about the Weimar Republic, it is important that students can identify those junctures or moments in the history of the Nazi Party's rise where individuals and groups made choices "for the good" that had horrific consequences. This helps to show that history isn't inevitable and that history is made through our individual and collective choices.

2. Vocabulary in the Nazi Party Platform

The reading National Socialist German Workers' Party Platform contains a number of vocabulary terms that students may find unfamiliar. You might need to pre-teach or be prepared to explain the following terms: *national self-determination*, *revocation*, *surplus*, and *alien* (in the context of a foreigner).

3. Previewing Vocabulary

In addition to the terms above in the Nazi Party platform, the following are key vocabulary terms used in this lesson:

- Platform
- Political party
- Coup

Add these words to your word wall, if you are using one for this unit, and provide necessary support to help students learn these words as you teach the lesson.

Activities

1. Reflect on Societal Values

As students transition from learning about various aspects of German society during the years of the Weimar Republic to tracing the rise of the Nazi Party during those same years, it can be helpful to pause for a moment to reflect on how the values of a society are shaped. Ask students to spend a few minutes responding in their journals to the following prompt:

> Who or what shapes the values of a society? What roles do political and business leaders, the media, artists, and education play? What roles do individual citizens play?

After students have had a few minutes to write, let them share their thinking in a brief discussion.

2. Analyze Key Events in the Nazis' Rise to Power

Explain to students that they are now going to learn about the rise of the Nazi Party in Germany, and throughout this unit they will observe how the Nazis shaped the values of German society.

The video Hitler's Rise to Power, 1918–1933 (09:30) provides an overview of the beginning of the Nazi Party in the early years of the Weimar Republic and the party's growth in relation and reaction to key events in Germany in the 1920s. Explain to students that as they watch this video, they will recognize events that they learned about in the previous two class periods about the Weimar Republic, but now they will focus on how those events affected the growth the Nazi Party in Germany.

Before beginning the video, write the full name of the Nazi Party, in both English and German, on the board:

The National Socialist German Workers' Party

Nationalsozialistische Deutsche Arbeiterpartei

Students can then see how "Nazi" is an abbreviation of the first word of the party's name in German. Tell students that they may see and hear a variety of related names for the Nazis in resources throughout this unit, including National Socialists and the initials NSDAP.

Pass out the handout *Hitler's Rise to Power, 1918–1933* Viewing Guide and instruct students to respond to the questions with information from the video as they watch. To help students prepare to answer, have them read the questions before watching.

Play the video Hitler's Rise to Power, 1918–1933 at facinghistory.org/thhb. You might choose to pause the video so students can add to their notes or, if time permits, consider showing the video twice in a row.

Debrief the video by reviewing the questions on the viewing guide and discussing the information students recorded, helping them fill in important ideas they may have missed. You might have students debrief in groups of three or four, or you might go over the viewing guide as a whole group.

As you discuss the video with students, emphasize the choices that individuals, other than Hitler, made during this time period that contributed to the Nazis' rise to popularity and power. You might ask students to underline on the viewing guide evidence of where individuals and groups made such choices and record a list of these key moments on the board.

3. Analyze the Nazi Party Platform

Pass out the reading National Socialist German Workers' Party Platform.

Explain that a political platform is an official statement by a party of its beliefs and positions on important issues. Read aloud with students the platform of the National Socialist German Workers' Party from the handout.

To help students comprehend the Nazi Party's platform, ask them to label each bullet point with a word or phrase that captures the promise of each provision. For example, students might write "citizenship" or "education" or "insurance" or "jobs." When you have finished the reading, you might ask students to share what they notice about their lists.

- Do any categories appear multiple times or seem to get more or less attention?
- What might the list of provisions suggest about the message the Nazis wanted to convey to German voters?

Pass out the handout What Did the Nazis Believe? and instruct students to answer the true/false statements using evidence from the Nazi platform. It is important for students, as they progress through this unit, to have a firm basic understanding of the Nazis' core beliefs, and this activity will allow students to examine the Nazi platform more closely. You might ask students to underline where in the platform they found evidence to support each of their true/false choices.

Use the Think, Pair, Share strategy to have students share and discuss their responses to the handout What Did the Nazis Believe? As students share their answers, make sure that they also cite the part of the platform that helped them determine each answer.

Finally, ask students to use the evidence they have so far to illustrate what the Nazis believe should be Germany's universe of obligation. They can draw concentric circles (similar to the handout they used in Lesson 4) in their journals to help illustrate the Nazi universe of obligation visually.

3. Discuss the Appointment of Hitler as Chancellor

It is important for students to end the lesson with the understanding that while Hitler was never elected president (and the Nazis never won a majority of the Reichstag seats), he was appointed chancellor by President Paul von Hindenburg as a result of the popularity of the Nazi Party and other political circumstances. If necessary, review the branches of government in the Weimar Republic in order to help students understand the relationship between the president and chancellor.

The reading Hitler in Power explains how Hitler's appointment came about. You might either read aloud this handout with the class or use it to create a mini-lecture if you don't have time for students to complete the reading in class.

4. Revisit the "Bubbling Cauldron" Metaphor

After discussing Hitler's appointment, return to the handout "The Bubbling Cauldron" from Lesson 8. Students completed the graphic organizer on this handout before learning about the rise of the Nazi Party during the years of the Weimar Republic. Now that they have learned about the Nazis' rise, ask them to revisit their work. What would they add now? Is there anything they would erase or change?

Give students a few minutes to complete the handout, and then lead a class discussion about how what students learned in this lesson has affected their understanding of the Weimar Republic.

Assessment

- Assign students to write a short reflection in response to the following prompt:

    What did the Nazis think were the most important problems facing Germany? What solutions did they propose? Why do you think so many Germans supported the Nazi Party by the 1930s?

- Re-examine students' "Bubbling Cauldron" handouts after they have added new ideas from this lesson. Look for evidence that students recognize the Nazis as one of many influences that shaped German society during the years of the Weimar Republic.

Extensions

1. Explore the 1932 German Elections in Depth

If you can devote an additional day to the rise of the Nazi Party in Germany, consider teaching the lesson "Choices in the Weimar Republic Elections." This lesson provides students with the opportunity to explore the issues at play in the 1932 Reichstag election from the viewpoints of German citizens with different perspectives and values. The lesson helps students understand the complexity of the choices citizens make at the voting booth and leads to additional insight into the appeal of not only the Nazi Party but also the Social Democratic and Communist Parties in Germany at the time.

2. Analyze an Image of the 1932 Ballot

To deepen their understanding of the challenges democracy faced during the Weimar years, show students the image "1932 Reichstag Election Ballot," and then lead a discussion with the following questions:

How many parties were on the ballot in 1932? How many parties are typically represented in the legislature of your country?

What might be the benefit of having so many political parties competing in an election? What might be the drawbacks?

In a democracy, is it important for election winners to receive a majority of the vote? Why or why not?

3. Share 1932 German Election Results

The handout titled "1932 Election Results" provides two tables of data showing the results of the 1932 elections for both president and the Reichstag. These tables are also available in this lesson's Context section. Share these two tables with students and lead a discussion about the results that focuses on the following questions:

- Which political parties in Germany gained and lost seats between 1928 and 1932? Why did some parties and candidates become more appealing as the depression took hold in 1929?

- If all Germans lived through the same economic, political, and cultural events, why didn't all Germans vote the same way?

- Is it significant that Hitler lost the presidential election and that the Nazis never held a majority of the seats in the Reichstag? How could other parties have worked together to keep the Nazis from controlling the government?

Visit **facinghistory.org/thhb** to access these additional resources.

Handout

Hitler's Rise to Power, 1918–1933 Viewing Guide

Directions: As you view the film *Hitler's Rise to Power, 1918–1933*, record notes that help you answer the questions on this handout. Watch for moments where choices made by people other than Hitler contributed to Hitler's and the Nazi Party's eventual rise to power. Put a star by these notes.

1. How did German soldiers who returned from World War I affect the way German politics was conducted?

2. How did the National Socialist German Workers' Party (the Nazi Party) explain Germany's loss in World War I to the public? Who did the party blame for the loss?

3. While in prison for his failed attempt at staging a coup in Munich, Hitler wrote *Mein Kampf* (My Struggle), a book in which he shares his idea for how to take control of a people. What is his main idea?

4. What was the Nazis' primary campaign message in the early 1930s? How was it different from what we now know were the Nazis' two primary goals for Germany?

Respond to the following question after viewing the film:

5. What choices did you learn about in this video, made by people other than Hitler, that contributed to the possibility that Hitler and the Nazi Party could eventually rise to power in Germany?

 Reading

National Socialist German Workers' Party Platform

The following list contains some of the provisions that Hitler proposed at the National Socialist German Workers' Party's first large party gathering in February 1920.

- We demand the unification of all Germans in a Greater Germany on the basis of the right of national self-determination.

- We demand . . . the revocation of the peace treaty of Versailles . . .

- We demand land and territory (colonies) to feed our people and to settle our surplus population.

- . . . Only those of German blood, whatever their creed, may be members of the nation. Accordingly, no Jew may be a member of the nation.

- Non-citizens may only live in Germany as guests and must be subject to laws for aliens.

- The right to vote . . . shall be enjoyed by the citizens . . . alone. We demand therefore that all official appointments, of whatever kind, whether in the Reich, in the states or in the smaller localities, shall be held by none but citizens.

- We demand that the State shall make its primary duty to provide a livelihood for its citizens. If it should prove impossible to feed the entire population, foreign nationals (non-citizens) must be deported . . .

- All non-German immigration must be prevented. We demand that all non-Germans who entered Germany after 2 November 1914 shall be required to leave immediately . . .

- . . . To facilitate the creation of a German national press we demand:

    - that all editors of, and contributors to newspapers appearing in the German language must be members of the nation;

    - that no non-German newspapers may appear without express permission of the State. They must not be printed in the German language;

    - that non-Germans shall be prohibited by law from participating financially in or influencing German newspapers . . .

    The Party . . . is convinced that our nation can achieve permanent health only from within on the basis of the principle: The common interest before self-interest . . .

 **Handout**

What Did the Nazis Believe?

Directions: Refer to the Nazi Party platform to answer true or false for the following statements about the Nazis' core beliefs.

☐ True ☐ False	The Nazis believed that only people who could prove they had "German blood" could be citizens.
☐ True ☐ False	The Nazis believed that Germans should not be blamed for World War I and should not have to pay money or give land to the winners of the war.
☐ True ☐ False	The Nazis believed that anybody living in Germany should have the same rights as German citizens.
☐ True ☐ False	The Nazis believed that Jews who had been living in Germany for hundreds of years and had fought in wars for Germany had "German blood."
☐ True ☐ False	The Nazis believed that Germany should be able to get more land for its growing population.
☐ True ☐ False	The Nazis believed that anyone should be able to publish a newspaper in Germany.
☐ True ☐ False	The Nazis believed that recent non-German immigrants were welcome in Germany.
☐ True ☐ False	The Nazis believed that all German citizens had the right to a job and food for their family.
☐ True ☐ False	The Nazis believed that if the country could not provide enough jobs and food for its own citizens, immigrants must leave so that they would not take jobs and food away from German citizens.
☐ True ☐ False	The Nazis believed that anyone living in Germany could vote and run for office.
☐ True ☐ False	The Nazis believed that anyone living in Germany who did not have German blood should follow special laws for non-citizens.

Reading

Hitler in Power

In April 1932, Paul von Hindenburg, at the age of 84, remained president by defeating Hitler and his other challengers. He began his new term in office that spring by naming a new chancellor—Franz von Papen, a close friend and member of the Center Party. Papen ran the country for the rest of the year. When he failed to end the depression, another of Hindenburg's friends, General Kurt von Schleicher, who belonged to no party, took over in December. He was also unable to bring about a recovery and was forced to resign.

Hindenburg and his advisors were all conservatives who represented wealthy landowners, industrialists, and other powerful people. As the depression persisted, their popular support was shrinking. So in January of 1933, they decided to make a deal with Hitler. He had the popularity they lacked, and they had the power he needed. They also agreed on a number of points, including a fierce opposition to communism, hostility to democracy, and eagerness for *Lebensraum*—additional land for the German *Volk*.

Hindenburg's advisors believed that the responsibility of being in power would make Hitler moderate his views. They convinced themselves that they were wise enough and powerful enough to "control" Hitler. Also, they were certain that he, too, would fail to end the depression. And when he failed, they would step in to save the nation. Hitler fooled them all.

On January 30, 1933, Hitler was sworn in as chancellor of Germany. Because the Nazi Party did not control a majority of the Reichstag, they joined with the German National People's Party to form a coalition government—that is, one run by multiple political parties, usually with different but overlapping agendas. Nevertheless, Hitler accepted the appointment as if he had been named emperor of Germany and ignored the wishes of the other party. He and his fellow Nazis boasted that they would soon restore the nation and the "Aryan race" to greatness by ending so-called "Jewish racial domination" and eliminating the Communist threat. The result would be a "third Reich" (*Reich* is the German word for "empire"). The Nazis considered the Holy Roman Empire (952–1806) the "first Reich" and the empire established after the unification of the German states in 1871 the "second." Hitler was confident that his Third Reich would be the greatest of all, and it would last a thousand years.

Unit Essential Question

What does learning about the choices people made during the Weimar Republic, the rise of the Nazi Party, and the Holocaust teach us about the power and impact of our choices today?

Lesson

European Jewish Life before World War II

Duration
One 50-minute class period

Materials

 Image Gallery
Pre-War Jewish Life in Eastern Europe

 Handout
Photo Analysis of Pre-War Jewish Life

 Video
A Day in Warsaw

 Teaching Strategies
Text-to-Text, Text-to-Self, Text-to-World
Wraparound

Find all materials referenced in this lesson at facinghistory.org/thhb.

Guiding Questions

- How can we describe Jewish life in Europe between the two twentieth-century world wars?
- How can isolation and unfamiliarity between groups influence the beliefs that members of one group form about members of another? How can this lead to the creation or reinforcement of "in" groups and "out" groups?

Learning Objectives

- Through an analysis of images and film, students will recognize that Jewish life in the 1920s was characterized by great variety in religious practice, culture, national affiliation, occupation, wealth, and status.
- Students will explore the idea that when groups in a society live separately and are unfamiliar with one another, they might develop myths and stereotypes about each other that can cause harm, especially to the less powerful group.

Overview

In previous lessons, students learned about the effect of World War I on Germany and how its aftermath created conditions that helped give rise to the Nazis in the years that followed. In this lesson, students will continue this unit's historical case study by learning more about Jewish life across Europe at the time of the Nazis' ascension to power. This lesson serves two crucial and related purposes:

1. It provides a counterbalance to the historical antisemitic and racist ideas and actions students learn about throughout this unit. Despite the efforts of the Nazis to reduce the lives and experiences of Jews to a "single story," Jewish life throughout Europe in the 1920s and 1930s was marked by great diversity, as it is today. Reality did not conform to the myths and stereotypes.

2. It will help students better appreciate the lives and cultures that were lost when they later learn about the devastation of European Jewry during the Holocaust. Students will also consider in this lesson the ways in which Jews were interwoven in the societies in which they lived and the ways in which they lived apart (by force or by choice). Students will think about how separation affected the beliefs and attitudes that non-Jewish Europeans developed about their Jewish neighbors.

Context

Over the course of this unit, students will come to see how, throughout history, many have sought to define Jews, incorrectly, as a single and uniform category of people with fixed characteristics, which racists and antisemites falsely believe are rooted in biology. But the lives Jews have lived around the world and throughout history can perhaps be characterized best by their immense diversity. Jews have always expressed their religious faith (or lack thereof) and connection to Jewish culture in myriad ways. It is important for students to understand and appreciate the richness and diversity of European Jewish life before the Third Reich, both to honor what was lost in the Holocaust and to counterbalance the "single story" about Jews spread through Nazi ideology and policy. As historian Doris Bergen writes:

> Nazi propaganda would create the category of "the Jews," a composite based on myths and stereotypes . . . In reality there was no such thing as "the Jew," only Jews who often differed as much, and in many cases more, from one another than they did from the Christians around them.[1]

Throughout history, Jews have always been a small minority in Europe that never made up more than 1 or 2% of the population. Yet, before World War II, Jews lived and thrived in varied communities, spanning eastern and western Europe, with diverse cultures and ways of life. Jews in Europe came from small towns as well as cities, and they held a variety of occupations. Bergen continues:

> [T]here were wealthy Jews in Europe around 1930 as well as middle-class and very poor Jews. There were Jewish bankers and shopkeepers, Jewish doctors, nurses, actors, professors, soldiers, typists, peddlers, factory owners, factory workers, kindergarten teachers, conservatives, liberals, nationalists, feminists, anarchists, and Communists.[2]

Many Jews identified more closely with the nations in which they lived than with Jewish religion and culture, while others lived apart from non-Jews and hewed to a more traditional and religious way of life. Bergen explains:

> European Jews, like European Christians, were and are a diverse group. By the early twentieth century many Jews were highly acculturated; neither their appearance, habits of daily life, or language distinguished them from their non-Jewish French, German, Italian, Polish, Greek, or other neighbors. Some attended religious services on high holidays only; others, never. Some maintained a strong sense of Jewish identity; others, very little or none at all . . .

---

1 Doris L. Bergen, *War and Genocide: A Concise History of the Holocaust,* 3rd ed. (Lanham: Rowman & Littlefield, 2016), 20.
2 Bergen, *War and Genocide,* 20.

In Europe in the early 1900s there were also more visible kinds of Jews. In some parts of eastern Europe many Jews lived in communities known as shtetls. Confined by the Russian tsars to an area in the west of the Russian empire called the Pale of Settlement, these Jews developed a lifestyle based on shared religious observance, the Yiddish language, a diet following kashrut—the Jewish dietary laws—and predominance of certain occupations. For example, many were small traders and craftspeople. Those lines of work did not require them to own land, something from which they were restricted and in some places prohibited altogether.[3]

In this lesson, students will glimpse a small part of Jewish rural and urban life before World War II by comparing and contrasting life in shtetls with life in Jewish communities in Warsaw, Poland. Nevertheless, it is important when explaining and debriefing the following activities to share with students this larger historical context, in which it is not possible to reduce the Jewish experience to just a few stories.

Notes to Teacher

1. Providing Context for the Photos of Pre-War Jewish Life

It is important to help students understand that although this lesson's photographs depict a variety of experiences, they do not begin to fully represent the richness and diversity of European Jewish life. Nevertheless, the photographs and analysis activity will help students glimpse the everyday lives of some European Jews living in shtetls and larger cities to get a sense of what life was like for them before World War II.

Before class begins, determine how students will access and view the photographs in the first activity so that you can have the materials and classroom prepared in advance. Options include the following: printed packets, a gallery walk, laptops, or mobile devices.

2. Previewing Vocabulary

The following are key vocabulary terms used in this lesson:

- Secular
- Isolation
- Shtetl

Add these words to your word wall, if you are using one for this unit, and provide necessary support to help students learn these words as you teach the lesson.

Activities

1. Analyze Photos of Pre-War Jewish Life in Eastern Europe

Students will begin to learn about pre-war Jewish life in eastern Europe by examining a series of photographs from the period. Students will need to see the entire Pre-War Jewish Life in Eastern Europe gallery of nine photographs, from which they will choose one to examine more closely.

3 Bergen, *War and Genocide*, 19.

Tell students that they are about to look at photographs depicting scenes from "everyday" Jewish life in eastern Europe in the 1920s and 1930s. Before introducing the photographs, ask students to think for a moment about what they expect they might see.

Then give students a few minutes to browse through all of the photographs in the collection. As they browse, instruct them to choose one photo that resonates with them for some reason. For instance, the photograph might remind them of a moment or experience in their own lives, or there might be something about the photograph that surprises or captivates them.

Pass out the handout Photo Analysis of Pre-War Jewish Life. This handout includes a version of the Text-to-Text, Text-to-Self, Text-to-World strategy modified for use with photographs.

Ask at least one student per image to share with the class their response to one of the questions on the handout.

Then ask students to think for a moment about the entire set of images. Have them respond to the following question in their journals:

> What do these pictures tell you about the lives of eastern European Jews during the period before World War II? What stories might be missing from this collection of pictures? What questions do the images leave unanswered?

After students have completed their journal writing, ask them to volunteer some of the conclusions they drew from the photo gallery activity while you record their ideas on the board.

2. Analyze Film Representations of Pre-War Life in Warsaw

Now that students have drawn some preliminary conclusions from their investigation of European Jewish life before World War II, share the following background information with them:

Before World War II, Jews lived in varied communities, spanning eastern and western Europe, with diverse cultures and ways of life. Jews in Europe came from small towns as well as cities, and they were active in music, theater, politics, the military, business, and education. While for many, being Jewish was central to their identity, for others it was just one part of who they were.

In the latter half of the nineteenth century, many European Jews lived in small villages called shtetls, where they were often isolated from many aspects of modern life, especially if the shtetl was not near a city or railway line, while many other Jews moved to cities. Some in the cities chose to live more secular and modern lives than shtetl Jews lived and worked to integrate themselves within a broader European society. Others strongly valued Jewish religious and cultural tradition. Still others lived somewhere in between tradition and modernity, and between the religious and the secular.

Introduce the documentary film A Day in Warsaw (10:18), available at at facing-history.org/thhb. Explain that this film was produced in 1938 and 1939, and its purpose was to encourage American Jews to visit Poland. (The filmmakers did not know, of course, that six years later, 90% of Polish Jewry would have been killed in the Holocaust.) Given this purpose, have students brainstorm what parts of life in Warsaw the filmmakers may have intentionally left out of the final version shown to Americans.

After showing the film, have students respond in their journals to the following questions:

- Looking at the film, what is your overall impression of life in eastern European cities such as Warsaw at the time this film was made?
- Based on what you've seen in this film, what opportunities do you think were available for Polish Jews in cities during this time period?
- Which of the photographs from the opening activity seem to connect most closely to this film clip? What answers does this film provide to questions raised from the photograph activity? What new questions does it raise?

Then ask students to return to the conclusions, written on the board, that they made about the lives of eastern European Jews before World War II. Discuss the following three questions as a class:

- How might you revise your conclusions based on the new information you encountered in the film?
- What new conclusions might you add?
- What questions remain unanswered?

3. Connect Separation and Stereotypes

Now share with students the following statement from sociologist David Schoem:

> The effort it takes for us to know so little about one another across racial and ethnic groups is truly remarkable. That we can live so closely together, that our lives can be so intertwined socially, economically and politically, and . . . yet still manage to be ignorant of one another is clear testimony to the deep-seated roots of this human and national tragedy. What we do learn along the way is to place heavy reliance on stereotypes, gossip, rumor, and fear to shape our lack of knowledge.[4]

Have students think about Schoem's statement and respond to the following questions in their journals:

- To what extent does Schoem's statement describe Warsaw in the 1920s and 1930s?
- To what extent does it describe your community or country today?
- How might the type of separation Schoem describes affect how individuals, communities, and countries define their universe of obligation?
- How can people break the isolation he describes?

Depending on time, ask students to share one line from their journals in a Wraparound activity, paired discussion, or class discussion.

---

[4] David Louis Schoem, *Inside Separate Worlds: Life Stories of Young Blacks, Jews, and Latinos* (Ann Arbor: University of Michigan Press, 1991), 3.

Assessment

- Read the connections students made with the photographs of pre-war Jewish life on the handout Photo Analysis of Pre-War Jewish Life. Look for evidence that students engaged emotionally in this activity by viewing the subjects of the photographs not through the lens of difference but by looking for common humanity.

- Listen carefully to students' contributions to the Wraparound activity that closes the lesson to hear how they are thinking about the connection between isolation and stereotypes, as well as the connections they are making to the world today.

Extension

Analyze a Film about Shtetl Life

Introduce the documentary film clip *Sholem Aleichem: Understanding the Life of Shtetl Jews* (04:28) by explaining that it is part of a documentary about one of the most renowned eastern European Jewish writers from the eighteenth and nineteenth centuries, Sholem Aleichem. He was born and raised in one of hundreds of small, predominantly Jewish villages, called shtetls, that once dotted the map of eastern Europe. His stories and plays were often set in shtetls, and the clip students will watch draws in part from his descriptions of the life and culture of these villages.

Show the clip, and then use the Connect, Extend, Challenge teaching strategy to help students analyze how what they learned from the film relates to what they learned from the previous activities in this lesson.

Visit facinghistory.org/thhb to access these additional resources.

Image Gallery

Pre-War Jewish Life in Eastern Europe

Shabbtai Sonenson and Teacher

Shabbtai (Shepske) Sonenson takes one of the shtetl's Hebrew teachers for a ride on his new motorcycle, 1941.

Jewish Family in Kalisz

A family in Kalisz, Poland, May 16, 1935.

Friends in Shtetl

United States Holocaust Memorial Museum, courtesy of The Shtetl Foundation

A group of friends sledding in the shtetl, January 12, 1932.

Kalecka Jewish Elementary School

United States Holocaust Memorial Museum, courtesy of Barbara Berkowicz Soloway

Pupils in the second grade work in their classroom at the Kalecka Jewish elementary school in Warsaw, Poland, ca. 1937–1938.

Bar Mitzvah at Zerrennerstrasse Synagogue

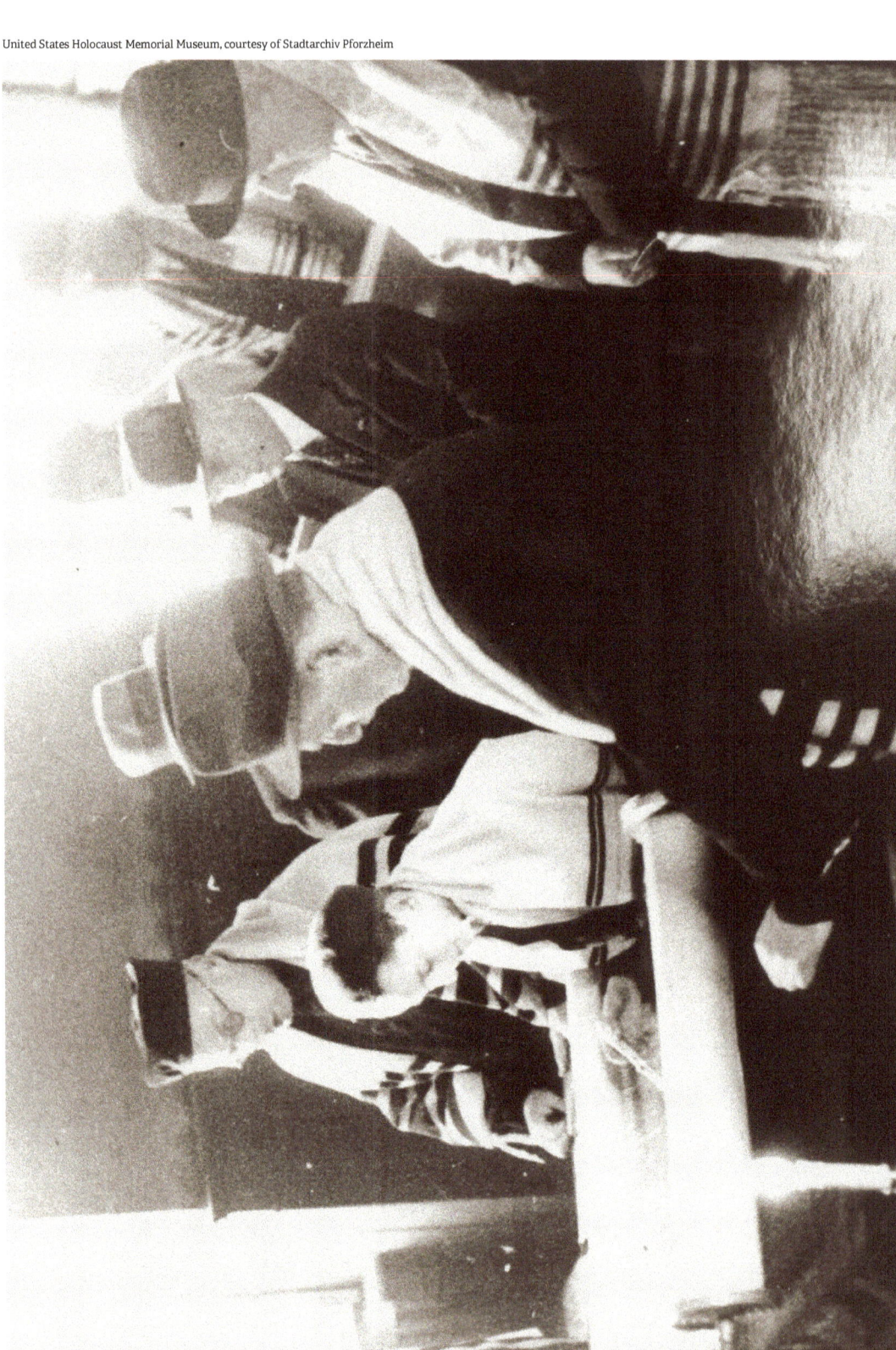

Ludwig Nachmann, the president of the congregation, follows the Torah reading during a bar mitzvah at the liberal Zerrennerstrasse synagogue in Pforzheim, Germany, 1936.

Three Generations of a Jewish Family, Vilnius, Lithuania

United States Holocaust Memorial Museum

Three generations of a Jewish family in Vilnius, the capital of Lithuania, in 1938 or 1939. In the eighteenth century, Vilnius (Vilna in Yiddish) was a center of Jewish learning. By the 1920s and 1930s, roughly a half of the city's inhabitants were Jews.

A Children's Volleyball Team in Szczuczyn, Poland

Yad Vashem

A volleyball team in Szczuczyn, Poland. In the interwar years, it was not uncommon for Jewish children to participate in school or community recreational activities with non-Jewish children. Despite the lurking danger of antisemitism, Jews often had close relationships with Christians, which led many to believe that Jewish integration was possible and might even be welcomed.

Huber Sisters in Czechoslovakia

Irenka and Eliska Huber, sisters, at their home in Czechoslovakia in 1920.

Ensemble of Jewish Musicians in Latvia

United States Holocaust Memorial Museum, courtesy of Samuel Heifetz

A small ensemble of Jewish musicians performs in Riga, Latvia, in the 1930s.

Handout

Photo Analysis of Pre-War Jewish Life

Directions: Spend at least a few minutes studying the image you selected. Look at the image as a whole. Look at specific places: around the corners and edges, in the shadows, behind central figures. Then answer the questions below.

Photo-to-Text

How does this photo remind you of another text (photo, story, book, movie, song, etc.)? Complete the following statement:

What I see reminds me of _____ (story/book/movie/song) because . . .

Photo-to-Self

How does this photo relate to your own life, ideas, and experiences? Complete one of the following statements:

What I see reminds me of the time when I . . .

I identify with this photo because in my life, I have experienced/learned . . .

Photo-to-World

How do the ideas or details in this photo relate to the larger world—past, present, and future? Complete one of the following statements:

What I see makes me think about (event from the past) because . . .

What I see makes me think about (event from today related to my own community, nation, or world) because . . .

What I see makes me wonder about the future because . . .

Unit Essential Question: What does learning about the choices people made during the Weimar Republic, the rise of the Nazi Party, and the Holocaust teach us about the power and impact of our choices today?

Lesson

Dismantling Democracy

Duration
One 50-minute class period

Materials

Videos
- From Democracy to Dictatorship
- Hitler's Rise to Power, 1933–1934

Handouts
- *Hitler's Rise to Power, 1933–1934* Viewing Guide
- Democracy to Dictatorship Reading Analysis

Readings
- Shaping Public Opinion
- Targeting Jews
- "Restoring" Germany's Civil Service
- Where They Burn Books
- Isolating Gay Men

Teaching Strategy
- Fishbowl

Find all materials referenced in this lesson at facinghistory.org/thhb.

Guiding Questions

- What steps did the Nazis take to transform Germany into a dictatorship during their first two years in power?
- What can we learn from the rise of the Nazis about what makes democracy fragile?

Learning Objective

- Students will learn about the transformation of Germany into a dictatorship in 1933–1934 and draw conclusions, based on this history, about the values and institutions that might serve as a bulwark against dictatorship and make democracy possible.

Overview

In previous lessons, students traced the rise of the Nazi Party during the years of the Weimar Republic in Germany, and they explored the political climate that led both to the Nazis becoming the most popular political party in Germany and to the appointment of Adolf Hitler as chancellor. In this lesson, students will continue this unit's historical case study by learning about the National Socialist revolution that followed Hitler's appointment as chancellor and analyzing the steps the Nazis took in 1933 and 1934 to dismantle democracy in Germany and establish a dictatorship. In the process, students will continue to deepen and extend their study of democracy and reflect on the idea of democracy's fragility. By examining how democracy was replaced with dictatorship in a relatively short period of time in Germany, students will begin to draw conclusions about the responsibilities shared by both leaders and citizens for democracy's survival.

Context

Historians point out that Hitler's political position upon his appointment as chancellor in January 1933 was precarious. Yet, by July of 1933, Hitler and the Nazis had succeeded in dismantling democracy and laying the foundation for dictatorship in Germany. Few Germans believed this could happen. In fact, many did not believe Hitler would remain in power for long. After all, in the 14 years since the creation of the Weimar Republic, Germany had had 14 chancellors, most of whom served for less than a year. Recalling a discussion with his father on the day Hitler became chancellor, journalist Sebastian Haffner wrote in 1939:

> I discussed the prospects of the new government with my father. We agreed that it had a good chance of doing a lot of damage, but not much chance of surviving very long . . . How could things turn out so completely different?[1]

The events described in this lesson begin to answer Haffner's question. The Nazis moved swiftly in early 1933 to take advantage of the weaknesses of the Weimar Republic. Previous chancellors had already invoked emergency powers under Article 48 of the Weimar Constitution (see Lesson 8) to bypass the Reichstag and enact their own laws to try to pull the country out of the Great Depression. According to the constitution, only the president could invoke Article 48, so Paul von Hindenburg had to approve each of the measures chancellors took under emergency powers. Hitler seized on those powers, relying on Hindenburg's willingness to sign off, to eliminate opposition, increase his power, and dismantle democracy.

On February 27, 1933, less than a month after Hitler became chancellor, the Reichstag building in Berlin was set on fire. While historians continue to debate who set the fire, Hitler chose to immediately blame the Nazis' chief political competitors, the Communists. The day after the fire, Hitler used emergency powers under Article 48 to issue two decrees that suspended every part of the constitution that protected personal freedoms and also legalized the arrest of Communists and other political opponents of the Nazis. A few weeks later, on March 21, Hitler issued another decree making it illegal to speak out against the government or criticize its leaders. And three days after that—while many Reichstag deputies from opposing parties were in prison, exile, or hiding—the Reichstag passed the Enabling Act, which gave Hitler and his cabinet the power to enact laws that overrode the constitution and the power to imprison anyone Hitler deemed an enemy of the state. That day, the Nazi government also announced the opening of the first concentration camp at Dachau to hold Communists and other political prisoners. The Nazis continued to attack opposing parties and organizations through the summer of 1933, dissolving trade labor unions in May and outlawing the Social Democratic Party in June. By July, remaining political parties dissolved and the Nazi Party was the only legal party in Germany.

In the first six months of Hitler's chancellorship, the Nazis also stepped up violence, intimidation, and terror toward the German people. The SA and SS attacked political dissenters in the streets, and the secret police force known as the Gestapo was created in April to spy on, interrogate, and imprison citizens in order

---

1 Sebastian Haffner, "Street-Level Coercion," in *How Was It Possible? A Holocaust Reader*, ed. Peter Hayes (Lincoln, NE: University of Nebraska Press, 2015), 118–19, excerpt from *Defying Hitler: A Memoir*, trans. Oliver Pretzel (New York: Farrar, Straus and Giroux, 2002), 106–08. Reproduced by permission from Farrar, Straus & Giroux.

to "protect public safety and order." The Nazis initiated attacks on homosexual men, imprisoning dozens under a long-existing law (Paragraph 175) that was not regularly enforced by the Weimar Republic. The Nazis also targeted Jews, imprisoning Jewish immigrants and attacking Jewish judges, lawyers, and shopkeepers. On April 1, the Nazis called for a nationwide day-long boycott of Jewish businesses. The boycott did not receive the widespread support the Nazis had hoped for; in some places in Germany people embraced the attack on Jewish businesses, but in other places people deliberately shopped in Jewish-owned businesses in defiance. Regardless, the event signaled the Nazis' intent to target German Jews and foreshadowed the onslaught of discrimination that would soon follow. On April 7, a new law to "restore" Germany's civil service went into effect, forcing the firing of Jews (and individuals deemed disloyal to the nation) who worked for government institutions.

In addition to people, the Nazis also began to attack ideas. On March 13, 1933, Hitler established the Reich Ministry of Public Enlightenment and Propaganda and put Joseph Goebbels in charge. The ministry set out to coordinate every form of expression in Germany—from music to radio programs to textbooks, artwork, newspapers, and even sermons—crafting language and imagery carefully to praise Nazi policies and Hitler himself and to demonize those who the Nazis considered enemies. On May 6, Goebbels led the first book burning, which the German Student Association declared was a nationwide "Action against the Un-German Spirit."

After July 1933, Hitler grew more concerned with his opposition within the Nazi Party itself. He feared that the SA, whose members outnumbered the German military, and its leader, Ernst Röhm, had become too powerful. On June 30, 1934—in what became known as "the Night of the Long Knives"—Hitler ordered the SS and the regular army to murder more than 200 SA leaders, including Röhm, and other high-profile political threats to the regime. According to historian Lucy S. Dawidowicz, the massacre was accepted by many Germans who "believed that the purge of the SA represented Hitler's wish to halt the arbitrary terror of the SA in the streets and to restore a measure of legality to the country."[2]

On August 2, 1934, President Hindenburg died and Hitler combined the positions of president and chancellor into a new position he called *Führer*. The dictatorship was complete.

In response to his own question—how could things turn out so differently?—Sebastian Haffner answered:

> Perhaps it was just because we were all so certain that they could not do so—and relied on that with far too much confidence. So we neglected to consider that it might, if worse came to worst, be necessary to prevent the disaster from happening . . .[3]

In this lesson, and especially in the lessons that follow, students will wrestle with the question of how Germans like Haffner might have tried to resist or prevent the Nazis' takeover and the atrocities that followed. The rapidity of the events that transformed Germany during that time suggests a sense of inevitability.

---

2 Lucy S. Dawidowicz, *The War against the Jews, 1933–1945* (New York: Holt, Rinehart and Winston, 1975), 82.
3 Haffner, "Street-Level Coercion."

However, it is important to help students look closely at each of these events and consider the agency of individuals, groups, and the public at large to influence the actions of the Nazi Party and resist the revolution. That level of agency varied from person to person and depended on circumstances and time.

There is evidence, after all, that Hitler and the Nazis were responsive to pressure against their policies from leaders such as Hindenburg as well as from public opinion. Historian Doris Bergen writes: "Hitler and his associates in the new German leadership struck in dramatic, decisive ways, but they also tested the public response to each move before proceeding further."[4] Yet public opinion did not stop Germany's descent into Nazi dictatorship. While a few Germans resisted or protested, others were true believers in the Nazi program. Still others were swept up in the energy and excitement of Nazi rallies and parades, or appreciated the order that the Nazis appeared to bring to German society in an unsettled time. Crucially, still others were troubled by the Nazis but felt intimidated and afraid to act. This lesson asks students to begin to consider the human behavior that may have influenced all of these responses, a topic that will be explored more deeply in subsequent lessons.

Notes to Teacher

1. Assigning Reading: Heterogeneous or Leveled Groupings of Students

To learn about the many ways the Nazis created a dictatorship in Germany, groups of students will read one of five articles highlighting significant events from 1933 and 1934. The readings vary in length from half a page to two pages, so you might consider in advance how you will group students for this activity. One option is to create heterogeneous groupings of readers so that the stronger readers can assist struggling ones with pacing, vocabulary, and comprehension. Alternatively, you might group students by level and work more closely with struggling readers to target specific literacy skills while allowing the more confident readers to tackle the content independently.

2. Reviewing Characteristics of Democracy

In Lesson 8, the class brainstormed characteristics of democracy. Students will refer to their notes from that discussion in this class. If you collected their ideas about democracy on chart paper, you might hang it in the room before class so it is ready to review in the first activity. As noted in Lesson 8, make sure that the chart paper includes "free and fair elections," "the rule of law," "equality before the law," "free expression," "free press," and "freedom of religion," if they are not already there.

3. Previewing Vocabulary

The following are key vocabulary terms used in this lesson:
- Dictatorship
- Fragile
- Dissent

---

[4] Doris L. Bergen, *War and Genocide: A Concise History of the Holocaust,* 3rd ed. (Lanham: Rowman & Littlefield, 2016), 73.

- Propaganda
- Civil service

Add these words to your word wall, if you are using one for this unit, and provide necessary support to help students learn these words as you teach the lesson.

Activities

1. Contrast Democracy and Dictatorship

Start the class by asking students to review their notes, or the class chart, from their Lesson 8 discussion about the characteristics of democracy. Then introduce the concept of *dictatorship*. You might create a similar chart for *dictatorship* as you did for *democracy*, or you can simply provide students with the following definition:

> A government ruled by a single person (or a small group) who has absolute power to make and enforce laws without the consent of the people or other branches of the government.

Then show students the video From Democracy to Dictatorship (03:00) at facinghistory.org/thhb, in which Holocaust survivor Alfred Wolf recalls how he realized that dictatorship was taking hold in Germany.

After watching the video, ask students to respond in their journals to the following prompt:

> For Alfred Wolf, what were the signs that a dictatorship was replacing democracy in Germany in 1933? What else do you imagine might be a sign of such a change? What might you be able to do if you lived in a democracy that you wouldn't be able to do if you lived in a dictatorship?

After a few minutes, ask students to share some of their ideas as you write them on the board.

2. Introduce Key Events in the Nazis' First Two Years in Power

Introduce the video Hitler's Rise to Power, 1933–1934 (7:45), available at facinghistory.org/thhb. It provides an overview of the two years following Hitler's appointment as chancellor of Germany. Explain to students that they will learn about some of the events that the video touches upon in more detail later in the lesson.

Pass out the handout Hitler's Rise to Power, 1933–1934 Viewing Guide and instruct students to respond to the first two questions on the handout as they watch the video. You might briefly pause the film two or three times to allow students some extra time to write their notes. After the film, ask students to complete the two reflection questions on the handout. They can complete this step independently or with a partner.

Debrief the video by reviewing the questions on the viewing guide and discussing the information students should have recorded.

3. Explore Pivotal Choices in the Dismantling of Democracy

Tell students that they will now work in groups to explore more deeply some specific choices the Nazis made to dismantle democracy and create a dictatorship in Germany. Each group will analyze the ways an individual event undermined democracy and share their conclusions about that event with the rest of the class.

Divide the class into small groups and provide each group with a copy of the handout Democracy to Dictatorship Reading Analysis and one additional reading: Shaping Public Opinion, Targeting Jews, "Restoring" Germany's Civil Service, Where They Burn Books, or Isolating Gay Men.

Give the groups time to complete their assigned reading and the handout. Tell students that they will be using the information they gather on their handouts for the next activity and should be prepared to share it with the class.

4. Discuss Democracy's Fragility

Have a short discussion with students about the meaning of the word *fragile*. What does it mean for something to be fragile?

Then have students review their Democracy to Dictatorship Reading Analysis handouts, and discuss with them the questions below. Time permitting, use the Fishbowl teaching strategy to structure this conversation.

- In what ways is democracy fragile?
- What makes democracy strong (or less vulnerable to becoming a dictatorship)?

Make sure that students support their thinking with information from their analysis handouts and the readings they analyzed. Record on the board important points that come up in the conversation, and instruct students to copy them into their journals at the end of the discussion.

Assessment

- To assess students' understanding of the factors that led to the destruction of democracy and rise of dictatorship in Germany, assign them to create a pie chart to represent the distribution of responsibility for that transformation between the groups listed below. They can create the chart individually or in pairs, and they should use evidence from the video Hitler's Rise to Power, 1933–1934 and the readings they analyzed in this lesson. Use the following prompt to spark their thinking:

    What role did each of the following individuals or groups play in the destruction of democracy in Germany?
    - Adolf Hitler
    - President Hindenburg
    - Members of the Reichstag
    - German citizens
    - Other (label who on your pie chart)

- Carefully observe the Fishbowl discussion about the fragility of democracy to assess students' ideas about what the history covered in this lesson suggests about the importance of protecting democracy. You might tell students in advance that they will be assessed on these conversations in order to ensure that everyone contributes.

Extensions

1. Watch *Hitler's First Victims*

The video *Hitler's First Victims* (11:00) details the Nazis' response to the Reichstag fire, the opening of Dachau, the first Nazi concentration camp, and the murders of four Jewish prisoners at the camp. The story of the murders and the response to them by investigators, bureaucrats, and Nazi officials sheds light on the relationship between the Nazi program, the law, the government bureaucracy, and public opinion in 1933, and it helps students consider the consequences of the choices made by a variety of individuals and groups at that crucial point in time.

2. Examine How the Nazis Stifled Dissent

The reading "Storm Troopers, Elite Guards, and Secret Police" introduces the Gestapo, or Nazi secret police. The resource book *Holocaust and Human Behavior* includes more information on the Gestapo and its tactics in the readings "Spying on Family and Friends" and "Speaking in Whispers." You might include one or both of these readings in the main activity above, or you can share these readings with students after the main activity and discuss the following questions:

- What is the role of dissent in a democracy?
- How did the Nazis use fear and suspicion to stifle dissent?
- Can democracy survive in a society in which neighbors do not trust each other?

Visit facinghistory.org/thhb to access these additional resources.

Handout

Hitler's Rise to Power: 1933–1934 Viewing Guide

Directions: While viewing the film, take notes in response to the first two questions listed below.

1. Why was Hitler vulnerable when he was appointed chancellor?

2. How did Hitler solidify his hold on power in 1933 and 1934? List as many details from the film as you can.

After watching the film, reflect on the following two questions:

3. Which one or two events described in this video do you think were most important in the transformation of Germany from democracy to dictatorship?

4. Which choices made by groups or by individuals seemed to have the greatest consequences?

Handout

Democracy to Dictatorship Reading Analysis

Directions: Read and discuss the reading your group has been assigned, and then respond to the following questions.

1. Write the title of your reading and a short summary (two or three sentences).

Title: _____

2. List the names and date(s) of important events discussed in this reading. Each reading has a different number of events, so you might not use the whole chart.

Date	Event

3. Explain how each of the events listed above contributed to the dismantling of democracy and the establishment of dictatorship in Germany.

4. What does this reading suggest about the values, institutions, and groups that must be protected and strengthened in order to make democracy possible?

 Reading

Shaping Public Opinion

As the Nazis eliminated civil liberties in Germany and opened the first concentration camps to imprison "enemies of the state," they were also trying to win public approval for their government. According to historian Robert Gellately,

> Hitler and his henchmen did not want to cower the German people as a whole into submission, but to win them over by building on popular images, cherished ideals, and long held phobias in the country. . . . [The Nazis] aimed to create and maintain the broadest possible level of popular backing. They expended an enormous amount of energy and resources to track public opinion and to win over people.[1]

The Reich Ministry of Public Enlightenment and Propaganda played a key role in the Nazis' efforts to cultivate favorable public opinion. Propaganda is biased or misleading information that is used to influence public opinion. Hitler created the new ministry on March 13, 1933, and put Joseph Goebbels in charge. It was his job "not just to present the regime and its policies in a positive light, but to generate the impression that the entire German people enthusiastically endorsed everything it did."[2]

To generate excitement and enthusiasm for the Nazi Party and for Hitler himself, Goebbels and his ministry created new festivals and holidays, such as the celebration of Hitler's birthday. They changed street names and other public signage to erase reminders of the Weimar Republic. They organized party rallies and dramatic torch-lit parades to demonstrate public support.

Writing in 1939, journalist Sebastian Haffner described these demonstrations and recalled the effect they had on many Germans.

> [O]ne was permanently occupied and distracted by an unending sequence of celebrations, ceremonies, and national festivities. It started with a huge victory celebration before the elections on March 4 . . . There were mass parades, fireworks, drums, bands, and flags all over Germany, Hitler's voice over thousands of loudspeakers, oaths and vows—all before it was even certain that the elections might not be a setback for the Nazis, which indeed they were. These elections, the last that were ever held in prewar Germany, brought the Nazis only 44 percent of the votes (in the previous elections they had achieved 37 percent). The majority was still against the Nazis.
>
> A week later, Hindenberg abolished the Weimar national flag, which was replaced by the swastika banner and a black, white, and red "temporary national flag." There were daily parades, mass meetings, declarations of gratitude for the liberation of the nation, military music from dawn to dusk, awards ceremonies for heroes, the dedication of flags. . . . Hitler swearing loyalty to something or other for the nth time, bells tolling, a solemn procession

---

1 Robert Gellately, *Backing Hitler: Consent and Coercion in Nazi Germany* (Oxford: Oxford University Press, 2001), vii.
2 Richard J. Evans, *The Third Reich in Power* (New York: Penguin, 2005), 121.

to church by the members of the Reichstag, a military parade, swords lowered in salute, children waving flags, and a torchlight parade.

The colossal emptiness and lack of meaning of these never-ending events was by no means unintentional. The population should become used to cheering and jubilation, even when there was no visible reason for it. . . . Better to celebrate, howl with the wolves, "Heil, Heil!" Besides, people began to enjoy doing so. The weather in March 1933 was glorious. Was it not wonderful to celebrate in the spring sunshine, in squares decked with flags? To merge with the festive crowds and listen to high-sounding patriotic speeches, about freedom and fatherland, exaltation and holy vows?[3]

Goebbels and his ministry also set out to coordinate every form of expression in Germany—from music to radio programs to textbooks, artwork, newspapers, and even sermons—crafting language and imagery carefully to praise Nazi policies and Hitler himself, and to demonize those who the Nazis considered enemies. While the ministry's work included censoring much German art and media, the Nazis also created an environment in which many artists, newspaper editors, and filmmakers censored themselves in order to gain favor with the regime, avoid punishment, or escape the Nazis' attention altogether.[4]

---

3 Sebastian Haffner, "Street-Level Coercion," in *How Was It Possible? A Holocaust Reader*, ed. Peter Hayes (Lincoln, NE: University of Nebraska Press, 2015), 122, excerpt from *Defying Hitler: A Memoir*, trans. Oliver Pretzel (New York: Farrar, Straus and Giroux, 2002), 128–29.

4 Doris Bergen to Facing History & Ourselves, comment on draft manuscript, December 23, 2015.

Targeting Jews

From the start, Adolf Hitler and his fellow Nazis were determined to resolve the so-called "Jewish question." In Hitler's words, Nazi leaders were to bring it up "again and again and again, unceasingly. Every emotional aversion, however slight, must be exploited ruthlessly." Julius Streicher, the publisher of an antisemitic newspaper known as *Der Stürmer* (the word means "attacker"), led the way in creating that kind of propaganda, claiming:

> The same Jew who plunged the German people into the bloodletting of the World War, and who committed on it the crime of the November Revolution [Weimar Republic,] is now engaged in stabbing Germany, recovering from its shame and misery, in the back. . . . The Jew is again engaged in poisoning public opinion.[1]

Propaganda was not the only weapon the Nazis used against the Jews. They also relied on terror. On March 9, 1933, just a few days after the elections, Nazi SA storm troopers in Berlin imprisoned dozens of Jewish immigrants from eastern Europe. In Breslau, they attacked Jewish lawyers and judges. On March 13 in Mannheim, they forced Jewish shopkeepers to close their doors. In other towns, they broke into Jewish homes and beat up the people living there.

Although these events were rarely reported in the German press, the foreign press wrote about them regularly. In the United States, many Jews and non-Jews were outraged by the violence. Some called for a boycott of German goods. Their outburst gave the Nazis an excuse for a "defensive action against the Jewish world criminal" on April 1, 1933.

That action—a boycott of Jewish-owned businesses—was the first major public event that specifically targeted Jews not as Communists or Social Democrats but as Jews. It was not a huge success. In some places, Germans showed their disapproval of the boycott by making a point of shopping at Jewish-owned stores on April 1.

Even in places where the boycott took place as planned, the Nazis quickly discovered that it was not always easy to decide if a business was Jewish-owned. There was no legal definition of who was a Jew and who was not. Also, many Jews had non-Jewish business partners, and nearly all had non-Jewish employees. Were those businesses to be closed as well? For example, Tietz, a chain of department stores in Berlin owned by Jews, had more than 14,000 employees, almost all of whom were non-Jews. At a time when unemployment was high and the economy fragile, did the Nazis really want to put those workers out of a job? In the end, the Nazis allowed Tietz to remain open—at least for the time being. A few years later, the owners were forced to turn over their stores to "Aryan" businessmen.

The boycott did succeed, however, in one of its goals: it terrorized Jews throughout Germany. Edwin Landau described what it was like in his hometown in West Prussia. On the Friday before the boycott, he recalled, "one saw the SA [storm troopers] marching through

---

1 Quoted in Nora Levin, *The Holocaust: The Destruction of European Jewry 1933–1945* (New York: Schocken, 1973), 46.

the city with its banners: 'The Jews are our misfortune.' 'Against the Jewish atrocity propaganda abroad.'" He wrote about the day of the boycott:

> I took my war decorations, put them on, went into the street, and visited Jewish shops, where at first I was also stopped. But I was seething inside, and most of all I would have liked to shout my hatred into the faces of the barbarians. Hatred, hatred—when had it become a part of me? — It was only a few hours ago that a change had occurred within me. This land and this people that until now I had loved and treasured had suddenly become my enemy. So I was not a German anymore, or I was no longer supposed to be one. That, of course, cannot be settled in a few hours. But one thing I felt immediately: I was ashamed that I had once belonged to this people. I was ashamed about the trust that I had given to so many who now revealed themselves as my enemies. Suddenly the street, too, seemed alien to me; indeed, the whole town had become alien to me. Words do not exist to describe the feelings that I experienced in those hours. Having arrived at home, I approached the one guard whom I knew and who also knew me, and I said to him: "When you were still in your diapers I was already fighting out there for this country." He answered: "You should not reproach me for my youth, sir . . . I've been ordered to stand here." I looked at his young face and thought, he's right. Poor, misguided young people![2]

---

[2] Edwin Landau, "My Life before and after Hitler," in *Jewish Life in Germany: Memoirs from Three Centuries*, ed. Monika Richarz, trans. Stella P. Rosenfeld and Sidney Rosenfeld (Bloomington, IN: Indiana University Press, 1991), 310–12.

 Reading

"Restoring" Germany's Civil Service

On April 7, 1933, a new law, known as the Law for the Restoration of the Professional Civil Service, went into effect. *Civil service* refers to the professionals who work in various agencies of a government, including public education, law enforcement, and more. The law required that all Jews and political opponents of the Nazis who were employed by the government in Germany be fired. The only Jews allowed to keep their positions were veterans, their fathers, and their sons. Similar laws dismissed all Jewish prosecuting attorneys and Jewish doctors who worked in the national health system.

On April 4, when he heard rumors of the new law, President Paul von Hindenburg wrote a letter to Hitler:

> Dear Mr. Chancellor!
>
> Recently, a whole series of cases has been reported to me in which judges, lawyers, and officials of the Judiciary who are disabled war veterans and whose record in office is flawless, have been forcibly sent on leave, and are later to be dismissed for the sole reason that they are of Jewish descent.
>
> It is quite intolerable for me personally . . . that Jewish officials who were disabled in the war should suffer such treatment, [especially] as, with the express approval of the government, I addressed a Proclamation to the German people on the day of the national uprising, March 21, in which I bowed in reverence before the dead of the war and remembered in gratitude the bereaved families of the war dead, the disabled, and my old comrades at the front.
>
> I am certain, Mr. Chancellor, that you share this human feeling, and request you, most cordially and urgently, to look into this matter yourself, and to see to it that there is some uniform arrangement for all branches of the public service in Germany.
>
> As far as my own feelings are concerned, officials, judges, teachers and lawyers who are war invalids, fought at the front, are sons of war dead, or themselves lost sons in the war should remain in their positions unless an individual case gives reason for different treatment. If they were worthy of fighting for Germany and bleeding for Germany, then they must also be considered worthy of continuing to serve the Fatherland. . . .

On April 5, Hitler replied to Hindenburg.

> Dear Mr. President!
>
> In a most generous and humane manner you, Mr. Field Marshal, plead the cause of those members of the Jewish people who were once compelled, by the requirements of universal military service, to serve in the war. . . .
>
> But, with the greatest respect, may I point out that members and supporters of my movement, who are Germans, for years were driven from all Government positions, without consideration for their wives and children or their war service. . . . Those responsible for this cruelty were the same Jewish parties which today complain when their supporters are denied the right to official positions, with a thousand times more justification, because they are of little use in these positions but can do limitless harm . . .
>
> Nevertheless, . . . the law in question . . . will provide consideration for those Jews who either served in the war themselves, were disabled in the war, have other merits, or never gave occasion for complaint in the course of a long period of service.
>
> In general, the primary aim of this cleansing process is only to restore a certain sound and natural balance, and, secondly, to remove from official positions of national significance those elements to which one cannot entrust Germany's survival. . . .
>
> I beg you, Mr. President, to believe that I will try to do justice to your noble feelings as far as is possible. I understand your inner motivations and myself, by the way, frequently suffer under the harshness of a fate which forces us to make decisions which, from a human point of view, one would a thousand times rather avoid.
>
> Work on the law in question will proceed as quickly as possible, and I am convinced that this matter, too, will then find the best possible solution.[1]

---

1 Yitzhak Arad, Yisrael Gutman, and Abraham Margaliot, eds., *Documents on the Holocaust: Selected Sources on the Destruction of the Jews of Germany and Austria, Poland, and the Soviet Union* (Jerusalem: Yad Vashem, 1987), 37–39.

 Reading

Where They Burn Books

On May 6, 1933, the German Student Association announced a nationwide "Action against the Un-German Spirit." At one gathering, Joseph Goebbels told a cheering crowd, "The soul of the German people can again express itself. Those flames not only illuminate the final end of an old era; they light up the new!"[1] Lilian T. Mowrer, an American journalist in Germany, described what happened next:

> I held my breath while he hurled the first volume into the flames: it was like burning something alive. Then students followed with whole armfuls of books, while schoolboys screamed into the microphone their condemnations of this and that author, and as each name was mentioned the crowd booed and hissed. You felt Goebbels's venom behind their denunciations. Children of fourteen mouthing abuse of Heine! Erich Remarque's *All Quiet on the Western Front* received the greatest condemnation . . . it would never do for such an unheroic description of war to dishearten soldiers of the Third Reich.[2]

The mobs also burned the books of Helen Keller, an American author who was a socialist, a pacifist, and the first deaf-blind person to graduate from college. Keller responded: "History has taught you nothing if you think you can kill ideas. . . . You can burn my books and the books of the best minds in Europe, but the ideas in them have seeped through a million channels and will continue to quicken other minds."[3]

---

[1] William L. Shirer, *The Rise and Fall of the Third Reich: A History of Nazi Germany* (New York: Simon & Schuster, 1990), 241.

[2] Quoted in *Witness to the Holocaust*, ed. Azriel Eisenberg (Cleveland, OH: Pilgrim Press, 1981), 79.

[3] Quoted in Rebecca Onion, "'God Sleepeth Not': Helen Keller's Blistering Letter to Book-Burning German Students," *The Vault* (blog), Slate.com, May 16, 2013, http://www.slate.com/blogs/the_vault/2013/05/16/helen_keller_her_scathing_letter_to_german_students_planning_to_burn_her.html?wpisrc=flyouts.

 Reading

Isolating Gay Men

After taking control of Germany, the Nazis increased their attacks on gay men. Many Germans applauded the move. Homophobia was not uncommon in German society; gay men had long been the target of bigotry and discrimination. In 1871, Germany had enacted a provision in the criminal code, known as Paragraph 175, that made sexual acts between men a crime. (Several other nations had similar laws at the time.) That law was still on the books, and many gay men were harassed or arrested by police throughout the years of the Weimar Republic. Nevertheless, in Berlin and a few larger German cities, tolerance of homosexuality increased in the 1920s and 1930s, and gay culture flourished. Many were able to live their lives openly without hiding their sexual orientation. The Reichstag was even considering abolishing Paragraph 175 before the Nazis came to power.[1]

The Nazis believed that gay men were "defective" and an obstacle to the goal of creating a master "Aryan" race. They did not embody, in the Nazis' view, the masculinity of the ideal German man. The Nazis also feared that if gay men held leadership positions in the Nazi Party or government, they would be vulnerable to manipulation or blackmail by anyone who threatened to expose their sexual orientation. The Nazis were not nearly as concerned about lesbians, who, as women, they presumed would be passive and could be forced to have children.[2]

When Hitler took over in 1933, enforcement of Paragraph 175 was stepped up. A man who lived near Hamburg recalled:

> With one blow a wave of arrests of homosexuals[3] began in our town. One of the first to be arrested was my friend, with whom I had had a relationship since I was 23. One day people from the Gestapo came to his house and took him away. It was pointless to inquire where he might be. If anyone did that, they ran the risk of being similarly detained, because he knew them, and therefore they were also suspect. Following his arrest, his home was searched by Gestapo agents. Books were taken away, note- and address books were confiscated, questions were asked among the neighbors. . . . The address books were the worst. All those who figured in them, or had anything to do with him were arrested and summoned by the Gestapo. Me, too. For a whole year I was summoned by the Gestapo and interrogated at least once every fourteen days or three weeks. . . . After four weeks my friend was released from investigative custody. The [Nazis] could not prove anything against him either. However, the effects of his arrest were terrifying. Hair shorn off, totally confused, he was no longer what he was before. . . . We had to be very careful with all contacts. I had to break off all relations with my friend. We passed each other by on the street, because we did not want to put ourselves in danger. . . . We lived like animals in a wild game park, always sensing the hunters.[4]

---

1 Geoffrey J. Giles, "Why Bother About Homosexuals? Homophobia and Sexual Politics in Nazi Germany," lecture, United States Holocaust Memorial Museum Center for Advanced Holocaust Studies, Washington, DC, May 30, 2001, accessed March 18, 2016, https://www.ushmm.org/m/pdfs/20050726-giles.pdf.

2 Doris L. Bergen, *War and Genocide: A Concise History of the Holocaust* (Lanham, MD: Rowman & Littlefield, 2003), 57.

3 **Note:** In earlier times, referring to members of the gay community as "homosexuals" was common. While not offensive in the past, today the term is outdated and inappropriate when used as a noun, unless one is reading aloud directly from a historical document.

4 Quoted in Michael Burleigh and Wolfgang Wippermann, *The Racial State: Germany 1933–1945* (Cambridge, UK: Cambridge University Press, 1991), 194.

Unit Essential Question	What does learning about the choices people made during the Weimar Republic, the rise of the Nazi Party, and the Holocaust teach us about the power and impact of our choices today?

Lesson 12

Do You Take the Oath?

Duration
One 50-minute class period

Materials

Readings
Pledging Allegiance
Do You Take the Oath?
Refusing to Pledge Allegiance

Teaching Strategies
Think, Pair, Share
Read Aloud
Exit Tickets

Find all materials referenced in this lesson at facinghistory.org/thhb.

Guiding Questions

- What factors influence our choices about whether to speak up or stay quiet in response to injustice?
- What choices did Germans have in the face of an emerging dictatorship? What opportunities for resistance were available?

Learning Objectives

- Through close reading, class discussion, and written reflection, students will recognize that while Germans went along with the Nazi regime for a variety of often complex reasons, dissent was possible in 1933 and 1934, though the consequences left some marginalized or unemployed and others imprisoned or even dead.
- Students will identify some of the universal human behaviors that influence individuals to look the other way, as well as those that influence individuals to speak out in response to injustice.

Overview

In the previous lesson, students analyzed the steps the Nazis took in 1933 and 1934 to dismantle democracy in Germany and establish a dictatorship. Students also began to think about the responsibilities shared by both leaders and citizens for democracy's survival. In this lesson, students will continue this unit's historical case study by engaging in a deeper analysis of the dilemmas many Germans experienced during the first few years of Nazi rule. In particular, they will examine how some individuals responded to demands that they show allegiance, and in some cases take an oath of fidelity, to Adolf Hitler and the Nazi government.

By carefully considering the choices and the reasoning of the individuals in this lesson, students will not only learn more about the human behaviors underlying Germans' choices in the mid-1930s but also deepen their understanding of the complex ethical dilemmas people often face over whether to stay quiet, speak up, or take action in response to injustices. Multiple extension activities bring additional complexity to the themes of this lesson by introducing opportunism and the desire to curry favor as motivating factors in the decision-making process. These extensions provide options for more in-depth units and classes with older students.

Context

As the Nazis consolidated power and established a dictatorship in Germany, they sought to align all individuals, institutions, and organizations in German society with their goals. They referred to this process as *Gleichschaltung*, or "coordination." They provided a mix of incentives, suspicion, fear, and brute force to bring about this alignment. As a result, individuals and institutions across the country were forced both to navigate the dangers that the Nazis posed to dissenters and to weigh the incentives they offered to encourage acceptance of the new government. Each person had to figure out how to live in a society under National Socialism, and even whether that would be possible at all.

How did individual Germans do it? Some were true believers in Nazism, some calculated that the benefits to them of Nazi government outweighed the parts they found unsettling, some who could do so left the country, some learned to stay quiet and retreat into "internal exile," and some protested openly. Over the course of the next several lessons, students will encounter stories of people who found themselves in all of these situations. In this lesson, they will explore the dilemmas faced by Germans in response to the 1933 Civil Service Law and the 1934 requirement that German soldiers and civil servants take an oath of fidelity to Hitler.

As students learned in the previous lesson, the Nazis enacted the Law for the Restoration of the Professional Civil Service on April 7, 1933. The law required that all Jews and political opponents of the Nazis who were employed by the government in Germany be fired. Historian Richard Evans writes that the civil service was

> a vast organization in Germany that included school teachers, university staff, judges, and many other professions that were not government-controlled in other countries. Social Democrats, liberals, and not a few Catholics and conservatives were ousted here too. To save their jobs, at a time when unemployment had reached terrifying dimensions, 1.6 million people joined the Nazi Party between 30 January and 1 May 1933.[1]

It was not difficult for the Nazis to win the support of many university professors, administrators, and students. At the time, a majority of them backed conservative political parties that had been hostile to the Weimar Republic. Many university professors immediately welcomed the Nazi-led government in 1933. Many student fraternities and other student groups already banned Jews and regularly protested against professors they believed did not support supposed traditional German values. Scholars who were Jewish or supported left-leaning parties struggled to find research and teaching positions in public, government-supported German universities and often worked in private ones instead. With the passage of the

---

1 Richard J. Evans, *The Third Reich in Power* (New York: Penguin, 2005), 14.

new law, the Nazis attempted to root out any dissent to their policies and ideology that remained in German higher education.

In August 1934, the Nazis issued a new demand to ensure loyalty to the regime. They required all German soldiers and civil servants to take an oath of fealty to Adolf Hitler himself, replacing a previous oath taken to the Weimar Constitution and to the office of president. Journalist William Shirer explains the oath's significance:

> The generals, who up to that time could have overthrown the Nazi regime with ease had they so desired, thus led themselves to the person of Adolf Hitler, recognizing him as the highest legitimate authority in the land and binding themselves to him by an oath of fealty which they felt honor-bound to obey in all circumstances no matter how degrading to them and the Fatherland. It was an oath which was to trouble the conscience of quite a few high officers when their acknowledged leader set off on a path which they felt could only lead to the nation's destruction and which they opposed. It was also a pledge which enabled an even greater number of officers to excuse themselves from any personal responsibility . . . [2]

The oath would trouble not only soldiers and their generals but also many civil servants who were required to take it, including the defense plant worker students will learn about in this lesson.

While many Germans experienced troubling dilemmas in response to the changes the Nazis brought, it is important to acknowledge that many others did not. Due either to feelings of adulation for Hitler's carefully presented persona as führer or to calculations of self-interest and self-preservation, many German soldiers, civil servants, and private citizens took it upon themselves to embrace, promote, and make a reality the vision for Germany articulated by Hitler. Historian Ian Kershaw writes:

> Individuals seeking material gain through career advancement in party or state bureaucracy, the small businessman aiming to destroy a competitor through a slur on his "aryan" credentials, or ordinary citizens settling scores with neighbors by denouncing them to the Gestapo were all, in a way, "working towards the Führer". . . [3]

Notes to Teacher

1. Considering the Effect of Hindsight

In this lesson, students will read excerpts from individuals' reflections, or, in one case, a son's recounting of his father's story, about whether or not to take the oath to Hitler or otherwise align themselves with the Nazi Party's policies. In some cases, these reflections were written many years after the choices they describe were made. Before reading each piece, ask students to consider the information provided in its introduction to determine who is telling the story and whether the reflection was made at the time the decision was made or years later. You might ask students to consider the effects that hindsight might have had on how the individuals in these readings remember and interpret their experiences.

---

2 William L. Shirer, *The Rise and Fall of the Third Reich: A History of Nazi Germany,* 50th ed. (New York: Simon & Schuster, 2011), 227.
3 Ian Kershaw, "'Working Towards the Führer': Reflections on the Nature of the Hitler Dictatorship," *Contemporary European History 2,* no. 2 (July 1993): 117.

2. Previewing Vocabulary

The following are key vocabulary terms used in this lesson:

- Oath
- Loyalty
- Allegiance
- Authority
- Obedience
- Führer

Add these words to your word wall, if you are using one for this unit, and provide necessary support to help students learn these words as you teach the lesson.

Activities

1. Reflect on Causes of Action and Inaction

Have students write a response to the following prompt in their journals:

> Think of a time when you obeyed a rule or an authority figure (a parent, teacher, group leader, etc.). Why did you obey? What were the consequences of your decision? Now think of a time when you ignored or disobeyed a rule or authority figure. Why did you resist authority? What were the consequences?

You can use the Think, Pair, Share strategy to have students share their reflections. Note that students may have written about choices they made that they would prefer not to share. Therefore it is not necessary that they share the details of their stories with other classmates. Instead, they can focus their discussion contribution on the reasons they obeyed or disobeyed (fear of punishment, sense of fairness, etc.).

Finally, hold a whole-group discussion in which you focus on the "whys" of the students' stories. Make two lists on the board, one titled "Reasons for Obedience" and the other titled "Reasons for Disobedience," and save them for use later in the lesson.

2. Reflect on the Significance of Oaths

Tell students that the Nazis pressured Germans to show their allegiance in a variety of ways, one of which was to take an oath to Hitler. Before looking at the text of the oath, ask students to think about the oaths, if any, that they are familiar with in their lives. Begin the discussion by asking the following questions:

- What oaths do people take today? For what reasons?
- How do such oaths affect people's choices? How should they, if they should at all?

Students may bring up oaths of office that government officials take, marriage vows, oaths that Boy Scout and Girl Scout members take, or oaths in religious ceremonies. While many students may not have been asked to take an oath before, they might have experienced a sense of obligation to stay true to their word or to care for others, and that sense of obligation may be similar to the commitment often expected from one who has taken an oath.

Then, read aloud the reading Pledging Allegiance, perhaps choosing to rotate among different students for each section. Ask students to compare and contrast the two oaths, using the following questions to guide the discussion:

- Summarize the two oaths in your own words.
- What is the main difference between the two oaths? How important is that difference? What are the implications of swearing an oath to an individual leader rather than to a nation?
- How might taking an oath affect the choices a person makes? How does an oath affect the level of responsibility a person has for their actions? Is keeping an oath an acceptable explanation for making a choice that a person later regrets?

3. Examine One German's Response to the Oath

Distribute the reading Do You Take the Oath? and begin reading aloud the first five paragraphs, stopping at "and it was I who lost it." Ask students to reflect on what this man has said so far by responding to the following questions in their journals:

- What do you think of his decision and his reasoning?
- What factors complicate his choice?
- How do you think he defines his universe of obligation?

Continue to read to the end of Do You Take the Oath? Ask students create a list of reasons why this man obeyed the Nazis' demand to take the oath, and then create a class list, drawing on the students' ideas. Be ready to ask follow-up questions that get students to analyze the defense plant worker's view about how the oath, and other Nazi policies, affected Germans.

Ask students to compare and contrast this list with the list of reasons for inaction they created in Activity 1 based on their journal entries. Make it clear to students that the goal here is not to equate their stories with events leading to the Holocaust, but to examine the human behaviors of conformity and obedience in difficult situations.

4. Explore Examples of Resistance

It is crucial for students to see that while the dilemmas faced by Germans such as the defense plant worker presented complex choices for many in the 1930s, some Germans chose to resist demands to pledge allegiance to Hitler and the Nazis.

Pass out the reading Refusing to Pledge Allegiance and have students take turns reading the two stories aloud. Ask students to consider the reasons why Fest and Huch chose not to pledge their allegiance to the Nazis, as well as the consequences of their choices. Use the following questions to lead a class discussion:

- Why did Fest and Huch each refuse to pledge allegiance to Hitler? What were the consequences of their decisions?

- Compare and contrast Fest's and Huch's situations with that experienced by the defense plant worker. How do you account for the different choices they made?

As a whole class, create a list of reasons why these individuals resisted the Nazis. Ask students to compare and contrast this list with the list of reasons for disobedience they created earlier and their discussion of the reading Do You Take the Oath? (see Activities 1 and 3).

5. Reflect on the Consequences of Resistance

Finish the lesson by asking students to respond to the following question in their journals. Or, you might choose to capture students' responses using the Exit Tickets strategy to assess their understanding of today's content.

- What were the positive and negative consequences of choosing to take the oath or show loyalty to Hitler in the mid-1930s?
- What have you learned in this lesson about why many people went along with Nazi policies even when they thought those policies were wrong?
- What have you learned about why some people chose to resist?

Assessment

- Applying the Found Poems strategy, assign students to create a poem using words and phrases from the reading Do You Take the Oath? or Refusing to Pledge Allegiance (or both). Students might focus their poems on the themes of "obedience" or "dissent," or they might choose their own themes to explore. You might also ask students to select two contrasting points of view to include in their poem that highlight the different perspectives represented in this lesson. When you evaluate the poems, look for evidence of students' emotional engagement with the text as well as their response to the ethical dilemmas described in these readings.

- Evaluate the exit tickets students submit at the end of the lesson to gauge how students understand and evaluate the dilemmas they encountered in this lesson.

Extensions

1. Analyze a Reading in a Socratic Seminar

The reading "No Time to Think" provides another powerful window into the thinking of those confronted with dilemmas over whether to speak out or stay silent during the first years of the Nazi regime. Many students find this account, by a German professor recounting his experiences seven years after World War II ended, to be compelling and impactful. Others approach the professor's reasons for inaction with skepticism due to the fact that he is writing with hindsight of the atrocities and genocide ultimately committed by the Nazis in the Third Reich. Use the connection questions that follow the reading to begin a discussion with students. Time permitting, you might consider using the reading as the basis for an activity based on the Socratic Seminar strategy, in which students analyze the professor's dilemma and his explanation for his inaction.

2. Create a "Lifted Line Poem"

The Lifted Line Poem strategy provides a way for the entire class to collaborate in creating a poem based on students' analysis of the words and experiences of the individuals who offer firsthand accounts in this lesson. The readings "Do You Take the Oath?" and "No Time to Think" both provide good source material for this activity. Students often become highly engaged in selecting their lines for this activity and arranging their contribution to create a powerful performance. Consider giving the class the opportunity to share their lifted line poem with other audiences in the school.

3. Introduce the "Working Toward the Führer" Dynamic

Historian Ian Kershaw points to a dynamic, called "working toward the führer," that was at play within both German government and society under the Nazis. This concept further complicates our understanding of the choices and motivations of individuals during this era. It is based on the observation that many German officials and citizens took it upon themselves (rather than being forced or coerced) to take actions that aligned with broader goals expressed by Hitler. In other words, the possibility of currying favor with the Nazi government became a powerful motivating factor for many Germans.

It is worth exploring this dynamic, especially with older students or more advanced classes. Have students read and discuss the reading "Working Toward the Führer," perhaps using the Save the Last Word for Me discussion strategy. In addition to the reading's connection questions, students should consider the following questions:

- How does "working toward the führer" add to or complicate the picture offered by the defense plant worker and the university professor?
- Who spells out the goals for the communities to which you belong? Who or what inspires individuals to try to meet those goals?

Visit facinghistory.org/thhb to access these additional resources.

 Reading

Pledging Allegiance

When German president Paul von Hindenburg died on August 2, 1934, Hitler combined the positions of chancellor and president. He was now the führer and Reich chancellor, the head of state, and the chief of the armed forces. In the past, German soldiers had taken this oath:

> I swear loyalty to the Constitution and vow that I will protect the German nation and its lawful establishments as a brave soldier at any time and will be obedient to the President and my superiors.

Now Hitler created a new oath.

> I swear by God this sacred oath, that I will render unconditional obedience to Adolf Hitler, the Führer of the German Reich and people, Supreme Commander of the Armed Forces, and will be ready as a brave soldier to risk my life at any time for this oath.

In his book *The Rise and Fall of the Third Reich*, William Shirer, an American journalist, writes that the new oath "enabled an even greater number of officers to excuse themselves from any personal responsibility for the unspeakable crimes which they carried out on the orders of the Supreme Commander whose true nature they had seen for themselves. . . . One of the appalling aberrations of the German officer corps from this point on rose out of this conflict of 'honor'—a word . . . often on their lips. . . . Later and often, by honoring their oath they dishonored themselves as human beings and trod in the mud the moral code of their corps."[1]

---

1 William Shirer, *The Rise and Fall of the Third Reich* (New York: Simon & Schuster, 1960), 227.

 Reading

Do You Take the Oath?

Soldiers were not the only ones required to take the new oath that pledged allegiance to Hitler. One German recalled the day he was asked to pledge loyalty to the regime:

> I was employed in a defense plant (a war plant, of course, but they were always called defense plants). That was the year of the National Defense Law, the law of "total conscription." Under the law I was required to take the oath of fidelity. I said I would not; I opposed it in conscience. I was given twenty-four hours to "think it over." In those twenty-four hours I lost the world. . . .
>
> You see, refusal would have meant the loss of my job, of course, not prison or anything like that. (Later on, the penalty was worse, but this was only 1935.) But losing my job would have meant that I could not get another. Wherever I went I should be asked why I left the job I had, and when I said why, I should certainly have been refused employment. Nobody would hire a "Bolshevik." Of course, I was not a Bolshevik, but you understand what I mean.
>
> I tried not to think of myself or my family. We might have got out of the country in any case, and I could have got a job in industry or education somewhere else.
>
> What I tried to think of was the people to whom I might be of some help later on, if things got worse (as I believed they would). I had a wide friendship in scientific and academic circles, including many Jews, and "Aryans," too, who might be in trouble. If I took the oath and held my job, I might be of help, somehow, as things went on. If I refused to take the oath, I would certainly be useless to my friends, even if I remained in the country. I myself would be in their situation.
>
> The next day, after "thinking it over," I said I would take the oath with the mental reservation, that, by the words with which the oath began, "Ich schwöre bei Gott," "I swear by God," I understood that no human being and no government had the right to override my conscience. My mental reservations did not interest the official who administered the oath. He said, "Do you take the oath?" and I took it. That day the world was lost, and it was I who lost it.
>
> First of all, there is the problem of the lesser evil. Taking the oath was not so evil as being unable to help my friends later on would have been. But the evil of the oath was certain and immediate, and the helping of my friends was in the future and therefore uncertain. I had to commit a positive evil there and then, in the hope of a possible good later on. The good outweighed the evil; but the good was only a hope, the evil a fact. . . . The hope might not have been realized—either for reasons beyond my control or because I became afraid later on or even because I was afraid all the time and was simply fooling myself when I took the oath in the first place . . .

There I was in 1935, a perfect example of the kind of person who, with all his advantages in birth, in education, and in position, rules (or might easily rule) in any country. . . . My education did not help me, and I had a broader and better education than most have had or ever will have. All it did, in the end, was to enable me to rationalize my failure of faith more easily than I might have done if I had been ignorant. And so it was, I think, among educated men generally, in that time in Germany. Their resistance was no greater than other men's.[1]

---

[1] From Milton Mayer, *They Thought They Were Free: The Germans 1933–45* (Chicago: University of Chicago Press, 1955), 177–81. Reproduced by permission from University of Chicago Press.

 Reading

Refusing to Pledge Allegiance

Joachim Fest's father—a devout Catholic and the headmaster of an elementary school—refused to demonstrate loyalty to the Nazis, even after the new law to "restore" the civil service. He remained active in the Catholic Central Party and the Reichsbanner (a pro-democracy group). Fest describes the consequences his father, a civil servant because he worked in a school, faced for his refusal to show loyalty:

> On April 20, 1933, my father was summoned to Lichtenberg Town Hall . . . and informed by Volz, the state commissar responsible for the exercise of the business of the borough mayor, that he was suspended from public service, effective immediately. When my father asked what he was accused of, the official responded in a sergeant-majorish manner: "You will be informed of that in due course!" But he was a civil servant, objected my father, to which Volz replied, "You can tell our Führer that. He'll be very impressed." . . .
>
> As he was on his way to the exit, all at once the building he knew so well seemed unfamiliar. It was the same with the staff, some of whom he had known for years; suddenly, one after the other, their eyes were avoiding his. At his school, to which he went immediately, it was no different, even in his office; everything from the cupboards to the stationery already seemed to have been replaced. The first person he bumped into was his colleague Markwitz who had clearly already been informed. "Fest, old man!" he said, after my father had spoken a few explanatory words. "Did it have to be like this?" And when my father replied, "Yes, it had to be!," Markwitz objected: "No, don't tell me that! It's something I learned early: there's no 'must' when it comes to stupidity!"
>
> On April 22 . . . my father was summoned again. Remaining seated and without offering my father a chair, the temporary mayor, reading from a prepared text, formally notified him that he was relieved of his duties as headmaster of the Twentieth Elementary School and was suspended until further notice. Given as grounds for the suspension were his senior positions in the [Catholic Center] party and in the Reichsbanner [a pro-democracy group founded during the Weimar years], as well as his "public speeches disparaging the Führer and other high-ranking National Socialists" . . . Under the circumstances there was no longer any guarantee that he would "at all times support without reservation the national state," as the law put it. . . . As he spoke these curt words, he continued leafing through my father's file and one of the pages fell to the floor—no doubt intentionally, thought my father. Volz clearly expected my father to pick it up. My father, however, remained motionless, as he later reported; not for one moment did he consider going down on his knees in front of the mayor.
>
> Volz then continued in a noticeably sharper tone. As well as being summarily suspended, my father was required within two days to formally transfer charge of the school to his successor, Markwitz. He would be informed in writing of the details. With a gesture that was

part dismissal, part shooing away to the door, the provisional mayor added that for the time being my father was not allowed to take up any employment. Everything proceeded as if according to a plan, said my father, when he came to talk about what happened.[1]

Ricarda Huch, a 70-year-old poet and writer, also refused to pledge allegiance to Hitler. She resigned from the prestigious Prussian Academy of Arts with this letter:

Heidelberg, April 9, 1933

Dear President von Schillings:

Let me first thank you for the warm interest you have taken in having me remain in the Academy. I would very much like you to understand why I cannot follow your wish. That a German's feelings are German, I would consider to be just about self-evident, but the definition of what is German, and what acting in a German manner means—those are things where opinions differ. What the present government prescribes by way of patriotic convictions is not my kind of Germanism. The centralization, the use of compulsion, the brutal methods, the defamation of those who hold different convictions, the boastful self-praise—these are matters which I consider un-German and disastrous. As I consider the divergence between this opinion of mine and that being ordered by the state, I find it impossible to remain in an Academy that is a part of the state. You say that the declaration submitted to me by the Academy would not prevent me from the free expression of my opinions. But "loyal cooperation, in the spirit of the changed historical situation, on matters affecting national and cultural tasks that fall within the jurisdiction of the Academy" requires an agreement with the government's program which in my case does not exist. Besides, I would find no newspaper or magazine that would print an opposition opinion. Thus the right to free expression of opinion would remain quite theoretical. . . .

I hereby resign from the Academy.

S. Ricarda Huch[2]

---

1 Joachim Fest, *Not I: Memoirs of a German Childhood,* trans. Martin Chalmers (New York: Other Press, 2006), 46–48. Reprinted by permission from Other Press, LLC, and Atlantic Books, UK.

2 Ricarda Huch, "'Not My Kind of Germanism': A Resignation from the Academy," in *The Nazi Years: A Documentary History,* ed. Joachim Remak (Prospect Heights, IL: Waveland Press, 1969), 162.

Unit Essential Question

What does learning about the choices people made during the Weimar Republic, the rise of the Nazi Party, and the Holocaust teach us about the power and impact of our choices today?

Lesson

13 Laws and the National Community

Duration
One 50-minute class period

Materials

Handouts
First Regulation to the Reich Citizenship Law

Law for the Protection of German Blood and Honor, Part 1

Law for the Protection of German Blood and Honor, Part 2

Reading
Discovering Jewish Blood

Teaching Strategies
Think, Pair, Share

Big Paper

Find all materials referenced in this lesson at facinghistory.org/thhb.

Guiding Questions

- What are the consequences when governments use laws to create "in" groups and "out" groups in a society?
- How do laws affect the ways that individuals think about their own identities and the identities of others? How do laws affect the relationships between individuals in a society?

Learning Objectives

- Through a close reading and discussion of the Nuremberg Laws, students will examine how the Nazis sought to create a racially pure "national community," one that stripped Jews of their citizenship rights and narrowed Germany's universe of obligation.
- By reflecting on a story of how the Nuremberg Laws affected one family, students will think more broadly about the power and limitations of laws to shape society and influence individual behavior.

Overview

In the previous lesson, students analyzed some of the dilemmas experienced by individual Germans during the National Socialist revolution in Germany. In this lesson, students will continue this unit's historical case study by turning their attention to what happened after the revolution was complete and the Nazis firmly established control over Germany. Specifically, students will be introduced to the Nazis' idea of a "national community" shaped according to their racial ideals, a concept students will continue to explore in two lessons that follow this one. While there were many ways in which the Nazis shaped and cultivated their ideal "national community," in this unit students will look closely at three of those methods. In this lesson, they will examine the way the Nazis used laws to define who belonged to the "national community" and then separate those who did not belong. In future lessons, students will look at the Nazis' use of propaganda and their creation of youth groups to shape German society.

Context

By 1934, Germany was firmly under Nazi control. After President von Hindenburg's death in August of that year, Adolf Hitler declared himself not only the nation's chancellor but also its führer. The revolution was over, he told his closest associates. It was now time to consolidate power and normalize life in the "new Germany" they had created. They were determined to create a *Volksgemeinschaft*—a "national community" or, literally, a "people's community."

The term had become popular during World War I as a way of rallying support for the conflict. At that time, it simply meant that all Germans, regardless of class, religious, and social differences, would work together to achieve a national purpose—winning the war. But the Nazis interpreted its meaning differently. They used the word to advance the idea of a racially pure and harmonious national community united in its devotion to the German people, their nation, and their leader. In the words of a popular Nazi slogan, the goal was "Ein Volk! Ein Reich! Ein Führer!" ("One People! One Empire! One Leader!")

In his book *Mein Kampf*, Hitler described the foundation he sought for the national community, a foundation based on false myths about race:

> Everything we admire on this earth today—science and art, technology and inventions—is only the creative product of a few peoples and originally perhaps one race [the "Aryans"]. On them depends the existence of this whole culture. If they perish, the beauty of this earth will sink into the grave with them.

In their effort to reshape the "national community" according to their racial ideals, the Nazis enacted hundreds of laws, policies, and decrees, including those that financially rewarded so-called Aryan couples for having children and those that allowed for the sterilization of people they considered "defective" or of supposedly inferior races.

Nearly 1,500 of the Nazis' laws, policies, and decrees enacted between 1933 and 1939 were designed to remove Jews from the country's political, economic, and cultural life. Among the most significant of these were the Nuremberg Laws. This set of laws included the Reich Citizenship Law and the Law for the Protection of German Blood and Honor, both announced at the Nuremberg Party Rally on September 15, 1935. The former stripped Jews of their rights to citizenship, including the rights to vote and hold a German passport. The latter unleashed a series of restrictions on the lives of German Jews, including the prohibition of sexual relationships between Jews and non-Jews as well as the forbiddance for Jews of flying the Reich flag.

These two laws raised an important question: What determined who was and who was not a Jew? According to many Jewish teachings, an individual was defined as a Jew if they were born to a Jewish mother or formally converted to Judaism. If a Jew converted to Christianity, they were no longer considered Jewish by many Jews. The Nazis did not accept that definition. They regarded Jews as members of neither a religious group nor an ethnic group (defined by their cultural heritage). Instead, they regarded Jews as members of a separate and inferior "race." Since, according to Nazi logic, "race" was not altered by conversion, people who were born Jewish would always be Jews, regardless of their religious beliefs or practices.

In reality, whether someone was German or Jewish could not be determined by medical or scientific tests. The question of defining German and Jewish identity was further complicated by the fact that there had been a great deal of intermarriage between the two groups, and there were thousands of people of mixed Jewish and non-Jewish ancestry, known to the Nazis as *Mischlinge* ("half-breeds" or "mixed-blood").

Responding to these questions, the Nazi government create precise legal definitions of who was a German and who was a Jew through an additional decree called the First Regulation to the Reich Citizenship Law, announced on November 14, 1935. (Debates about how to classify *Mischlinge* went on for years and were never completely resolved.) The detailed definitions the Nazis created are included in the resources in this lesson.

The Nuremberg Laws turned Jews from German citizens into "residents of Germany." The laws transformed the lives of Jews all over Germany, including thousands of people who had not previously known that their families had Jewish heritage. They placed Jews squarely outside of Germany's "universe of obligation."

Notes to Teacher

1. Connotation of the Term "National Community"

The German word for "national community," *Volksgemeinschaft*, implies a specific kind of community that the Nazis aspired to foster and has a meaning that is more specific in connotation than the English common-noun translation signifies. For this reason, we chose to include quotation marks around the English translation of this term to highlight this distinction. (Review the Context section for more information on the meaning of this term.)

2. Preparing Students for a Big Paper Activity

Activity 3 below uses the Big Paper teaching strategy, which we encourage you to familiarize yourself with before teaching the lesson. Note that in order for students to have a totally silent conversation with the text and with each other, you must provide very clear and explicit instructions for students prior to the start of the activity and answer any questions in advance. To get a sense of the final product for a Big Paper activity, refer to the "example" on the Big Paper teaching strategy page on Facing History's website.

3. Previewing Vocabulary

The following are key vocabulary terms used in this lesson:
- "National community"
- Reich
- Citizen

Add these words to your word wall, if you are using one for this unit, and provide necessary support to help students learn these words as you teach the lesson.

4. The Unit Assessment

If your students are writing the final essay assessment for this unit, after teaching this lesson, instruct students to add evidence from the last four lessons to their evidence logs. For suggested activities and resources, see Adding to Evidence Logs, 1 of 3.

Activities

1. Briefly Introduce the Nazi Concept of "National Community"

Open by telling students that in this lesson, and the two following lessons, they are going to examine closely the "national community" that the Nazis envisioned for Germany and the ways in which they tried to create it in the 1930s. To illustrate for students the importance of the concept of "national community" to the Nazis, you might tell them that the Nazis had a specific word for this special community: *Volksgemeinschaft*. Tell students that defining who belonged in the Nazis' idea of a "national community" is similar to defining who belonged in their universe of obligation.

2. Reflect on Responding to Injustice in Our Own Lives

Now, before looking at laws enacted by the Nazis, ask students to reflect on unfair laws or rules that they have experienced or witnessed in their own lives. Use the following journal prompt:

> How do laws help to define a nation's universe of obligation? Can you think of an example of a current or past law that excludes people from your country's universe of obligation? Explain your example.

Students can share and discuss their thinking in a brief Think, Pair, Share activity.

3. Analyze Laws Used to Shape the National Community

Tell students that there are a variety of measures a government can take to shape society—and a variety of ways a government can exclude those who leaders consider to be outsiders from enjoying the benefits of belonging to the nation. Laws were one powerful tool the Nazis used for these purposes; between 1933 and 1939 they enacted nearly 1,500 laws, policies, and decrees that privileged "Aryans" and excluded, discriminated against, and persecuted Jews and other supposedly inferior groups.

In this activity, students will examine a set of laws known as the Nuremberg Laws using the Big Paper silent discussion strategy. (For classes with additional time, an extension to this lesson analyzes a variety of additional laws enacted by the Nazis.)

Divide the class into groups of three or four, and prepare a piece of chart paper for each group with one of the following handouts taped in the middle:

- First Regulation to the Reich Citizenship Law
- Law for the Protection of German Blood and Honor, Part 1
- Law for the Protection of German Blood and Honor, Part 2

Make sure that each student has a pen or marker to write with, and then give them eight minutes to have a written discussion about their assigned handout in complete silence. The following questions can help guide their discussion:

- What is the purpose of this law?
- Who benefits from it and who is harmed by it?
- What does the law suggest about who is included in Germany's "national community"?
- How does the law define Germany's universe of obligation?

The written conversation should start with students' responses to these questions, but it can continue wherever the students take it. Students should feel free to annotate the text. If someone in the group writes a question, another member of the group should answer it. Students can draw lines connecting a comment to a particular question. Make sure students know that more than one of them can write on the big paper at the same time.

After the ten minutes, rotate each group to a different big paper, and give them two or three minutes to read the document and the written conversation on that paper. They can add new comments and questions if they have them. Then rotate the groups one more time, making sure that each group has seen each of the three handouts at least once.

Finally, debrief the activity with the class, asking the following questions as checks for understanding:

- How would you summarize the purpose of the Nuremberg Laws?
- How did the laws you read and discussed contribute to creating the type of "national community" that the Nazis desired?
- How might these laws have influenced the attitudes and actions of the German people? How might their lives and beliefs have changed as a result of this law?

4. Examine the Impact of the Nuremberg Laws

Tell students that they will now read a personal account of how one family was affected by the enactment of the Nuremberg Laws. Instruct students that as you read aloud from the reading Discovering Jewish Blood, they should underline any information that helps them answer the following question:

> How did the enactment of the Nuremberg Laws affect the lives of Marianne Schweitzer and her family?

After you finish reading, discuss with students their annotations as well as the effects of the Nuremberg Laws on the Schweitzer family using the Think, Pair, Share strategy.

End the lesson by giving students a few minutes to respond in their journals to one or more of the questions below. If necessary, they can complete their reflections for homework:

- How did the Nuremberg Laws affect Marianne Schweitzer and her family members' status in German society? How did the laws influence how they thought about their own identities?
- How might discriminatory laws influence the way we think about others in our society? About ourselves?
- What other examples can you think of from history, literature, or your own life of laws or rules affecting how people think about and treat others? Of laws and rules affecting how people think about themselves?
- What can be done to change laws that you disagree with? What would be required to change laws in your community (local, state, or national)? Which of these options, if any, were available to people in Germany in the 1930s?

Assessment

- The **Big Paper** activity provides a visual representation of students' thinking throughout the lesson that you can use to evaluate their understanding of the relationship between discriminatory laws and the way Germans thought about and treated each other.

- Assign students to respond to one of the prompts at the end of the lesson on notecards instead of in their journals, so that you can collect the responses. Evaluate their responses to gain insight into students' understanding of the power of laws to shape society and individual behavior. Connections students are able to make to other examples from history, literature, or current events can provide evidence of a deeper level of understanding.

Extensions

1. View and Discuss *A Class Divided*

The film *A Class Divided* tells the story of teacher Jane Elliott's third-grade classroom experiment, in which she temporarily separated her students by eye color. The results of her experiment provide powerful insight into how rules and laws created by authority figures can impact how we view our own identities and those of others. This film was offered as an extension to Lesson 5. If you viewed it then, consider reminding students of the film. If you did not view it then, consider showing it after this lesson. Either way, ask students how the results of Elliott's classroom experiment might provide insight into the impact of the Nuremberg Laws (and other regulations enacted by the Nazis) on families such as the Schweitzers. The Connect, Extend, Challenge teaching strategy can help you structure the discussion.

2. Delve More Deeply into the Concept of "National Community"

Share the reading "The Common Interest before Self-Interest" with students. It is short enough that you might simply project it for the class to read together. Ask students to take turns reading aloud each of the questions and answers on the pamphlet.

Lead a brief discussion with the class that focuses on the following questions:

- How does this pamphlet define what it means to be German?
- What does the phrase "racial comrade" suggest about the way Goebbels defined "Germanness"?
- What did National Socialism offer to these "honestly creative" Germans? What did it ask of them?

3. Examine Additional Laws Designed to Shape the "National Community"

The readings "Breeding the New German 'Race'" and "A Wave of Discrimination" provide additional important examples of laws enacted by the Nazis to shape their ideal "national community" of Aryans. These laws included dozens of discriminatory measures passed by national, state, regional, and local governments to exclude Jews from even the seemingly mundane aspects of German society, as well as laws that put into place national programs to encourage so-called Aryans to reproduce and prevent non-Aryans from doing so. Consider sharing these readings with students and discussing the following questions:

- How do these laws contribute to creating the type of "national community" that the Nazis desired?
- How might some of these laws have influenced the attitudes and actions of the German people? How might their lives and beliefs have changed as a result of some of these laws?
- How can laws affect the relationship between individuals and society? How do they affect the relationships individuals have with each other?

Visit facinghistory.org/thhb to access all materials referenced in these activities.

 Handout

First Regulation to the Reich Citizenship Law

Note: This law, passed on November 14, 1935, amended the original Reich Citizenship Law, passed on September 15, 1935.

Article 3
Only the Reich citizen, as bearer of full political rights, exercises the right to vote in political affairs or can hold public office . . .

Article 4
1. A Jew cannot be a citizen of the Reich. He has no right to vote in political affairs and he cannot occupy public office.

2. Jewish [government] officials will retire as of December 31, 1935 . . .

Article 5
1. A Jew is anyone who is descended from at least three grandparents who are racially full Jews . . .

2. A Jew is also one who is descended from two full Jewish parents, if (a) he belonged to the Jewish religious community at the time this law was issued, or joined the community later, (b) he was married to a Jewish person, at the time the law was issued, or married one subsequently, (c) he is the offspring of a marriage with a Jew, in the sense of Section I, which was contracted after the Law for the Protection of German Blood and German Honor became effective, (d) he is the offspring of an extramarital relationship with a Jew, according to Section I, and will be born out of wedlock after July 31, 1936 . . .[1]

---

1 Jeremy Noakes and Geoffrey Pridham, eds., *Documents on Nazism 1919–1945* (New York: Viking Press, 1974), 463–67.

 Handout

Law for the Protection of German Blood and Honor, Part 1

Moved by the understanding that purity of German blood is the essential condition for the continued existence of the German people, and inspired by the inflexible determination to ensure the existence of the German nation for all time, the Reichstag has unanimously adopted the following law, which is promulgated herewith:

Article 1

Marriages between Jews and subjects of the state of German or related blood are forbidden. Marriages nevertheless concluded are invalid, even if concluded abroad to circumvent this law . . .

Article 2

Extramarital relations between Jews and subjects of the state of German or related blood are forbidden.

Article 5

1. Any person who violates the prohibition under Article 1 will be punished with a prison sentence.

2. A male who violates the prohibition under Article 2 will be punished with a jail term or a prison sentence.[1]

---

1 "Reich Citizenship Law of September 15, 1935," trans. by the United States Holocaust Memorial Museum.

Handout

Law for the Protection of German Blood and Honor, Part 2

Moved by the understanding that purity of German blood is the essential condition for the continued existence of the German people, and inspired by the inflexible determination to ensure the existence of the German nation for all time, the Reichstag has unanimously adopted the following law, which is promulgated herewith:

Article 3

Jews may not employ in their households female subjects of the state of German or related blood who are under 45 years old.

Article 4

1. Jews are forbidden to fly the Reich or national flag or display Reich colors.

2. They are, on the other hand, permitted to display the Jewish colors. The exercise of this right is protected by the state.

Article 5

Any person violating the provisions under Articles 3 or 4 will be punished with a jail term of up to one year and a fine, or with one or the other of these penalties . . .[1]

---

[1] "Reich Citizenship Law of September 15, 1935," trans. by the United States Holocaust Memorial Museum.

Reading

Discovering Jewish Blood

The Nuremberg Laws turned Jews from German citizens into "residents of Germany." The laws transformed the lives of Jews all over Germany, including thousands of people who had not previously known their families had Jewish heritage. Among them were Marianne Schweitzer and her siblings.

> Although we were not a churchgoing family, we observed Christmas and Easter in the traditional ways and belonged to the Lutheran church. My parents, my three siblings and I were all baptized and I took confirmation classes with Martin Niemöller, the former U-boat commander and his brother who substituted when Martin was in prison for anti-Nazi activities.
>
> It was in 1932 that my [older] sister Rele provoked my father to reveal our Jewish ancestry for the first time. She played the violin and rejected a violin teacher because he "looked too Jewish." Our father had responded in a rather convoluted way by saying, "Don't you know that your grandmother came from the same people as Jesus . . . ?"
>
> Our mother's side, the Körtes, were "Aryan" by Hitler's standards. But our father's parents, Eugen Schweitzer and Algunde Hollaender were Jews born in Poland who had been baptized as adults. My father and his two brothers were considered Jews by Hitler's laws. Though all were married to non-Jewish wives, our lives were dramatically changed. The whole family was devastated and worried about our future. My mother's "Aryan" side stood by my father. My Körte grandmother said, "If Hitler is against Ernst [my father], I am against Hitler."
>
> We heard no anti-Jewish remarks at home, but the antisemitism of that time was so pervasive and the images in periodicals such as *Der Stürmer* so ugly, that Rele later wrote of her shock at learning her relation to "monsters." She considered herself "the typical German girl with blond, curly hair." I took the news more in stride. I was happy to be able to stay in school and glad not to be eligible to join Hitler Youth. . . .
>
> In September of 1935, the Nuremberg Laws were introduced. My "Jewish" father was barred from treating "Aryan" patients, employing "Aryans," attending concerts or the theater, or using public transportation. Rele had passed her Abitur, the certification of completing a high school degree, but as a Mischling, was ineligible to attend university. She couldn't marry her "Aryan" boyfriend Hans, a medical student.[1]

The Schweitzers were certainly not the only Germans to be penalized for having "Jewish blood." By 1935, explains historian Martin Gilbert,

> The search for Jews, and for converted Jews, to be driven out of their jobs was continuous. On 5 September 1935 the SS newspaper published the names of eight half-Jews and converted Jews, all of the Evangelical Lutheran faith, who had been "dismissed without notice

---

1 Marianne Schweitzer, afterword to Melita Maschmann, *Account Rendered: A Dossier on My Former Self,* trans. Geoffrey Strachan (Cambridge, MA: Plunkett Lake Press, 2013).

and deprived of any further opportunity of acting as organists in Christian churches." From these dismissals, the newspaper commented, "It can be seen that the Reich Chamber of Music is taking steps to protect the church from pernicious influence."[2]

---

[2] Martin Gilbert, *The Holocaust: A History of the Jews of Europe During the Second World War* (New York: Holt, 1985), 47.

STEP 3

Adding to Evidence Logs, 1 of 3

After completing Lesson 13, students are ready to think about the next step of the writing prompt, the Nazi Party's rise to power and what they can learn about the impact and power of their own choices from the events they studied in Lessons 8 through 13. In addition to addressing the writing prompt in a journal reflection, students will start to evaluate the quality and relevance of the evidence they are gathering.

Suggested Activities

Visit facinghistory.org/thhb to access all materials referenced in these activities.

1. **Journal Reflection**

    Ask students to reread their last essay journal response that they completed after Lesson 8 and then respond to the following question:

    > What does learning about the choices people made during the Weimar Republic and the rise of the Nazi Party teach us about the power and impact of our choices today?

    To allow students to interact with a number of their peers after they have finished writing, have them first share their journal responses with a partner. Then ask each pair to join another pair so the class is now divided into groups of four. After they share, have the groups combine into groups of eight or come together as a class. Remind students that they can add ideas from the discussions to their journal entries that extend or challenge their thinking.

2. **Evaluate Evidence**

    Facilitate a class discussion in which students suggest documents or videos from Lessons 8 to 13 that are relevant to the essay topic. Write the list on the board.

    Have students break into pairs or groups to review the documents on the list, adding to their annotations and writing relevant evidence in their evidence logs. If you feel like your students would benefit from a lesson about evaluating evidence, you might consult Strategy 9: Evaluating Evidence and Strategy 10: Relevant or Not? in the Common Core Writing Prompts and Strategies supplement.

    After they gather their evidence, use the Give One, Get One strategy to have students share the evidence they have collected and identify questions they have about what they are learning.

3. Final Reflection

In a final journal response or on exit tickets, ask students to respond to the following questions:

- How has what you have learned about the Nazi Party's rise to power changed your thinking about the prompt?

- Which choices made by individuals, groups, and nations in the history that you have learned about so far in this unit seemed most significant? What made those choices powerful or impactful?

- What questions do you have about the essay topic, thesis statement, evidence logs, or evidence that you didn't ask in class today?

| Unit Essential Question | What does learning about the choices people made during the Weimar Republic, the rise of the Nazi Party, and the Holocaust teach us about the power and impact of our choices today? |

Lesson

The Power of Propaganda

Duration

Two 50-minute class periods

Materials

 Image
The Eternal Jew

 Image Gallery
Propaganda Posters

 Readings
The Impact of Propaganda

 Teaching Strategies
Think, Pair, Share
Crop It
Read Aloud
3-2-1

Find all materials referenced in this lesson at facinghistory.org/thhb.

Guiding Questions

- How did the Nazis use propaganda to influence individuals' attitudes and actions and to cultivate public support for their idea of a "national community"?
- How do explicit and implicit messages in the media (including television, the internet, film, radio, etc.) influence people's beliefs, feelings, and actions?

Learning Objectives

- Students will analyze several examples of Nazi propaganda to determine how it communicates powerful messages about who should be included in and who should be excluded from German society.
- Students will recognize that the effects of propaganda are more complex than simple brainwashing, and that Hitler succeeded because many German people shared some of the beliefs that were transmitted through Nazi propaganda.

Overview

In the previous lesson, students were introduced to the Nazis' idea of a "national community" shaped according to their racial ideals, and the way the Nazis used laws to define and then separate those who belonged to the "national community" from those who did not. In this lesson, students will continue this unit's historical case study by considering the nature of propaganda and analyzing how the Nazis used media to influence the thoughts, feelings, and actions of individuals in Germany. While the Nazis used propaganda as a tool to try to condition the German public to accept, if not actively support, all of their goals (including rearmament and war), this lesson focuses specifically on how they used propaganda to establish "in" groups and "out" groups in German society and cultivate their ideal "national community." After carefully analyzing several propaganda images created by the Nazis, students will consider the ways in which this material influenced individuals, and they will be encouraged to consider how the effects of propaganda are more complicated than simple brainwashing.

Context

Propaganda—information that is intended to persuade an audience to accept a particular idea or cause, often by using biased material or by stirring up emotions—was one of the most powerful tools the Nazis used to consolidate their power and cultivate an "Aryan national community" in the mid-1930s.

Hitler and Goebbels did not invent propaganda. The word itself was coined by the Catholic Church to describe its efforts to discredit Protestant teachings in the 1600s. Over the years, almost every nation has used propaganda to unite its people in wartime. Both sides of World War I used propaganda, for example. For additional context, watch the film *Propaganda during World War I*. But the Nazis were notable for making propaganda a key element of government even before Germany went to war again. One of Hitler's first acts as chancellor was to establish the Reich Ministry of Public Enlightenment and Propaganda, demonstrating his belief that controlling information was as important as controlling the military and the economy. He appointed Joseph Goebbels as director. Through the ministry, Goebbels was able to penetrate virtually every form of German media, from newspapers, film, radio, posters, and rallies to museum exhibits and school textbooks, with Nazi propaganda.

Whether or not propaganda was truthful or tasteful was irrelevant to the Nazis. Goebbels wrote in his diary, "No one can say your propaganda is too rough, too mean; these are not criteria by which it may be characterized. It ought not be decent nor ought it be gentle or soft or humble; it ought to lead to success."[1] Hitler wrote in *Mein Kampf* that to achieve its purpose, propaganda must "be limited to a very few points and must harp on these in slogans until the last member of the public understands what you want him to understand by your slogan. As soon as you sacrifice this slogan and try to be many-sided, the effect will piddle away."[2]

Some Nazi propaganda used positive images to glorify the government's leaders and its various activities, projecting a glowing vision of the "national community." Nazi propaganda could also be ugly and negative, creating fear and loathing by portraying those the regime considered to be enemies as dangerous and even sub-human. The Nazis' distribution of antisemitic films, newspaper cartoons, and even children's books aroused centuries-old prejudices against Jews (see Lesson 6) and also presented new ideas about the racial impurity of Jews. The newspaper *Der Stürmer* (The Attacker), published by Nazi Party member Julius Streicher, was a key outlet for antisemitic propaganda.

This lesson includes a selection of Nazi propaganda images, both "positive" and "negative." It focuses on posters that Germans would have seen in newspapers like *Der Stürmer* and passed in the streets, in workplaces, and in schools. Some of these posters were advertisements for traveling exhibits—on topics like "The Eternal Jew" or the evils of communism—that were themselves examples of propaganda.

---

1 Quoted in Joachim C. Fest, *The Face of the Third Reich: Portraits of the Nazi Leadership* (New York: Da Capo Press, 1999), 90.
2 Adolf Hitler, *Mein Kampf*, trans. Ralph Manheim (Boston: Houghton Mifflin Company, 1943).

Notes to Teacher

1. Propaganda and Stereotypes

The poster The Eternal Jew and other images in this lesson portray inaccurate, offensive stereotypes of Jews. Teachers have the responsibility to acknowledge that these images contain stereotypes and to prepare their students to discuss the material in a thoughtful and respectful manner.

Devoting time on the first day of the lesson to a whole-group analysis of The Eternal Jew provides the opportunity to set an appropriate tone for students throughout the lesson and the unit. You might set this tone by asking students to refer back to the concept maps they created for *stereotype* in Lesson 3, as well as their journal responses to Chimamanda Adichie's "The Danger of a Single Story," before working with the images in this lesson.

2. The Pervasiveness of Nazi Propaganda: An Important Reminder

Even with two days devoted to this lesson, it is not possible to provide students with examples of every form of Nazi propaganda. They need to understand that it pervaded every aspect of society—radio, the press, feature films and newsreels, theater, music, art exhibits, books, the school curriculum, sports, and more. Propaganda was not a separate stream of information; it was embedded in all of the existing information streams in German society.

While not explicitly addressed in this lesson, it is also important to note that the Nazis created propaganda for a variety of other purposes as well, most notably to encourage adulation of Hitler and, eventually, to encourage support for war.

3. Crop It: A Teaching Strategy for Analyzing Images

Students will use the Crop It teaching strategy to analyze several propaganda images in this lesson. Before beginning, make sure that you have prepared cropping tools for students to use. (You might also have students create them if you think that you will have time during class.) Each tool consists of two *L*-shaped strips of paper (cut from the border of a blank sheet of 8 ½ x 11-inch paper), and each student will need two *L*-shaped cropping tools to work with.

4. Previewing Vocabulary

The following are key vocabulary terms used in this lesson:

- Media literacy
- Persuade
- Coerce
- Brainwash

Add these words to your word wall, if you are using one for this unit, and provide necessary support to help students learn these words as you teach the lesson.

Activities

Day 1

1. Introduce the Concept of Propaganda

Explain to students that in this lesson, they will continue to examine the Nazis' efforts to shape the German "national community" according to their racial ideals. This meant privileging "Aryans" and discriminating against those of so-called inferior races, such as Jews. In the last lesson, students looked at how the Nazis used laws to accomplish this goal. In this lesson, they will look at the way the Nazis used propaganda—through radio, the press, feature films and newsreels, theater, music, art exhibits, books, the school curriculum, sports, and more—to influence the beliefs, feelings, and actions of individuals to help further this goal.

Begin by having students reflect on the power of media to persuade. Ask them to respond to the following question in their journals:

> Do you think people are generally skeptical? Or are they too willing to believe what they learn on the internet, see on television, or hear from politicians or celebrities? How do <u>you</u> decide whether or not to believe what you see and hear?

You might have students discuss their responses using the Think, Pair, Share strategy, or briefly hear a few students' thoughts as a whole group.

Then tell students that when governments or politicians use media to persuade people, we often call that *propaganda*. In the Lesson 11 reading "Shaping Public Opinion," students learned about how Hitler established the Bureau of Propaganda and Public Enlightenment in 1933 and appointed Joseph Goebbels as its leader. It is worth reviewing or reminding students of that reading and then establishing a definition for *propaganda*. Provide students with the following definition:

> Propaganda: Information that is intended to persuade an audience to accept a particular idea or cause, often by using biased material or by stirring up emotions.

2. Analyze "The Eternal Jew" Poster

Tell students that in the activities that follow today and in the next class, they will analyze specific propaganda images used by the Nazis. If you haven't already, take a moment to pause and set the tone for viewing the images by asking students to revisit the *stereotype* concept maps they created (or the one the class created together) as part of Lesson 3 (see Notes to Teacher).

Then guide students through the Crop It strategy to analyze a propaganda image together as a whole class. Post or project the image The Eternal Jew and tell students that this is a poster representing a museum exhibit in Germany in 1937 and 1938 that was titled "The Eternal Jew."

Give students a few moments to simply observe the image. Then lead them through the series of instructions below, selecting one or two students to approach the image, use their cropping tool to respond to each prompt, and explain their choice. Move through the prompts one at a time, calling on different students for each prompt to allow for an array of ideas to be contributed. Use the following prompts:

- Identify a part of the image that first caught your eye.
- Identify a part of the image that raises a question for you.
- Identify a part of the image that is designed to make you feel rather than think.
- Identify a part of the image that is designed to make certain individuals feel included in or excluded from the German "national community."

3. "The Eternal Jew" Class Discussion

Remind students that propagandists meticulously pervaded all aspects of German society and used a wide range of forms of propaganda to serve particular purposes and convey specific messages. Students should assume that every detail has a purpose. Finish this activity by discussing the following questions with the class:

- What is the message the creator of this image is sending?
- What does the maker of this image want the viewer to feel?
- What does the creator of this image want the viewer to do?

Day 2

1. Propaganda Warm-Up

Before introducing new examples of Nazi propaganda, spend a few minutes reviewing with students the key ideas from the previous day. Ask students to look back at their journal responses about the influence of media to see how their thinking might have changed as a result of analyzing the poster The Eternal Jew.

Alternatively, you might project the poster again and ask students to work with a partner to make a short list of strategies that the creator(s) of the image used to convey an intended message. You could solicit ideas from each pair and record a list on the board to reference later in the lesson.

2. Analyze Additional Nazi Propaganda Images

There are three additional examples of Nazi propaganda images in the gallery Propaganda Posters for students to examine in this activity using the Crop It teaching strategy that you modeled the previous day. By analyzing a collection of such images, students can see that the Nazis created some propaganda that denigrated Jews and other so-called inferior races, while they created other propaganda that glorified "Aryans." The goal of both approaches was to influence the beliefs, feelings, and actions of individuals in Germany about who should be included and excluded from the "national community."

Divide students into groups of three or four to work together at analyzing these three images. Distribute the following images from the image gallery, and cropping tools, to each group.

- Nazi Recruitment Propaganda
- Hitler Youth Propaganda
- Antisemitic Children's Book

Lead students through the same series of instructions for the Crop It strategy listed in Day 1. You might project the list of prompts on the board for each group to reference as students work, or copy and paste them onto a handout for each table.

Depending on the amount of time you have available, have each member of each group analyze a separate image, taking notes in response to each prompt and then sharing their observations with the other members of their group. Alternatively, if you have more time to devote to this activity, you might have every student work with the same image simultaneously, discussing their thinking in their groups along the way. If you choose the second strategy, consider passing out the images one at a time so that the groups don't rush through the process.

After students have analyzed all of the images, lead a class discussion in which students describe the picture that this collection of propaganda paints of the "national community" the Nazis wished to create. Consider drawing from the following questions:

- Do you notice any themes or patterns in this group of propaganda images?
- Based on the images you have analyzed in this lesson, how do you think the Nazis used propaganda to define the identities of individuals and groups?
- Based on the images you have analyzed and what you have learned thus far in this unit about the rise of the Nazi Party and the Nazi Party's platform, what can you conclude about the ideal "national community" the Nazis strove to foster? How did they use propaganda to further their goal of creating this ideal "national community"?

3. Consider the Impact of Propaganda

Now that students have seen and analyzed several examples of Nazi propaganda, ask them to think about the impact these forms of media might have had on the beliefs, feelings, and actions of the people who were exposed to them. It is common for students to conclude after studying propaganda that the Nazis succeeded at brainwashing the German population, but it is important to help them think carefully about this idea. The quotations in the reading The Impact of Propaganda, one from a woman who lived in the Netherlands during this period and another from a contemporary scholar, can help to complicate the idea of a brainwashed populace.

Give students the reading The Impact of Propaganda. Read aloud Marion Pritchard's reflection on viewing a film at the museum exhibit "The Eternal Jew" and ask students to respond to the questions in a class discussion or with a partner. Then read aloud scholar Daniel Goldhagen's ideas about the limits of the power of propaganda and ask students to respond to the questions in a class discussion.

4. 3-2-1 Exit Ticket

On an index card or half-sheet of paper, ask students to complete an exit ticket using the 3-2-1 strategy format before leaving the classroom. They should address the following prompts, which you can project on the board or distribute on the cards:

- Write down 3 things you learned about how the Nazis used propaganda to influence the way Germans defined their universe of obligation.
- Write down 2 questions you have about Nazi propaganda or propaganda and brainwashing.
- Write down 1 thing you learned that supported or challenged your thinking in your journal response at the beginning of the lesson about the way media can influence our beliefs and actions.

Assessment

- Assign students to independently complete the Crop It viewing protocol that they used in this lesson with a new image. Assign students a piece of propaganda, or allow them to choose their own, and have them record their answers to the prompts outside of class. Review their work to check for the quality of their observations and the depth of their analysis of the propaganda's purpose. There are additional examples of Nazi propaganda in the *Holocaust and Human Behavior* online image gallery "The Impact of Propaganda."

- Evaluate students' responses on their exit tickets to find evidence of their thinking about how propaganda influences people's beliefs, attitudes, and actions. Look for nuance in students' thinking that resists the notion that propaganda succeeds simply by brainwashing its audience.

Extensions

1. Watch and Analyze the Video *Art as Propaganda: The Nazi Degenerate Art Exhibit*

To expose students to another form of Nazi propaganda, consider showing the short video *Art as Propaganda: The Nazi Degenerate Art Exhibit* (08:18). In addition to explaining the importance of this traveling 1937 exhibit, Dr. Jonathan Petropoulos also discusses the role of propaganda in the 1930s as a means of spreading the Nazis' message and how it contributed to their rise to power.

Because it is important for students to view the images as they watch the short film, ask them to complete an activity based on the Connect, Extend, Challenge strategy after they have finished watching. Be sure that students are making connections with what they have learned in the prior activities in this lesson.

2. Watch and Analyze *Triumph of the Will*

The film *Triumph of the Will* (01:44:27), directed by Leni Riefenstahl, is both a powerful work of Nazi propaganda and a landmark in the art of filmmaking. It portrays the massive 1934 Nazi Party rally in Nuremberg, and it includes scenes that strongly suggest the Nazi vision for "national community." Consider showing students a clip from the film, such as the opening scene of Hitler's arrival at and parade through Nuremberg (00:00–09:15) or the Nazi Youth Encampment (13:40–18:05). You can use the Close Viewing Protocol to guide your students through a more thorough examination of the film and how it attempts to communicate its messages.

3. Discuss the Use of Propaganda Today

It is worth engaging students in a reflection on and analysis of propaganda in our society today. The following questions can help start the discussion:

- Can you think of examples of propaganda in society today?
- How is propaganda similar to advertising? How is it different?
- How do you think such propaganda influences the attitudes and actions of people today?
- Is there a difference between the impact of propaganda in a democracy that has a free press and an open marketplace of ideas and the impact of propaganda in a dictatorship with fewer non-governmental sources of information?

Visit **facinghistory.org/thhb** to access these additional resources.

Image

The Eternal Jew

This 1938 poster advertises a popular antisemitic traveling exhibit called *Der ewige Jude* (The Eternal Jew).

Image Gallery

Propaganda Posters

Nazi Recruitment Poster

This mid-1930s poster says, "The NSDAP [Nazi Party] protects the people. Your fellow comrades need your advice and help, so join the local party organization."

Hitler Youth Propaganda

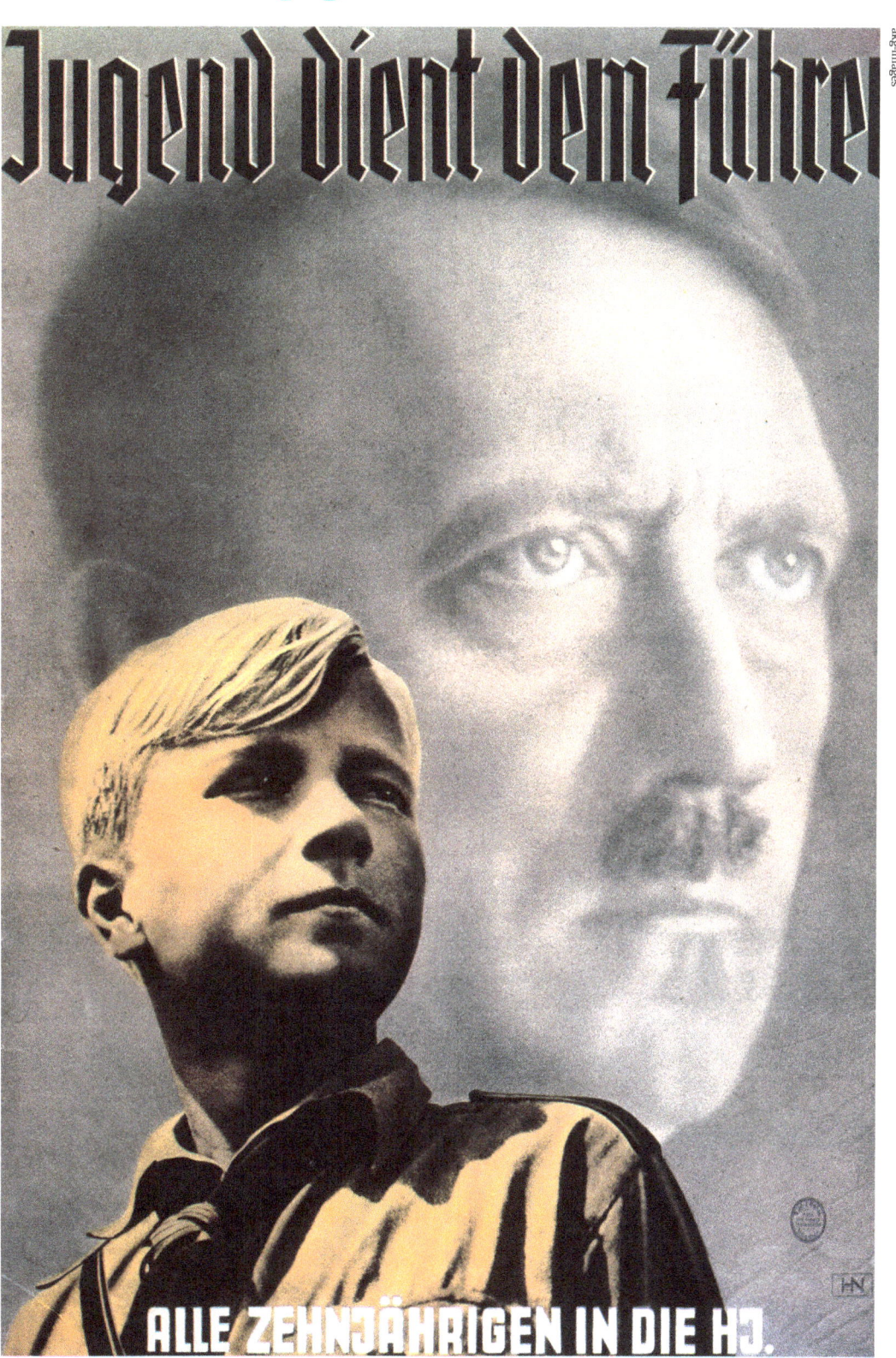

This 1935 poster promotes the Hitler Youth by stating: "Youth serves the Führer! All ten-year-olds into the Hitler Youth."

Antisemitic Children's Book

From the 1938 antisemitic children's book *The Poisonous Mushroom*. The boy is drawing a nose on the chalkboard, and the caption reads: "The Jewish nose is crooked at its tip. It looks like a 6."

Reading

The Impact of Propaganda

1. The museum exhibit *Der ewige Jude* (The Eternal Jew), represented by the poster you analyzed, also included a film. Filled with blatant antisemitic lies, the film was presented as a documentary but was in fact propaganda. Marion Pritchard, then a graduate student in the Netherlands, recalled seeing the film:

   > We went to see this movie and sat and made smart remarks all the way through and laughed at it because it was so outrageous. And yet when we came out of the movie, one of my Gentile [non-Jewish] friends said to me, "I wish I hadn't seen it. I know that it was all ridiculous and propaganda, but for the first time in my life I have a sense of them and us—Jews and Gentiles. I'm going to do everything I can to help them, but I wish I didn't have this feeling."[1]

   What did Marion Pritchard's friend mean when she said, "I know that it was all ridiculous propaganda, but for the first time in my life I have a sense of them and us—Jews and Gentiles"? How do you explain her statement? What does her statement suggest about the way that propaganda can affect people?

2. Some scholars caution that there are limits to the power of propaganda; they think it succeeds not because it persuades the public to believe an entirely new set of ideas but because it validates beliefs people already hold. Scholar Daniel Goldhagen writes:

   > No man, [no] Hitler, no matter how powerful he is, can move people against their hopes and desires. Hitler, as powerful a figure as he was, as charismatic as he was, could never have accomplished this [the Holocaust] had there not been tens of thousands, indeed hundreds of thousands of ordinary Germans who were willing to help him.[2]

   Do you agree or disagree with Goldhagen's ideas about the power of propaganda? Would people have rejected Nazi propaganda if they did not already share, to some extent, the beliefs it communicated? How do Goldhagen's ideas help you understand Marion Pritchard's friend's reaction to the exhibit's film in a new, different, or deeper way?

---

1 Carol Rittner and Sondra Myers, eds., *The Courage to Care* (New York: New York University Press, 1986), 28. Reproduced by permission from New York University Press.

2 Daniel Jonah Goldhagen, interview with Richard Heffner, "Hitler's Willing Executioners, Part I," *The Open Mind* (TV program), PBS, July 9, 1996, http://www.pbs.org/video/1512022073/.

Unit Essential Question

What does learning about the choices people made during the Weimar Republic, the rise of the Nazi Party, and the Holocaust teach us about the power and impact of our choices today?

Lesson

Youth and the National Community

Duration

One 50-minute class period

Materials

Handout
Youth in Society Anticipation Guide

Videos
Changes at School under the Nazis
Friendship and Betrayal

Handouts
Youth in Nazi Germany Reading Set 1
Youth in Nazi Germany Reading Set 2

Teaching Strategies
Four Corners
Big Paper
Connect, Extend, Challenge

Find all materials referenced in this lesson at facinghistory.org/thhb.

Guiding Questions

- How did the Nazis attempt to enlist young people in their efforts to create "in" groups and "out" groups in German society in the 1930s? How did young people respond to these attempts?
- What were the consequences for young people who were excluded from the Nazi vision for a "national community"?
- What is the role of education in preparing young people for their role as citizens? What might be the difference between preparing students to live in a dictatorship versus a democracy?

Learning Objectives

- Through close reading and discussion, students will identify the range of choices that young people faced in Nazi Germany and how the Nazis used schools and youth organizations to mold young people to embrace their nationalist and racist ideologies.
- Students will also develop their ideas about the role young people should play in any society and how they should best be educated for the future.

Overview

In the previous two lessons, students learned about how the Nazis used laws and propaganda to compel and persuade the German public to accept, if not support, their idea of a "national community" shaped according to their racial ideals. In this lesson, students will continue this unit's historical case study by looking at how the Nazis trained young people, through schools and youth groups, in an effort to build a foundation for the future of that "national community." Students will learn about the experiences of people who grew up in Nazi Germany through a variety of firsthand accounts that show the appeal the Nazi program held for many youth and the limits of that appeal for others. This lesson also reveals some of the dilemmas and isolation experienced by those young people who were deliberately excluded from the Nazi universe of obligation. The lesson both begins and concludes by providing students with the opportunity to discuss the role of young people in any society and the proper goals and methods for their education.

Context

In his book *Mein Kampf,* written in the 1920s, Hitler said, "Whoever has the youth has the future." As the Nazi Party grew during the Weimar era, they devoted substantial time, effort, and resources to winning over Germany's youth. Hitler hoped, once he was in power, that "these young people will learn nothing else but how to think German and act German. . . . And they will never be free again, not in their whole lives."

Schools had a key role to play in the Nazi efforts to inculcate in German youth a philosophy centered on the idea of a racially pure "national community." Throughout the 1920s, German schools adhered to a conservative educational philosophy—emphasizing social hierarchy and obedience to authority—that was already consistent with the Nazi worldview. After they came to power in 1933, the Nazis quickly passed new laws to make public education further reflect and teach their nationalist and racial ideologies. Jewish teachers were fired from their posts, and other teachers were encouraged to join the National Socialist Teachers League; by 1936, over 97% of teachers were members. Nazi leaders also created new curricula and textbooks to be used throughout the country. All students took classes in "race science," while Nazi racism infused materials in every class, including literature selections in reading and word problems in math.

The Nazis also sought to win over Germany's children and teenagers through party-sponsored youth groups. In the 1920s, the Nazis had already begun to organize groups that would train young people according to their principles. By 1936, all "Aryan" children in Germany over the age of six were required to join a Nazi youth group. At ten, boys were initiated into the Jungvolk (Young People), and at 14 they were promoted to the Hitler Youth. Their sisters joined the Jungmädel (Young Girls) and were later promoted to the League of German Girls. Although membership in the Hitler Youth organizations was compulsory, many young people did not have to be forced to join. In fact, they were eager to do so, because membership in Nazi youth groups offered a feeling of excitement, belonging, and even power.

Yet support for the Hitler Youth was never as widespread and strong as Nazi leaders would have liked. Young people skipped some meetings and activities, even though attendance was compulsory, and their loyalty could be inconsistent. Their reasons for losing enthusiasm for Hitler Youth activities were not always political or moral; sometimes young people grew tired of the many requirements or just got bored. In 1939, the Social Democratic Party, which had been outlawed by the Nazis and was operating in secrecy, published a report on German youth that described some of this discontent. It said that "young people are starting to feel particularly burdened by the lack of freedom and the mindless drills practiced by National Socialist organizations. So it is no wonder that signs of fatigue would be particularly prominent in their ranks."[1]

The resources in this lesson explore more deeply both the allure of the Hitler Youth to some young Germans and the reluctance felt by others. Examining these resources closely reveals not only the range of reactions but also a range of choices available to German youth in response to the Nazis' efforts to win them over in the 1930s—and a range of consequences for those choices, as well.

Meanwhile, those young Germans who were excluded from the "national community" by the Nazis had markedly fewer choices and faced difficult and often dangerous dilemmas. Jewish children were prohibited from joining Nazi youth groups and excluded from that social world so central to many of their classmates in the process. Their supposed inferiority was pronounced repeatedly before them and their peers in school every day. And the seemingly infinite number of laws and rules that singled them out in Nazi Germany emphasized their "otherness" in the eyes of true "Aryans" in painful ways. The resources in this lesson include reflections by both a Jehovah's Witness woman and a Jewish man who attended school in Nazi Germany, both of whom faced excruciating dilemmas related to their use of the ubiquitous "Heil Hitler" greeting.

Notes to Teacher

1. Setting Up for Four Corners

The first activity in this lesson includes the Four Corners teaching strategy. We recommend that you set up the room for this activity before class begins. Create four signs that read "Strongly Agree," "Agree," "Disagree," and "Strongly Disagree," and hang them in different corners of the room.

2. Considerations for the Little Paper Activity

In this lesson, students will be using a variation of the Big Paper strategy, "Little Paper," to analyze accounts of the lives of young people in Nazi Germany told from a variety of perspectives. Because it is likely not practical for every student to analyze every document in this lesson, this activity is designed to enable each student to look at accounts of four or five different experiences.

One thing to keep in mind with this activity is timing. Some students may be slower readers, or take longer to comment on a text, while others are faster. To account for these differences, consider asking students to swap readings with another student who finishes at the same time as them, rather than rotating the handouts clockwise. In addition, you'll want to ensure that students have plenty of margin space to comment on their little papers, so be sure to tape the handouts on a larger sheet of paper in advance.

---

[1] "SOPADE: Reports on German Youth" (1938), in *The Third Reich Sourcebook,* ed. Anson Rabinbach and Sander L. Gilman (Berkeley: University of California Press, 2013), 252.

3. Previewing Vocabulary

The following are key vocabulary terms used in this lesson:

- Educate
- Indoctrinate
- Disillusion
- Comradeship

Add these words to your word wall, if you are using one for this unit, and provide necessary support to help students learn these words as you teach the lesson.

Activities

1. Reflect on the Role of Young People in Society

Tell students that in this lesson, they will be looking at the experiences of young people in Nazi Germany, and especially how the Nazis attempted to enlist many of them in the process of building a "national community" that excluded non-"Aryans." But first, students will engage in an activity to help them think about and discuss the role of young people in society more broadly.

Pass out the handout Youth in Society Anticipation Guide and give students a few minutes to respond to each statement.

Then lead a Four Corners activity in which students position themselves in corners of the room near signs reading "Strongly Agree," "Agree," "Disagree," and "Strongly Disagree" to indicate their opinion about each statement.

Discussing every statement on the anticipation guide could easily take the entire class period, so choose two or three of the statements that you think are of especially high interest to your students for the activity. Read one of the statements and instruct students to move to the corner of the room that represents their opinion.

Then let students from each corner explain their opinions. Make sure at least one person from each corner has the opportunity to speak, and tell students that if they are persuaded by the argument of a classmate in another corner, they may change their mind and move.

Repeat this process with as many statements as you can discuss in about ten minutes.

2. Analyze Accounts of Youth Experiences in Nazi Germany

Tell students that they will now examine a variety of firsthand accounts from people who were teenagers in Nazi Germany. Many of the ideas they responded to on the anticipation guide in the opening activity will come up in these readings.

Begin by projecting (or writing on the board) and previewing the following questions for students, which they will respond to in their journals after watching a short video.

- What messages were being sent to young Germans about the proper way to think and act in Germany in the 1930s? What messages were sent about how young people should think about their universe of obligation?
- Why might these messages have appealed to some German youth? Why might they have frightened, angered, or confused others?
- What options did young Germans have about how they could respond to the pressures they faced? What factors may have expanded or shrunk the number of options available to them?
- How were young people from groups targeted by the Nazis affected by the changes in German society in the 1930s?

Next, show students one or both of the following video testimonies at facinghistory.org/thhb:

- Changes at School under the Nazis (04:13): testimony by Kurt Klein
- Friendship and Betrayal (02:55): testimony by Ellen Kerry Davis

After watching the videos, briefly discuss how Klein's and Davis's testimonies help to answer the questions above.

Tell students that they will now use the same series of questions to respond to a variety of documents about youth in Nazi Germany in a "Little Paper" activity (a variation of Big Paper).

Divide the class into groups of four or five, and have each group sit in a circle. Then give each group either Youth in Nazi Germany Reading Set 1 or Youth in Nazi Germany Reading Set 2. Each student should start with one reading from their assigned reading set. As students read, they should annotate the text by highlighting or underlining portions that help to answer the questions above. They can also write comments and observations in the margins about young people's experiences.

After a few minutes, students will then pass their handouts to the person on their right, and they will repeat the process with the new handout. This time, however, they can respond to the comments and annotations the previous student made. Repeat this process at least once more, or (time permitting) until students have had a chance to work with each handout in their group.

When the process is complete, have students return each handout to the student who read it first so that student can see the written discussions that followed their initial comments.

Finally, bring the class together as a whole group and debrief the activity with the following questions:

- How did the Nazis attempt to educate young people to accept, if not support, the dictatorship? How would education be different if the goal were to teach young people how to be citizens in a democracy?
- What did you notice about the variety of ways young people responded to education and youth groups in Nazi Germany? Did any of the responses surprise you?

- What options did German teenagers have in terms of how they could respond to the pressures they faced? What were the consequences of some of those choices?

3. Revisit the Role of Young People in Society

To close the lesson, or for homework, ask students to review their responses to the anticipation guide they completed at the beginning of the lesson.

After they review the anticipation guide, assign students to select two of the statements from the list and copy them into their journals. After each statement, they should write a short reflection explaining how the firsthand accounts they studied in this lesson affected their initial opinions about them from the beginning of the lesson. For this reflection, use the Connect, Extend, Challenge teaching strategy.

Assessment

- Evaluate students' reflections from the closing activity of this lesson to help you assess both their understanding of the role young people played in the Nazis' ideal "national community" and their thinking about the broader question of the role of young people in society. To use these reflections as an assessment, ask students to write them on a separate piece of paper or notecard to turn in (if you have established that their journals are private).

- For a more formal assessment, assign students to write an argumentative paragraph in response to the following prompt:
  - In his book *Mein Kampf,* written in the 1920s, Hitler said, "Whoever has the youth has the future." How did Hitler and the Nazi Party use schools and youth organizations to reflect this idea? How did young people choose to respond, and how did these choices challenge the way they saw themselves and understood their identities?
  - Support your argument with evidence from the materials (videos, readings, and handouts) in Lesson 14 and Lesson 15. Be sure to include a thesis statement and explain how your evidence supports your thesis.

Extensions

1. Explore the Roles of Obedience and Conformity

The reading "Models of Obedience" explores the roles that obedience and conformity played in the upbringing of children in Nazi Germany. You might use this reading to extend this lesson's exploration of young people's role in society and the proper goals of education. The connection questions following the reading probe the tension between the importance of teaching children to obey and the possibility that at some point the inclination to obey can become harmful. Use the questions as the basis for a class discussion about the differences between obedience and conformity and the times or circumstances in which each of these behaviors may be useful or dangerous.

2. Further Explore Resistance to Nazi Education and Propaganda

The reading "Even If All Others Do—I Do Not!" explores how one German parent, Johannes Fest, coped with his opposition to Nazi policies and shared his opinions with his family. To more fully explore the question of choices and resistance, share this reading with students and discuss the connection questions that follow.

3. Do the Children Have the Power?

The reading "The Birthday Party" describes a situation in which a 14-year-old Hitler Youth leader felt empowered to challenge another boy's father for keeping his son home from training exercises because he had a cold. You might read and discuss this reading with students and ask them what light it sheds on both the allure of the Hitler Youth for some young Germans and the influence it had on their behavior. You might also ask students how this helps them interpret the meaning of Hitler's belief that "Whoever has the youth has the future."

Visit **facinghistory.org/thhb** to access these additional resources.

 **Handout**

Youth in Society Anticipation Guide

Directions: The statements below express a variety of viewpoints about the role of young people in society. Read each statement in the left column. Decide if you strongly agree (SA), agree (A), disagree (D), or strongly disagree (SD) with it. Circle your response and provide a one- to two-sentence explanation of your opinion (on separate paper if needed).

Statement	Your Opinion
1. It's easier to manipulate teenagers than adults.	SA A D SD **Explain:**
2. Students should be taught about the history of their country from different points of view, even if some of those perspectives reveal that their country might have made mistakes in its past.	SA A D SD **Explain:**
3. It comes more naturally to teenagers to create "in" groups and "out" groups than it does to adults.	SA A D SD **Explain:**
4. Children should be taught that it is always important to obey authority, especially government officials and the laws of the country.	SA A D SD **Explain:**
5. Public schools (which are run by the government) should teach only the perspective of the political party that controls the government.	SA A D SD **Explain:**
6. Young people should be required to participate in community service.	SA A D SD **Explain:**

7. The most effective way to change the values of a society is to change what students are taught in schools.	SA A D SD	**Explain:**
8. The most important job of education is to teach students skills they will need to get jobs when they are adults.	SA A D SD	**Explain:**

 **Handout**

Youth in Nazi Germany Reading Set 1

Schooling for the National Community

Gregor Ziemer was a teacher and headmaster at the American School in Berlin (a school for the children of American citizens living in Germany) for most of the 1930s. During this time, Ziemer toured German schools and eventually wrote a book called *Education for Death*, which was first published in 1941. In it, Ziemer describes the schools he visited:

> A teacher is not spoken of as a teacher (Lehrer) but an Erzieher. The word suggests an iron disciplinarian who does not instruct but commands, and whose orders are backed up with force if necessary.
>
> Matters of the spirit are frankly and energetically belittled. Physical education, education for action, is alone worthy of the Nazi teacher's attention. All else can be dismissed as non-essential . . .
>
> The Nazi schools are no place for weaklings. All children must, of course, finish the primary school before they are ten; but after that the schools are proving-grounds for the Party. Those who betray any weakness of body or have not the capacities for absolute obedience and submission must be expelled. . . .
>
> The regime draws a sharp distinction between girls, inherently weak, and boys, natural exponents of strength. Boys and girls have nothing in common. Their aims, their purposes in life, are fundamentally different. Boys will become soldiers; girls will become breeders. Co-educational schools are manifestations of decadent democracies and hence are taboo.
>
> [Dr. Bernhard Rust, the Nazi Minister of Education] decrees that in Nazi schools the norm is physical education. After that, German, biology, science, mathematics, and history are for the boys; eugenics and home economics for the girls. Other subjects are permissible if they are taught to promote Nazi ideas. Spiritual education is definitely unimportant.[1]

History and science were the subjects most influenced by Nazi ideology. Soon after Hitler took power, a new course in "race science" was added to the curriculum in every German school. But racial instruction was not limited to a single course. It was included in all classes, even arithmetic. One book, titled *Germany's Fall and Rise—Illustrations Taken from Arithmetic Instruction in the Higher Grades of Elementary School*, asks, "The Jews are aliens in Germany—in 1933 there were 66,060,000 inhabitants of the German Reich, of whom 499,682 were Jews. What is the percentage of aliens?"[2]

---

[1] Gregor Ziemer, *Education for Death: The Making of the Nazi* (Oxford: Oxford University Press, 1941), 15–16.

[2] Ziemer, *Education for Death*, 16.

Indoctrination

Hede von Nagel grew up in Nazi Germany. She wrote of her childhood:

> As my parents' second daughter, I was a great disappointment to my father, who wanted to produce sons for the Führer and the nation—and, because he was of the nobility, to carry on the family name.
>
> He was furious that, unlike my fair-haired older sister, who looked so Nordic, I had been cursed with auburn hair and dark brown eyes. Then came a third child, this time a male, but he was a dark-eyed redhead—another let down for my patriotic father. Only when another son was born and proved to be the very model of a tow-headed, blue-eyed Aryan was my father satisfied. "At last," he said, "the child I wanted."
>
> Our parents taught us to raise our arms and say "Heil Hitler" before we said "Mama." This type of indoctrination was universal. Children experienced it in kindergarten, at home—everywhere. We grew up believing that Hitler was a super-god, and Germany an anointed nation. . . .
>
> At the same time, our parents and teachers trained my sister and me to be the unquestioning helpmates of men; as individuals, we had no right to our own opinion, no right to speak up.[3]

---

[3] Hede von Nagel, "The Nazi Legacy—Fearful Silence for Their Children," *Boston Globe*, October 23, 1977.

Joining the Hitler Youth

Alfons Heck was an enthusiastic participant in the Nazi Youth organizations. In a memoir written many years after World War II, Heck reflected on what made him want to join:

> Far from being forced to enter the ranks of the *Jungvolk*, I could barely contain my impatience and was, in fact, accepted before I was quite 10. It seemed like an exciting life, free from parental supervision, filled with "duties" that seemed sheer pleasure. Precision marching was something one could endure for hiking, camping, war games in the field, and a constant emphasis on sports. . . . To a degree, our pre-war activities resembled those of the Boy Scouts, with much more emphasis on discipline and political indoctrination. There were the paraphernalia and the symbols, the pomp and the mysticism, very close in feeling to religious rituals. One of the first significant demands was the so-called . . . "test of courage," which was usually administered after a six-month period of probation. The members of my Schar, a platoon-like unit of about 40–50 boys, were required to dive off the three-meter board—about 10 feet high—head first in the town's swimming pool. There were some stinging belly flops, but the pain was worth it when our *Fahnleinführer*, the 15-year-old leader of *Fahnlein* (literally "little flag"), a company-like unit of about 160 boys, handed us the coveted dagger with its inscription Blood and Honor. From that moment on we were fully accepted.[4]

---

[4] Alfons Heck, *A Child of Hitler: Germany in the Days When God Wore a Swastika* (Phoenix, AZ: Renaissance House, 1985), 9.

Disillusionment in the Hitler Youth

Hans Scholl, who later founded the White Rose resistance movement with his sister Sophie and was executed by the Nazis, was at one point a member of the Hitler Youth. His sister Inge Scholl describes how Hans slowly became disillusioned with the group:

> Hans had assembled a collection of folk songs, and his young charges loved to listen to him singing, accompanying himself on his guitar . . .
>
> But some time later a peculiar change took place in Hans; he was no longer the same . . . His songs were forbidden, the leader had told him. And when he had laughed at this, they threatened him with disciplinary action. Why should he not be permitted to sing these beautiful songs? Only because they had been created by other peoples? . . . [T]his depressed him, and his usual carefree spirit began to wane.
>
> At this particular time he was given a very special assignment.
>
> He was to carry the flag of his troop to the party's national rally at Nuremberg. He was overjoyed. But when he returned we hardly dared trust our eyes. He looked tired, and on his face lay a great disappointment . . . gradually we learned that the youth movement which had been held up to him as an ideal image was in reality something totally different from what he had imagined the Hitler Youth to be. Their drill and uniformity had been extended into every sphere of personal life. But he had always believed that every boy should develop his own special talents . . .
>
> Ultimately it came to an open break.
>
> One evening, as they stood with their flag in formation for inspection by a higher leader, something unheard-of happened. The visiting leader suddenly ordered the tiny standard-bearer, a frolicsome twelve-year-old lad, to give up the flag. "You don't need a special flag. Just keep the one that has been prescribed for all." Hans was deeply disturbed. Since when? Didn't the troop leader know what this special flag meant to its standard-bearer?
>
> Once more the leader ordered the boy to give up the flag. He stood quiet and motionless. Hans knew what was going on in the little fellow's mind and that he would not obey. When the high leader in a threatening voice ordered the little fellow for the third time, Hans saw the flag waver slightly. He could no longer control himself. He stepped out of line and slapped the visiting leader's face. From then on he was no longer the standard-bearer.[5]

---

5 Inge Scholl, *Students Against Tyranny: The Resistance of the White Rose, Munich, 1942–1943,* trans. Arthur R. Schultz (Middletown, CT: Wesleyan University Press, 1970), 7–10. Reproduced by permission from Wesleyan University Press.

 **Handout**

Youth in Nazi Germany Reading Set 2

Youth on the Margins, Part 1

When Elizabeth Dopazo and her brother were very young, their parents were sent to concentration camps because of their religious beliefs; they were Jehovah's Witnesses whose faith required that they pledge allegiance only to God. Jehovah's Witnesses therefore refused to say "Heil Hitler" as a matter of religious conviction. After their parents were arrested, seven-year-old Elizabeth and her six-year-old brother went to live with their grandparents. Elizabeth later recalled:

> We had to quickly change our way of speaking so maybe we wouldn't be so noticeable. In school right away it started, you see. We had to raise our right arm and say "Heil Hitler" and all that sort of thing and then we didn't do it a few times. A few times was all right. You can drop a handkerchief, you can do a little something, but quickly they look and they say, "Ah, you're different and you're new in the school." So you're watched a little more closely. You might get one or two children who'd tell on you but it was rare. The teacher would bring you to the front of the class and say "Why don't you say Heil Hitler?" and you were shaking already because you knew, unlike other children, if you told them the real reason there'd be trouble. For us to say "Heil Hitler" and praise a person would be against our belief. We shouldn't because we had already pledged our allegiance to God and that's it. So we could stand and be respectful to the government, but we were not to participate in adulation for political figures. . . .
>
> Later, around age twelve or thirteen, we joined the Hitler Youth, which we actually didn't want to do, but the Gestapo came to my grandparents' house, just like you've seen in the movies with the long leather coats on and they stood at the front door and they were saying, "Your grandchildren have to join the Hitler Youth and if they don't by Thursday we will take stronger measures." After they'd left we told our grandparents we'll join tomorrow, even if we hate all that stuff. They agreed we'd better do it and we very quickly donned those uniforms. . . .
>
> As time went on, my brother, when he was thirteen or fourteen, sort of was swayed. You know, you have to believe in something. He wanted to be a German officer and said our father had been wrong all along and that we went to the dogs for our father's beliefs. He [our father] died for his ideals and where are we? [My brother] was very angry. I was too, but not as much. I was torn between what would be the good thing to do and what would not. . . .[1]

---

[1] Elizabeth Dopazo, "Reminiscences," unpublished interview, 1981, Facing History & Ourselves.

Comradeship

In 1938, a boy named Hans Wolf wrote a story about his experiences in the Hitler Youth that was published in a school textbook. The story was called "Comradeship." It begins:

> It was a hot day and we had far to march. The sun was burning down on the heath, which was bereft of trees. The sand was glistening, I was tired. My feet were hurting in those new walking shoes, every step was hurting and all I could think about was rest, water, and shade. I clenched my teeth to keep walking. I was the youngest, and this was my first outing. In front of me strode Rudolf, the leader. He was tall and strong. His backpack was heavy and pressed down on his shoulders. Rudolf carried the bread for us six boys, the cooking pot, and a pile of books, from which he would read us wonderfully thrilling stories, at night in the hostel. My backpack only contained a shirt, a couple of sneakers, washing utensils, and some cooking gear, apart from a tarpaulin for rainy days and straw beds. And yet I thought I could not lug this backpack any longer. My comrades all were somewhat older and had camping experience. They hardly felt the heat and hardship of the march. Every now and then they would sigh and drink lukewarm coffee from their canteens. More and more, I remained behind, even though I tried to make up for my slack by running. Suddenly Rudolf turned around. He stopped and watched me crawling up to him from a distance, while our comrades continued in the direction of a few trees on the horizon. "Tired?" Rudolf asked me, kindly. Ashamed, I had to say yes. Slowly, we walked side by side. I was limping. But I did not want to let on to Rudolf. When we got to a juniper bush, the leader sat down and said: "For a little rest!" Relieved, I threw myself down. I did not want to talk, for I was shy. Rudolf gave me something to drink. I thanked him and leaned back comfortably, glad to be able to stretch my aching feet, and before I knew it I was sleeping. . . . When we resumed our march, my feet hurt much less and my backpack did not press down on me so. I was very glad about that.[2]

2 Hans Wolf, "Comradeship," trans. Michael H. Kater, in Michael H. Kater, *Hitler Youth* (Cambridge, MA: Harvard University Press, 2004), 13–14.

"Heil Hitler!": Lessons of Daily Life

In 1938, writer Erika Mann published a book called *School for Barbarians: Education Under the Nazis.* Mann had emigrated from Germany to the United States in 1937. Her book criticized the Nazis' efforts to shape young people's ideas and feelings. In it, she describes how daily life in Germany was a kind of "school" that educated children in accordance with Nazi ideals:

> Every child says "Heil Hitler!" from 50 to 150 times a day . . . The formula is required by law; if you meet a friend on the way to school, you say it; study periods are opened and closed with "Heil Hitler!"; "Heil Hitler!" says the postman, the street-car conductor, the girl who sells you notebooks at the stationery store; and if your parents' first words when you come home for lunch are not "Heil Hitler!" they have been guilty of a punishable offense and can be denounced. "Heil Hitler!" they shout in the Jungvolk and Hitler Youth. "Heil Hitler!" cry the girls in the League of German Girls. Your evening prayers must close with "Heil Hitler!" if you take your devotions seriously . . .
>
> . . . You leave the house in the morning, "Heil Hitler" on your lips; and on the stairs of your apartment house you meet the Blockwart [block warden]. A person of great importance and some danger, the Blockwart has been installed by the government as a Nazi guardian. He controls the block, reporting on it regularly, checking up on the behavior of its residents . . . All the way down the street, the flags are waving, every window colored with red banners, and the black swastika in the middle of each. You don't stop to ask why; it's bound to be some national event . . . Only the Jews are exempted under the strict regulation. Jews are not Germans; they do not belong to the "Nation," they can have no "national events." . . .
>
> There are more placards as you continue past hotels, restaurants, indoor swimming pools, to school. They read "No Jews allowed"—"Jews not desired here"—"Not for Jews." And what do you feel? Agreement? Pleasure? Disgust? Opposition? You don't feel any of these. You don't feel anything, you've seen these placards for almost five years. This is a habit, it is all perfectly natural, of course Jews aren't allowed here. Five years in the life of a child of nine—that's his life, after four years of infancy, his whole personal, conscious existence . . . [3]

---

3 Erika Mann, *School for Barbarians: Education Under the Nazis* (Mineola, NY: Dover Publications, 1938), 21–24. Reproduced by permission from Dover Publications.

Rejecting Nazism

Some German young people refused to join Nazi youth organizations. One group who refused to join called themselves the *Swing-Jugend* ("swing kids") after a style of American jazz music and dancing they loved. Historian Richard Bessel describes the "swing kids":

> The swing youth were not anti-fascist in a political sense—their behavior was indeed emphatically anti-political—both Nazi slogans and traditional nationalism were of profound indifference to them. They sought their counter-identity in what they saw as the "slovenly" culture of . . . England and America. They accepted Jews and "half-Jews" into their groups . . . and gave ovations to visiting bands from Belgium and Holland.[4]

A Hitler Youth report on a 1940 swing festival attended by more than 500 teenagers in Hamburg describes the kind of behavior that upset Nazi officials:

> The dancers made an appalling sight. None of the couples danced normally; there was only swing of the worst sort. Sometimes two boys danced with one girl; sometimes several formed a circle, linking arms and jumping, slapping hands, even rubbing the backs of their heads together; and then, bent double, with the top half of the body hanging loosely down, long hair flopping into the face, they dragged themselves round practically to their knees. When the band played a rumba, the dancers went into wild ecstasy. They all leaped around and mumbled the chorus in English. The band played wilder and wilder numbers; none of the players was sitting any longer, they all "jitterbugged" on the stage like wild animals. Frequently boys could be observed dancing together, without exception with two cigarettes in the mouth, one in each corner . . .[5]

---

[4] Richard Bessel, *Life in the Third Reich* (Oxford: Oxford University Press, 1987), 39.

[5] Bessel, *Life in the Third Reich*, 37.

Youth on the Margins, Part 2

Daily life in school was difficult for a boy named Frank, one of two Jewish students in a school in Breslau in the mid-1930s. He recalled:

> People started to pick on me, "a dirty Jew," and all this kind of thing. And we started to fight. . . . There was my friend, and he was one class above me, he fought in every break. . . . I started to fight, too, because they insulted too much or they started to fight, whatever it was.
>
> We were very isolated, and one order came after another. . . . [One] order says all Jews must greet with the German greeting. The German greeting was "Heil Hitler" and raising your hand. Then the next order came out, and it says the Jews are not allowed to greet people with the "Heil Hitler" signal. Okay, so, in Germany you had to greet every teacher. When you see a teacher on the street, you had to respect them and you had to greet him—you had to bow down. . . .
>
> Now we were in an impossible situation, because when we went up the stairs and we saw one teacher, and we said "Heil Hitler." And he turned around. "Aren't you a Jew? You're not allowed to greet me with 'Heil Hitler.'" But if I didn't greet him at all, then the next teacher would say "Aren't you supposed to greet [me with] 'Heil Hitler'?" And this was always accompanied with a punishment. . . . Not all of them but some of them, the teachers that knew me and would pick on me—they'd punish me, put me in a corner, or humiliate me in one way or another. . . .
>
> You had to raise your hand and salute when the flag passed and Jews weren't allowed to do it. . . . If you don't salute, you immediately were recognized as a Jew, and you really were left to the mercy of the people who saw you, what they would do with you. They could perfectly well kill you on the street and, you know, nobody really said anything because there was no such thing as a court and after all, it was only a Jew. . . . We were at the mercy of people.[6]

---

6 *Childhood Experiences of German Jews* (New Haven, CT: Fortunoff Video Archive for Holocaust Testimonies, ca. 1987), VHS.

| **Unit Essential Question** | What does learning about the choices people made during the Weimar Republic, the rise of the Nazi Party, and the Holocaust teach us about the power and impact of our choices today? |

Lesson

Kristallnacht

Duration

Two 50-minute class periods

Materials

Videos

"Kristallnacht": The November 1938 Pogroms

Elsbeth Lewin Remembers Kristallnacht

Handouts

The November 1938 Pogroms Viewing Guide

Kristallnacht Testimony Viewing Guide

Decision Making in Times of Fear and Crisis

The Range of Human Behavior Vocabulary Terms

Readings

Responses to Kristallnacht (various)

Teaching Strategies

Think, Pair, Share

Wraparound

Exit Tickets

Find all materials referenced in this lesson at facinghistory.org/thhb.

Guiding Question

- What do the variety of responses to Kristallnacht teach us about the ways that people respond in times of fear and crisis?

Learning Objectives

- Students will cite evidence from a mini-documentary to understand the historical significance of Kristallnacht as a major escalation of the Nazi campaign against Jews, and they will respond to the video testimony of a survivor of the pogroms to reflect on the personal impact of the violence and terror that occurred across Germany.

- Students will define the terms *perpetrator*, *victim*, *bystander*, and *upstander* and use first-person testimonies about Kristallnacht to demonstrate how these roles that people play in times of fear and crisis do not describe fixed identities; individuals move into and out of these roles depending on circumstances.

Overview

In the previous lessons, students explored the variety of methods the Nazis used to marginalize Jews and other supposedly inferior groups and to create a "national community" shaped according to Nazi racial ideals. In this lesson, students will continue this unit's historical case study by learning about a major escalation of the Nazi campaign against Jews, the violent pogroms of Kristallnacht on November 9–10, 1938. Students will learn about these events by watching a short documentary and examining a range of firsthand accounts. They will then look closely at the range of choices made by individuals, groups, and countries—to participate in the attacks, to oppose them, to help the victims, or to look the other way—and connect those choices to universal concepts about human behavior in times of crisis.

Context

In the second half of the 1930s, the Nazis became openly aggressive toward neighboring countries and increasingly violent against Jews and other targeted minorities within Greater Germany.

By 1935, Hitler's efforts to rebuild the German military forces (which had begun in 1933 in violation of the Treaty of Versailles) became public, and Germany began taking steps toward expanding the Third Reich across all of Europe. The first steps included annexing Austria (an act known as the *Anschluss*) and the part of Czechoslovakia called the Sudetenland, territories inhabited by so-called "true Germans" who Hitler believed ought to be part of the Reich. Fearful of igniting a new world war, the leaders of other countries were unwilling to oppose with military force Hitler's demands for these territories. As a result, Germany expanded into Austria and Czechoslovakia without firing a shot. (The Nazis' plans to expand Germany's "living space" are explored in more detail in the next lesson.)

The German takeover of Austria and the Sudetenland increased the number of Jews affected by Nazi restrictions, while at the same time discrimination intensified to the point where Jews were effectively removed from German public life. This meant that Germany's aggressive steps to expand its borders touched off both an international political crisis, as world leaders scrambled to avoid war, and a humanitarian refugee crisis, as hundreds of thousands of people, mostly Jews, sought safety from the Nazis.

The ineffective international response deepened the peril in which Jews in the Reich found themselves. The danger became even more dire on November 9–10, 1938, in what was called Kristallnacht (Night of Broken Glass)—the worst outbreak of terror and violence against Jews all over Germany since the Nazis came to power.

On that night, according to the Nazi propaganda, "the German people" spontaneously took revenge on the Jewish people for the murder of a Nazi diplomat in Paris by a young Jewish man named Herschel Grynszpan. In reality, the violence had been planned and organized by the Nazis, and carried out by the SS, SA, Hitler Youth, and other Nazi groups.

By the morning of November 10, they had destroyed thousands of Jewish homes and businesses, and they had set fire to 191 synagogues, the centers of Jewish social and spiritual life, in every part of Greater Germany. Fire departments were instructed not to put out the fires but merely to stand by and make sure that adjacent property did not go up in flames. Although the exact figure is not known, it is likely that anywhere from 1,500 to 3,000 Jews died as a result of the violence and 30,000 others were afterward sent to concentration camps. Two days later, the German government fined the Jewish community one billion marks for "property damaged in the rioting."

In this lesson, students will learn about the events of November 9–10, 1938, and they will explore the choices a variety of people made during and after this violent crisis to participate in the violence, help those who were targeted, or look the other way. This lesson introduces important terms that help us understand this range of human behavior in times of crisis. The roles of *perpetrator*, *victim*, *bystander*, and *upstander* can be assumed by individuals, groups, or even nations. But it can be difficult to define each term clearly. For example, under the label *upstander*, we often list those who take a variety of actions, including resistance and rescue. However, upstanders might also include those who are able to maintain a part of their identity despite opposition, such as people who continue to secretly practice their religious faith or others who refuse to give up hope. The term *bystander* can be even more complicated. In most dictionaries, it means a person who is simply "standing by" or who is present without taking part in what is going on—a passive spectator. But some scholars, like psychologist Ervin Staub, believe that even passive spectators play a crucial role in defining the meaning of events by implicitly approving the actions of perpetrators. The choice not to act or speak up is still a choice.

It is important to recognize that it is not these labels themselves, as words, that matter; it is the way we think and talk about the actions (or inactions) of others that helps us both understand history and make connections to the choices we all make in the present. In addition, it is important to remember that individuals and groups usually do not fit into only one category. Instead, they may move into and out of these roles throughout their lives.

But studying this history and others with these terms in mind, despite those limitations, allows us to think about the agency of individuals, groups, and nations—their ability to recognize the options available to them and make choices that impact their own lives, the lives of others, and the course of history. By reflecting on the agency of individuals, groups, and nations in historical context, we can better understand the possibility and power of the choices available to us today.

Notes to Teacher

1. Defining *Bystander* and *Upstander*: Understanding Their Nuances

The terms *bystander* and *upstander* are difficult to define clearly because they can apply to a variety of different kinds of choices in different circumstances. It is important that students understand the nuances of these two terms before applying them to choices from the past they learn about in this lesson and their own personal choices. To help you guide students through the nuances, make sure to read carefully the discussion of these terms in the Context section before teaching this lesson.

Students will be asked to develop their own definitions for each term before also considering dictionary definitions. They will reference the handout they use to define these terms when they study the Holocaust in later lessons, so it is important that they keep it accessible with their journals and notes.

2. Assigning Reading: Heterogeneous or Leveled Groupings

The readings in this lesson vary in length, so you might consider in advance how you will group students for Activity 2 on Day 2 ("Analyze Responses to Kristallnacht"). One option is to create heterogeneous groupings of readers so the stronger readers can assist struggling ones with pacing, vocabulary, and comprehension. Alternatively, you might group students by level and work more closely with struggling readers to target specific literacy skills while allowing the more confident readers to tackle the content independently.

3. Previewing Vocabulary

The following are key vocabulary terms used in this lesson:

- Pogrom
- Perpetrator
- Victim
- Bystander
- Upstander

Add these words to your word wall, if you are using one for this unit, and provide necessary support to help students learn these words as you teach the lesson.

Activities

Day 1

1. Discuss the Value of Studying Choices in a Time of Fear and Crisis

Tell students that in this lesson they will learn about an explosion of violence against Jews in Germany in November 1938, and they will examine the choices a variety of individuals made in response to these events. Then ask them to respond in their journals to the following prompt:

> What can we learn by thinking about the choices people make in times of fear and crisis?

After students have taken a few minutes to respond in writing, discuss their thoughts using the Think, Pair, Share teaching strategy. Alternatively, you might ask some students to share their ideas with the class, keeping a list of what they can learn on the board or chart paper to add to over the course of the lesson.

2. Introduce the Kristallnacht Pogroms

Students will initially learn about what happened on November 9 and 10, 1938, by watching two videos: one in which historians discuss the causes, events, and aftermath, and another in which a survivor whose family was targeted on Kristallnacht describes her experiences. Students will hear the word *pogrom* in this lesson, so if they have not yet learned it, provide the *Merriam-Webster* dictionary definition:

> *pogrom:* an organized massacre of helpless people; *specifically:* such a massacre of Jews

Pass out the handouts The November 1938 Pogroms Viewing Guide and Kristallnacht Testimony Viewing Guide. Then show the video "Kristallnacht": The November 1938 Pogroms (09:40) at facinghistory.org/thhb. There are powerful images of destruction in this video, so it is important that your students are able to watch the film and not focus solely on their papers. You might ask students to read the questions in advance, and then pause the film a few times to allow them to record their reactions, or give them time to write after viewing the film.

After briefly discussing students' responses to the first video, show the next one, the video Elsbeth Lewin Remembers Kristallnacht (09:43) at facinghistory.org/thhb. Students will record on the handout a phrase or sentence from Lewin's testimony that resonates with them. When the video is over, ask students to also write a word or phrase that describes their experiences of hearing her account.

Use the Wraparound teaching strategy to provide each student with the opportunity to share both the sentence from the video they recorded and the words they chose to describe their experiences. If you have the space in your classroom, you might ask the students to form a circle and share their sentences in the first "wraparound" and their experiences of watching Elsbeth Lewin's testimony in the second. Remind students that it is fine if multiple students chose similar sentences and used the same words to describe their personal responses.

3. Complete Exit Tickets

So far in this lesson, students have encountered stories of escalating violence toward Jews in Nazi Germany in 1938 and a powerful firsthand account of Kristallnacht. Before ending the period, ask students to briefly respond to two prompts on an exit ticket to help you understand how they are processing what they have learned:

- Write down one thing you learned or observed in class today that you found surprising or troubling.
- Record one question, about history or human behavior, that arose for you in response to what you learned about in class today.

Day 2

1. Acknowledge Exit Tickets

Begin the second day of this lesson by acknowledging the exit tickets that students completed at the end of the previous day. Point out any patterns that you noticed. It can be helpful for students to know that others had similar responses to emotionally challenging material they encountered. Hearing some of their peers' questions can also help to promote more thoughtful and sensitive contributions from students as they proceed together into lessons about violence, war, and mass murder that will likely challenge them both emotionally and intellectually.

2. Analyze Responses to Kristallnacht

Students will now read about a variety of experiences and choices that people made in response to the pogroms that occurred on Kristallnacht. If necessary, remind students of their opening journal reflections about what we can learn about human behavior from reflecting on the choices people make in times of fear and crisis.

Remind the class that in the last session, they heard Elsbeth Lewin's testimony of surviving Kristallnacht and the deep impact that night had on her family. Explain that her story is just one example of how personal testimonies from those who lived through particular moments in history can help us understand more than simply what happened; they can help us consider the complexity of the dilemmas that individuals faced along with the deep emotional impact that can be felt over the course of a lifetime.

Tell students that today, they will be reading and analyzing a testimony about Kristallnacht with a group and then reporting on what they learned to the rest of the class.

Give each student a copy of the handout Decision Making in Times of Fear and Crisis to record their notes. For now, they should only complete the first three columns of the handout. Because each reading includes information about the choices of more than one person or group, they should use as many rows of the grid on the handout as necessary to capture the choices they discussed.

Divide the class into small groups and assign each group one of the following readings:

- The Night of the Pogrom
- Opportunism during Kristallnacht
- A Family Responds to Kristallnacht
- Thoroughly Reprehensible Behavior
- A Visitor's Perspective on Kristallnacht
- World Responses to Kristallnacht, Part 1

After groups have completed their charts and the discussion question, have a spokesperson for each group report to the class about one of the choices made in the reading that the group discussed, the reasons the individual made that choice, the role that the choice played in perpetuating or preventing injustice, and what this source suggests about human behavior in times of fear and crisis.

After each spokesperson's report, ask the class to respond by briefly discussing how each individual they learned about seems to define their universe of obligation and how that individual's sense of responsibility toward others influenced their actions.

3. Consider the Range of Human Behavior

Studying Kristallnacht and the responses from individuals and nations to that event provides an opportunity to introduce students to terms that describe a range of human behavior in response to unjust and troubling actions. For the final activity of this lesson, students will use context clues to help establish the definitions of four concepts that can be used to describe this range of behavior.[1]

Pass out the handout The Range of Human Behavior Vocabulary Terms and instruct students to use the context clues in the sentences of the first column to predict the definition of the underlined words.

---

1 Kelly Gallagher, *Deeper Reading: Comprehending Challenging Texts*, 4–12 (Portland, ME: Stenhouse Publishers, 2004), 77–78.

After asking a few students to share their predicted meanings of each word and how they came to that conclusion, you can share the dictionary definition and have them record the information in the third column of the chart.

- **Perpetrator:** A person carrying out a harmful, illegal, or immoral act.
- **Victim:** A person being targeted by the harmful, illegal, or immoral acts of a perpetrator.
- **Bystander:** A person who is present but not actively taking part in a situation or event.
- **Upstander:** A person speaking or acting in support of an individual or cause, particularly someone who intervenes on behalf of a person being attacked or bullied.

Invite students to critique the dictionary definitions. Do they have any questions about these definitions? How are they similar to or different from the students' own definitions? Are the dictionary definitions adequate, or do they need to be further revised?

You might point out to students that these dictionary definitions are written in the present tense ("carrying out" and "being targeted") and ask them to consider the fact that a person may act as a perpetrator or bystander at one moment in time and be targeted as a victim at another moment in time. Therefore, these are roles that people play rather than permanent identities.

Then ask students to return to the handout Decision Making in Times of Fear and Crisis from the previous activity and complete the fourth column by labeling the actions they identified as *victim*, *perpetrator*, *bystander*, and/or *upstander* behavior.

Finally, lead a discussion in which students reflect on the task of using these terms to label specific actions in the readings about Kristallnacht:

- Which terms were hardest to define?
- Which actions were most difficult to label?
- What has analyzing the variety of responses to Kristallnacht suggested to you about the ways people often respond to episodes of violence and terror?
- What roles can people who are not targeted by violence and terror play in perpetuating or preventing injustice?

Assessment

- Collect the handouts used in this lesson to assess students' understanding of the range of human behavior and how they are analyzing the choices individuals made in response to Kristallnacht.

- Apply the Text-to-Text, Text-to-Self, Text-to-World teaching strategy by assigning students to make connections to resources from this lesson. They can choose one or more of the readings or videos they encountered in this lesson and write a paragraph that describes how those stories connect to other literature, histories, current events, or personal experiences they know about. It is important to give students the choice about which of these three types of connections they want to write about, since their knowledge of literature, history, and, especially, their personal experiences will vary.

Extensions

1. Reflect on "The Hangman"

The allegorical poem "The Hangman" by Maurice Ogden explores the consequences of inaction after a hangman arrives and constructs his gallows in the center of a small town. You can either read the poem or watch the animated version. Conclude with an activity based on the Connect, Extend, Challenge strategy, in which students reflect on how the poem enhances their thinking about the range of choices in times of crisis and the reasons and explanations that bystanders might give for their choices.

2. Nazi Telegram Close Reading and Analysis

For classes with older students, the primary source reading "Nazi Telegram with Instructions for Kristallnacht" details the instructions sent from Reinhard Heydrich, major general of the SS, on November 10, 1938, that explained to local German officers how to carry out the anti-Jewish measures that became known as Kristallnacht. Consider sharing this document with students and asking the students to reflect in their journals on the following prompt:

> What new, different, or deeper understanding of Kristallnacht do you have as a result of reading this Nazi telegram? What new questions does the document raise for you?

Visit facinghistory.org/thhb to access these additional resources.

 Handout

The November 1938 Pogroms Viewing Guide

Directions: In the video *"Kristallnacht": The November 1938 Pogroms,* scholars discuss the events of Kristallnacht ("The Night of Broken Glass"), a series of violent attacks against Jews in Germany, Austria, and part of Czechoslovakia in November 1938. As you watch the film, record notes that help you answer the first two questions on this handout. Then respond to the third question after you have finished viewing the film.

1. What did Jews experience during and immediately after Kristallnacht?

2. What do you imagine other Germans would have seen and experienced that night and in the following days?

3. To what extent was Kristallnacht similar to what had come before? How was Kristallnacht different?

 Handout

Kristallnacht Testimony Viewing Guide

1. **While watching Elsbeth Lewin's testimony,** write down a phrase or sentence that resonates with you.

2. **After watching Elsbeth's testimony,** write a word or a short phrase that describes how you felt while listening to her story.

3. What can you learn about Kristallnacht from the personal testimony of Elsbeth Lewin that you could not learn from other sources, such as readings or videos, that focus on the historical aspects of the event?

Handout

Decision Making in Times of Fear and Crisis

Directions: After finishing your assigned reading with your group, work together to complete the first three columns of the graphic organizer together. Do not write anything in the fourth column until your teacher directs you to do so.

Name/Position	**Reaction to Kristallnacht** How did this person react to Kristallnacht? What choices did they make?	**Motivating Factors** What factors may have motivated this person and/or influenced their choices? How might this person's universe of obligation have influenced their choices?	**Label This Person's Actions**

228 FACING HISTORY & OURSELVES

Name/Position	**Reaction to Kristallnacht** How did this person react to Kristallnacht? What choices did they make?	**Motivating Factors** What factors may have motivated this person and/or influenced their choices? How might this person's universe of obligation have influenced their choices?	**Label This Person's Actions**

After your group has finished the reading and the first three columns of the chart, discuss the following question to prepare for the class discussion:

What does this source suggest about the variety of ways humans might respond to fear and crisis?

Reading

The Night of the Pogrom

Hugo Moses described what he experienced on Kristallnacht and in the days that followed:

> On the evening of 9 November 1938, the SA brown-shirts and the SS black-shirts met in bars to celebrate the fifteenth anniversary of [the Nazis'] failed putsch in Munich. Around eleven o'clock in the evening, I came home from a Jewish aid organization meeting and I can testify that most of the "German people" who a day later the government said were responsible for what happened that night lay peacefully in bed that evening. Everywhere lights had been put out, and nothing suggested that in the following hours such terrible events would take place.
>
> Even the uniformed party members were not in on the plan; the order to destroy Jewish property came shortly before they moved from the bars to the Jewish houses. (I have this information from the brother of an SS man who took an active part in the pogroms.)
>
> At 3 a.m. sharp, someone insistently rang at the door to my apartment. I went to the window and saw that the streetlights had been turned off. Nonetheless, I could make out a transport vehicle out of which emerged about twenty uniformed men. I recognized only one of them, a man who served as the leader; the rest came from other localities and cities and were distributed over the district in accordance with marching orders. I called out to my wife: "Don't be afraid, they are party men; please keep calm." Then I went to the door in my pajamas and opened it.
>
> A wave of alcohol hit me, and the mob forced its way into the home. A leader pushed by me and yanked the telephone off the wall. A leader of the SS men, green-faced with drunkenness, cocked his revolver as I watched and then held it to my forehead and slurred: "Do you know why we've come here, you swine?" I replied, "No," and he went on, "Because of the outrageous act committed in Paris, for which you are also to blame. If you even try to move, I'll shoot you like a pig." I kept quiet and stood, my hands behind my back, in the ice-cold [draft] coming in the open door. An SA man, who must have had a little human feeling, whispered to me: "Keep still. Don't move." During all this time and for another twenty minutes, the drunken SS leader fumbled threateningly with his revolver near my forehead. An inadvertent movement on my part or a clumsy one on his and my life would have been over. If I live to be a hundred, I will never forget that brutish face and those dreadful minutes.
>
> In the meantime, about ten uniformed men had invaded my house. I heard my wife cry: "What do you want with my children? You'll touch the children over my dead body!" Then I heard only the crashing of overturned furniture, the breaking of glass and the trampling of heavy boots. Weeks later, I was still waking from restless sleep, still hearing that crashing, hammering, and striking. We will never forget that night. After about half an hour, which seemed to me an eternity, the brutish drunks left our apartment, shouting and bellowing. The leader blew a whistle and as his subordinates stumbled past him, fired his revolver close to my head, two shots to the ceiling. I thought my eardrums had burst but I stood there like a wall. (A few hours later I showed a police officer the two bullet holes.) The last SA man

who left the building hit me on the head so hard with the walking stick he had used to destroy my pictures that a fortnight later the swelling was still perceptible. As he went out, he shouted at me: "There you are, you Jewish pig. Have fun." . . .

Towards dawn, a police officer appeared in order to determine whether there was any damage visible from the outside, such as broken window glass or furniture thrown out into the street. Shaking his head, he said to us, as I showed him the bullet holes from the preceding night: "It's a disgrace to see all this. It wouldn't have happened if we hadn't had to stay in our barracks." As he left, the officer said, "I hope it's the last time this will happen to you."

Two hours later, another police officer appeared and told Moses, "I'm sorry, but I have to arrest you."

I said to him, "I have never broken the law; tell me why you are arresting me." The officer: "I have been ordered to arrest all Jewish men. Don't make it so hard for me, just follow me." My wife accompanied me to the police station. . . .

At the police station, the officers were almost all nice to us. Only one officer told my wife: "Go home. You may see your husband again after a few years of forced labor in the concentration camp, if he's still alive." Another officer, who had been at school with me, said to his comrade: "Man, don't talk such nonsense." To my wife he said: "Just go home now, you'll soon have your husband back." A few hours later my little boy came to see me again. The experiences of that terrible night and my arrest were too much for the little soul, and he kept weeping and looking at me as if I were about to be shot. The police officer I knew well took the child by the hand and said to me: "I'll take the child to my office until you are taken away. If the boy saw that, he'd never forget it for the rest of his life."[1]

After several weeks in prison, Moses was released, thanks to the wife of an "Aryan" acquaintance. Soon after, he and his family managed to leave Germany. Moses told his story for the first time in 1940, just a year and a half after the pogrom. He refused to reveal the name of his town or the identities of those who helped him, because he did not want to endanger those left behind.

---

1 Uta Gerhardt and Thomas Karlauf, eds., *The Night of Broken Glass: Eyewitness Accounts of Kristallnacht* (Cambridge, UK: Polity Press, 2012), 21–23. Reproduced by permission from Polity Press.

 Reading

Opportunism during Kristallnacht

Despite Gestapo chief Heinrich Müller's instructions to state police that plundering be held to a minimum, the theft of goods, property, and money from Jews by German police, SS members, and civilians amid the chaos of Kristallnacht was widespread.

> German newspapers reported the looting of and theft from Jewish-owned businesses. According to Berlin's *Daily Herald* newspaper, "The great shopping centers looked as though they had suffered an air raid . . . Showcases were torn from the walls, furniture broken, electric signs smashed to fragments." The *News Chronicle* newspaper, also from Berlin, reported looters "smashing with peculiar care the windows of jewellery shops and, sniggering, stuffing into their pockets the trinkets and necklaces that fell on the pavements."[1]

In Vienna, Helga Milberg, who was eight years old during Kristallnacht, recalled that all of the goods and equipment from her father's butcher shop were stolen during the pogrom. "My father saw that the other storekeepers had helped themselves to everything," she wrote.[2] According to historian Martin Gilbert, when a British reporter asked a Nazi official about the widespread theft of goods from Jewish businesses during Kristallnacht in Vienna, the official responded:

> "We began seizing goods from Jewish shops because sooner or later they would have been nationalised [confiscated by the government] anyway." The goods thus seized, the official added, "will be used to compensate us for at least part of the damage which the Jews have been doing for years to the German people."[3]

Gilbert also describes how Kurt Füchsl's family lost their home.

> Seven-year-old Kurt Füchsl was bewildered by the events of Kristallnacht, and by being forced to leave home with his family early on the morning of November 10. He later recalled: "What happened, as recounted to me by my Mother, was that an interior decorator had taken a picture of our beautiful living room and displayed the picture of our apartment in his shop window. A Frau [Mrs.] Januba saw the picture and heard that we were Jewish. She came around to the apartment and asked if it was for sale. She was told it wasn't, but a few days later, on the morning of Kristallnacht, she came back with some officers and said, 'This apartment is now mine.' She showed a piece of paper with a swastika stamped on it and told us that we would have to leave by six that evening." Kurt Füchsl's mother protested to the officers who were accompanying Frau Januba that she had a sick child at home who was already asleep. "All right," they told her, "but you have to get out by six in the morning."[4]

---

1 Martin Gilbert, *Kristallnacht: Prelude to Destruction* (New York: HarperCollins, 2006), 46–47.
2 Gilbert, *Kristallnacht: Prelude to Destruction*, 54.
3 Gilbert, *Kristallnacht: Prelude to Destruction*, 59.
4 Gilbert, *Kristallnacht: Prelude to Destruction*, 62.

German officials also stole cash from Jewish businesses and families. Two weeks after Kristallnacht, Margarete Drexler wrote the following letter to the Gestapo, requesting the return of the money officials had taken from her home in Mannheim, Germany:

> Mannheim, 24 November 1938
>
> Margarete Drexler, Landau Pfalz Suedring St. 10
>
> To the Secret State Police Landau (Pfalz) The sum of 900 Marks in cash was confiscated from me in the course of the action of 10 November. I herewith request to act for the return of my money, as I need it urgently for me and my child's livelihood. I hope that my request will be granted, as my husband died as a result of his injuries during the war — he fought and died for his fatherland with extreme courage — and I am left without any income. Until recent years you could have found a photo of my husband on the wall next to the picture of Generalfeldmarschall [Paul] von Hindenburg in the canteen of the 23 Infantry regiment in Landau. This was done to honour his high military performance. His medals and decorations prove that he fought with great courage and honour. He received: The Iron Cross First Class, The Iron Cross Second Class, The Military Order of Merit Fourth Class with swords. The Military Order of Sanitation 2 class with a blue-white ribbon. This ribbon is usually bestowed only upon recipients of the Max Joseph Order, which accepts only members of the nobility. I can only hope that as a widow of such a man, so honoured by his country, my request for the return of my property will not be in vain.
>
> With German greetings,
> (signed) Frau Margarete Drexler
> Widow of reserve staff surgeon
> Dr. Hermann Drexler[5]

In 1940, Drexler was arrested and imprisoned in a concentration camp in France, where she died.

---

[5] Yad Vashem, "Looting during 'Crystal Night,'" accessed June 29, 2016, http://www.yadvashem.org/odot_pdf/Microsoft%20Word%20-%203238.pdf.

 Reading

A Family Responds to Kristallnacht

Marie Kahle (a teacher), her husband (a university professor and Lutheran pastor), and their sons witnessed the events of Kristallnacht in the city of Bonn and the effects those events had on their Jewish neighbors and colleagues. Marie Kahle wrote about the choices she and her family made the next day:

> On 10 November, 1938, at 11:30 in the morning, the wife of a Jewish colleague came to me and reported that both the synagogues in Bonn had been set on fire and that SS men had destroyed the Jewish shops, to which I replied: "That can't be true!" She gave me a manuscript to keep, her husband's life work. Then one of my sons brought the same news.
>
> My third son immediately went, without my knowing it, to a Jewish clockmaker's shop, helped the man's wife hide a few things and brought home a chest with the most valuable jewelry and time-pieces. Then he went to a chocolate shop, warned the owner and helped her move tea, coffee, cocoa, etc. to a room in the very back of the building. While three SS men were destroying everything in the front of the shop, he slipped out the back door with a suitcase full of securities and rode home with it on his bicycle. Later on, he spent weeks selling these hidden things to our acquaintances and thus made money for the two shop owners that the Gestapo knew nothing about. A Jewish colleague of my husband's stayed with us all day long on 10 November and thus avoided being arrested.
>
> From 11 November on, my sons worked furiously to help the Jewish shopkeepers clear out their shops. I couldn't take part in this myself because I did not want to endanger my husband's position. I could only visit the poor people. During one of these visits, my eldest son and I were surprised by a policeman, who wrote down my name. The consequence was a newspaper article . . . for 17 November 1938 headed "This is a betrayal of the people: Frau Kahle and her son help the Jewess Goldstein clear out."
>
> On the basis of this newspaper article, my husband was immediately suspended and he was forbidden to enter . . . the university buildings. My eldest son was also forbidden to enter the university. He was convicted by a disciplinary court. . . . During the night, our house was attacked. Window panes were broken, etc. . . . The police came a short time later but went away again immediately. One of the policemen advised me to look out into the street: there, we found written in large red letters on the pavement: "Traitors to the People! Jew-lovers!" We washed the writing away with turpentine.
>
> However, since the people were constantly coming back in their car, I openly rode away on my bicycle. I did not want to be beaten to death in front of my children and I was also only a danger to my family. I found shelter in a small Catholic convent, where the nuns were kind enough to look after me and my youngest child. During the interrogation by the Gestapo a few days later, I was asked whether I knew the license number of the car whose occupants

had made the attack. When I said "no", I was released. As I came out of the Gestapo building, this same car stood in front of the door. I even recognized the driver.

Particularly important in this whole period was a visit in 1939 by a well-known neurologist who, as Reich Education Director . . . was well up on Jewish matters. He told me, on two afternoons when we were alone, what would happen to me and my family along the lines of "Jews and friends of Jews must be exterminated. We are exterminating friends of Jews and all their offspring." Then he said that I could not be saved, but my family could. When I asked what I should do, he gave his answer in the form of a couple of stories in which the wife committed suicide and thereby saved her family. Then he asked: "How much Veronal [a sleeping pill] do you have?" When I answered, "Only two grams," he wrote me a prescription for the quantity that I was lacking. I carried the Veronal around with me for a few days, but then decided not to die, but instead to try to escape abroad with my family.

In four months, only three of my husband's colleagues dared to visit us. I was not allowed to go out during the day. When one evening I met a colleague's wife and complained that no friends or acquaintances had dared to visit me, she said: "That's not cowardice; we are just facing facts."[1]

Soon after, the family left Germany.

---

[1] Marie Kahle, in *The Night of Broken Glass: Eyewitness Accounts of Kristallnacht,* ed. Uta Gerhardt and Thomas Karlauf (Cambridge, UK: Polity Press, 2012), 88–90. Reproduced by permission from Polity Press.

Reading

Thoroughly Reprehensible Behavior

Wilhelm Kahle, Marie Kahle's eldest son, was a student at the University of Bonn. He was called before the university's disciplinary court for helping a Jewish storekeeper restore order to her shop after Kristallnacht. His "crimes" are spelled out in this "Disciplinary Judgment."

> The student of musicology Wilhelm Kahle will be punished, because of behavior unworthy of a student in regard to the protest action against Jewish businesses, by dismissal from the university and denial of credit for the semester's work.
>
> On 10 November 1938, there occurred in Bonn, as a result of the murder of the legation councilor vom Rath, a demonstration against Jews, in which the corset shop owned by the Jewess E. Goldstein was affected. On the late afternoon of 12 November 1938, the accused went with his mother to this shop, in which the latter had earlier made purchases. When they arrived at the shop, around 6 or 6:30 p.m., three Jewish females were leaving it. In the shop they met the owner and another Jewish person named Herz. The shop owner was busy putting boxes back on the shelves. After they had been there for about three minutes, Police Sergeant Peter Stammen entered the shop and wrote down the names of the Jewish persons and then also the name of the student Kahle's mother, and in doing so had some difficulties with the latter. He then turned to the student Kahle, who was putting the boxes that were on the counter back on the shelves, and asked him whether he was an interior decorator. The student said he was not, and then gave his name.
>
> Contrary to the charge, the Disciplinary Court has not been able to determine that the accused intended from the outset . . . to go to the Jewish shop. It is more of the opinion that no preconceived intention lay behind this visit, but rather that the visit took place only on the occasion of passing by the demolished shop. Further, the Disciplinary Court has not derived from the proceedings the impression that the student helped the Jewess put her merchandise back on the shelves but sees the student's actions simply as an effort, without any special intention, to help the Jewess in her work or to support her in some way.
>
> Nonetheless, the student's behavior is thoroughly reprehensible. By finding it justifiable to enter a Jewish shop after the given incidents, he seriously endangered the reputation and dignity of the university and thereby violated his academic duties. Articles II and III of the Disciplinary Code for Students, 1 April 1935. He was to be penalized.
>
> The accused's behavior requires a vigorous atonement. Since the accused seemed to be a little inept and awkward during the proceedings and was obviously under the influence of his mother, the Disciplinary Court has decided in mitigation merely to dismiss him from the university and deny him the credit for the entire semester's work.

In imposing this punishment, which is mild in relation to the offense, the Disciplinary Court has acted on the basis of the expectation that the student will pursue his further education at a greater distance from his parents' home, so that in the future he can mature into a more independent, more self-confident and more responsible person.[1]

---

1 Uta Gerhardt and Thomas Karlauf, eds., *The Night of Broken Glass: Eyewitness Accounts of Kristallnacht* (Cambridge, UK: Polity Press, 2012), 90–91. Reproduced by permission from Polity Press.

Reading

A Visitor's Perspective on Kristallnacht

René Juvet, a Swiss merchant, was visiting friends in the countryside during the events of Kristallnacht. The next morning he drove to the town of Bayreuth, where he saw people watching as houses burned to the ground. At one point, he got out of his car to take a closer look at a crowd gathered in front of a warehouse where dozens of Jews were being held.

> I was reluctant to add myself to the assembled crowd but I had to see with my own eyes what was happening there. Through the great windows you could see perhaps fifty people in a bleak, empty hall. Most of them stood against the wall, staring gloomily, a few walked restlessly about, others were sitting—in spite of the severe cold—on the bare floor. Almost all of them, incidentally, were inadequately dressed; some only had thrown on a topcoat over their nightclothes. The SA people who had picked them up during the night had apparently not allowed them time to put on more clothing. Compared to what happened later, this was only a small beginning.

At the end of his description of Kristallnacht, Juvet writes:

> To the credit of my [non-Jewish German colleagues] I can report that they—with the exception of Neder, who took part in the operation in his role as an SA Führer—disapproved of the excesses. Some more, others less. Waldmeyer said nothing, but he was very thoughtful in ensuing days; Hoffmann, who could almost count himself as one of the old guard, made no attempt to conceal his horror from me. I also heard that the workers were outraged. . . .
>
> A little while after this I met our Nuremberg representative, a harmless and industrious person. He was a member of the SA but was, by chance, kept away from home that evening. . . .
>
> "I am happy I was not in Nuremberg that evening, it certainly would have rubbed me the wrong way," said our representative.
>
> I asked him whether he would have taken part if he had been there. "Of course," he said, "orders are orders."
>
> His words clarified a whole lot of things for me.[1]

---

[1] René Juvet, "Kristallnacht," in *Travels in the Reich, 1933–1945: Foreign Authors Report from Germany*, ed. Oliver Lubrich (Chicago: University of Chicago Press, 2010), 176–78.

 Reading

World Responses to Kristallnacht, Part 1

Newspapers around the world reported on the events of Kristallnacht. The following story by Otto D. Tolischus of the *New York Times* was typical of many.

> A wave of destruction, looting and incendiaries [fires] unparalleled in Germany since the Thirty Years War and in Europe generally since the Bolshevist revolution, swept over Greater Germany today as National Socialist cohorts took vengeance on Jewish shops, offices and synagogues for the murder by a young Polish Jew of Ernst vom Rath, third secretary of the German Embassy in Paris.
>
> Beginning systematically in the early morning hours in almost every town and city in the country, the wrecking, looting and burning continued all day. Huge but mostly silent crowds looked on and the police confined themselves to regulating traffic and making wholesale arrests of Jews "for their own protection."
>
> All day the main shopping districts as well as the side streets of Berlin and innumerable other places resounded to the shattering of shop windows falling to the pavement, the dull thuds of furniture and burning shops and synagogues. Although shop fires were quickly extinguished, synagogue fires were merely kept from spreading to adjoining buildings.[1]

People everywhere were outraged. As the archbishop of Canterbury, Cosmo Gordon Lang, wrote in a November 12 letter to the editor of the *London Times*, "There are times when the mere instincts of humanity make silence impossible." Thousands of Americans agreed. They showed their outrage at huge rallies held in support of German Jews. In reporting these events to Berlin, the German ambassador expressed a fear that such protests might jeopardize the agreement concerning the Sudetenland in Czechoslovakia.

Leaders in Britain and France were very careful in how they responded. When members of Britain's Parliament asked Neville Chamberlain to condemn the pogrom, he simply said that newspaper reports were "substantially correct." He also expressed "deep and widespread sympathy" for those who were "to suffer so severely" for the "senseless crime committed in Paris."[2]

Similar comments from French leaders led the editor of a newspaper called *La Lumière* to warn, "In the past, when we protested against massacres in Ethiopia, China, Spain, we were told, 'Silence! You are warmongering.' When we protested against the mutilation of Czechoslovakia, we were told 'Keep quiet! You are a war party.' Today, when we protest against the contemptible persecution of defenseless Jews and their wives and children, we are told, 'Be silent! France is afraid.'"[3]

---

1 Otto D. Tolischus, "The Pogrom," *New York Times*, November 19, 1938.
2 "Chamberlain Deplores Nazi Pogroms; Acts to Aid British Jews in Reich," *Jewish Telegraphic Agency*, November 14, 1938, accessed April 26, 2016, http://www.jta.org/1938/11/15/archive/chamberlain-deplores-nazi-pogroms-acts-to-aid-british-jews-in-reich.
3 Quoted in Anthony Read and David Fisher, *Kristallnacht: The Unleashing of the Holocaust* (New York: Peter Bedrick Books, 1989), 155.

Condemnation from leaders in the United States was broad-based and widespread. Clergymen of all faiths spoke out against the burning of synagogues; politicians of all parties—Republicans and Democrats, isolationists and interventionists—denounced the violence against Jews and their houses of worship. The only world leader to take a stand was President Franklin D. Roosevelt. On November 15, six days after the pogrom, he opened a press conference by stating, "The news of the last few days from Germany has deeply shocked public opinion in the United States. Such news from any part of the world would produce a similar profound reaction among American people in every part of the nation. I myself could scarcely believe that such things could occur in a twentieth-century civilization."

But Roosevelt's response had to take into account widespread isolationist and antisemitic feelings in his administration, in Congress, and in the country. At his press conference, Roosevelt announced that the United States was withdrawing its ambassador to Germany, but he did not offer to help the thousands of Jews who were trying desperately to leave the Third Reich.

Handout

The Range of Human Behavior Vocabulary Terms

Directions: Use the context clues in the sentence in the first column to predict the meaning of each underlined term, and write your definition in the center column. Leave the third column blank.[1]

Sentence	Predicted Meaning	Actual Meaning
The **perpetrator** of the crime was caught not long after robbing the convenience store and fleeing on foot down the crowded street.		
The **victim** of bullying didn't want to go to school and instead crawled back into bed and pretended to be sick.		
Despite feeling a knot in her stomach while reading the hateful comments on her childhood friend's social media feed, the **bystander** put away her phone and headed to the gym for volleyball practice.		
After three days of reading the increasing number of homophobic comments and threats on his friend's blog, the **upstander** picked up his phone and texted: "You don't deserve this treatment."		

1 Kelly Gallagher, *Deeper Reading: Comprehending Challenging Texts, 4–12* (Portland, ME: Stenhouse Publishers, 2004), 77–78.

Unit Essential Question What does learning about the choices people made during the Weimar Republic, the rise of the Nazi Party, and the Holocaust teach us about the power and impact of our choices today?

Lesson

Responding to a Refugee Crisis

Duration
One 50-minute class period

Materials

Readings
Jewish Refugees from Austria
The Evian Conference
World Responses to Kristallnacht, Part 2

Videos
Turned Away on the M.S. *St. Louis*
Preparing for the Kindertransport

Teaching Strategies
Barometer
Jigsaw
S-I-T

Find all materials referenced in this lesson at facinghistory.org/thhb.

Guiding Questions

- What challenges prevented many Jews from leaving Nazi Germany?
- What responsibility does a country have to help those from another country who are facing danger?

Learning Objectives

- Students will analyze texts describing the choices countries made in response to the European Jewish refugee crisis in the late 1930s in order to deepen their thinking about the responsibilities of governments and individuals to people outside their borders.

- Students will respond to video testimony of Holocaust survivors describing the difficulties of escaping Nazi Germany in 1939.

Overview

In the previous lesson, students learned about Kristallnacht and explored the range of choices people made in response to the violence and destruction of those coordinated attacks on Jews in Nazi Germany. In this lesson, students will learn about one significant consequence of Kristallnacht and other instances of Nazi aggression in 1938: an intensifying refugee crisis. They will explore how countries around the world responded to thousands of European Jews trying to escape the danger of Nazi Germany. Students will think deeply about the rights and responsibilities of governments to respond to events that take place within the borders of other countries, and they will hear the testimonies of Holocaust survivors describing their experiences as they tried to escape from Nazi Germany before World War II.

Context

Germany's aggressive steps to expand its borders in 1938 touched off both an international political crisis, as world leaders scrambled to avoid war, and a humanitarian refugee crisis, as hundreds of thousands of people, mostly Jews, sought safety from the Nazis.

The annexation of Austria into the Third Reich spelled terror for the 200,000 Jews in that country. Within weeks of the *Anschluss* (a term used to refer to the union of Germany and Austria in 1938), foreign journalists in Austria were reporting hundreds of antisemitic incidents throughout the nation. Some noted a sharp increase in suicides, as thousands of Jews tried desperately to emigrate only to encounter roadblocks wherever they turned. Their difficulty in leaving "Greater Germany" was not with the Nazis, who, faced with the problem of including an additional 200,000 Jews in the Reich, were eager to see Jews leave the country as long as they left their money and other possessions behind. The problem was with other nations, most of whom had no interest in accepting thousands of penniless Jewish refugees. US President Franklin Roosevelt believed he did not have the public's support to ask Congress to change the quota system under which immigrants were admitted. In one poll, 67% of Americans said that the United States should keep Jewish refugees out.[1]

Instead, Roosevelt called for an international conference at Evian, France, to discuss the growing crisis. Yet none of the countries that gathered, except the Dominican Republic, pledged to help. Only M. J. M. Yepes of Colombia, a professor who also served as the legal advisor to his country's permanent delegation to the League of Nations, addressed the real issue at the Evian conference. He told delegates that there were two central questions that they must confront. One was a question of fact that each nation had to answer for itself: How many refugees would it admit? The other question involved a matter of principle: "Can a State, without upsetting the basis of our civilization, and, indeed, of all civilization, arbitrarily withdraw nationality from a whole class of its citizens, thereby making them Stateless Persons whom no country is compelled to receive on its territory?"[2] Yepes went on to say that as long as that central problem was not decided, the work of the conference would not be lasting and a dangerous example would be set—an example that in his view would make the world "uninhabitable." But most delegates did not want to deal with either issue.[3]

The events of Kristallnacht in November 1938 only increased the urgency felt by hundreds of thousands of Jews to leave the Third Reich. But both public opinion and political will against admitting refugees held strong in most countries, including the United States.

Nevertheless, there were some successful rescue efforts, as some individual activists and diplomats devised ways to issue visas to allow Jews to emigrate. Also, a group of Christians and Jews in England responded with a plan to rescue Jewish

---

1 Ishaan Tharoor, "What Americans thought of Jewish refugees on the eve of World War II," *Washington Post*, November 17, 2015, accessed June 29, 2016, https://www.washingtonpost.com/news/worldviews/wp/2015/11/17/what-americans-thought-of-jewish-refugees-on-the-eve-of-world-war-ii/.
2 Debórah Dwork and Robert Jan van Pelt, *Flight from the Reich: Refugee Jews, 1933–1946* (New York: W. W. Norton, 2009), 100.
3 Dwork and van Pelt, *Flight from the Reich*, 100.

children from the Nazis. In the operation known as the Kindertransport, 10,000 children under the age of 17 were brought to England between December 1938 and September 1939. The rescue effort was focused on children because the organizers feared the British would see adults as competitors for jobs, housing, and social services. Children were forced to separate from their parents (often permanently), and they were placed in English homes, schools, and farms, where they were raised at least through the war years.

Despite the difficulties of emigration, by 1939, nearly half of the 1933 Jewish population of Germany had left the country. Many more were desperate to obtain visas to get out. Among those who had the "right papers" were the 937 men, women, and children who boarded a ship, the *St. Louis*, in Hamburg, Germany, on May 14. The voyage of the *St. Louis* has become both a symbol of the refugee crisis and a cautionary tale about the indifference of countries to the plight of those in danger outside their borders. As the *St. Louis* neared Cuba, the Cuban government, in response to pressure from Cubans opposed to increased Jewish immigration, suddenly canceled the landing permits of all Jewish passengers (30 non-Jews were permitted to enter the country). The ship left Havana and sailed along the Florida coast, hoping to obtain permission for the passengers to enter another country in North or South America. No permission was granted. On June 7, the captain had no choice but to return to Germany with most of his passengers still on board. The Nazis turned the incident into propaganda. They claimed that it demonstrated that Jews were universally disliked and distrusted. On June 10, Belgium accepted 200 passengers from the *St. Louis*. Two days later, the Netherlands promised to take in 194. Britain and France admitted the rest.

Furious at the role the US government had played in the crisis, a resident of Richmond, Virginia, wrote:

> [The] press reported that the ship came close enough to Miami for the refugees to see the lights of the city. The press also reported that the U.S. Coast Guard, under instructions from Washington, followed the ship . . . to prevent any people landing on our shores. And during the days when this horrible tragedy was being enacted right at our doors, our government in Washington made no effort to relieve the desperate situation of these people, but on the contrary gave orders that they be kept out of the country. . . . The failure to take any steps whatsoever to assist these distressed, persecuted Jews in their hour of extremity was one of the most disgraceful things which has happened in American history and leaves a stain and brand of shame upon the record of our nation.[4]

Notes to Teacher

1. Discussing the Anschluss and the Sudetenland

This unit does not explore the history of the *Anschluss* (the German annexation of Austria) and the Nazi occupation of the Sudetenland in Czechoslovakia. Yet these are two significant events in 1938 that contributed to the refugee crisis and to international tensions that led to World War II. It is important to explain briefly to students that Germany began to expand its borders in 1938 so that

---

4 Quoted in Arthur Morse, *While Six Million Died: A Chronicle of American Apathy* (New York: Overlook Press, 1985), 280.

they can understand why some of the stories included in the resources they encounter took place in Austria and Czechoslovakia. Consult Chapter 7 of *Holocaust and Human Behavior* for additional resources that can provide background knowledge or classroom activities.

2. Previewing Vocabulary

The following are key vocabulary terms used in this lesson:

- Refugee
- Visa
- Quota

Add these words to your word wall, if you are using one for this unit, and provide necessary support to help students learn these words as you teach the lesson.

Activities

1. Reflect on the Rights and Responsibilities of Countries to Act

Tell students that in this lesson they will learn about the efforts of many Jews to leave Nazi-controlled areas and the barriers they faced, in large part, because of other countries' unwillingness to help them. Begin by asking students to copy the statement below into their journals and then respond to it. Do they agree or disagree with the statement. Why?

> When a government commits violence against the people of its own country, other countries have a responsibility to intervene, stop the violence, and help the victims.

After students have had a few minutes to respond, encourage them to share their viewpoints in a short class discussion. If you have time, you might debrief their responses using the Barometer teaching strategy.

2. Analyze World Responses to German Aggression

Explain to students that in 1938, Nazi Germany expanded into Austria and Czechoslovakia without other nations acting in those countries' defense. Germany's expansion put millions more Jews in danger of persecution by the Nazis, and the violence of Kristallnacht (in November 1938) caused many fearful Jews in these countries to try to emigrate to other countries. But emigration wasn't so simple, because other countries weren't willing to take them in.

Prepare the class for Jigsaw discussions by arranging students in groups of three. Assign one of the following three readings to each group:

- Jewish Refugees from Austria
- The Evian Conference
- World Responses to Kristallnacht, Part 2

Each group will read its reading together and then discuss the following questions:

> How did the countries in this reading respond to the refugee crisis? What reasons did they give for their response? What determined whether or not countries were willing to accept Jewish refugees? What do the countries' responses say about how each of them defined its universe of obligation?

Let students know that they will each be required to share their group's response to these questions with a new group, and encourage them to each write down their group's response in preparation for that task.

After students have had time to read and discuss their readings, instruct the class to form "expert" groups of three. Set up these groups so that each member of an expert group will bring a different reading to the group. In their new groups, students should take turns summarizing their readings and sharing their first group's response to the discussion question.

After the expert groups have completed their tasks, ask students to take a moment to complete an S-I-T reflection in their journals. They should name and write about one thing they learned about world responses to the refugee crisis that *surprises* them, one thing that they find *interesting*, and one thing that *troubles* them.

3. Respond to Personal Accounts of the Refugee Crisis

Tell students that they will watch two videos of Holocaust survivors discussing their efforts to leave Germany in 1939.

Before showing the first video, Turned Away on the M.S. *St. Louis* (06:28), share with students the following context. Then play the video at facinghistory.org/thhb.

> On May 14, 937 men, women, and children boarded a ship, the *St. Louis*, in Hamburg, Germany. Each had paid $150—a significant sum of money in 1939—for written permission to enter Cuba. While the ship crossed the Atlantic Ocean, the Cuban government changed its mind and prohibited the refugees from entering the country. The ship sailed along the coast of Florida, hoping the US government would accept the refugees, but the United States turned the ship away, and it sailed back to Europe. The passengers were eventually admitted into Belgium, the Netherlands, Britain, and France. In this video, Holocaust survivor Sol Messinger describes his experiences aboard the M.S. *St. Louis*.

Before showing the second video, Preparing for the Kindertransport (07:06), share with students the following context. Then play the video at facinghistory.org/thhb.

> Between December 1938 and September 1939, a group of Christians and Jews organized an effort to rescue Jewish children, under the age of 17, by bringing them to England to live with families or at schools and on farms. They focused their efforts on children because they feared the British would see adults as competitors for jobs, housing, and social services. In all, the operation rescued 10,000 children, though it forced them

to separate from their families (often permanently). In this video, Vera Gissing, a Holocaust survivor from Czechoslovakia, recalls how her family prepared her for the Kindertransport.

After viewing the videos, ask students to respond to the following questions in their journals:

- What did watching these videos make you think and feel?
- How does hearing a firsthand account from a survivor add to your understanding of the difficulties Jews experienced in attempting to flee Nazi Germany?

Finish the lesson by asking students to review their journal response from the beginning of the lesson. Ask them now to write for a moment about how what they learned and experienced in this lesson either changed or confirmed their initial thinking about whether or not countries have a responsibility to intervene when other countries act violently toward the people living within their own borders.

Assessment

- Collect the S-I-T reflections from Activity 2 to gauge students' understanding of and reaction to the plight of refugees in 1938 and the refusal of so many countries to help. If you have established that journals are private in your classroom, have students complete the reflection on a separate sheet of paper to turn in.

- Listen carefully to students' contributions to the Jigsaw discussions in this lesson to check for understanding and the quality of their contributions to each other's learning.

Extensions

1. Make Connections to the Contemporary Refugee Crisis

In the 2010s, Europe has faced its greatest humanitarian and refugee crisis since the 1930s. The reading "Memory and Decision Making in Europe Today" explores the historical parallels between these two crises. You might share this reading with students and use the connection questions that follow to begin a class discussion about the echoes of history in contemporary Europe. You might also assign students to research the current state of the refugee crisis in Europe (as well as those taking place in Myanmar and other parts of the world) to extend their exploration.

2. Show *America and the Holocaust*

The film *America and the Holocaust* (01:21:00) traces the history of the US response to the actions of the Nazi government through the 1930s, World War II, and the Holocaust. One particular clip (05:00–20:30) is worth showing to students to help them better understand the extent of antisemitism and fear of refugees in the United States in the 1930s. After watching the clip, use the Connect, Extend, Challenge strategy to debrief with students.

3. Go Deeper in *Holocaust and Human Behavior*

Chapter 7 of *Holocaust and Human Behavior* includes several readings that explain Nazi Germany's takeover of Austria (known as the Anschluss) and expansion into Czechoslovakia. The chapter also includes additional information about the refugee crisis, the refusal of countries to take in refugees, and efforts to rescue Jews from Nazi Germany on the eve of World War II. Consider using these resources in additional activities with students, or read the chapter for your own background information.

Visit **facinghistory.org/thhb** to access these additional resources.

Reading

Jewish Refugees from Austria

The incorporation of Austria into Germany spelled terror for the 200,000 Jews in that country. Between 1,500 and 3,500 Austrian Jews applied for immigration visas (documents needed for permission to enter a country) to come to the United States. President Franklin Roosevelt was sympathetic to their plight but believed that he did not have the public's support to ask Congress to change the quota system under which immigrants were admitted. A poll published in *Fortune* magazine in 1938 reveals much about public opinion in the United States.

Attitudes toward Allowing German, Austrian, and Other Political Refugees into the United States, July 1938

We should encourage their arrival even if our immigration quotas are raised.	4.9%
We should allow their arrival but not raise our immigration quotas.	18.2%
Given our current conditions, we should keep them out.	67.4%
I don't know.	9.5%

Source: *Fortune* magazine, July 1938.

Reading

The Evian Conference

US President Franklin Roosevelt called for an international conference in 1938 to discuss the growing Jewish refugee crisis intensified by the German takeover of Austria.

In July 1938, delegates from 32 nations met in Evian, France. They were joined by representatives from dozens of relief organizations and other groups, as well as hundreds of reporters. At the conference, each delegate formally expressed sorrow over the growing number of "refugees" and "deportees," boasted of his nation's traditional hospitality, and lamented that his nation was unable to do more in the "present situation."

Canadian Prime Minister Mackenzie King wrote in his diary around that time, "We must . . . seek to keep this part of the Continent free from unrest and from too great an intermixture of foreign strains of blood." In his view, nothing was to be gained "by creating an internal problem in an effort to meet an international one."[1]

The British, noting that many refugees wanted to go to Palestine, which was then under British rule, said they would like to admit more refugees, but in view of the ongoing conflict between Arabs and Jews, it was not a practical solution. The French claimed that their country had already done more than its fair share. The Americans noted that Congress would have to approve any change in the nation's immigration laws—legislation that set a limit on the number of immigrants the United States would accept from each country each year.

Historians Richard Breitman and Allan Lichtman describe the responses of other countries at the conference:

> Nicaragua, Costa Rica, Honduras, and Panama stated that they wanted no traders or intellectuals, code words for Jews. Argentina said it had already accommodated enough immigrants from Central Europe. Canada cited its unemployment problem. Australia said that it had no "racial problems" and did not want to create any by bringing in Jewish refugees. Imperial countries such as Britain, France, and the Netherlands said that their tropical territories offered only limited prospects for European refugees. League of Nations High Commissioner Sir Neill Malcolm was openly hostile to the idea of a new refugee organization . . . The *Washington Post* headlined one story on the conference, "YES, BUT—." It noted, "it has been a disappointment, if not altogether a surprise . . . that delegates take the floor to say, We feel sorry for the refugees and potential refugees but—."[2]

The Dominican Republic was the only country that agreed to accept Jewish immigrants. In 1937, the nation's leader, Rafael Trujillo, had ordered his soldiers to massacre thousands of Haitians at the Dominican border. Historians believe he hoped that accepting Jewish refugees might repair his image internationally. He also hoped that Jews would marry local inhabitants and "lighten" the population. He granted visas to a thousand Jews who were to live in Sosúa, a special community established for them.

---

1 Quoted in Irving Abella and Harold Troper, *None Is Too Many: Canada and the Jews of Europe, 1933–1948* (New York: Random House, 1983), 17.
2 Richard Breitman and Allan J. Lichtman, *FDR and the Jews* (Cambridge, MA: Belknap Press of Harvard University Press, 2013), 109.

 Reading

World Responses to Kristallnacht, Part 2

Despite the outrage against the violence in Germany, there was not much support for lifting or modifying immigration restrictions. Since the beginning of the Great Depression in 1929, Americans had been worried about unemployment and the economy and coping with labor unrest. They had been unwilling to confront racism in their own country and fearful of being drawn into foreign conflicts in which they felt their country had no interest. All these matters seemed much more important than the problem of stateless Jews in Europe. Although many were willing to accept a few famous writers, artists, and scientists who happened to be Jews, they were not willing to let in thousands of other Jews.

Few Americans were violently antisemitic, but many felt that Jews should be "kept in their place." Enforcement of the nation's immigration laws reflected these views. The United States could legally admit 27,000 immigrants from Germany each year. Yet in 1934, the State Department had allowed only about 5,000 to enter the country. Approximately 6,000 were permitted to enter in 1935 and less than 11,000 in 1936.

In February 1939, Senator Robert Wagner of New York and Representative Edith Nourse Rogers of Massachusetts sponsored a bill based on a popular British program. Between 1938 and 1939, the British admitted 10,000 unaccompanied Jewish children from "Greater Germany" as part of a program known as the Kindertransport (children's transport). Wagner and Rogers wanted Congress to temporarily admit 20,000 Jewish children until it was safe for them to return home. The first 10,000 would arrive in 1939 and the remaining 10,000 in 1940. Most of these children were too young to work, so they would not take away jobs from Americans. Furthermore, their stay would not cost taxpayers a penny because various Jewish groups had agreed to assume financial responsibility for the children.

Yet the bill encountered strong opposition. In January 1939, Gallup, a polling organization, began asking Americans the following question: "It has been proposed to bring to this country 10,000 refugee children from Germany—most of them Jewish—to be taken care of in American homes. Should the government permit these children to come in?"[1] In response, 61% said that the government should not permit the children to come into the country, 30% said that the children should be permitted to come, and 9% said that they had no opinion.[2]

Why, some opponents asked, were Christian children from countries threatened by the Nazis or Chinese children (Japan had invaded China in 1935) not included? Others made openly antisemitic remarks. The wife of the US commissioner of immigration (and the cousin of

---

1 Ishaan Tharoor, "What Americans thought of Jewish refugees on the eve of World War II," *Washington Post*, November 17, 2015, accessed June 29, 2016, https://www.washingtonpost.com/news/worldviews/wp/2015/11/17/what-americans-thought-of-jewish-refugees-on-the-eve-of-world-war-ii/.

2 Frank Newport, "Historical Review: Americans' Views on Refugees Coming to U.S.," Gallup, last modified November 19, 2015, accessed June 29, 2016, http://www.gallup.com/opinion/polling-matters/186716/historical-review-americans-views-refugees-coming.aspx.

President Roosevelt) warned that those "20,000 charming children would all too soon grow into 20,000 ugly adults."[3] The bill was never passed.

In the summer of 1940, after World War II had begun and the Germans were bombing British cities, the US Congress did vote to accept thousands of British children, mostly non-Jewish, into the country.

---

[3] Marc Lee Raphael, *Judaism in America* (New York: Columbia University Press, 2003), 297.

Unit Essential Question	What does learning about the choices people made during the Weimar Republic, the rise of the Nazi Party, and the Holocaust teach us about the power and impact of our choices today?

Lesson 18

Race and Space

Duration
One 50-minute class period

Materials

Video
Hitler's Ideology: Race, Land, and Conquest

Map
The Growth of Nazi Germany

Handout
Notes on the Growth of Nazi Germany, 1933–1939

Readings
Colonizing Poland
"Cultural Missionaries"

Teaching Strategies
S-I-T
Save the Last Word for Me

Find all materials referenced in this lesson at facinghistory.org/thhb.

Guiding Question

- How did the Nazis' beliefs about "race and space" influence Germany's violent aggression toward other nations, groups, and individuals in the first years of World War II?

Learning Objectives

- Students will be able to explain the relationship between the Nazis' beliefs about race and their quest for "living space," and how these ideas played a central role in Germany's aggression toward other nations, groups, and individuals in the first years of World War II.
- After analyzing two firsthand accounts, students will be able to explain how the "race and space" ideology provided justification and motivation for many Germans to participate in the Nazi plans for expansion and conquest, just as it led to dire consequences for those of so-called inferior races who lived in the newly conquered lands.

Overview

In the previous lesson, students analyzed the violent pogroms of Kristallnacht, a major escalation in the Nazis' campaigns against Jews. In this lesson, students will continue this unit's historical case study by examining the Nazi ideology of "race and space," a belief system that provided a rationale for their instigation of World War II and their perpetration of genocide. Students will then connect this ideology to Germany's expansion throughout Europe, including the annexation of Austria and the Sudetenland, the invasion of Poland, and eventually the conquest of most of mainland Europe. Finally, students will examine the effects of the Nazis' beliefs about "race and space" on individuals, through a close reading of eyewitness accounts by two individuals affected in different ways by the Germans' 1939 invasion of Poland.

Context

Hitler and the Nazis believed that the driving force of history was a struggle between races, a struggle that would only end when the superior race—in Hitler's view, the Aryans—achieved supremacy over all the other races. By 1939, when Germany invaded Poland and touched off World War II in Europe, the Nazis' vision of dominance increasingly necessitated the conquest and occupation of other countries. Historian Doris Bergen writes, "For Hitler, these two notions of race and space were intertwined. Any race that was not expanding, he believed, was doomed to disappear. Without living space—land to produce food and raise new generations of soldiers and mothers—a race could not grow."[1]

Germany's annexation of Austria and the Sudetenland in 1938 was a significant first step in the Nazis' efforts to expand the Reich. The acquisitions represented a symbolic as well as territorial victory. By regaining most of Germany's World War I losses, Hitler sought to unite ethnic Germans—people of German descent, sharing supposed "German blood"—into one nation. Emboldened by success in Austria and the Sudetenland, in 1939 the Nazis and many Germans were ready to go to war for additional "living space" for their nation. The invasion of Poland that year instigated war in Europe and a succession of German military victories throughout the continent. By December 1941, Germany had conquered most of mainland Europe, from France in the west to the outskirts of Moscow in the Soviet Union in the east. This conquest brought about what Hitler saw as a "New Order" in Europe.

This lesson provides insight into how the Nazis' racial ideology shaped their military and expansion strategies, ultimately sparking the outbreak of World War II. But it also highlights the cultural aspects of conquest, demonstrating how ordinary Germans' belief in their ethnic superiority and the righteousness of their work as "cultural missionaries" in foreign countries justified increasingly egregious acts of violence and mass murder. Indeed, the "New Order" the Nazis imposed on Europe carried significant benefits for many Germans. These included enhanced national and racial pride and material gains for German citizens in the form of cheap goods, as well as new jobs, homes, and land in conquered countries.

By reading eyewitness accounts, students will also gain an understanding of how Jews and other people deemed inferior by the Nazis experienced German occupation. For non-Germans, consequences of the Nazi plans for "race and space" were economic loss, horrible suffering, and the death of millions who the Nazis believed could not be productive members of the Reich. These groups included mentally and physically disabled people, whose murder the Nazis justified as a necessity of war. They also included members of what the Nazis considered to be inferior races—such as Poles, Slavs, Roma, and Sinti—who were taken from their homes and often confined to camps and murdered, as well. And of course the Nazi "race and space" worldview involved special contempt for Jews, who were killed in increasing numbers as the war wore on.

---

1 Doris L. Bergen, *War and Genocide: A Concise History of the Holocaust,* 3rd ed. (Lanham, MD: Rowman & Littlefield, 2016), 52.

Notes to Teacher

1. **Explaining *Ideology***

    This lesson focuses on the meaning and consequences of the Nazi ideology that historians refer to as "race and space." *Ideology* can be a complicated concept to explain. In this lesson, it is defined as "a framework of beliefs and ideals about the way the world works." The first activity in this lesson provides some suggestions for how to explain what an ideology is. Examples of ideologies can be helpful in explaining the concept to students, but it is important for you to choose a few examples that your students likely know about. For instance, if students have taken an American history course that covers westward expansion, they may be familiar with the basic tenets of manifest destiny, making it a good example of an ideology to offer in this lesson. If students are struggling to grasp the meaning of *ideology*, you might ask them to use the definition and the examples you provide to brainstorm together some additional examples of ideologies that influence people's choices in the world today. Through the ensuing discussion, evaluating the examples students brainstorm, you can help them zero in on a firmer understanding of the concept.

2. **Creating a Mini-Lecture**

    One activity in this lesson includes a mini-lecture, which you may choose to transfer to a PowerPoint presentation or some other format for students. If you would like to add images and other multimedia resources, you might choose to incorporate the following related images, available at **facinghistory.org/thhb**:

    - "League of German Girls in the Warthegau"
    - "Jews in German-Polish Border Town"
    - "Exhibit on Germany's Colonization of Poland"

3. **Previewing Vocabulary**

    The following are key vocabulary terms used in this lesson:

    - Ideology
    - Expel
    - Missionary

    Add these words to your word wall, if you are using one for this unit, and provide necessary support to help students learn these words as you teach the lesson.

4. **The Unit Assessment**

    If your students are writing the final essay assessment for this unit, after teaching this lesson, instruct your students to add evidence from the last four lessons to their evidence logs. For suggested activities and resources, see **Adding to Evidence Logs, 2 of 3**.

Activities

1. Introduce the Nazi Ideology of "Race and Space"

Explain to students that Hitler and the Nazis were motivated by a specific ideology, or a framework of beliefs and ideals about the way the world works. If necessary, take a moment to explain the meaning of *ideology*, using examples of ideologies students might have heard about (i.e., manifest destiny, nonviolence, white supremacy, environmentalism, capitalism, and other political worldviews).

Tell students that historians have referred to the ideology that motivated the Nazis' actions that started World War II and led to genocide as "race and space."

In the short video Hitler's Ideology: Race, Land, and Conquest (05:50), available at facinghistory.org/thhb, historian Doris Bergen introduces this ideology and explains how it is foundational to understanding World War II and the Holocaust. Watch the video with students, and then use the S-I-T teaching strategy to engage students in a discussion.

As the discussion continues, you might pose the following questions to check for understanding:

- Why does Bergen use the terms *race* and *space* to describe Hitler's ideology? What does she mean by each term?
- How was Hitler's belief in a superior Aryan race related to his desire for the conquest of new land? How did this ideology make war necessary, in Hitler's view?

2. Provide Historical Context

Before students look closely at some effects that the Nazi "race and space" ideology had on the lives of individuals at the beginning of World War II, it is important to provide some basic historical context.

Pass out the map The Growth of Nazi Germany and the handout Notes on the Growth of Nazi Germany, 1933–1939 to students. As you give a mini-lecture covering the numbered notes on the latter handout, have students write the number of each note in the appropriate location on the map.

Finish the mini-lecture by reading aloud to students the testimony of the Polish woman Mrs. J. K. in the reading Colonizing Poland. You might give students a moment to jot down any thoughts or feelings they have about the story in their journals before moving on to the next activity.

3. Analyze a Firsthand Account

After considering basic facts about the German invasion of Poland, students will now analyze a firsthand account describing the experiences and consequences of German colonization.

The class will use the Save the Last Word for Me teaching strategy to discuss and analyze the reading "Cultural Missionaries." Provide each student with three notecards and a copy of the reading.

As the class reads Melita Maschmann's account together, each student should highlight three sentences that they find especially surprising, interesting, troubling, or otherwise noteworthy.

Then have students copy each sentence onto the front of one of their notecards, and on the back of each notecard they should write a few sentences explaining why they chose the quotation on the front.

Divide the class into groups of three, where they will take turns sharing one of their quotations. After reading the quotation to the group, the other two group members will discuss its significance for a minute before the student who shared the quotation explains their reasons for choosing it. Each student should have the opportunity to share one quotation before the activity ends.

Debrief the activity with a whole-group discussion of the following question:

> What motivated Melita Maschmann to participate in Germany's policies of expelling Poles and colonizing their land? How did the Nazis' "race and space" ideology connect to how she thought about her work in Poland?

4. Reflect on the Influence of Ideology

Finish the lesson by asking students to write a response in their journals to the following prompt:

> What are some examples of ideologies that are influential in the world today? Choose one that you have encountered in your own life or have read about in the news and write about how it influences, positively or negatively, people's choices and experiences.

Assessment

- Collect the notecards that students completed as part of the Save the Last Word for Me activity to gauge their understanding of the text, the "race and space" ideology, and how it influenced Germans like Maschmann.

- Students' responses to the closing journal prompt about ideology in the world today can help you verify their understanding of the concept and see how they are thinking about the influence of powerful systems of belief on human behavior. If you have established that student journals are private in your classroom, assign students to complete the reflection on a separate piece of paper to turn in if you want to use this reflection for assessment.

Extensions

1. Further Investigate the Invasion and Colonization of Poland

To help students further contextualize the political, cultural, and social effects of the German occupation of Poland, you might share the following readings from Chapter 8 of *Holocaust and Human Behavior*: "The War against Poland: Speed and Brutality," "Dividing Poland and Its People," and "Colonizing Poland." Each reading is followed by connection questions that you can use to help guide students' analysis and discussion.

2. Explore the Nazis' Secret War against People with Disabilities

The Nazis' "race and space" ideology also led them to target people with disabilities, who Hitler believed were "marginal human beings." Programs such as the T4 "euthanasia" program involved the medical killing of about 70,000 people with epilepsy, alcoholism, birth defects, hearing loss, mental illnesses, and personality disorders, as well as those who had vision loss or developmental delays or who even suffered from certain orthopedic problems. You can share the following resources with students to introduce them to the Nazis' medical killing program and the range of responses to it, from complicity to protest, by a variety of Germans:

- Reading: "'Unworthy to Live'"
- Reading: "Bystanders at Hartheim Castle"
- Reading: "Protesting Medical Killing"
- Video: *Bishop von Galen and the War against the Disabled* (07:04)

Visit **facinghistory.org/thhb** to access these additional resources.

 Map

The Growth of Nazi Germany

Between 1933 and 1939, Greater Germany expanded significantly as a result of the Third Reich's annexations and conquests in eastern Europe.

 Handout

Notes on the Growth of Nazi Germany, 1933–1939

1. The Nazi ideology of "race and space" inspired their plans for Germany's expansion throughout Europe, their desire to acquire new "living space" for the so-called Aryan race.

2. In 1938, the Nazis took advantage of inaction from world leaders and annexed Austria and part of Czechoslovakia (known as the Sudetenland), two areas with a large number of people who considered themselves of German descent.

3. In 1939, Germany and the Soviet Union signed a nonaggression pact (an agreement not to attack each other) and divided up Poland and the Baltic countries between them.

4. In September 1939, Germany invaded Poland and quickly defeated the Polish army. This was the beginning of World War II.

5. Hitler issued the order: "Poland is to be depopulated and settled with Germans." Therefore, the Nazis divided Poland into two parts. One part (the General Government) was designated for Poles, who the Nazis believed were an inferior race to Aryans, and for Jews. The other part (the Warthegau) was adjacent to Germany and designated for "true Germans."

6. The Germans expelled hundreds of thousands of Poles, Jews, and Sinti and Roma from the Warthegau to the General Government and gave their homes and property to "Aryan" Germans. Jews were confined to ghettos.

 Reading

Colonizing Poland

A Polish woman identified as "Mrs. J. K." described her expulsion from her home by the Nazis:

> On 17 October 1939, at 8 a.m., I heard someone knocking at the door of my flat. As my maid was afraid to open it, I went to the door myself. I found there two German gendarmes [police], who roughly told me that in a few hours I had to be ready to travel with my children and everybody in the house. When I said that I had small children, that my husband was a prisoner of war, and that I could not get ready to travel in so short a time, the gendarmes answered that not only must I be ready but that the flat must be swept, the plates and dishes washed and the keys left in the cupboards, so that the Germans who were to live in my house should have no trouble. In so many words, they further declared that I was entitled to take with me only one suitcase of not more than 50 kilograms [110 pounds] in weight and a small handbag with food for a few days.
>
> At 12 noon they came again and ordered us to go out in front of the house. Similar groups of people were standing in front of all the houses. After some hours waiting, military lorries [trucks] drove up and they packed us in one after the other, shouting at us rudely and also striking us. Then they took us to the railway station, but only in the evening did they pack us into [boxcars], the doors of which they then bolted and sealed. In these [cars], most of which were packed with forty people, we spent three days, without any possibility of getting out. I hereby affirm that in my [car] there were six children of under ten years of age and two old men, and that we were not given any straw, or any drinking utensils, that we had to satisfy our natural needs in the tightly packed [car], and that if there were no deaths in our transport it was only because it was still comparatively warm and we spent only three days on the journey. We were unloaded, half dead at Czestochowa [in the General Government part of Poland,] where the local population gave us immediate help, but the German soldiers who opened the truck exclaimed, "What! Are these Polish swine still alive?"[1]

---

1 Quoted in *Nazism: A History in Documents and Eyewitness Accounts,* 1919–1945, vol. 2, ed. Jeremy Noakes and Geoffrey Pridham (New York: Schocken Books, 1988), 937–38.

Reading

"Cultural Missionaries"

Melita Maschmann, who was then in her early 20s and held a leadership position in the BDM (the German initials of the League of German Girls), was among the first to live and work in the Warthegau. She recalled:

> My colleagues and I felt it was an honor to be allowed to help in "conquering" this area for our own nation and for German culture. We had all the arrogant enthusiasm of the "cultural missionary." . . .
>
> How could young people, in particular, fail to enjoy such a life? It is true that if one visited the eastern parts of the Warthegau it was impossible to imagine oneself to be standing on lost German soil which had simply to be reclaimed for the Reich. This country was Polish through and through. Hitler had not reclaimed it but conquered it in battle. We knew that might had triumphed over right there. In those days we should probably have agreed that "the right of the strongest" had triumphed in the struggle for Lebensraum [living space for "Aryans"]. . . .
>
> Our existence at that time was for us like a great adventure. . . . All through our childhood the lament over Germany's defeat in the First World War and her misery in the postwar years had never ceased. I believe that growing up in a country where people's minds are dominated by such a mood has a fateful effect. Young people do not want to be ashamed of their fatherland. They depend more than older people on being able to honor, admire and to love it.
>
> The fact that we were allowed to perform a kind of "colonization work" in "advanced posts" there healed the wounds which our sense of honor had suffered in our childhood and early youth. Germany required us not merely to do a job of work but to give our entire selves. This feeling rose on many occasions to a sensation of intoxication. . . .
>
> It goes without saying that in this situation we were inclined to romanticize our existence in the "front line," and developed much of the colonial's presumptuous arrogance towards the "stay at homes." . . .
>
> I was the first Reich German B.D.M. leader to be sent to the Warthegau, and for a long time I was the only one. It is true that I had no leadership task—I had simply come to Posen to run the press department for the Regional leadership of the Hitler Youth—but I quickly made close contact with the local . . . B.D.M. leaders and was drawn into their work.[1]

---

1 Melita Maschmann, *Account Rendered: A Dossier on My Former Self* (London: Abelard-Schuman, 1965), 73.

STEP 4

Adding to Evidence Logs, 2 of 3

Before introducing the final historical topic for the essay, the Holocaust and its legacy, now is an appropriate time in the unit for students to review the documents and videos from Lessons 14 to 18 and consider which information supports, expands, or challenges their thinking about the writing prompt.

Suggested Activities

Visit **facinghistory.org/thhb** to access all teaching strategies referenced in these activities.

1. Share Ideas

By using the Learn to Listen, Listen to Learn discussion strategy, students can share and build on each other's ideas about the significant choices they are learning about in this unit. Start by having students reflect in their journals on the following question:

> Which choices made by individuals, groups, and nations in the history that you have learned about so far in this unit seemed most significant? What made those choices powerful or impactful?

Since students have been asked to reflect on this question in earlier evidence log activities, they can review their writing and either add to their previous thinking or write about a choice they learned about in Lessons 14 to 18.

Next, divide students into groups of four or five. Each student will have the opportunity to share part of their journal reflection with the rest of the group. It is helpful to provide a time limit for each student's sharing. The other group members will practice listening without interrupting the speaker. When it is their turn to share, tell students to refrain from responding to other students' ideas; they should focus only on sharing their own thoughts and reflections from their journals. Encourage students to take notes from each other and record ideas or evidence that supports or challenges their ideas.

After all group members have shared, each group will have an open conversation in which they ask each other questions and respond to each other's ideas. They should decide on three or four main ideas from their discussion that they will share with the whole group.

Then ask each group to report to the entire class on the main ideas from their conversation.

Finish the activity by giving students a few minutes to return to their journals and write down any ideas they heard from their classmates that contributed to or changed their thinking about the impact and power of people's choices in history and today.

2. Journal Response

Ask students to take out their journals and choose an idea or question they heard from a classmate during the Learn to Listen, Listen to Learn activity that they found interesting, provocative, or confusing. They should record the idea and then write a journal entry in response. If they finish before the time is up, they can choose a different idea from the previous activity to respond to in their journals. Students might share their new journal responses with a partner or in a class discussion that also allows them to share their observations about the Learn to Listen, Listen to Learn discussion as a whole.

3. Revisit Skills: Annotating, Paraphrasing, and Relevant Evidence

If you have noticed students struggling with annotation or paraphrasing, you might review those skills with one or more of the readings from this section of the unit before asking them to add to their evidence logs.

If you have observed that students are writing every piece of evidence rather than the most relevant ones on their evidence logs, you might create a mini-lesson in which you give students a mock thesis statement (it could be for a different topic question) and a list of ten pieces of evidence. Ask students to label the evidence "R" for relevant and "I" for irrelevant, explaining their choices. Or you might ask students to rank the evidence in a ladder from most to least relevant.

4. Evidence Logs

Students should add to their evidence logs any information from Lessons 14 to 18 that helps them answer the essay question:

> How does learning about the choices people made during Weimar Germany and the rise of the Nazi Party help us understand the power and impact of our choices in the world today?

5. Final Reflection

In a final journal response or on exit tickets, ask students to respond to the following questions:

- What did you learn from the Learn to Listen, Listen to Learn activity today that extends or challenges your thinking about the essay topic question?
- What do you feel you need to learn more about in order to answer the writing prompt and write your essay?

Unit Essential Question

What does learning about the choices people made during the Weimar Republic, the rise of the Nazi Party, and the Holocaust teach us about the power and impact of our choices today?

Lesson

The Holocaust: Bearing Witness

Duration
Two 50-minute class periods

Materials

 Reading
Take This Giant Leap

 Videos
Step by Step: Phases of the Holocaust
The Nazis in Vilna

 Handouts
Phases of the Holocaust
Creating a Found Poem

 Gallery Walk
Jewish Ghettos in Eastern Europe
Main Nazi Camps and Killing Sites
The Boy in the Warsaw Ghetto
Mobile Killing Units
Auschwitz
We May Not Have Another Chance
Diary from the Łódź Ghetto

(Continued on next page)

Find all materials referenced in this lesson at facinghistory.org/thhb.

Guiding Questions

- What was the Holocaust? Why is it important to confront the brutality of this history?
- What did it mean to resist the Nazis? What kinds of resistance were those targeted by the Nazis able to carry out?
- What is the meaning of human dignity? How did the Nazis seek to deprive their victims of basic human dignity, and how did those targeted attempt to preserve or reclaim their dignity?

Learning Objectives

- Students will be able to explain the range of Nazi methods of mass murder, including the establishment of Jewish ghettos, mobile killing units, concentration camps, and killing centers.
- Students will bear witness to the atrocities committed by the Nazis during the Holocaust, as well as extraordinary acts of resistance and efforts to preserve human dignity on the part of victims and survivors.

Overview

The purpose of this lesson is to introduce students to the enormity of the crimes committed during the Holocaust and to help them bear witness to the experiences of those targeted by the Nazis. In this lesson, students will continue this unit's historical case study by learning about four phases of the Holocaust and then looking closely at stories of a few individuals who were targeted by Nazi brutality. Students will also examine firsthand accounts of individuals who worked to preserve their human dignity in the face of dehumanization, and they will use those stories to help them think about the meaning and purpose of resistance during the Holocaust.

Materials *Continued*

Reading
A Basic Feeling of Human Dignity

Teaching Strategies
Gallery Walk
Graffiti Board
Read Aloud
Think, Pair, Share
Found Poem
Exit Ticket

Find all materials referenced in this lesson at facinghistory.org/thhb.

The next lesson focuses on the role of perpetrators and bystanders, as well as acts of resistance and courage by upstanders and rescuers during the Holocaust. The material in these two lessons reminds students of the importance of living in a democracy whose institutions safeguard civil and human rights and whose citizens are capable of making informed judgments, not only on behalf of themselves but on behalf of a larger community.

Context

Holocaust survivor Sonia Weitz begins her poem "For Yom Ha'Shoah" with these lines: "Come, take this giant leap with me / into the other world . . . the other place / where language fails and imagery defies, / denies man's consciousness . . . and dies / upon the altar of insanity."[1] To study the history in this lesson is to take Weitz's "giant leap." Learning about the Holocaust requires us to examine events in history and examples of human behavior that both unsettle us and elude our attempts to explain them.

When Germany invaded the Soviet Union in June 1941, its goal was to claim "living space" for the "Aryan" race that the Nazis had long wanted. But in order for Germans to settle in the territory of eastern Europe they had conquered from the Soviet Union in 1941 and 1942, they would have to empty it of so-called inferior races, including the millions of Jews who lived there. Early in the war, the Germans had forced Jews from the territories they conquered into ghettos and concentration camps and killed scores of them in mass shootings by mobile killing units. They had also considered plans to move the populations of Jews and other "non-Aryans" to far-off places like Madagascar or Siberia.

Eventually, however, the Nazi leadership decided that these plans would be too impractical or expensive; they chose instead a policy to annihilate all of the Jews of Europe. Historians believe this decision was made by Hitler and his advisors toward the end of 1941. As mobile killing units continued to operate throughout eastern Europe, the Nazis began to establish killing centers—camps designed for the purpose of murdering large numbers of victims, primarily in gas chambers, as quickly and efficiently as possible. By the end of the war in 1945, more than six million Jews and millions of other civilians—including Roma and Sinti, Slavs (Poles, Russians, and others), the disabled, and many of the Nazis' political enemies—were murdered by the Third Reich.

To gain an understanding of the Holocaust, it is important to look not only at the acts of perpetrators but also at the experiences of victims and survivors. Yet it is impossible to truly understand their experiences. Nobel Prize winner and Holocaust survivor Elie Wiesel explains, "Ask any survivor and he will tell you, and his children will tell you. He or she who did not live through the event will never know it. And he or she who did live through the event will never reveal it. Not entirely. Not really. Between our memory and its reflection there stands a wall that cannot be pierced."[2]

---

1 Sonia Schreiber Weitz, *I Promised I Would Tell* (Brookline, MA: Facing History & Ourselves, Inc., 2012), 66.

2 Elie Wiesel, "The Holocaust as Literary Inspiration," as quoted in *Dimensions of the Holocaust* (Evanston: Northwestern University Press, 1977), 7.

Still, even though it is impossible to truly understand the victims' experiences, and even though nothing can prepare us to encounter the horror of this crime, it is still important to take stock of the scope of this genocide—to appreciate how humanity was stripped from millions of people. This lesson helps students bear witness to the stories of some of the people who suffered under Nazi brutality.

This lesson also includes the stories of individuals who, in spite of the danger, violence, and suffering around them, resisted the Nazis' program of dehumanization and murder. Some individuals imprisoned in the concentration camps made enormous efforts to preserve human dignity for themselves and others. A small percentage of prisoners in camps and ghettos found ways to carry out armed resistance.

This lesson challenges students to expand their ideas about resistance to include forms of "spiritual resistance," or the struggle to maintain a sense of identity, dignity, faith, and culture in the degrading and dehumanizing systems of the ghettos and camps. While perhaps less perceptible, acts of spiritual resistance such as secretly providing education for children in concentration camps (see the reading A Basic Feeling of Human Dignity) or creating a secret archive representing the individual lives lost (see the reading Voices from the Warsaw Ghetto) are equally powerful.

It is important to recognize the incredible challenges that confronted Jews trying to resist Nazi oppression and violence. For some victims it was impossible to believe what lay ahead. Even once Jews recognized the gravity of their situation, during the war it was difficult for anyone, and especially Jews, to gain the resources or arms to resist the Nazis. Resistance was not possible for many other Jews who were confronted with what scholar Lawrence Langer has labeled *choiceless choices*. For example, consider the circumstances of the *Sonderkommandos*—Jewish prisoners who were kept alive and forced to help German guards murder other prisoners. According to Langer, there are no moral equivalents in the "normal" world for these experiences, no way to understand or judge their actions.

Answering the question, asked by some, of why more Jews did not resist, Elie Wiesel explains, "The question is not why all the Jews did not fight, but how so many of them did. Tormented, beaten, starved, where did they find the strength—spiritual and physical—to resist?"[3]

The history and the stories that students encounter in this lesson are disturbing and difficult to fathom yet necessary to confront. They show the importance of honoring human dignity by showing us what can happen when it is taken away and what can be prevented when it is preserved.

Notes to Teacher

1. Preparing to Teach Emotionally Challenging Content

In this lesson, students will encounter emotionally challenging content. Carefully consider each of these suggestions before engaging with this material with your students:

---

[3] Elie Wiesel, *The New Leader* 46 (August 5, 1963): 21.

Teachers know their students best. Preview each resource in this lesson before you share it with your students. Let students know in advance when they are about to encounter material that some may find upsetting. If necessary, omit resources that you believe will be too disturbing for your students.

Briefly review the class contract with students before beginning the lesson. This will help reinforce the norms you have established and reinforce the idea of the classroom as a safe space for students to voice concerns, questions, or emotions that may arise.

Be prepared for a variety of responses from students. Students often react to the Holocaust with sadness, anger, or frustration, yet it is also the case that many students do not have an immediate public response to learning about the Holocaust. Many teachers have been surprised by some students' lack of emotion during a lesson on the Holocaust. Experience has taught us that it can take time before students are able and ready to make sense of this material. In the meantime, many students report that their journals provide a safe space where they can begin to process their emotions and ideas. Therefore, we recommend that students are invited to write in their journals at many points throughout this lesson.

2. Defining Terms

The resources in this lesson refer to *ghettos*, *concentration camps*, and *killing centers*. It may be helpful to post simple definitions of each of these words in the room to help students understand and distinguish between them:

- *Ghetto*: a specific area of a city or town in which Jews were forced to live (and often not permitted to leave). Ghettos were overcrowded and deprived of sufficient food and other basic supplies.
- *Concentration camp*: a camp created to confine large numbers of prisoners (including political opponents and those deemed racially inferior) in harsh and unhealthy conditions.
- *Killing center*: a camp designed for the purpose of murdering large numbers of victims, primarily in gas chambers, as quickly and efficiently as possible.

The reality of the Nazi ghetto and camp system is quite complex, as the Nazis operated more than 40,000 ghettos and camps that served a variety of purposes and varied in size and operation. But for this lesson, these three definitions will suffice.

3. Previewing Vocabulary

In addition to *ghetto, concentration camp,* and *killing center,* the following are key vocabulary terms used in this lesson:

- Holocaust
- Shoah
- Resistance
- Spiritual resistance
- Dignity
- Genocide

Add these words to your word wall, if you are using one for this unit, and provide necessary support to help students learn these words as you teach the lesson.

4. Setting Up a Gallery Walk and Graffiti Board

The first day's activities in this lesson include a gallery walk and a graffiti board. Prepare in advance by placing the gallery walk resources around the room and setting up a whiteboard or large paper to use as a graffiti wall. We recommend leaving up the graffiti wall for a few days, so make sure it does not occupy space you anticipate needing.

Graffiti boards can offer the richest opportunity for reflection and written discussion when students can revisit them over time to observe new contributions from classmates. You might help to make this a more rewarding activity, and save some class time in the process, if you are able to find time outside of the normal class period (such as homeroom or study hall time) when students are able to visit your room and work on the graffiti wall.

Activities

Day 1

1. Prepare Students to Confront the Holocaust

Project the poem "For Yom Ha'Shoah," from the reading Take This Giant Leap, by Sonia Weitz, a Holocaust survivor. We suggest having students read the poem aloud at least two times. After reading, ask students to respond to the following questions in their journals:

- What does this poem mean to you?
- What does this poem suggest it is like to learn about the Holocaust?
- What questions does the poem raise for you?

Then ask students to share their responses to these prompts. Their questions about the poem can be recorded on the board so that they can be revisited at the end of the lesson, when students have greater familiarity with the Holocaust.

2. Understand the Steps Leading to Mass Murder

While the primary goal of this lesson is to provide students with the opportunity bear witness to some specific stories and experiences of individuals who lived or died during the Holocaust, it is first necessary to briefly give students a framework to understand what happened.

In the video Step by Step: Phases of the Holocaust (06:47), available at facinghistory.org/thhb, historian Doris Bergen divides the history of the Holocaust into four phases, described on the handout Phases of the Holocaust. Pass out the handout and give students a few moments to read through the information. Then show the video so that students can hear Bergen's description of the four phases.

3. Reflect on a Range of Primary Sources

In this activity, students will have the opportunity to work independently to reflect on and bear witness to a variety of stories and experiences during the Holocaust.

First, students will watch a short video with testimony from a Holocaust survivor from the city of Vilna, Lithuania. The Jews of Vilna were forced into ghettos after the German invasion in 1941, and tens of thousands of them were then murdered either in mass shootings or at the Sobibór killing center. Show the class the video The Nazis in Vilna (05:06) at facinghistory.org/thhb. After the clip is over, give students a few minutes to write in their journals in response to the following questions:

- What about Jack Arnel's testimony is most striking to you? What does it make you think about or feel?
- What is the value of hearing this kind of firsthand account? How does it change how you understand the Holocaust?

Tell students that in order to bear witness to the many ways that people experienced and responded to the brutality of the Holocaust, they will be looking at images from the period and reading the words of people who were there. They will also view two maps to get a sense of the scope of the Nazi atrocities.

Set up a gallery walk by placing the following resources on tables or hanging them around the room:

- Map: Jewish Ghettos in Eastern Europe
- Map: Main Nazi Camps and Killing Sites
- Image: The Boy in the Warsaw Ghetto
- Handout: Mobile Killing Units
- Handout: Auschwitz
- Handout: We May Not Have Another Chance
- Handout: Diary from the Łódź Ghetto

Ask students to silently "tour" the gallery. Give them eight minutes (or longer if you have more time) to view or read as many of the resources as they can. For each one they view, ask them to do the following in their journals:

- Record the name of the resource.
- If it is a text-based resource: Record a sentence, phrase, or detail you think is striking or significant.
- If it is an image: Describe a part of the image that provokes a question, observation, or emotional response from you.

When students are finished, rather than return to their desks, ask them to visit the graffiti board you have set up in advance and write a response to the resources they encountered. They might add one or more of the notes they took during the gallery walk to the graffiti board, or they might write a new thought, observation, or feeling they are experiencing after viewing the resources.

Give students five minutes to finish their silent writing, but leave the graffiti board up in the classroom for the next day or longer so that students have additional time to reflect on the activity, view their peers' responses, and add new comments.

Day 2

1. Acknowledge Graffiti Board Responses

Begin class by encouraging students to continue interacting with the graffiti board. You might read aloud a few responses from the board so that students can hear each other's thoughts. If you have the time, you might also give students a few minutes to go up to the graffiti board, read comments from yesterday (especially if other classes added to the same graffiti board since you last met), and add new thoughts and observations.

2. Explore Resistance

Explain to students that it is crucial in a study of the Holocaust to acknowledge the various ways that Jews and others targeted by the Nazis resisted.

Students will often associate the idea of resistance with violent or armed rebellion. It is important to acknowledge that such actions did occur, such as the efforts of Jewish partisan groups, the sabotage of the crematoria by Jewish prisoners at Auschwitz, or the Warsaw ghetto uprising (see the extension "Explore Additional Examples of Jewish Resistance" below). Tell students that scholar Michael Berenbaum writes that for those who resisted violently, "Death was a given." Ask students to consider the question: If death was a given, why might Jews resist anyway?

Then explain to students that there are other types of resistance for them to consider. Pass out the reading A Basic Feeling of Human Dignity and read it aloud with the class.

After reading, ask students to respond in their journals to the following questions:

- What is dignity? What do you think Lévy-Hass means by the phrase "a basic feeling of human dignity"? How did the Germans try to deprive Lévy-Hass and her fellow prisoners of this feeling?
- How did Lévy-Hass attempt to restore dignity for some of those imprisoned in her camp? Were her efforts an act of resistance?

Lead a class discussion in response to these questions, using the Think, Pair, Share strategy. Then introduce students to the idea of *spiritual resistance* by providing them with the following definition:

> *spiritual resistance:* the struggle to maintain a sense of identity, dignity, faith, and culture in the degrading and dehumanizing systems of the ghettos and camps.

3. Create a Found Poem with the Words of a Survivor

Students will finish this lesson by returning to the words of Hannah Lévy-Hass to create a found poem.

Read aloud **A Basic Feeling of Human Dignity** once more. This time, as students read along, they will highlight or copy down words and phrases from the diary entry that they find especially powerful. Their goal is to eventually narrow down their list of words and phrases to 15 or 20.

Then pass out the handout **Creating a Found Poem** and go over the instructions with students. Students might want to copy the words and phrases they selected onto notecards or separate scraps of paper so that they can easily rearrange them. Tell students to try to arrange the words in a way that captures the essence of Lévy-Hass's testimony, as well as their experience of hearing it.

When students are satisfied with their poems, tell them to add titles. Ask them to turn in their poems or complete them for homework. At the beginning of the next class period, you might ask a few students to share their poems aloud with the class.

4. Exit Tickets

End this lesson by having students complete an **exit ticket** to give you a sense of how they are responding to this emotionally challenging content. Have students read the poem "For Yom Ha'Shoah" again, and then ask them to write on their cards about what this poem means to them after learning more about the Holocaust.

Assessment

This lesson prioritizes emotional engagement over ethical reflection and intellectual rigor. While it is important for students to know what happened during the Holocaust, it is crucial that they have the opportunity to confront the brutality of this history and to process individually and together the emotions and questions this history evokes. Therefore, it is most important for you to look at student contributions to the graffiti wall, their found poems, and their exit tickets for evidence of how they are processing what they have encountered in this lesson. If necessary, follow up with individual students to offer support, or set aside additional class time for students to talk through and articulate their thoughts and feelings about this challenging history.

Extensions

1. Bring Survivor Testimony into the Classroom

Many Facing History teachers arrange to have a Holocaust survivor visit their classroom to tell their story. Hearing a survivor's story in person is an extraordinary experience that often changes the way students feel about history and themselves. Because the Holocaust occurred more than seven decades ago, however, the number of survivors alive and available to speak to students is shrinking. In some cases, children of survivors are also visiting classrooms and sharing their families' powerful stories with students. To learn more, visit facinghistory.org.

If you are unable to schedule an in-person visit with a survivor, Facing History has produced a collection of films of testimony called "Survivors and Witnesses." The videos are divided into three sections: "The Nazis in Power: Voices from Europe," "The Holocaust," and "After the Holocaust." Consult the lesson "Using Testimony to Teach" for suggestions and strategies for viewing testimony and facilitating purposeful reflection with students.

2. Explore the Concept of a "Choiceless Choice"

Throughout this unit, we have focused on examining the choices people made throughout the history of Nazi Germany as a way of reflecting more deeply on the choices we make in our own lives. However, there are some choices and some situations in this history for which analysis and judgment of individuals' actions is not appropriate or useful. Scholar Lawrence Langer labels the circumstances many victims were confronted with as *choiceless choices*. These are situations in which no meaningful choices are available. For instance, Langer argues that the circumstances of Sonderkommandos—Jewish prisoners who were kept alive and forced to help German guards murder other prisoners—were unimaginable to us, and "surviving in extremity meant an existence that had no relation to our system of time and space." Therefore, it is not possible to judge their actions according the standards we might use to judge people's actions under more normal circumstances.

The concept of *choiceless choices* is abstract and difficult for younger students to grasp. But if you teach older students, consider sharing the reading Choiceless Choices with them. You can use the connection questions that follow the reading to begin a discussion, and you might ask students how Langer's concept connects to the "giant leap" Sonia Weitz describes in her poem "For Yom Ha'Shoah."

3. Explore Additional Examples of Jewish Resistance

Chapters 8 and 9 of *Holocaust and Human Behavior* include a variety of additional resources about Jewish resistance during the Holocaust. Among these are examples of both spiritual (see the reading "Voices from the Warsaw Ghetto") and armed resistance (see the reading "The Warsaw Ghetto Uprising") in the Warsaw ghetto. Facing History also offers the unit "Resistance During the Holocaust: An Exploration of the Jewish Partisans." All of these resources can help deepen students' understanding of resistance by those who were targeted by the Nazis.

Visit facinghistory.org/thhb to access these additional resources.

Reading

Take This Giant Leap

Sonia Weitz was born in Kraków, Poland. She was 11 years old when her family and other Polish Jews were herded into ghettos by the Nazis. Of the 84 members of her extended family, she and her sister Blanca were the only survivors of years in ghettos and concentration camps during the Holocaust. At an early age, she turned to poetry to help her cope with her emotions. Years after the Holocaust, Weitz wrote the poem "For Yom Ha'Shoah." *Yom Ha'Shoah* is Hebrew for "Day of Holocaust Remembrance."

FOR YOM HA'SHOAH

Come, take this giant leap with me

into the other world . . . the other place

where language fails and imagery defies,

denies man's consciousness . . . and dies

upon the altar of insanity.

Come, take this giant leap with me

into the other world . . . the other place

and trace the eclipse of humanity . . .

where children burned while mankind stood by

and the universe has yet to learn why

. . . has yet to learn why[1]

---

1 Sonia Schreiber Weitz, *I Promised I Would Tell* (Brookline, MA: Facing History & Ourselves, Inc., 2012), 66.

 **Handout**

Phases of the Holocaust

In the video *Step by Step: Phases of the Holocaust,* historian Doris Bergen divides the history of the Holocaust into four phases:

1. Planning and Propaganda: 1933–1939

Key events:

- German Jews and other so-called inferior races and people are isolated from the rest of the population.
- Germany rebuilds military in violation of Treaty of Versailles.
- Germany annexes Austria and part of Czechoslovakia.
- German government attacks Jewish lives and property on Kristallnacht.
- Nazi government prepares German public for war.

2. Expansion and Violence: September 1939 – June 1941

Key events:

- World War II begins with German invasion of Poland.
- Nazi violence expands into Poland and across Europe.
- Nazis establish ghettos and new concentration camps to imprison millions of Jews.
- Einsatzgruppen (mobile killing units) murder millions of Jews and other targeted groups in mass shootings in eastern Europe.
- Germany invades Soviet Union.

3. Dedication to Mass Killing: 1941–1944

Key events:

- Decision is made by Hitler and his advisors to annihilate all of the Jews in Europe.
- Six killing centers are established, where millions of Jews, Sinti and Roma, and other targeted groups are murdered in gas chambers. The most infamous killing center is Auschwitz.

4. Death Marches: January 1945 – May 1945

- As Germany is losing the war, and the Soviets are pushing the German military west, killing centers and camps are closed or liberated.
- Nazis force prisoners from camps to march from eastern Europe toward Germany. Hundreds of thousands die along the way.

Map

Jewish Ghettos in Eastern Europe

Historians estimate that about 1,100 Jewish ghettos were established by the Nazis and their allies in Europe between 1933 and 1945. This map shows the locations of the largest ghettos.

 Map

Main Nazi Camps and Killing Sites

Between 1933 and 1945, the Nazis established more than 40,000 camps for the imprisonment, forced labor, or mass killing of Jews, Sinti and Roma, Communists, and other so-called "enemies of the state."

 Image

The Boy in the Warsaw Ghetto

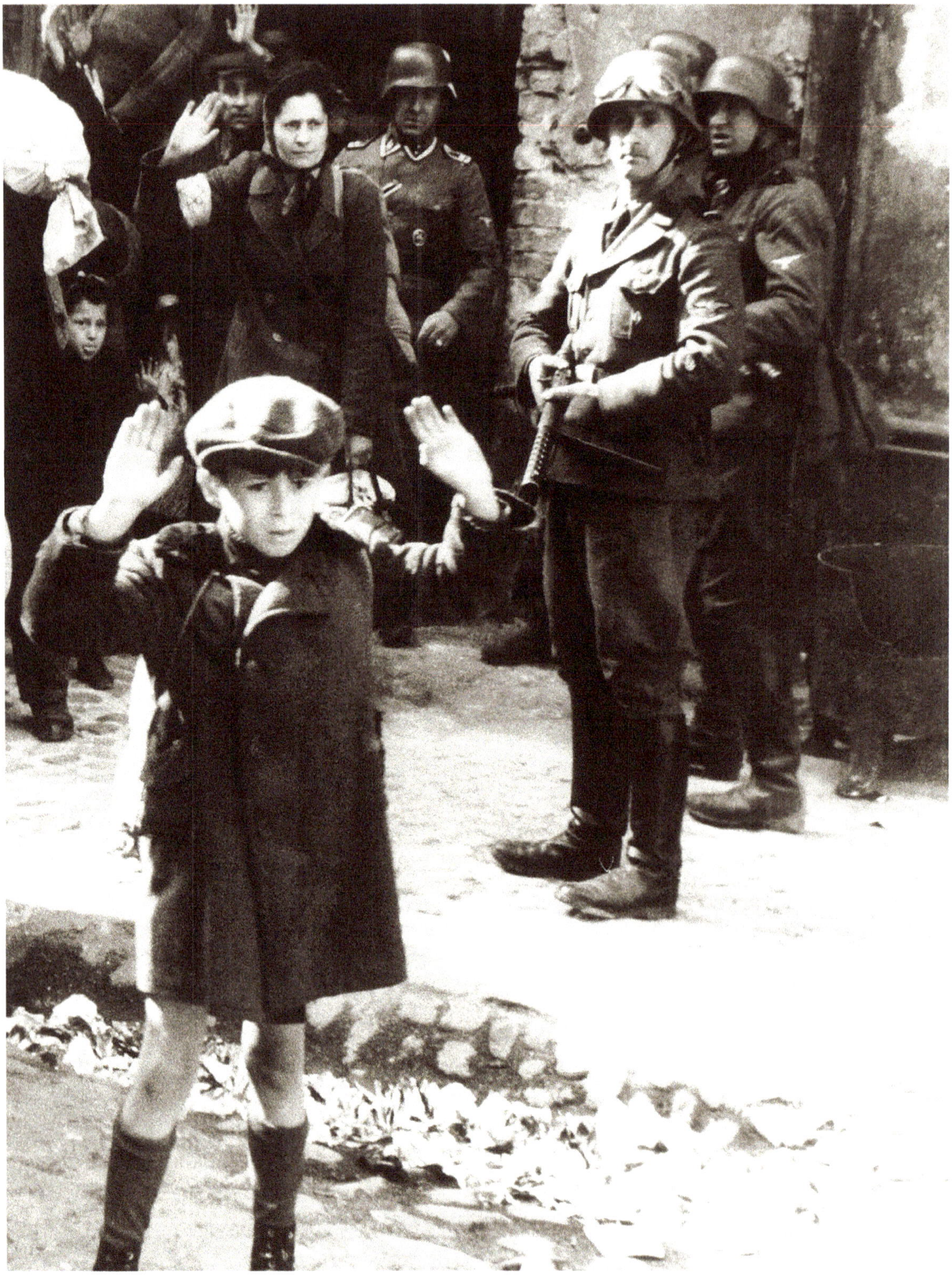

This picture shows seven-year-old Tsvi Nussbaum in the Warsaw ghetto in 1943. The photo was taken by a Nazi photographer. There are conflicting accounts of whether this boy survived the war.

Handout

Mobile Killing Units

Physician Y. Kutorgene, who was not Jewish, witnessed the German invasion of her country, Lithuania. She wrote in her diary, "Thousands of people humiliated, without any protection, worse than animals, and that because they have 'other blood.'" On October 30, 1941, Dr. Kutorgene wrote about what had happened the previous day in the city of Kovno as the Nazis prepared to murder (by shooting) the Jews in the ghetto there:

> On [October 29] there was an announcement that everybody [every Jew] must come at six in the morning to the big square in the ghetto and line up in rows, except workers with the documents which were recently distributed to specialists and foremen. . . . The square was surrounded by guards with machine guns. It was freezing. The people stood on their feet all through that long day, hungry and with empty hands. Small children cried in their mothers' arms. Nobody suspected the bitter fate that awaited them. They thought that they were being moved to other apartments. . . . [There] was a rumor that at the Ninth Fort . . . prisoners had been digging deep ditches, and when the people were taken there, it was already clear to everybody that this was death. They broke out crying, wailed, screamed. Some tried to escape on the way there but they were shot dead. . . . [1]

---

[1] Y. Kutorgene, "Kaunaski Dnievnik (Kovno Diary) 1941–1942," *Druzhba Narodov* ("Amity of Nations"), VIII, 1968, 210–11, in *Documents on the Holocaust: Selected Sources on the Destruction of the Jews of Germany and Austria, Poland, and the Soviet Union*, ed. Yitzhak Arad, Israel Gutman, and Abraham Margaliot, trans. Lea Ben Dor (Lincoln and Jerusalem: University of Nebraska Press and Yad Vashem, 1999), 405–06.

Handout

Auschwitz

Auschwitz was a complex of camps where Jews, Sinti and Roma, prisoners of war, and Polish resisters were imprisoned and forced to perform slave labor. In October 1941, it also became the site of the largest killing center built by the Nazis.

This photograph shows Jewish women and children from Ukraine walking toward the gas chambers at Auschwitz, where they would be murdered.

United States Holocaust Memorial Museum, courtesy of Yad Vashem

Primo Levi, an Italian Jew, described his first few days as a prisoner in Auschwitz:

Nothing belongs to us any more; they have taken away our clothes, our shoes, even our hair; if we speak, they will not listen to us, and if they listen, they will not understand. They will even take away our name. . . . My number is 174517 . . . we will carry the tattoo on our left arm until we die.[1]

---

1 Primo Levi, *Survival in Auschwitz* (New York: Touchstone, 1996), 26.

 Handout

We May Not Have Another Chance

Sonia Weitz was a young teenager in Poland when, in 1941, she and her family were forced to enter the Kraków ghetto. In 1943, Sonia, her older sister Blanca, and their father were sent to Płaszów, a slave-labor camp south of Kraków. In her book *I Promised I Would Tell*, she writes:

> Although men and women lived in separate parts of the camp, the two groups did manage to have contact with each other. For example, on one occasion I was sent to the ghetto with a cleanup detail. While there I found a jacket, a precious warm jacket. I smuggled it back to Płaszów to my father. It was comforting to think that the jacket would keep him warm that winter. On another day, I sneaked into my father's barracks on the other side of the barbed wire fence. While I was there, I met a boy who was about my age—14 or 15. The boy was playing a harmonica, an offense punishable by death. My father and I listened to the music, and my father said to me, "You and I never had a chance to dance together" . . . and so we danced. It is such a precious image, a bizarre and beautiful gift.[1]

Weitz and her sister were separated from their father soon after this moment. In December 1944, the two sisters were transferred to Auschwitz. They would never see their father again. The sisters were forced to march across Poland from Auschwitz to Bergen-Belsen, a concentration camp in Germany. They were later transferred to two other camps and at last liberated from Mauthausen, in Austria, in May 1945 by US troops.

---

1 Sonia Schreiber Weitz, *I Promised I Would Tell* (Brookline, MA: Facing History & Ourselves, Inc., 2012), 35.

Handout

Diary from the Łódź Ghetto

In early 1942, a young girl living in the ghetto in Łódź (a Polish city) kept a diary of her experiences. Her name remains unknown, but her diary entries evoke the fear and suffering of life in the ghetto.

[No Date]

There is no justice in the world, not to mention in the ghetto… People are in a state of panic. And this hunger. A struggle against death from starvation. Life is terrible, living conditions are abominable, and there is no food . . .

Wednesday March 11, 1942

. . . Today I had a fight with my father. I swore at him, even cursed him. It happened because yesterday I weighed twenty decagrams of zacierki [egg noodles] and then sneaked a spoonful. When my father came back, he immediately noticed that some zacierki were missing. My father started yelling at me and he was right. But since the chairman [Mordechai Chaim Rumkowski, the head of the Jewish Council of Łódź] gave out these zacierki to be cooked, why can't I have some? I became very upset and cursed my father. What have I done? I regret it so much, but it can't be undone. My father is not going to forgive me. How will I ever look him in the eyes? He stood by the window and cried like a baby. Not even a stranger insulted him before. The whole family witnessed this incident. I went to bed as soon as possible, without dinner. . . . We would be a happy family, if I didn't fight with everybody. All the fights are started by me. I must be manipulated by some evil force. I would like to be different, but I don't have a strong enough will. . . .

Saturday March 14, 1942

. . . O freedom! Will I have to stay behind this barbed wire forever? Will that sign be on the big board forever, [Entering Jewish residential area forbidden]? Will there always be a booth with a German guard who has a rifle on his shoulder? Has it always been like this? Will it stay like this? Oh, no! But who is going to live through it? I miss freedom. Especially on a warm sunny day. O sun! It's you who make me yearn for freedom. My heart is bleeding and my eyes are full of tears. Someone reading this in the future may sneer at me, say I'm an idiot . . .[1]

---

1 Alexandra Zapruder, *Salvaged Pages: Young Writers' Diaries of the Holocaust* (New Haven: Yale University Press, 2002), 230–40.

 Reading

A Basic Feeling of Human Dignity

Hanna Lévy-Hass was a Yugoslavian teacher imprisoned in the Bergen-Belsen concentration camp in Germany. She was held in a part of the camp for "exchange prisoners"—prisoners that the Nazis thought they might be able to exchange for Germans held prisoner by other countries. The exchange prisoners included many children.

Lévy-Hass wrote in her diary about both the loss of human dignity she and others suffered and how they sought to restore it.

> November 8, 1944
>
> I would love to feel something pleasant, aesthetic, to awaken nobler, tender feelings, dignified emotions. It's hard. I press my imagination, but nothing comes. Our existence has something cruel, beastly about it. Everything human is reduced to zero. Bonds of friendship remain in place only by force of habit, but intolerance is generally the victor. Memories of beauty are erased; the artistic joys of the past are inconceivable in our current state. The brain is as if paralyzed, the spirit violated.
>
> . . . We have not died, but we are dead. They've managed to kill in us not only our right to life in the present and for many of us, to be sure, the right to a future life . . .
>
> I turn things over in my mind, I want to . . . and I remember absolutely nothing. It's as though it wasn't me. Everything is expunged from my mind. During the first few weeks, we were still somewhat connected to our past lives internally; we still had a taste for dreams, for memories . . .
>
> November 18, 1944
>
> In spite of everything, my work with the children continues. . . . I cling desperately to every chance, however slight, to gather the children together to foster in them and in me even the slightest mental sharpness, as well as a basic feeling of human dignity.
>
> It was decided in the camp that Saturdays will be devoted to children's entertainment, mostly of a religious nature. In our barracks, we are also taking advantage of Saturdays to provide the children with some amusement, but adapted mostly to the overall mentality of the people here: oral recitations, singing solo or in chorus, small theatrical productions. Given the total lack of books, I collect and write down the material for these performances based on the children's memories and my own and more often than not, we must resort to improvising texts or poetic lines. A whole throng of known tunes have been recovered thanks to the tireless efforts and concentration of all my students—but the words escape

us as if they had been sucked into a pit. So we begin to invent lines, to rhyme, to create texts that affect us deeply, to invoke our distant homeland, glorious and heroic . . .

I carry out this task spontaneously, even instinctively I would say, through an irresistible need in my soul—in the rare moments when I manage to awaken it—and by an irresistible need that I can clearly sense coming from the children's souls. Because they take my lead, they get excited, they want to live, they want to rejoice, it's stronger than them. What heartbreak![1]

---

[1] Hanna Lévy-Hass and Amira Hass, *Diary of Bergen-Belsen,* trans. Sophie Hand (Chicago, IL: Haymarket Books, 2009), 85–88.

 Handout

Creating a Found Poem

Creating a "found poem" from a Holocaust survivor's testimony can be a way to pay respectful attention to and honor their experiences. A found poem is one that is created using only words that have been copied and rearranged from another text.

Directions: Use the following steps to create your poem:

1. Read the selected testimony at least two to three times. If possible, read it aloud at least once.
2. While reading the testimony one additional time, copy down at least 15 to 20 words or phrases from it that you find memorable or powerful.
3. Arrange the words and phrases you have selected into a poem. You might want to copy the words and phrases onto notecards or separate sheets of paper so that you can easily rearrange them. Try to arrange the words in a way that captures what you think is the essence of the testimony, as well as your experience of hearing it.

Here are a few more guidelines for creating your poem:
- You DON'T have to use all of the words and phrases you chose.
- You CAN repeat words or phrases.
- You CAN'T add other words besides those you copied from the testimony.
- Your poem DOESN'T have to rhyme.

4. When you are satisfied with your poem, give it a title.

Unit Essential Question

What does learning about the choices people made during the Weimar Republic, the rise of the Nazi Party, and the Holocaust teach us about the power and impact of our choices today?

Lesson

The Holocaust: The Range of Responses

Duration
Two 50-minute class periods

Materials

Video
Facing History Scholar Reflections: Bystanders and Resisters

Readings
A Commandant's View

Bystanders at Hartheim Castle

Protests in Germany

Deciding to Act

Le Chambon: A Village Takes a Stand

Denmark: A Nation Takes Action

Handouts
Perpetrators, Bystanders, Upstanders, and Rescuers

Choices and Consequences

Teaching Strategies
Think, Pair, Share

3-2-1

Find all materials referenced in this lesson at facinghistory.org/thhb.

Guiding Question

- What choices did individuals, groups, and nations make in response to the events of the Holocaust? What factors influenced their choices to act as perpetrators, bystanders, upstanders, or rescuers?

Learning Objectives

- Students will analyze, discuss, and explain the range of choices available to individuals, groups, and nations during the Holocaust and explore the possible motivations and reasons for decision making in this time of crisis.

- Students will recognize that the range of choices available in the 1940s was not as wide as the range available in the decades before the outbreak of war, but that despite these constraints, many upstanders and rescuers still chose to take action and help people targeted by the Nazis.

Overview

In the last lesson, students learned about the atrocities the Nazis committed during the Holocaust, the experiences of many who were targeted for murder, and some of the ways those imprisoned in the ghettos and camps resisted. In this lesson, students will continue this unit's historical case study by deepening their examination of human behavior during the Holocaust and considering the range of choices available to individuals, communities, and nations in the midst of war and genocide. Students will read firsthand accounts in which perpetrators, bystanders, upstanders, and rescuers describe their choices during this period of time and reflect on both the reasons behind their actions and the consequences. Students will grapple with questions about how circumstances of time and place played a role in the choices available to people, and they will reflect on why some people decided to help—in both dramatic and subtle ways—while others stood by or even participated in the atrocities that occurred.

Context

The history of the Holocaust reveals a range of behavior of which people are capable when confronted with extreme brutality toward their fellow human beings. While the Nazis carried out their plans to murder millions of Jews and other supposedly inferior groups, individuals, groups, towns, and even entire nations risked their own safety to protect, hide, or evacuate those in danger. However, opportunities to resist or rescue were not available to everyone, and among those who had such opportunities, many did not seize them. Indeed, thousands participated actively in the Nazi plan of annihilation, while many more knew what was happening and did nothing. The efforts of rescuers and resisters, therefore, were the exception rather than the rule, and the Nazis largely succeeded in their plan to annihilate European Jews. Historian Peter Hayes writes:

> A few diplomats rose to the occasion, but most did not. More clergy accepted the challenge, but a majority did not. Minority group members expressed solidarity with Jews more frequently than the surrounding population, but not reliably or uniformly. Cosmopolitan residents of Warsaw may have been more inclined to aid Jews than Poles in the countryside, but not dependably so. Rescue was always the choice of the relatively few.[1]

Hayes adds that "at most, 5 to 10% of the Jews who survived the Holocaust in Europe did so because a non-Jew or non-Jewish organization . . . concealed and sustained them." In the end, the Nazis succeeded in murdering 6 million of the estimated 9 million Jews who lived in Europe in 1939.

Because of the magnitude of the tragedy of the Holocaust, it is necessary to confront the reasons why so many participated as perpetrators or looked the other way as bystanders. The Nazis persuaded or coerced thousands to participate. Many others participated willingly; they were true believers in Nazi ideology and did not need to be persuaded. By doing nothing, one could also indicate tacit approval of the persecution and killing of certain groups, or at least the belief that the victims' lives were not worth risking one's own life or livelihood to stand up for. Some people cooperated in the Nazi program of mass murder, or at least looked the other way despite the evidence that millions were perishing, because they stood to gain personally by taking the homes and possessions of Nazi victims. Many people did nothing in response to what they knew because they feared punishment for interfering or were consumed by their own wartime difficulties.

If the action and inaction of perpetrators and bystanders represents some of the worst of which human beings are capable, the courage of resisters and rescuers represents the best. Nearly all Jews who went into hiding relied on others to help them, and they often felt that they were totally dependent on their helpers—for food and water, for news from the outside world, and especially for a willingness to continue to keep their secret. Sometimes Jews were hidden by neighbors or former employees whom they knew, and sometimes they were helped by strangers. Sometimes entire communities provided shelter, food, and fake documents for dozens of families, actively taking part in the rescue or choosing to remain silent and not report their neighbors' activities. Some diplomats created false papers and exit or transit visas, saving the lives of thousands of Jews at great risk to

---

1 Peter Hayes, "Rescuing Jews—Means and Obstacles: Introduction," in *How Was It Possible? A Holocaust Reader*, ed. Peter Hayes (Lincoln: University of Nebraska Press, 2015), 647.

their own safety. On an even larger scale, one nation, Denmark, evacuated nearly all of its Jewish residents to safety after hearing that the Germans were planning to deport its entire Jewish population.

Sometimes rescuers acted after great deliberation, or after having taken smaller measures of resistance against the Nazi regime before accepting greater amounts of responsibility for the fate of others. In his study of rescuers, psychologist Ervin Staub states, "Goodness, like evil, often begins in small steps. Heroes evolve; they aren't born. Very often the rescuers made only a small commitment at the start—to hide someone for a day or two. But once they had taken that step, they began to see themselves differently, as someone who helps. What starts as mere willingness becomes intense involvement."[2]

Other rescuers say that the decision to act was neither gradual nor complicated. Magda Trocmé, who helped hide thousands of Jews in the French village of Le Chambon, explains:

> We had no time to think. When a problem came, we had to solve it immediately. Sometimes people ask me, "How did you make a decision?" There was no decision to make. The issue was: Do you think we are all brothers or not? Do you think it is unjust to turn in the Jews or not? Then let us try to help![3]

By examining the stories and choices of perpetrators, bystanders, upstanders, and rescuers during the Holocaust, we are not only better able to understand what happened during this crucial period of the twentieth century but can reach a deeper understanding of the range of human behavior in any time of crisis. By examining what led some to limit their universes of obligation and see the lives of others as not worth protecting, we can gain insight into the forces in our own lives that might encourage us to act cruelly or inhumanely, or to ignore such actions by others. By hearing and honoring the stories of those who took risks, large and small, on behalf of others, we might better find within ourselves the desire to be "someone who helps" and to act with caring toward others when circumstances require.

Notes to Teacher

1. Decision Making in Times of Crisis

It is important to remind students, as discussed in Lesson 16, that the terms *perpetrator*, *victim*, *bystander*, *upstander*, and now *rescuer* refer not to fixed identities but to the behavior of individuals, groups, or even nations at specific moments in time. The same person may act as a bystander in one situation and then as a rescuer or perpetrator in another situation. You might reread the final paragraphs of the Context section in Lesson 16 before teaching this lesson. It is not these categories themselves, as words, that matter; it is the way we—and our students—think and talk about the actions (or inactions) of others that helps us both understand history and make connections to the choices we all make in the present.

---

2 Quoted in Daniel Goleman, "Great Altruists: Science Ponders Soul of Goodness," *New York Times*, March 5, 1985, accessed May 25, 2016, http://www.nytimes.com/1985/03/05/science/great-altruists-science-ponders-soul-of-goodness.html?pagewanted=all.

3 Carol Rittner and Sondra Myers, *The Courage to Care: Rescuers of Jews During the Holocaust* (New York: New York University Press, 1986), 102.

2. Creating Time and Space for Reflection

Like the previous lesson, the content of this lesson can be emotionally challenging for many students. It is important to be responsive to how students are processing this material and to give them time to reflect and write quietly in their journals when they need it, even if it is not explicitly specified in the lesson.

It is important that students have time to complete the final journal response activity on Day 2 of this lesson so that they can synthesize the material from the Holocaust lessons and make connections between what they have read, seen, and discussed and their own understanding of human behavior and decision making. If you are concerned about having enough time, please consult "Abbreviating the Poster Activity" below for suggestions about shortening that activity. Students' emotional well-being is more important than completing all of the activities in the lesson.

3. Helping Students Make Connections

When discussing the choices of perpetrators, bystanders, upstanders, and rescuers during the Holocaust, invite students to reconsider the choices they analyzed in readings from previous lessons in their discussion contributions. This exercise provides the opportunity for students to review past material in a new context, thus deepening their understanding of agency at different times within this historical period. You might ask students to consider both what they now perceive to be the consequences of some of the choices made in earlier years and how the range of available choices narrowed after the Nazis went to war and began to carry out mass murder.

4. Abbreviating the Poster Activity

If you would like to devote more class time on Day 2 to the discussion and journal entry, students can forgo making the posters, which can be a time-consuming affair. To help the class follow the oral presentations, you or a member of each group could record key information on the board while the students are speaking. Alternatively, if you have access to a document camera, you might project one copy of each group's completed handout Perpetrators, Bystanders, Upstanders, and Rescuers on the board during each presentation.

5. Previewing Vocabulary

The following are key vocabulary terms used in this lesson:

- Rescuer
- Intervene

Add these words to your word wall, if you are using one for this unit, and provide necessary support to help students learn these words as you teach the lesson.

Activities

Day 1

1. Reflect on the Influence of Stories

Explain to students that they will continue their study of the Holocaust by learning about stories of people who were perpetrators and bystanders as well as those of people who took risks to help and rescue those targeted by the Nazis. Begin by having students respond to the following question in their journals:

> What does it take to intervene to try to save someone from violence and injustice? When do you think it is necessary to do so? When might it be dangerous or unwise? Explain your thinking.

Students can respond in an activity based on the Think, Pair, Share strategy, or you can facilitate a whole-group discussion.

2. Provide an Overview of Bystanders and Resisters during the Holocaust

In the short video Facing History Scholar Reflections: Bystanders and Resisters (05:11), available at facinghistory.org/thhb, Dr. Paul Bookbinder discusses the range of choices people made during the Holocaust. In the next activity, students will be reading about some of the individuals he highlights in this video.

Share the 3-2-1 analysis prompts below with students, and then show the video. Students will listen for information that addresses the prompts and then respond to them after viewing the video.

- Identify three acts of rescue or resistance you learned about from watching the video.
- Identify two debates among scholars that Bookbinder mentions about the choices groups made in response to the Holocaust.
- Think of one question the video raises for you about perpetrators, rescuers, or resisters.

Review the possible answers to the first two 3-2-1 prompts, and then ask students to share some of the questions they wrote in response to the third prompt. If you record their questions on chart paper, you can refer back to them over the course of this two-day lesson to see which ones get answered and if any need to be added.

3. Analyze Specific Choices People Made

Remind students of some of the dilemmas and choices they have analyzed in past lessons, including the following:

- The choices Germans made during the Weimar Republic that either strengthened or weakened democracy
- The decision of the German worker (in the reading "Do You Take the Oath?" in Lesson 12) about whether or not to take the oath to Hitler
- The choices young people made about participating in Nazi youth groups
- The range of responses by individuals and groups to the violence and destruction of Kristallnacht

Take a moment to reflect with students on how the circumstances of each of these situations were different and how the range of possible choices (and the associated consequences) may have been different in each instance.

Explain to students that in this lesson, they are going to read the stories of individuals, groups, and nations that faced difficult, often life-altering decisions under even more intense circumstances: war, the mass imprisonment and murder of Jews and other groups, and violent retribution for dissent.

Before distributing the readings for this next activity, ask students to take out the handout "The Range of Human Behavior Vocabulary Terms" from Lesson 16 to review the definitions of *perpetrator, bystander*, and *upstander*. To this list, you can add *rescuer*, a subcategory of *upstander*. Explain to students that while "upstanding" included a wide range of actions to oppose Nazi injustice, some upstanders took action to directly save people from the Nazis by hiding them, taking their children into their homes, helping them get visas to flee to safe countries, and helping in other critical ways. We refer to these upstanders as *rescuers*.

Divide the class into six groups, and assign each group one of the following readings:

- A Commandant's View
- Bystanders at Hartheim Castle
- Protests in Germany
- Deciding to Act
- Le Chambon: A Village Takes a Stand
- Denmark: A Nation Takes Action

Explain to the class that today they will be collaborating with their group members to read stories of Holocaust perpetrators, bystanders, upstanders, and rescuers and then answering questions. Each group will make a presentation about its reading in the next class period.

Distribute one of the readings to each group, along with the handout Perpetrators, Bystanders, Upstanders, and Rescuers for each student. Read the instructions on the handout aloud so the groups are clear about the steps for reading, annotating, and discussing the questions together.

Tell students that they will have time to prepare their presentation at the start of the next lesson. If any groups did not finish responding to their reading's questions, they should do so outside of class for homework.

Day 2

1. Prepare Poster Presentations

Tell students that they will be presenting their readings to the class, focusing on the choices, motivations, and consequences of the decisions that were made. So they can be mindful of time, let students know at the outset of the activity at what time they will begin their presentations.

Each group should prepare a poster that draws from the information they collected yesterday on the handout Perpetrators, Bystanders, Upstanders, and Rescuers and includes the following information:

- The setting of the reading
- One significant choice that individuals, groups, or nations made in the reading
- A motivation, reason, or explanation for this choice
- The possible or actual consequences of this choice
- A sentence describing how the individuals, groups, or nations in the reading define their universe of obligation
- A significant quotation from the reading

After the groups have finished preparing their posters, ask them to select two people to provide a <u>brief</u> summary of their reading and present the information on their poster to the class. Alternatively, you might ask each group to present, with each student sharing one or more aspects of the poster.

2. Present Posters to the Class

Pass out the handout Choices and Consequences for students to record notes during the group presentations, and have one pair from each group present their information to the class.

Students in the class should record notes on the handout as they listen to their peers. There is space at the bottom of the handout for students to add their own questions.

3. Discuss Decision Making in a Time of Crisis

To help students synthesize the material presented in this lesson, lead a class discussion about decision making in times of crisis. While you might not have time to address all of the questions, consider selecting one or more of the following to explore with the class:

- When looking at these readings as a whole, what similarities and differences do you notice when considering the circumstances under which people chose to perpetuate violence, stand by, or take action?
- How did circumstances of time, place, and opportunity factor into the choices that individuals, groups, and nations made in the 1940s?
- Reflect back on recent lessons to compare the choices that might have been open to individuals, groups, and nations in the 1920s and 1930s with those choices available in the 1940s.
    - Which choices were no longer possible?
    - Which choices seemed riskier than they might have been in previous years of Nazi rule?

The two Holocaust lessons (Lesson 19 and Lesson 20) expose students to a *range of choices* that individuals made during the Holocaust. You might want to start the discussion of this topic by making a list of choices on the board to visually capture the range for students and asking questions such as these:

- Were such choices available to all people who were part of this history?
- How does thinking about the range of choices extend or challenge your thinking about the Holocaust?
- How does thinking about the range of choices extend or challenge your understanding of human behavior?

4. Reflect on the Holocaust

Before moving to the next phase of Facing History's scope and sequence—"Judgment, Memory, and Legacy"—it is important that students have time and space to reflect quietly in their journals about what they have learned so far in this unit. You might simply give students a few minutes to freewrite in their journals about the experience of learning about the Holocaust in the past several class periods. Or you can have them respond to one of the following prompts:

- Describe what you thought about and what you felt while learning about people's experiences and choices during the Holocaust. What did you learn about human behavior? What did you learn about yourself?
- What information, stories, ideas, or questions from your study of the Holocaust do you think are most important to share or for you to remember?
- What questions about the Holocaust or individual and group choices during this time of crisis do you still have?

You might collect students' journals to get a sense of what they are thinking and their questions at this point in the unit. If you do collect the journals, it is important to inform students of this before they write, or have them write their response on a separate sheet of paper to collect if you have established in your class that student journals are private.

Assessment

- Evaluate the group posters and presentations, looking for evidence of students' deep thinking about the dilemmas people faced in determining how to respond to the events of the Holocaust and the factors that influenced them to make the choices they did. Even before the presentations, listen carefully to the groups' conversations as they read, annotate, and respond to questions about this lesson's core readings to gauge students' individual contributions and the evolution of their thinking.

- Collect this lesson's Perpetrators, Bystanders, Upstanders, and Rescuers and Choices and Consequences handouts to check for understanding and observe students' ethical reflections on the choices they learned about in this lesson.

Extensions

1. Examine Perpetrator Behavior

Consider pairing the reading "Reserve Police Battalion 101" with an examination of psychologist Stanley Milgram's famous experiments about circumstances under which individuals are willing and able to inflict pain on other people. Together, these resources provide a powerful way to discuss the behavior of perpetrators, as well as the conditions in which each of us might be drawn into harming others.

Use the connection questions following the reading to discuss the content with students, and then deepen their exploration of human behavior by introducing the Milgram experiments. Use the reading "A Matter of Obedience?" to provide background information on the experiments, and then show a clip from the film *Obedience: The Milgram Experiment* (21:55–39:15).

Preview these resources to ensure that they are appropriate for your students. Watching the clip of the experiments is a powerful and often uncomfortable experience for many students. Sometimes students show that discomfort by laughing. Instead of disciplining students for such responses, you might use them as an entry point for a discussion about why the video elicits such discomfort and what it suggests about the potential of any individual to be willing to harm another under the right circumstances.

For a still deeper exploration of perpetrator behavior, consider showing students the video *The Psychology of Genocidal Behavior*.

2. Extended Focus on Rescue

The Facing History & Ourselves website offers a variety of additional resources to support an extended focus on rescuers during the Holocaust. If you decide to extend this lesson to provide a more in-depth focus on rescue, begin by asking students to consider the question: How did people make the choice to rescue? You might also share this statement from psychologist Ervin Staub: "Goodness, like evil, often begins in small steps. Heroes evolve; they aren't born." Then share one or more of the following videos, to help students consider the qualities and motivations that enable one to be a rescuer and look for evidence to support Staub's statement:

- *The Courage to Care* (28:40) profiles both Jews who were rescued during the Holocaust and rescuers from France, Holland, and Poland, and it raises questions about the moral and ethical dilemmas that rescuers confronted.
- *Life or Death in the Netherlands* (05:12) features Marion Pritchard describing her decision to murder a Dutch policeman in order to protect a Jewish family hiding in her home. (This is the same story told in the reading Deciding to Act.)
- *Finding Safety in Italy* (05:47) features the testimony of Holocaust survivor Esther Bem and her description of the people in northern Italy who protected her and her family during World War II.
- *Weapons of the Spirit* (35:07) provides an in-depth profile of the French town of Le Chambon and the beliefs that motivated its residents to save 5,000 Jews during World War II. (This is the same story told in the reading "Le Chambon: A Village Takes a Stand.")

You can extend your study of rescuers even further with additional Facing History resources, including "Defying the Nazis: The Sharps' War," "The Rescuers," and other readings from Chapters 7, 8, and 9 of *Holocaust and Human Behavior*.

Visit **facinghistory.org/thhb** to access these additional resources.

 Reading

A Commandant's View

In 1971, journalist Gitta Sereny interviewed Franz Stangl, who had been the commandant of the death camp at Sobibór and, later, the camp at Treblinka.

"Would it be true to say that you were used to the liquidations?"
He thought for a moment. "To tell the truth," he then said, slowly and thoughtfully, "one did become used to it."

"In days? Weeks? Months?"
"Months. It was months before I could look one of them in the eye. I repressed it all by trying to create a special place: gardens, new barracks, new kitchens, new everything: barbers, tailors, shoemakers, carpenters. There were hundreds of ways to take one's mind off it; I used them all."

"Even so, if you felt that strongly, there had to be times, perhaps at night, in the dark, when you couldn't avoid thinking about it."
"In the end, the only way to deal with it was to drink. I took a large glass of brandy to bed with me each night and I drank."

"I think you are evading my question."
"No, I don't mean to; of course, thoughts came. But I forced them away. I made myself concentrate on work, work, and again work."

"Would it be true to say that you finally felt they weren't really human beings?"
"When I was on a trip once, years later in Brazil," he said, his face deeply concentrated and obviously reliving the experience, "my train stopped next to a slaughterhouse. The cattle in the pens, hearing the noise of the train, trotted up to the fence and stared at the train. They were very close to my window, one crowding the other, looking at me through that fence. I thought then, 'Look at this; this reminds me of Poland; that's just how the people looked, trustingly, just before they went into the tins . . .'"

"You said tins," I interrupted. "What do you mean?" But he went on without hearing, or answering me.
" . . . I couldn't eat tinned meat after that. Those big eyes . . . which looked at me . . . not knowing that in no time at all they'd all be dead." He paused. His face was drawn. At this moment he looked old and worn and sad.

"So you didn't feel they were human beings?"
"Cargo," he said tonelessly. "They were cargo." He raised and dropped his hand in a gesture of despair. Both our voices had dropped. It was one of the few times in those weeks of talks that he made no effort to cloak his despair, and his hopeless grief allowed a moment of sympathy.

"When do you think you began to think of them as cargo? The way you spoke earlier, of the day when you first came to Treblinka, the horror you felt seeing the dead bodies everywhere—they weren't 'cargo' to you then, were they?"

"I think it started the day I first saw the Totenlager [death camp] in Treblinka. I remember [Christian Wirth, the man who set up the death camps] standing there next to the pits full of blue-black corpses. It had nothing to do with humanity—it couldn't have; it was a mass—a mass of rotting flesh. Wirth said, 'What shall we do with this garbage?' I think unconsciously that started me thinking of them as cargo."

"There were so many children; did they ever make you think of your children, of how you would feel in the position of those parents?"

"No," he said slowly, "I can't say I ever thought that way." He paused. "You see," he then continued, still speaking with this extreme seriousness and obviously intent on finding a new truth within himself, "I rarely saw them as individuals. It was always a huge mass. I sometimes stood on the wall and saw them in the tube. But—how can I explain it—they were naked, packed together, running, being driven with whips like . . . " The sentence trailed off.

. . . *"Could you not have changed that?"* I asked. *"In your position, could you not have stopped the nakedness, the whips, the horror of the cattle pens?"*

"No, no, no. This was the system. . . . It worked. And because it worked, it was irreversible."[1]

---

1 Gitta Sereny, *Into that Darkness: An Examination of Conscience* (London: Pan Books, 1977), 200–02. Reproduced by permission of the Estate of Gitta Sereny and The Sayle Literary Agency.

Reading

Bystanders at Hartheim Castle

While the Nazis loudly proclaimed the campaigns to demonize and isolate Jews and "Gypsies" (the name Germans gave to two ethnic groups known as the Sinti and Roma) in newspapers and magazines, on billboards, and over the radio, they attempted to keep secret the program to murder mentally and physically disabled "Aryans." And yet by the end of 1940, most Germans were aware of some if not all aspects of the killings.[1] As historian Gordon J. Horwitz investigated the history of Mauthausen, a small Austrian town 90 miles from Vienna, he uncovered evidence of what the residents of a nearby village had known about the "euthanasia," or medical killing, program taking place there.

Soon after Austria became part of the Third Reich in 1938, the Germans built a labor camp for political prisoners in Mauthausen. As the camp expanded, German officials took over buildings in a number of nearby villages. One of those buildings was Hartheim Castle, which was a home for mentally handicapped children. In researching the history of Hartheim Castle, Horwitz discovered a letter written by a man he identified as "Karl S." The letter recalls events in 1939.

> [The] house of my parents was one of the few houses in Hartheim from which one could observe several occurrences. After Castle Hartheim was cleared of its inhabitants (around 180 to 200 patients) in the year 1939, mysterious renovations began which, to an outsider, however, one could hardly divine, since no [local] labor was used for it, and the approaches to the castle were hermetically sealed. Following completion of the renovation work, we saw the first transports come and we could even recognize some of the earlier residents who showed joy at returning to their former home.[2]

Karl S. watched the buses arrive from a window in his father's barn. He recalled that groups of two or three buses came as frequently as twice a day. Soon after they arrived, "enormous black clouds of smoke streamed out of a certain chimney and spread a penetrating stench. This stench was so disgusting that sometimes when we returned home from work in the fields we couldn't hold down a single bite."[3]

A woman called Sister Felicitas, who had formerly worked with children kept in the castle, had similar memories:

> My brother Michael, who at the time was at home, came to me very quickly and confidentially informed me that in the castle the former patients were burned. The frightful facts which the people of the vicinity had to experience first hand, and the terrible stench of the burning gases, robbed them of speech. The people suffered dreadfully from the stench. My own father collapsed unconscious several times, since in the night he had forgotten to seal up the windows completely tight.[4]

---

1 Carol Poore, *Disability in Twentieth-Century German Culture* (Ann Arbor: University of Michigan Press, 2007), 87.
2 Quoted in Gordon J. Horwitz, *In the Shadow of Death: Living Outside the Gates of Mauthausen* (New York: Free Press, 1990), 59.
3 Quoted in Horwitz, *In the Shadow of Death*, 59.
4 Quoted in Horwitz, *In the Shadow of Death*, 60.

Horwitz notes, "It was not just the smoke and stench that drew the attention of bystanders. At times human remains littered parts of the vicinity. In the words of Sister Felicitas, 'when there was intense activity, it smoked day and night. Tufts of hair flew through the chimney onto the street. The remains of bones were stored on the east side of the castle and in ton trucks driven first to the Danube [River], later also to the Traun.'"[5]

As evidence of mass murders mounted, Christian Wirth, the director of the operation, met with local residents. He told them that his men were burning shoes and other "belongings." When they asked about the strong smell, he told them it came from a device that turned old oil and oil byproducts into a water-clear, oily fluid that was of "great importance" to German submarines. Wirth ended the meeting by threatening to send anyone who spread "absurd rumors of burning persons" to a concentration camp.[6] The townspeople took him at his word. They did not break their silence.

The castle at Hartheim was one of six facilities, most of which were hospitals, that the Nazis outfitted with gas chambers and ovens in 1940 and 1941 in order to murder physically and mentally disabled people and burn their remains. Between May 1940 and May 1941, 18,269 patients were murdered at Hartheim.[7]

---

5 Quoted in Horwitz, *In the Shadow of Death*, 60–61.

6 Quoted in Horwitz, *In the Shadow of Death*, 61–62.

7 Robert N. Proctor, "Culling the German Volk," in *How Was It Possible? A Holocaust Reader*, ed. Peter Hayes (Lincoln: University of Nebraska Press, 2015), 267.

 Reading

Protests in Germany

By 1942, people living in Germany were increasingly aware of the mass murders in places to the east.

Some of the first Germans to speak out against Nazi injustices were a group of students at the University of Munich. In winter 1942, Hans Scholl, his sister Sophie, and their friend Christoph Probst formed a small group known as the White Rose. Hans, a former member of the Hitler Youth, had been a soldier on the eastern front, where he witnessed the mistreatment of Jews and learned about deportations. In 1942 and 1943, the White Rose published four leaflets condemning Nazism. The first leaflet stated the group's purpose: the overthrow of the Nazi government. In the second leaflet, the group confronted the mass murders of Jews:

> We do not want to discuss here the question of the Jews, nor do we want in this leaflet to compose a defense or apology. No, only by way of example do we want to cite the fact that since the conquest of Poland three hundred thousand Jews have been murdered in this country in the most bestial way. Here we see the most frightful crime against human dignity, a crime that is unparalleled in the whole of history. For Jews, too, are human beings—no matter what position we take with respect to the Jewish question—and a crime of this dimension has been perpetrated against human beings.[1]

In February 1943, the Nazis arrested the Scholls and Probst and brought them to trial. All three were found guilty and were guillotined that same day. Soon afterward, others in the group were also tried, convicted, and beheaded.

In March 1943, German author Friedrich Reck-Malleczewen wrote in his diary:

> The Scholls are the first in Germany to have had the courage to witness for the truth. . . . On their gravestones let these words be carved, and let this entire people, which has lived in deepest degradation these last ten years, blush when it reads them: . . . "He who knows how to die can never be enslaved." We will all of us, someday, have to make a pilgrimage to their graves, and stand before them, ashamed.[2]

Although the Nazis were able to destroy the White Rose by executing its members, they could not keep its message from being heard. Helmuth von Moltke, a German aristocrat, smuggled the group's leaflets to friends in neutral countries. They, in turn, sent them to the Allies, who made thousands of copies and then dropped them over German cities. As a lawyer who worked for the German Intelligence Service, von Moltke had been aware of the murders for some time but had taken no action. By late October, he was asking, "May I know this and yet sit at my table in my heated flat and have tea? Don't I thereby become guilty too?"[3]

---

1 "The Second Leaflet," The White Rose Society, accessed May 24, 2016, http://www.whiterosesociety.org/WRS_pamphets_second.html.
2 Friedrich Reck-Malleczewen, *Diary of a Man in Despair,* trans. Paul Rubens (New York: Collier Books, 1970), 179–81.
3 Helmuth James von Moltke, *Letters to Freya, 1939–1945,* ed. and trans. Beate Ruhm von Oppen (New York: Knopf, 1990), 175.

Reading

Deciding to Act

In 1942, Marion Pritchard was a graduate student in German-occupied Amsterdam. She was not Jewish, but she observed what was happening to the Jews of her city. One morning, while riding her bicycle to class, she witnessed a scene outside an orphanage for Jewish children that changed her life:

> The Germans were loading the children, who ranged in age from babies to eight-year-olds, on trucks. They were upset, and crying. When they did not move fast enough the Nazis picked them up, by an arm, a leg, the hair, and threw them into the trucks. To watch grown men treat small children that way—I could not believe my eyes. I found myself literally crying with rage. Two women coming down the street tried to interfere physically. The Germans heaved them into the truck, too. I just sat there on my bicycle, and that was the moment I decided that if there was anything I could do to thwart such atrocities, I would do it.
>
> Some of my friends had similar experiences, and about ten of us, including two Jewish students who decided they did not want [to] go into hiding, organized very informally for this purpose. We obtained Aryan identity cards for the Jewish students, who, of course, were taking more of a risk than we were. They knew many people who were looking to . . . "disappear," as Anne Frank and her family were to do.
>
> We located hiding places, helped people move there, provided food, clothing, and ration cards, and sometimes moral support and relief for the host families. We registered newborn Jewish babies as gentiles . . . and provided medical care when possible.[1]

The decision to rescue Jews often led to other difficult choices. Pritchard described what happened when she agreed to hide a Jewish family:

> The father, the two boys, and the baby girl moved in and we managed to survive the next two years, until the end of the war. Friends helped take up the floorboards, under the rug, and build a hiding place in case of raids. . . . One night we had a very narrow escape.
>
> Four Germans, accompanied by a Dutch Nazi policeman came and searched the house. They did not find the hiding place, but they had learned from experience that sometimes it paid to go back to a house they had already searched, because by then the hidden Jews might have come out of the hiding place. The baby had started to cry, so I let the children out. Then the Dutch policeman came back alone. I had a small revolver that a friend had given me, but I had never planned to use it. I felt I had no choice except to kill him. I would do it again, under the same circumstances, but it still bothers me. . . . If anybody had really tried to find out how and where he disappeared, they could have, but the general attitude was that there was one less traitor to worry about. A local undertaker helped dispose of the body, he put it in a coffin with a legitimate body in it. . . .

---

1   Carol Rittner and Sondra Myers, eds., *The Courage to Care: Rescuers of Jews During the Holocaust* (New York: New York University Press, 1986), 29. Reproduced by permission from New York University Press.

> Was I scared? Of course, the answer is "yes." . . . There were times that the fear got the better of me, and I did not do something that I could have. I would rationalize the inaction, feeling it might endanger others, or that I should not run a risk, because what would happen to the three children I was now responsible for, if something happened to me, but I knew when I was rationalizing.[2]

In reflecting on her choices and those made by others during the war, Pritchard was troubled by a "tendency to divide the general population during the war into a few 'good guys' and the large majority of 'bad guys.' That seems to me to be a dangerous oversimplification . . . The point I want to make is that there were indeed some people who behaved criminally by betraying their Jewish neighbors and thereby sentencing them to death. There were some people who dedicated themselves to actively rescuing as many people as possible. Somewhere in between was the majority, whose actions varied from the minimum decency of at least keeping quiet if they knew where Jews were hidden to finding a way to help when they were asked."[3]

---

[2] Carol Rittner and Sondra Myers, eds., *The Courage to Care: Rescuers of Jews During the Holocaust* (New York: New York University Press, 1986), 29–31. Reproduced by permission from New York University Press.

[3] Rittner and Myers,, eds., *The Courage to Care*, 32–33. Reproduced by permission from New York University Press.

 Reading

Le Chambon: A Village Takes a Stand

All over Europe, a small number of individuals tried to save Jews. But in Le Chambon, a village in southern France, the entire community became involved in rescue. Le Chambon was a Protestant village in a predominantly Roman Catholic region, which before and even during the war a center of tourism. Now its residents turned their tiny mountain village into a hiding place for Jews from every part of Europe. Between 1940 and 1944, Le Chambon and other nearby villages provided refuge for more than 5,000 people fleeing Nazi persecution, about 3,500 of whom were Jews.[1] Magda Trocmé, the wife of the local minister, explained how it began.

> Those of us who received the first Jews did what we thought had to be done—nothing more complicated. It was not decided from one day to the next what we would have to do. There were many people in the village who needed help. How could we refuse them? A person doesn't sit down and say I'm going to do this and this and that. We had no time to think. When a problem came, we had to solve it immediately. Sometimes people ask me, "How did you make a decision?" There was no decision to make. The issue was: Do you think we are all brothers or not? Do you think it is unjust to turn in the Jews or not? Then let us try to help![2]

Almost everyone in the community of 5,000 took part in the effort. Even the children were involved. When a Nazi official tried to organize a Hitler Youth camp in the village, the students told him that they "make no distinction between Jews and non-Jews. It is contrary to Gospel teaching."[3]

The majority of the Jewish refugees were children. The villagers provided them with food, shelter, and fake identity papers. They also made sure that those they sheltered were involved as much as possible in the life of the town, in part to avoid arousing suspicion from other visitors. Whenever residents of Le Chambon learned of an upcoming police raid, they hid those they were protecting in the surrounding countryside. The values of the village were perhaps expressed best by its minister, André Trocmé, who concluded his sermons with the words, "You shall love the Lord your God with all your heart, with all your mind and with all your strength and love your neighbor as yourself. Go practice it."[4]

In February 1943, the police arrested André Trocmé and his assistant, Edouard Theis. Although they were released after 28 days, the Gestapo continued to monitor their

---

1 "Le Chambon-sur-Lignon," United States Holocaust Memorial Museum, last modified January 2016, accessed May 17, 2016, https://www.ushmm.org/wlc/en/article.php?ModuleId=10007518.
2 Carol Rittner and Sondra Myers, *The Courage to Care: Rescuers of Jews During the Holocaust* (New York: New York University Press, 1986), 102. Reprinted by permission from New York University Press.
3 Philip Hallie, *Lest Innocent Blood Be Shed* (London: Michael Joseph, 1979), 102.
4 Hallie, *Lest Innocent Blood Be Shed*, 170.

activities. In summer 1943, the Gestapo offered a reward for André Trocmé's capture, forcing him into hiding for ten months. Many knew where he was, but no one turned him in.[5]

Historian Marianne Ruel Robins notes:

> The fact that an entire community participated (or watched and said nothing) is remarkable indeed. The silence observed by the people of the Plateau was an important condition for its success, not simply because it sheltered Jews from external threats, but also because it minimized internal dissent. To refrain from talking meant that one would not shame one's neighbor for his lack of participation; it also meant that different rationales for behavior would not conflict with another, be they commitment to pacifism, nationalism, Christian charity or judeophilia. Silence did not necessarily imply that everyone implicitly agreed on the reasons for hiding Jews, but rather that most people came to agree that something ought to be done.[6]

The rescuers of Le Chambon also drew support from people in other places. There was an extensive network of sympathizers throughout the region who could be called upon for help with communication and organization. Jewish rescue organizations brought Jewish children to the area for protection. Church groups, both Protestant and Catholic, helped fund their efforts. So did the World Council of Churches. Also, a group known as the Cimade led hundreds of Jews across the Alps to safety in Switzerland.

When Magda Trocmé reflected on her choices years after the war, she said, "When people read this story, I want them to know that I tried to open my door. I tried to tell people, 'Come in, come in.' In the end I would like to say to people, 'Remember that in your life there will be lots of circumstances where you will need a kind of courage, a kind of decision on your own, not about other people but about yourself.' I would not say more."[7]

---

5 "Le Chambon-sur-Lignon," United States Holocaust Memorial Museum, http://www.ushmm.org/wlc/en/article.php?ModuleId=10007518.
6 Marianne Ruel Robins, "A Grey Site of Memory: Le Chambon-sur-Lignon and Protestant Exceptionalism on the Plateau Vivarais-Lignon," *Church History* 82, no. 2 (2013).
7 Carol Rittner and Sondra Myers, *The Courage to Care: Rescuers of Jews During the Holocaust* (New York: New York University Press, 1986), 107. Reproduced by permission from New York University Press.

 Reading

Denmark: A Nation Takes Action

By 1943, anyone in German-occupied Europe who wanted to know was aware of what was happening to Jews. For a variety of reasons—including fear, self-interest, passivity, and even sympathy with German policies—few in occupied nations acted to protect Jewish residents. Many government officials in the occupied countries turned over documents that allowed Germans to quickly identify Jews, and local police often helped Germans find and arrest those Jews. The exception was in Denmark.

After the Germans conquered Denmark in 1940, Hitler had allowed the pre-war government to stay in power and kept only a token military force in the nation. German policy regarded Danes as members of a superior race, similar to Germans. Nevertheless, the Danes deeply resented the occupation of their country, and some fought back with acts of sabotage, riots, and strikes. In summer 1943, the Nazis decided to retaliate. They limited the power of King Christian X, forced the pre-war Danish government to resign, and disbanded the Danish army. They also ordered the arrest of a number of Christian and Jewish leaders.

A few weeks later, the Danes learned that the Germans were planning to deport the nation's entire Jewish population. That news came from Georg Ferdinand Duckwitz, a German diplomat in charge of overseeing shipping between Germany and Denmark. In the early 1930s, Duckwitz was drawn to the Nazis' ultranationalist propaganda and joined the party. However, as Hitler's violent intentions came to light, he became disillusioned with the party. And when the Germans took over Denmark, he sympathized with the hardships and challenges of the Danish people. When Duckwitz learned in late September of secret orders to prepare four cargo ships for transporting Danish Jews to Poland, he immediately passed on the information to leaders in the Danish resistance. They, in turn, informed the Danish people.

When leaders of the Danish church were told of the Germans' plan, they sent an open letter to German officials. On Sunday, October 3, 1943, that letter was read from every pulpit in the nation.

> Wherever Jews are persecuted because of their religion or race it is the duty of the Christian Church to protest against such persecution, because it is in conflict with the sense of justice inherent in the Danish people and inseparable from our Danish Christian culture through the centuries. True to this spirit and according to the text of the Act of the Constitution all Danish citizens enjoy equal rights and responsibilities before the Law and full religious freedom. We understand religious freedom as the right to exercise our worship of God as our vocation and conscience bid us and in such a manner that race and religion per se can never justify that a person be deprived of his rights, freedom or property. Our different religious views notwithstanding, we shall fight for the cause that our Jewish brothers and sisters may preserve the same freedom which we ourselves evaluate more highly than life itself.[1]

---

1 Quoted in Leo Goldberger, ed., *The Rescue of the Danish Jews: Moral Courage Under Stress* (New York: New York University Press, 1988), 6–7.

The Danes responded in the following weeks with a plan to keep Jews from being deported by hiding them until they could be evacuated to nearby Sweden, a neutral nation. It was a collective effort—organized and paid for by hundreds of private citizens, Jews and Christians alike. Fishermen, many of whom could not afford to lose even one day's pay, were paid to transport the Jews to Sweden. The money was also used for bribes. It was no accident that all German patrol ships in the area were docked for repairs on the night of the rescue.

Not every Jew was able to leave. Some were captured as they waited for a boat, while others were picked up at sea. But, in the end, the Nazis were able to deport only 580 of Denmark's 7,000 Jews to the Terezín camp-ghetto, and the Danish government constantly inquired about their status. No Danish Jews were shipped to a death camp, and with the exception of a few who died of illness or old age in Terezín, all of them returned safely to Denmark after the war.

 **Handout**

Perpetrators, Bystanders, Upstanders, and Rescuers

Directions:

1. Read the story out loud together, pausing at the end of each one- to two-paragraph section to annotate *choices, consequences,* and *questions.* There will be sections of the text with no choices or consequences, so every paragraph won't necessarily have an annotation.
   - Write *choice* in the margin alongside any moments where the individual, group, or nation faced a decision and made a significant choice.
   - Underline information in the text that helps you understand what might have led the individual, group, or nation to make those choices.
   - Write *consequence* in the margin alongside any moments where the story discusses the possible or actual consequences for the individual, group, or nation's choices.
2. Discuss the questions below and record your group's answers on this handout. The information you gather today will help you prepare your presentation in the next lesson.

Reading Title: _____

1. Where does your reading take place?

2. What are the significant choices discussed in your reading? Who made them?

3. What reasons or explanations did each individual, group, or nation give for their choices?

4. What were the possible (or actual) consequences of these choices for the individual, group, or nation? In other words, what did the individual(s) know could happen if they made this choice, and/or what actually did happen to them as a consequence of making the choice?

5. How do you think the individual, group, or nation in this reading defined its universe of obligation?

6. What were the impacts of the choices?

7. In this unit, you have learned about the range of human behavior in times of crisis and heard stories about *survivors, resisters, perpetrators, bystanders, upstanders,* and now *rescuers.* It is important to understand that individuals and groups don't fit neatly into one category, even when talking about a single event, and that during the Holocaust, there was a range of choices available at any given moment, although this range was more limited in the 1940s than in earlier decades, especially in Germany, Austria, and Poland.

    Where on the range of behavioral categories (see list above) does your reading's individual, group, or nation fall, and why? (Remember that they could fall into more than one category.) What makes you say that?

 **Handout**

Choices and Consequences

Directions: As each group presents, record notes in this chart about the choices, motivations, and consequences that they discuss. There is room below the chart for you to record any questions that arise during the presentations.

Name of the individual, group, or nation making the choice	What was one choice that they made?	What were the possible motivations for the choice? Did the individual telling the story give a possible explanation or reason for the choice?	What were the possible (or actual) consequences for the choice?	Label the action(s): perpetrator, bystander, upstander, rescuer

Name of the individual, group, or nation making the choice	What choice did they make?		What was the reason or explanation for the choice?	Label the action(s)

My questions:

Unit Essential Question: What does learning about the choices people made during the Weimar Republic, the rise of the Nazi Party, and the Holocaust teach us about the power and impact of our choices today?

Lesson 21

Justice and Judgment after the Holocaust

Duration

Two 50-minute class periods

Materials

Handouts

Justice after the Holocaust Anticipation Guide

An Overview of the Nuremberg Trials

Video

Facing History Scholar Reflections: The Nuremberg Trials

Teaching Strategies

Four Corners

Exit Tickets

3-2-1

Fishbowl

Barometer

Find all materials referenced in this lesson at facinghistory.org/thhb.

Guiding Questions

- Who was responsible for the crimes committed during the Holocaust? Who should be held accountable, and how?
- What challenges did the Allies face once they agreed to bring the Nazi leaders to trial after World War II and the Holocaust? How did the Allied leaders and others involved in the trials respond to these challenges?

Learning Objectives

- Students will recognize some universal dilemmas of justice and judgment faced by societies in the aftermath of mass violence and genocide.
- Students will connect universal dilemmas of justice and judgment to the challenges that Allies faced when deciding how to hold Nazi Germany accountable for the crimes committed during World War II and the Holocaust.

Overview

In the last lesson, students examined choices made by perpetrators, bystanders, upstanders, and rescuers during the Holocaust. In this lesson, students will engage with dilemmas, both universal and specific to this history, about how to hold perpetrators accountable for their actions and to help society recover after the trauma of war and genocide. The study of these dilemmas begins the "Judgment, Memory, and Legacy" stage of the Facing History scope and sequence. Students will recognize that the process of seeking justice is complex and raises questions about accountability, fairness, and punishment. They will grapple with the meaning of justice and the purpose of trials as they learn how the Allies responded to the atrocities of Nazi Germany and attempted to establish a precedent they hoped would prevent such crimes from occurring again. Students will gather evidence to help them evaluate at the end of the lesson whether or not justice was achieved at Nuremberg.

Context

What kind of justice is possible after mass murder on a scale never seen before? Legal scholar Martha Minow writes that seeking justice for war and mass atrocities like the Holocaust requires balance between two opposite responses: vengeance and forgiveness. Vengeance, in response to war and genocide, means revenge or retaliation against those who instigated the war and committed atrocities; it is usually carried out by the victims themselves, and it can perpetuate a cycle of violence. Forgiveness has the power to break the cycle of violence, but it often leaves the perpetrators unpunished and it may often be too much to ask of the victims of heinous crimes.[1]

A spectrum of justice lies between the two poles of vengeance and forgiveness. Trials, like those held by the Allies in Nuremberg after the war, occupy one place on that spectrum. At a trial, a court with established rules and procedures is given the responsibility of responding to a crime, rather than the victims themselves. Evidence is presented to prove or disprove that defendants committed the crimes of which they are accused, and they have an opportunity to defend themselves. Perpetrators are punished, but only after their guilt has been proven. Minow writes, "Resisting revenge and the continuation of war, the [Nuremberg] tribunal turned to principle, fact-finding, and public debate."[2]

Long before the war was over, the Allied powers began to discuss how to hold Germany accountable for its wartime actions. They agreed that Germany had violated several internationally accepted rules of war. Germany's war crimes included its aggressive invasion of other countries, its violation of international treaties, and its inhumane treatment of prisoners of war, hostages, and civilians. Soviet Premier Joseph Stalin suggested executing as many as 50,000 members of the German army. British Prime Minister Winston Churchill was in favor of executing high-ranking Nazi officials without a trial. At the Yalta Conference in February 1945, US President Franklin D. Roosevelt proposed holding international trials for German leaders. Stalin, seeing the propaganda value that public trials would provide, enthusiastically supported the plan. The British, though worried that such trials would simply be seen as "victor's justice," eventually agreed, as well.

Yet the Allies' decision to hold trials led to additional dilemmas: Who, exactly, should be brought to trial? What crimes, specifically, should the defendants be charged with? Can defendants be held responsible for breaking international laws that did not yet exist when they broke them? After a war, can the victorious nations be trusted to conduct fair trials of the leaders of the nations they fought against and defeated?

In June 1945, after Germany's surrender, the Allied powers wrote a charter answering many of these questions and establishing an international tribunal, or court, to conduct trials of Germany's leaders. The charter articulated the crimes for which individuals and corporations could be charged, which included crimes against peace, war crimes, and crimes against humanity. Furthermore, individuals brought to trial could not use the plea that they were following orders as

---

1 Martha Minow, *Between Vengeance and Forgiveness: Facing History after Genocide and Mass Violence* (Boston: Beacon Press, 1998), 10–21.
2 Minow, *Between Vengeance and Forgiveness*, 29.

their defense. Most individuals who had participated in the war and mass killings would never be brought to trial. Instead of trying to prosecute everyone who played a part, the tribunal decided to focus on the most prominent Nazi leaders.

In November 1945, the first trial began in Nuremberg. Of the 22 men tried, five were military leaders and the rest were prominent German government or Nazi Party officials. The Nuremberg trials addressed all German crimes associated with World War II together, not the Holocaust in particular (at that time, the concept of the Holocaust as we know it did not exist). On October 1, 1946, after months of testimony, examination and cross-examination of the defendants, and deliberation by the judges from the four Allied powers who presided over the trials, the verdicts were announced. Twelve defendants received a death sentence, three were sentenced to life in prison, four received prison terms ranging from 10 to 20 years, and three of the defendants were acquitted.

After the first trial ended in October 1946, the United States held 12 other trials at Nuremberg under the authority of the International Military Tribunal. Among those brought to trial were top military leaders, high-ranking SS and other police officers, leaders of the mobile killing units, doctors who participated in the Nazi medical killing program, and officials of other Nazi organizations that engaged in racial persecution.

The Nuremberg trials were not without controversy. Some people argued that it was unfair to indict Nazi leaders for violating laws that had not yet existed at the time they committed the acts of which they were accused. This is called *ex post facto* ("after the fact") justice, and it is specifically forbidden by the US Constitution and the laws of many other nations. Others worried that the trials would result in a "victor's justice" in which the Allied powers would impose their own laws to indict those individuals charged with crimes. Yet today the Nuremberg trials are viewed largely as an effort by the Allies to, in the words of American Nuremberg prosecutor Robert Jackson, "stay the hand of vengeance and voluntarily submit their captive enemies to the judgment of law."[3]

The trials and the judgments that were reached after the war in courtrooms in Nuremberg gave life to long-standing international laws and inspired new ones over time. Each of the trials was intended to give expression to the horror of the crimes and the pain of the victims. The trial proceedings were made public so that people could not only learn but also judge for themselves what had happened and whether justice was done. The evidence was recorded, and every judgment included the reasoning it was based on, so that the truth could be established and tested and retested over time.

US Supreme Court Justice Stephen Breyer has observed that when we learn about the Holocaust, "We think: There are no words. There is no compensating deed. There can be no vengeance. Nor is any happy ending possible." But Nuremberg "reminds us of those human aspirations that remain a cause for optimism. It reminds us that after the barbarism came a call for reasoned justice."[4] Studying this call and evaluating its successes and its difficulties allows us to reflect more deeply

---

[3] Robert H. Jackson, "Opening Statement before the International Military Tribunal," The Robert H. Jackson Center, accessed June 7, 2016, https://www.roberthjackson.org/speech-and-writing/opening-statement-before-the-international-military-tribunal/.

[4] Stephen Breyer, "Crimes Against Humanity: Nuremberg, 1946," *New York University Law Review* 71, no. 5 (November 1996): 1164.

on the complexity of human behavior, the possibility of judging today the choices made by people in past generations, and the existence of universal standards of right and wrong.

Notes to Teacher

1. An Overview of the Nuremberg Trials

You may need additional background information to answer questions that come up in class about the Nuremberg trials. To support your own background knowledge before teaching this lesson, consider reading "Establishing the Nuremberg Tribunal" and "The First Trial at Nuremberg" from Chapter 10 of *Holocaust and Human Behavior*.

2. Setting Up for "Four Corners"

The first activity in this lesson includes the Four Corners teaching strategy. We recommend that you set up the room for this activity before class begins. Create four signs that read "Strongly Agree," "Agree," "Disagree," and "Strongly Disagree," and hang them in different corners of the room.

3. Defining *Genocide*

If you have not already introduced the term *genocide* to your students, it would be helpful to provide them with the definition, coined in 1944 by lawyer Raphael Lemkin: "the destruction of a nation or an ethnic group." The United Nations Genocide Convention defines *genocide* in significantly more detail. The reading "Raphael Lemkin and the Genocide Convention" from Chapter 10 of *Holocaust and Human Behavior* includes the more detailed United Nations definition, as well as information and links to additional resources about Lemkin's development of the term and his campaign to establish genocide as an international crime.

4. Previewing Vocabulary

In addition to *genocide*, the following are key vocabulary terms used in this lesson:

- Justice
- Responsibility
- International community
- Tribunal
- Trial
- Legacy
- Conspiracy

Add these words to your word wall, if you are using one for this unit, and provide necessary support to help students learn these words as you teach the lesson.

5. The Unit Assessment

If your students are writing the final essay assessment for this unit, after teaching this lesson, instruct your students to add evidence from the last three lessons to their evidence logs. For suggested activities and resources, see Adding to Evidence Logs, 3 of 3.

Activities

Day 1

1. ### Explore the Complexities of Achieving Justice

   Before examining the specific dilemmas of justice after the Holocaust, ask students to think about the meaning of justice in their own experiences by responding to the prompt below. Let students know that their responses will be kept private:

   > Identify a time when someone wronged you or someone you care about. It might be a situation in which you or someone you love was treated unfairly, or it might be an accident that resulted in a loss or injury. After this event, what would have needed to happen for "justice to be served"?

   Then tell students that the question of what would need to happen for "justice to be served" had to be answered after the Holocaust and World War II. Tell students that even before the war ended, the Allied leaders (Roosevelt, Churchill, and Stalin) were discussing ways to hold Germany accountable for the war and the murder of millions of civilians. In those discussions, the Allies encountered a variety of dilemmas and disagreements about what justice might look like and how it might be achieved.

   Some of the dilemmas the Allies faced are probed on the handout **Justice after the Holocaust Anticipation Guide**. Distribute the handout and ask students to complete it on their own by circling their response to each statement (strongly agree, agree, disagree, strongly disagree) and explaining their thinking in the space provided.

   After students have completed the anticipation guide, use the **Four Corners** strategy to discuss their responses. Remember that students can change their positions in the room if they are persuaded by their classmates in the course of the discussion. To ensure that you hear everyone's voice, try to create space for each student to share at least one idea with the class during the discussion.

   Finally, debrief the activity with the class by leading a whole-group discussion based on the following question:

   > What does this activity suggest about the challenges faced by the Allies in seeking justice after World War II and the Holocaust?

2. ### Provide an Overview of the Nuremberg Trials

   Explain to students that they will now learn about the Nuremberg tribunal, an international court established by the United States, Britain, France, and the Soviet Union to put Nazi leaders on trial. The first trial in Nuremberg involved the prosecution of 22 Nazi Party officials, prominent members of the German government, and German military leaders.

   Show the video **Facing History Scholar Reflections: The Nuremberg Trials** (04:27) at **facinghistory.org/thhb** for a brief overview of the trials. If you have time, show the video twice, sharing the questions below with students before they watch for the second time. Note that this video includes a few photographs depicting violence and mass murder.

Help students recall key pieces of information from the video to record in their notes by leading a class discussion in which you draw from the following text-dependent questions:

- Which four Allied countries made up the international tribunal?
- What was the purpose of the Nuremberg trials?
- What were four charges on which a Nazi leader could be indicted (charged with a serious crime)?
- What was significant about the charge of "crimes against humanity"?
- What was significant about the charge of "conspiracy"?
- According to Bookbinder, what evidence suggests that the Nuremberg trials were fair?

3. Assess Student Understanding

To formatively assess each student's understanding of the content covered in today's lesson, ask them to respond to the following questions on an exit ticket.

- List three things that you learned about the Nuremberg trials and the challenges that the Allies faced when seeking justice after World War II and the Holocaust.
- Write one question that you have about a statement on the anticipation guide, a detail in the video, or something that was said during class discussion.

Day 2

1. Address Exit Tickets

Start the class by spending a few minutes reading comments from the exit tickets. To provide continuity with yesterday's lesson, you might read a sampling of the things students wrote that they learned, hitting on a range of ideas. Then respond to a few of the students' questions to help clear up any misunderstandings.

Unless students have given you permission to use their names, we recommend that you keep them anonymous and address any significant individual misunderstandings one-on-one with students outside of class.

2. Connect Nuremberg to Dilemmas of Justice

Yesterday students grappled with some of the dilemmas that the Allied nations faced when deciding how to seek justice for the atrocities committed by Germany during World War II and the Holocaust. They also watched a video that provided an overview of the crimes for which defendants could be charged and the lasting effects of the trial on how justice has been sought after genocides in recent decades. Today students will read about what happened at the first Nuremberg trial and those that followed.

Divide the class into groups of four or five students, and ask them to take out their anticipation guides from the previous class period. Pass out the handout An Overview of the Nuremberg Trials, and read the instructions aloud with the class. Complete the first statement on the handout as a whole group to make sure that students understand the instructions.

LESSON 21: JUSTICE AND JUDGMENT AFTER THE HOLOCAUST   315

As students are working, circulate around the room, encouraging them to refer to their anticipation guides and discuss each section together before writing their notes.

After the groups have finished reading, have them complete the 3-2-1 activity included on the handout. Debrief these responses as a class, asking each group to share at least one thing they learned or one question they debated together.

3. Discuss Trials and the Goal of Achieving Justice

In these two lessons, students have learned about the dilemmas involved in seeking justice after World War II and the Holocaust and some key events from the Nuremberg trials. Now they will consider the broader goal of seeking justice, and the specific role a trial plays: its purpose, its advantages, and its limitations.

To prepare for a Fishbowl discussion, ask students to respond to the following questions in their journals:

- What conflicts and challenges might remain, after the violence has ended, in a society that has experienced war and the mass murder of civilians?
- How might a trial address some of those challenges? In what ways might a trial be insufficient to bring about healing and justice?
- What else might be needed for a society to be repaired after war and a crime as severe as genocide?

After students have had some time to reflect on the questions, ask six to ten students to form a circle in the center of the room while the rest of the class gathers around the outside of the circle to listen to the conversation. You might ask the first group to address the first question in their discussion and then have the students switch places so that a new group can discuss the last two questions.

4. Evaluate the Nuremberg Trials

To finish this lesson, tell students that they will evaluate the following statement:

> The Nuremberg war crimes trials were effective at achieving justice for the crimes of World War II and the Holocaust.

Instruct them to copy the statement at the top of a sheet of paper, or in their journals, and then draw a T-chart underneath it. The columns of the T-chart should be labeled *Agree* and *Disagree.*

Ask students to work individually or in pairs to use the handouts as well as their notes from the video and discussions in this lesson to list facts, evidence, and ideas in each column of the T-chart. Which facts, evidence, and ideas might one use to justify their agreement with the statement? Which facts, evidence, and ideas might one use to justify disagreement?

After completing the chart, students might use their work to decide which column offers the more convincing case. Time permitting, the class can debrief this activity in a discussion using the Barometer strategy.

Assessment

- Evaluate the T-charts that students complete in the "Evaluate the Nuremberg Trials" activity that ends the lesson for evidence of students' understanding of the issues of justice explored in this lesson. You might ask students to take the activity one step further and use the ideas and evidence from their T-charts to write a paragraph explaining their agreement or disagreement with the statement.

- Collect the anticipation guides and An Overview of the Nuremberg Trials handouts in order to gauge students' understanding of and critical thinking about issues of justice and judgment.

Extensions

1. Explore Legacies of World War II and the Holocaust

World War II and the Holocaust left a variety of crucial institutional legacies that are still highly relevant in the world today. These legacies include:

- The United Nations
- The Universal Declaration of Human Rights
- The Convention on the Prevention and Punishment of the Crime of Genocide
- The International Criminal Court

Each of these topics deserves its own lesson and unit to help provide students with a deeper understanding of twentieth- and twenty-first-century history. To incorporate these topics into your class, begin with readings in Chapter 11 of *Holocaust and Human Behavior*. Those readings include links and recommendations for videos and other Facing History resources about these topics.

2. Introduce Transitional Justice

While this lesson focuses on the strengths and limitations of trials in delivering justice, other models exist through which societies can respond to traumatic conflict and attempt to repair themselves. A discussion of the concept of *transitional justice* can help students better understand such questions as:

- Can a nation as a whole be held responsible for crimes?
- Is it possible to make amends for genocide and crimes against humanity? What is owed to the victims?
- Is it possible to restore peace between different groups and to repair society?

These questions are the focus of transitional justice, the term scholars use to describe the variety of actions a society can take as it emerges from a period of war, injustice, and mass violence and tries to move toward a better future. The readings "Transitional Justice in Germany" and "Transitional Justice in South Africa" can help you broaden your students' ideas about justice and the possibility of healing after war and genocide.

3. Explore the Concept of Moral Luck

Any exploration of justice and judgment in history can lead to a more philosophical question about how, in the present day, we can judge the choices people made in the past when different standards of behavior and morality may have existed. The reading "Moral Luck and Dilemmas of Judgment" might stimulate a rich and provocative discussion about both our ability to judge choices people made in the past and the ways in which people in the future might judge our choices today. Consider sharing the reading with students and using the connection questions that follow to begin a class discussion.

Visit **facinghistory.org/thhb** to access these additional resources.

 Handout

Justice after the Holocaust Anticipation Guide

Directions: The statements below represent some of the main issues that the Allies faced as they tried to figure out how to achieve justice after World War II and the Holocaust. Read each statement in the left column. Decide if you strongly agree (SA), agree (A), disagree (D), or strongly disagree (SD) with it. Circle your response and provide a one- to two-sentence explanation of your opinion (on separate paper if needed).

Statement	Your Opinion
1. It is possible to achieve justice for the crimes committed during the Holocaust.	SA A D SD **Explain:**
2. The victors in a war have the right to punish the defeated countries however they wish.	SA A D SD **Explain:**
3. Those responsible for the Holocaust should be immediately killed or jailed; they do not have the right to a fair trial in a court of law.	SA A D SD **Explain:**
4. Bringing perpetrators to justice in courts is an effective way to prevent future crimes.	SA A D SD **Explain:**

5. Since each country has its own laws, citizens should be brought to trial by the courts of their own country. It is unfair for some nations, or the international community, to impose their laws on citizens of other nations.	SA A D SD	**Explain:**
6. Bystanders allowed the Holocaust to happen. If more people had stood up rather than looking the other way, millions of lives could have been saved. The bystanders should be punished along with the perpetrators.	SA A D SD	**Explain:**
7. Spreading hateful lies that influence people to harm others is a crime against humanity.	SA A D SD	**Explain:**
8. The only person responsible for the Holocaust was Adolf Hitler. Nazi leaders were following the laws of their country and the orders of their elected leader. They should not be punished.	SA A D SD	**Explain:**

Handout

An Overview of the Nuremberg Trials

Directions: Below are eight descriptions of key events from the Nuremberg trials. Read each description, and then choose one or more statements from the Justice after the Holocaust Anticipation Guide handout that relate to the event. Write the statement number (1–8) from the anticipation guide on the line after the event to which it relates. Then, in the space provided on this handout, explain the connection that you see between the two.

1. Soviet Premier Joseph Stalin suggested executing 50,000 members of the German army. Winston Churchill, the British leader, thought that high-ranking Nazi leaders should be hanged. But other leaders thought they should go to trial.
   Statement #: _____

2. The Allied countries agreed to put Nazi leaders on trial for two reasons: 1) to punish those responsible, and 2) to prevent future crimes against humanity. Those who organized the trials wanted future leaders to know that if they acted like Hitler and other Nazi leaders, they would be punished for their actions; they could not just get away with murdering their own citizens.
   Statement #: _____

3. Beginning in November 1945, an international trial—a court case involving many countries—was held in the city of Nuremberg in Germany, so the trials were called the Nuremberg trials. The trials included judges and lawyers from each of the winning countries (Britain, France, the United States, and the Soviet Union). The Nazi defendants also had lawyers to defend them. Some argued that it was unfair for the Allied powers to bring the Nazis to trial because they had not broken any laws. (At this point in time, there were no international laws forbidding a government from murdering its own citizens.)
   Statement #: _____

4. Twenty-four men were indicted (charged with a crime) during the first set of trials at Nuremberg. These defendants included military leaders, Nazi Party leaders, and officers who worked at the concentration camps. Hitler and several other Nazi leaders were not indicted because they had committed suicide or escaped at the end of the war. Some lower-ranking officers, soldiers, and bureaucrats who participated in the Holocaust were indicted in later trials. Bystanders also were not put on trial at Nuremberg or in future trials.
Statement #: _____

5. The defendants in the first set of trials were charged with four types of crimes. One of these crimes was "crimes against humanity." One of the men charged with crimes against humanity was Julius Streicher. He was minister of propaganda of the Nazi Party. He was responsible for spreading hateful lies about Jews in the newspaper and in other forms, such as children's books.
Statement #: _____

6. Many Nazis charged with "crimes against humanity" argued that they were only following orders and that they had not broken any laws by their actions.
Statement #: _____

7. Nineteen of the defendants were found guilty in the first Nuremberg trial. Twelve were sentenced to death by hanging. Three were given life in prison, and four were given prison terms ranging from 10 to 20 years. In the three years that followed, many more trials of Germans were held in Nuremberg. By 1949, more than 200 German officials, including the highest-ranking surviving Nazi leaders, members of the Einsatzgruppen mobile killing units, and dozens of physicians and industrialists, were brought to trial for their roles in the war and in the mass murder of civilians. The vast majority were convicted and sentenced to death or given prison sentences of varying lengths.
Statement #: _____

8. After the war, the Allied powers also had to consider what Germany should do to "pay back" the survivors of the Holocaust and the families of the victims. After all, the Nazis had taken all of their money and property and had caused immeasurable suffering. A program was set up to provide money (reparations) to those who could prove they were victims of the Nazis, and Germany was supposed to give back stolen property to its rightful owners (if they were still alive).
Statement #: _____

9. After you have finished discussing each section and making connections to the anticipation guide, work together to complete a 3-2-1 activity, described below, that you will share in a class discussion.

    A. Write **three** things you learned about the Nuremberg trials and the complexities of seeking justice after World War II and the Holocaust after reading this overview.

    B. Write **two** questions that your group has about the Nuremberg trials and the complexities of seeking justice after World War II and the Holocaust after reading this overview.

    C. Write **one** idea from this overview that you found particularly interesting or confusing (you can do this one individually).

STEP 5

Adding to Evidence Logs, 3 of 3

UNIT ASSESSMENT

Students are now ready to reflect on, gather evidence for, and discuss the unit writing prompt in its entirety:

> What does learning about the choices people made during the Weimar Republic, the rise of the Nazi Party, and the Holocaust teach us about the power and impact of our choices today?

In addition to reflecting on the entire prompt and adding evidence from Lessons 19 to 21 to their evidence logs, you might also ask students to engage in structured conversations or mini-debates that challenge them to support their ideas about the writing topic with evidence and listen actively to their peers. For many students, the process of talking before writing helps them organize their thoughts, explain their thinking, and develop a clear point of view.

Suggested Activities

Visit facinghistory.org/thhb to access all materials referenced in these activities.

1. Journal Reflection

Ask students to reread their journal entries in response to the essay topic. Challenge them to look for, and maybe even mark with a star, places where their thinking about the question evolved or changed. Then ask them to respond to the writing prompt in their journals:

> What does learning about the choices people made during the Weimar Republic, the rise of the Nazi Party, and the Holocaust teach us about the power and impact of our choices today?

Use the Wraparound strategy to allow each student to share an idea from their journal with the class.

2. Evidence Logs

Students should add to their evidence logs any information from Lessons 19 to 21 that helps them respond to the essay question.

3. Take a Stand on Controversial Issues

Although students will continue to gather evidence throughout the final two lessons of this unit, this is an appropriate time for them to begin the process of developing their position in response to the writing prompt by engaging in structured discussions with their peers. You might select from the Common Core Writing Prompts and Strategies supplement's Strategy 14: Taking a Stand on

Controversial Issues: Speaking and Listening Strategies or Strategy 15: Building Arguments through Mini-Debates. Or you might select a different pre-writing teaching strategy from the website.

4. Final Reflection

In a final journal response or on exit tickets, ask students to respond to the following questions:

- How has your thinking about the essay topic question changed over the course of the unit? Which text (reading, image, video), lesson, or activity contributed the most to this change?
- What do you feel you need to learn more about in order to answer the essay topic question and write your essay?

Unit Essential Question What does learning about the choices people made during the Weimar Republic, the rise of the Nazi Party, and the Holocaust teach us about the power and impact of our choices today?

Lesson 22: How Should We Remember?

Duration
One 50-minute class period

Materials

Image Gallery
Holocaust Memorials

Handout
Creating a Memorial

Teaching Strategy
Jigsaw

Find all materials referenced in this lesson at facinghistory.org/thhb.

Guiding Questions

- How should we remember the past? What impact do memorials and monuments have on the way we think about history?
- What parts of the history of the Holocaust are most important for us to remember today? How can we ensure that this history is not forgotten?

Learning Objectives

- Students will analyze several examples of Holocaust memorials to see how the communities and individuals that designed them sought to shape future generations' understanding of this history.
- By designing their own memorials, students will become familiar with the many choices artists and communities make in their commemorations about what aspects of a particular history are worth remembering and what parts are intentionally left out.

Overview

The previous lesson began the "Judgment, Memory, and Legacy" stage of the Facing History scope and sequence by helping students wrestle with dilemmas of justice after the Holocaust. This lesson continues that stage of the scope and sequence by helping students think deeply about the impact of memory and history on the present day. In particular, this lesson engages students in the processes of both responding to and creating memorials to the Holocaust. By doing so, they are forced to grapple with key questions about why history is important and how our memory of history is shaped and influenced. Students will begin by learning about several Holocaust memorials around the world and analyzing the choices that artists and communities made when creating them. Then they will design, plan, and create their own memorial to represent an idea, event, or person they believe is important to remember from the history of the Holocaust.

Context

As students explored in the previous lesson, judgment and justice were crucial components of the aftermath of the Holocaust. Testimony in the Nuremberg trials provided the world with clear evidence of the human devastation wrought by the Nazis and preserved this information in the historical record. In this way, these trials were a step toward another stage of the postwar process: remembrance. This process of reckoning, or coming to terms, with the history of the Holocaust is one that continues today among historians, survivors and their descendants, politicians, citizens, and students. As American author James Baldwin has said, in writing about America's history of slavery:

> History, as nearly no one seems to know, is not merely something to be read. And it does not refer merely, or even principally, to the past. On the contrary, the great force of history comes from the fact that we carry it within us, are unconsciously controlled by it in many ways, and history is literally *present* in all that we do.[1]

Baldwin suggests that we won't really understand history or ourselves unless we consider how the past is "present" in our world. And the Holocaust—which historians describe as not merely a significant moment in history but a "collapse in human civilization"[2] and a "symbol of evil"[3]—exerts an especially powerful force. Author Eva Hoffman, the daughter of Holocaust survivors, has observed, "Sixty years after the Holocaust took place, our reckoning with this defining event is far from over. Indeed, as this immense catastrophe recedes from us in time, our preoccupation with it seems only to increase."[4]

There are many ways in which individuals, groups, and nations, in Germany and around the world, have confronted the memory of the Holocaust. Some countries, including Germany and France, have made Holocaust denial a crime, punishable by a fine and imprisonment. Governments have also encouraged or mandated education about the Holocaust. German schools are required to teach their students about the Nazi era and the Holocaust, and in addition to classroom learning, most German students visit either a concentration camp or a Holocaust memorial.[5] Scholars, journalists, survivors, and novelists have helped the public remember the Holocaust through their writing. When Holocaust survivor and author Elie Wiesel was awarded the Nobel Peace Prize in 1986, the chairman of the Nobel committee remarked, "Through his books, Elie Wiesel has given us not only an eyewitness account of what happened, but also an analysis of the evil powers which lay behind the events."[6]

Another way that communities around the world have remembered the Holocaust is through building memorials and monuments. These buildings are created for many reasons: to preserve the past, to honor heroes (such as the resisters of the Warsaw ghetto uprising or the rescuers of Le Chambon), to commemorate

---

1 James Baldwin, "The White Man's Guilt," *Ebony*, August 1965, 47.
2 "The President's Commission on the Holocaust: Guiding Principles," United States Holocaust Memorial Museum, accessed June 1, 2016, https://www.ushmm.org/information/about-the-museum/presidents-commission/guiding-principles.
3 Yehuda Bauer, *Rethinking the Holocaust* (New Haven, CT: Yale University Press, 2001), x.
4 Eva Hoffman, *After Such Knowledge: Memory, History, and the Legacy of the Holocaust* (New York: Public Affairs, 2011), ix.
5 "Holocaust Education in Germany: An Interview," PBS website, accessed January 23, 2009.
6 Egil Aarvick, "The Nobel Peace Prize 1986," PBS website, accessed January 23, 2009.

tragedies, and to inspire action or reflection. These monuments raise questions about appropriate ways to study and remember the Holocaust. To what extent can any memorial help us truly understand the experiences of victims of the Holocaust? How can we symbolize the vast number of victims while still honoring each unique life that was lost—the schoolchild, the aunt, the tailor, the physicist, the sister? Who should decide how the Holocaust is represented and remembered—what symbols are used, what facts are presented, and whose stories are told?

As the process of reckoning and remembrance continues to unfold, one thing is certain: What happened then continues to have a profound influence on the lives of individuals to this day. As Rabbi Jonathan Sacks has written, there is a difference between history and memory: "History is information. Memory, by contrast, is part of identity. . . . Memory is the past as present, as it lives on in me."[7] Survivors, witnesses, the descendants of those who lived this history, and all those who learn about it today face the question of how to remember the past and how that memory might shape our understanding of ourselves and our present world.

Notes to Teacher

1. Helpful Background on Memorials and Monuments

The images in this lesson are taken from the visual essay "Holocaust Memorials and Monuments" in *Holocaust and Human Behavior*. The introduction to the visual essay provides an in-depth discussion of the relationship of memorials to history and public memory, as well as the variety of roles memorials can serve in a community or country. We recommend that you read this introduction in preparation to teach this lesson in order to help you answer questions that may arise and guide students to a deeper level of understanding of the power of memory. You might also decide to share some of this introduction with your students.

2. Building in Time for Memorial Planning

The last activity in this lesson provides students with the opportunity to plan their own Holocaust memorial. This is a task that may warrant more time for reflection than is available in the class period. Consider assigning this activity for homework. You might even give students multiple nights to complete and submit the Creating a Memorial handout so that they have time to develop their ideas more thoroughly.

Also consider devoting an extra class period to this lesson, if possible. Doing so will give students time to workshop their ideas for memorials with each other, as well as time to sketch or build models of their ideas using clay, construction paper, or other materials you are able to provide.

3. Providing Models for Student Memorials

The last activity in this lesson requires students to plan their own memorials related to the Holocaust, and many teachers also ask students to build a physical model of the memorial they have conceptualized. In addition to the examples of existing, real-world memorials and monuments students will analyze in

---

7 Jonathan Sacks, *Rabbi Jonathan Sacks's Haggadah: Hebrew and English Text with New Essays and Commentary* (New York: Continuum, 2006), 29.

this lesson, it may be helpful to provide students with examples of memorials designed and created using the instructions provided in this lesson. In other words, consider sharing with students one or two examples of memorials that students from past years created, or a memorial you created yourself. These examples can help inspire students' creativity and set standards for the quality and depth of thought you are expecting.

4. Previewing Vocabulary

The following are key vocabulary terms used in this lesson:

- Memorial
- Monument
- Commemoration

Add these words to your word wall, if you are using one for this unit, and provide necessary support to help students learn these words as you teach the lesson.

Activities

1. Define the Purpose of Memorials and Monuments

Begin by asking students to take a few moments to describe in their journals one or more monuments or memorials that they are familiar with. Perhaps it is one in their neighborhood that they pass every day, or one they have seen elsewhere in the city, country, or world that they found memorable. Have them describe both what it looks like and what they think its purpose is. What do they think the designer of the monument wanted people to think, remember, or feel?

After writing, give students a few moments to share their examples with one or more classmates, and then lead a short whole-group discussion in response to the question: Why do people build monuments and memorials? What purposes do they serve? Record students' ideas on the board.

2. Introduce Choices Reflected in Holocaust Memorials and Monuments

Continue the whole-group discussion about memorials and monuments by reading the following paragraph to students:

> Across Europe, and even around the globe, people have built memorials to commemorate the Holocaust. Each tries to preserve the collective memory of the generation that built the memorial and to shape the memories of generations to come. Memorials raise complex questions about which history we choose to remember. If a memorial cannot tell the whole story, then what part of the story, or whose story, does it tell? Whose memories, whose point of view, and whose values and perspectives will be represented?

Ask students to write down their thoughts in their journals in response to the following question: What do you think the author means when she says that memorials "cannot tell the whole story"?

LESSON 22: HOW SHOULD WE REMEMBER? 329

- Ask a few students to share their thoughts in a brief, informal whole-group discussion. You might ask students to think again about the memorial or monument they wrote about at the beginning of class. What parts of the story might it leave out?

3. Analyze Examples of Holocaust Memorials and Monuments

The class will now use the Jigsaw teaching strategy to analyze a variety of Holocaust memorials. Divide the class into six groups and assign each group one of the following images from the Holocaust Memorials gallery:

- Warsaw Ghetto Uprising Memorial
- Aschrott Fountain
- Stolpersteine
- Memorial to Roma and Sinti Victims of National Socialism
- Holocaust Memorial Miami Beach
- Shoes on the Danube Bank Memorial

Students can analyze these Holocaust memorials and monuments using the Jigsaw strategy. First, divide the class into "expert" groups of three to four students; each group will analyze one handout that shows one memorial or monument. Depending on the size of your class, you may have more than one group working with a particular memorial. In their journals, have each group answer the following questions, using what they observe in the image and the information in the caption, if necessary:

- Who is the intended audience for the memorial?
- What, specifically, is the memorial representing or commemorating?
- What story or message do you think the artist was trying to convey to the intended audience? What might the memorial be leaving out?
- How does the memorial convey its intended story or message? What materials did the artist use? What might the audience's experience be like when they visit the memorial?

Once the "expert" groups have completed their work, students will reorganize themselves into "teaching" groups, with three students in each group. The members of each "teaching" group should have analyzed a different voice in their "expert" groups. Each "teaching" group also has two tasks:

1. Share their "expert" group's work (the answers to the above questions).
2. Discuss the following questions with the group: What similarities and differences do you notice between the memorials/monuments? What do you think accounts for these similarities and/or differences?

Complete the activity by asking members of each "teaching" group to report to the whole class the takeaways from their discussions.

4. Plan Your Own Holocaust Memorial

Conclude the lesson by asking students to submit a written plan for their own Holocaust memorial (see the Extensions section for an activity that involves creating a visual representation). Pass out the handout Creating a Memorial. Ask students to complete the questions individually and then follow the instructions at the end of the handout to create a simple sketch of their memorial, give it a title, and write an artist's statement.

Assessment

- Assess students' understanding of the ideas in this lesson by observing the depth of their thinking in their oral participation and written responses in the Jigsaw activity.

- Students' work on the Creating a Memorial handout can also provide evidence of their understanding of the role and meaning of memorials and monuments. Look at the choices they make in planning their own monument, as well as their explanations of those choices and how well they connect to themes, events, and individuals in the history they studied in this unit.

Extensions

1. Create a Model of Your Memorial

While the "Creating a Memorial" handout directs students to create a visual representation of the memorials they have planned, many teachers take the activity a step further by giving students the opportunity to actually build something (usually on a smaller scale than their plan may call for). This can be accomplished at school by devoting additional class time to the project and providing a selection of materials and supplies (such as modeling clay or construction paper) for students to work with. The intent is not to judge students' skills as artists and craftspeople but to give them an opportunity to make their thinking visible with a tangible product. Remind students that even simple shapes, arranged thoughtfully, can communicate powerful ideas, and that the title and artist's statement that accompany the model of their monument will help explain to classmates and teachers their intent and overall vision.

After students have completed their models, consider giving them the opportunity to share their memorials with their classmates and other audiences in the school. You can give each student a few minutes to present their memorial to the class, or students can set up an exhibit in the classroom or another public space in the school to showcase their memorials.

2. Read about Debates over Symbols of the Past in the United States

Memorials and monuments, and the way they relate to the public memory of history, have often been controversial. In the United States, persistent debates have intensified in recent years about the how the Civil War and the related history of racial injustice is represented (or omitted) in the memorials and monuments that occupy public spaces. The lesson "After Charlottesville: Contested History and the Fight Against Bigotry" can help you introduce to your students some of the debates over symbols of the past in the United States. You might also share with students the readings "Acknowledging the Past to Shape the Present" and "Creating a New Narrative."

All of these resources can help you address the following questions with your students:

- What role does history play in a healthy democracy? Is it necessary to acknowledge past injustices to achieve a more just and equitable society?
- No matter where you live, your community has a history. Is any part of your community's history unacknowledged or forgotten today? How might you discover and explore such histories? Could awareness of the past change your understanding of the place you call home?

Visit **facinghistory.org/thhb** to access these additional resources.

Image Gallery

Holocaust Memorials

Warsaw Ghetto Uprising Memorial

This memorial was built on the site of Warsaw's Jewish ghetto. When it was unveiled in 1948, the city still lay in ruins all around it.

Aschrott Fountain

In Kassel, Germany, artist Horst Hoheisel created a "counter-memorial" marking the site where a majestic fountain built by a Jewish citizen once stood; it had been destroyed by the Nazis in 1939.

Stolpersteine

Stolpersteine (stumbling stones) in Sušice, Czech Republic, mark the site where the four members of the Gutmann family lived before they were murdered in the Holocaust.

Memorial to Roma and Sinti Victims of National Socialism

Michael Brooks / Alamy Stock Photo

This memorial in Berlin, Germany, was designed by Dani Karavan and opened in 2012. The triangular stone at the center of the pool holds a fresh flower, which is replaced every day.

Holocaust Memorial Miami Beach

Miami Beach is home to a large number of Holocaust survivors, who commissioned this memorial by architect Kenneth Treister in 1990. The outstretched arm is almost four stories tall.

Shoes on the Danube Bank Memorial

Sixty pairs of shoes mark the site in Budapest, Hungary, where fascist Arrow Cross militiamen shot Jews and threw their bodies into the river in 1944 and 1945. The memorial opened in 2005.

 **Handout**

Creating a Memorial

Directions: If you were to design a memorial to commemorate the Holocaust, what events, people, or ideas would you want it to represent? Take some time to reflect on what you've learned about the Holocaust and what you think is most important for you and others to remember.

Create a plan for your memorial. Your plan should answer the following questions:

What message do you want the memorial to convey?

Who is the audience for the memorial?

How will the memorial communicate your ideas? What specific materials, forms, imagery, or words will it include?

After you've thought it over, create something—it can be as simple as a sketch or as complex as a model made from physical materials. Finally, give your memorial a title and write a brief description, or artist's statement, to accompany it.

| Unit Essential Question | What does learning about the choices people made during the Weimar Republic, the rise of the Nazi Party, and the Holocaust teach us about the power and impact of our choices today? |

Lesson

Choosing to Participate

Duration

One 50-minute class period

Materials

 Handout
Analyzing Levers of Power

 Readings
What Difference Can a Word Make?
Bullying at School
The Voices of Millions
Acknowledging the Past to Shape the Present
Seeking a Strategy that Works
Believing in Others
Walking with the Wind

 Teaching Strategy
Wraparound

Find all materials referenced in this lesson at facinghistory.org/thhb.

Guiding Questions

- What must individuals do and value in order to bring about a more humane, just, and compassionate world and a more democratic society?
- How can we determine the most effective way to make a difference in our neighborhood, our nation, and the world? Which strategies are best for bringing about the changes we want to see?

Learning Objectives

- Students will be able to explain the term "levers of power" and recognize how individuals strategically use organizations, institutions, and technologies to make social or political change.
- Students will use the "levers of power" framework to identify ways they can bring about positive change in their communities.

Overview

The previous lesson engaged students in an examination of how societies remember and represent their history, especially through memorials and monuments. This lesson brings students into the "Choosing to Participate" stage of the Facing History scope and sequence by asking them to consider how our memory and understanding of history inspires and guides our choices in the world today. In particular, this lesson invites students to envision the ways that they themselves might contribute to the process of creating a more humane, just, and compassionate world.

Legal scholar Martha Minow has observed that one of the biggest barriers that individuals face in getting involved is that it is hard to know what actual steps to take: "Often times we see something that's unjust and we wonder, 'Where do I go? What do I do?'" In an effort to help individuals identify concrete actions to take when they "choose to participate," Minow developed a "levers of power" framework to map out the organizations, institutions, and technologies that can enable us to strengthen the impact of our voices and our actions. In this lesson, students will learn about these "levers" of power and analyze how some individuals and communities have strategically used them to make change. Students will then have the opportunity to think about which levers are most accessible to them personally and how they might use these to bring about changes they would like to see in their own communities.

Context

How does learning about the history of Nazi Germany and the Holocaust educate us about our responsibilities in the world today? Racism, antisemitism, and other forms of bigotry—which were at the root of so much of the inhumanity of the twentieth century—have not gone away. The principles of international law and the institutions that enforce those principles, which were created after World War II in response to the problems of war, genocide, and statelessness, continue to face daunting challenges. The news from around the world can be overwhelming, and people often wonder how they can help with the enormous job of bringing about a more humane, just, compassionate world and a more democratic society.

This lesson includes stories of individuals and groups who did "choose to participate," and their stories can help us reflect on the values and actions that will strengthen our communities rather than make them more fragile. But the goal of this final step in the Facing History & Ourselves scope and sequence is not to force students to take action. Instead, its aim is to open their eyes to the different ways of participating that are happening around them and to the tools that others have used to make positive changes in their own communities. Encountering these examples offers an opportunity for students to reflect on who they are, who they want to be, and what kind of world they want to help create. As students explore the stories in this lesson, they should pay close attention to what inspires the individuals who appear in them, to the goals and strategies of those individuals, and to the ways those individuals enlist allies and respond to success and failure.

We often think about civic participation as a matter of politics, activism, and voting. Many people participate in organized campaigns to elect candidates, change laws, and influence the actions of governments and other institutions in our society, such as corporations and the media. But these are not the only ways of choosing to participate. Scholar Ethan Zuckerman, who studies civic engagement around the world, has noticed a trend toward types of participation that do not rely on the power of government and other institutions to make change. The readings in this lesson provide examples of both types of initiative: individuals choosing to participate through politics, activism, and institutions, and others who are attempting to make change through creative uses of art and technology, the formation of small businesses, and attempts to influence the norms and traditions of communities and cultures. Zuckerman concludes:

> If you feel like you can change the world through elections, through our political system, through the institutions we have—that's fantastic, so long as you're engaged in making

change. If you mistrust those institutions and feel disempowered by them, . . . I challenge you to find ways you can make change through markets, through norms [unspoken rules], through becoming a fierce and engaged monitor of the institutions we have and that we'll build. The one stance that's not acceptable, as far as I'm concerned is that of disengagement, of deciding that you're powerless and remaining that way.[1]

Ultimately, Facing History & Ourselves hopes to create a society of thoughtful citizens who think deeply about the way they live—when they are riding the subway to work as much as when they hear about incidents of mass violence that demand a global response. Indeed, at the conclusion of the Facing History & Ourselves journey, we hope that students will believe that their choices do matter and will feel compelled to think carefully about the decisions they make, realizing that their choices will ultimately shape the world.

Notes to Teacher

1. Capitalizing on Student Energy and Creativity

Teachers must sometimes approach the end of a Facing History unit with flexibility and creativity, as students may be inspired to invest themselves in a class project, or series of projects, to make a difference in their school, community, country, or the world. While this lesson is designed to provide students with some models and inspiration for the various ways in which they might "choose to participate" in creating a more humane world, students may already feel galvanized to do something beyond the scope of this lesson's activities. We urge you to follow their passion and energy, to be willing to deviate from this lesson's activities, and to use the resources here (especially the "levers of power" framework) to help guide projects in the school, community, and beyond that are conceived, created, and led by your students. If such energy does not emerge from the class, you cannot force it, and it does not mean that you have failed to produce the desired outcome. Every class is different, and the effects of the learning and growth students experienced in this unit may not reveal themselves until some time has passed, perhaps even when the students are adults.

2. Choosing and Assigning Resources

A variety of different resources will work with activities in this lesson. Feel free to browse additional readings Chapter 12 of *Holocaust and Human Behavior* and use different readings for the third activity listed below.

Also consider using resources from the Not In Our School project. Their website, www.niot.org/nios, hosts a variety of videos describing examples of student-led projects to address issues of bullying, hatred, and intolerance in their own schools and communities. These provide additional examples of participation that are tangible and directly relevant to students' lives.

---

1 Ethan Zuckerman, "Insurrectionist Civics in the Age of Mistrust," . . . *My heart's in Accra* (blog), entry posted October 19, 2015, accessed October 29, 2015, http://www.ethanzuckerman.com/blog/2015/10/19/insurrectionist-civics-in-the-age-of-mistrust/.

3. Previewing Vocabulary

The following are key vocabulary terms used in this lesson:

- Participation
- Strategy
- Levers of power

Add these words to your word wall, if you are using one for this unit, and provide necessary support to help students learn these words as you teach the lesson.

4. The Unit Assessment

If your students are writing the final essay assessment for this unit, after teaching this lesson, instruct them to finalize their evidence logs. For suggested activities and resources to help you guide your class through the remaining steps of the writing process, see Refining the Thesis and Finalizing Evidence Logs, as well as *Common Core Writing Prompts and Strategies: Holocaust and Human Behavior*.

Activities

1. Reflect on What It Means to Be an Upstander

Tell students that they have learned about a variety of choices and actions from history in this unit that we might categorize as "upstander behavior." To begin this lesson, ask them to review some of those examples and then respond to the following prompt:

> What examples of upstander behavior from this unit were most meaningful to you? Which provide models for how you might act as an upstander in your life today?

Ask students to share some of their examples, perhaps using the Wraparound strategy. As students name examples, emphasize the range of ways that an individual can act as an upstander—a range that includes both public and private acts, as well as extraordinary and mundane ones. Tell students that in this lesson, they will analyze a variety of contemporary examples of upstander behavior.

2. Introduce "Levers of Power"

Explain to students that they are going to think about what it takes to get involved in making their school, community, and country better, more humane places. Explain that one of the biggest barriers that individuals face in getting involved is that it is hard to know what actual steps to take. As legal scholar Martha Minow puts it: "Often times we see something that's unjust and we wonder, 'Where do I go? What do I do?'"

Now explain to students that they will look at a framework for planning what to do in order to respond to injustice and make positive changes in society.

Distribute the handout Analyzing Levers of Power. Spend a moment exploring the metaphor of the lever in the title. Ask students to define the meaning of the word *lever*, and then ask them to make an inference about what the phrase "levers of power" might mean. Tell students that in a literal sense, a lever is a tool that allows one to pick up or move something much heavier than could be lifted without it. In other words, a lever allows someone to use a small amount of force to have a big impact.

Briefly walk students through each category on the second side of the handout, which outlines the individuals, organizations, and technology platforms that can have this sort of amplifying effect at a societal level. By influencing or making use of these "levers," individuals might have a larger impact on their community or society.

Ask students to come up with examples of individuals or groups that belong to each category in order to make sure that everyone understands them.

3. Analyze Strategies for Making Change

Students will use the "levers of power" framework to analyze examples of individuals who "chose to participate."

In teams of two, assign students one of the following readings:

- What Difference Can a Word Make?
- Bullying at School
- The Voices of Millions
- Acknowledging the Past to Shape the Present
- Seeking a Strategy that Works
- Believing in Others

Alternatively, if time permits, you can preview each reading for students and have them select the reading that appeals to them the most from a table at the front of the classroom. (See the Notes to Teacher section for suggestions about customizing the readings for this activity.)

After they choose or are assigned their reading, pairs should read and answer the questions on the first side of the handout Analyzing Levers of Power.

In each row on the second side of the handout, students should write a sentence or two explaining how the individual(s) in the readings used the lever described in the heading. If such a lever was not used, students can write "N/A" in the row. If a "lever of power" was involved that is not listed on the handout, students should describe it at the bottom of the page.

4. Share "Levers of Power" Analyses

After students have completed their handouts, have them meet briefly with a classmate who worked with a different reading. When they meet, they should introduce the story they each read, describe the strategies that the people they read about used, and explain which levers of power were most useful to those people. Time permitting, ask students to change partners one or two more times so that they can learn about additional examples of choosing to participate.

Finally, lead a whole-group discussion in which you ask students to share their observations. Guide the discussion with the following questions:

- What patterns did you notice? Did certain "levers of power" seem to come up in more readings than others?
- Which of the strategies for change that you learned about seem most effective? Most difficult? Most creative?
- Which of the "levers of power" on the handout seem most accessible to you? Which seem most difficult to influence? Which are you struggling to understand?

4. Discuss the Persistent Need for Participation

End this lesson, and this unit, with a broader reflection on our responsibilities to participate together in the process of creating a more humane society. Share with students the reading Walking with the Wind.

Read aloud John Lewis's story, and then discuss its meaning with the class: What does Lewis suggest about the work of citizens in a democracy?

Finally, ask students to write a reflection in their journals in response to the following question: What does choosing to participate mean to you? In what ways might you participate in the communities around you?

Assessment

- Assign students to write a paragraph outlining an issue that they care about and a change they would like to bring about regarding that issue. The paragraph should describe specific actions they could take to try to help make that change happen. Their plans should also include at least two of the "levers" of power outlined in this lesson, and students should describe how the specific action they could take might make use of those levers to increase their impact.

- Collect students' reflections in response to the Walking with the Wind reading, in which they have interpreted the meaning of John Lewis's allegory and described what choosing to participate means to them. If you have established that journals are private in your classroom, ask students to write their reflections on a separate sheet of paper to turn in.

Extensions

1. Analyze the Role of the Internet in Civic Participation

Ask students to analyze the potential benefits and pitfalls of using the internet for civic participation. Pass out the reading "Online Civic Participation" and ask students to read through Danielle Allen's ten questions. Then lead a discussion using the following questions:

- What examples do you know about of people using the internet in their attempts to bring about change? How might they have answered Allen's questions?

- What do Allen's questions suggest about the potential opportunities and difficulties in using the internet to make positive change? Do you think these questions would be helpful even if one's plan of action does not involve the internet?

2. Explore a Community Response to Bigotry

The reading "Not in Our Town" tells the story of how the town of Billings, Montana, responded to intolerance in their community. Analyzing this story can provide students with additional insight and inspiration for how to work together to create a more humane and democratic society. Consider sharing the reading with students, discussing the connection questions that follow, and using the "levers of power" framework to think about the strategy used by the residents of Billings to address the incidents of hate in their community.

Visit **facinghistory.org/thhb** to access these additional resources.

Handout

Analyzing Levers of Power

Reading name: _____

1. What change did the individual(s) in this reading want to make?

2. What strategies did the individual(s) use in order to make the change happen?

3. Which powerful people or organizations ("levers of power") did the individual(s) attempt to influence? How?

4. Which strategies led to the most success? Which failed?

Lever of Power	Strategy
Government (National, State, Local)	
Nonprofit Organizations/Charities	
Industry/Commercial Organizations	
Professional Media	
Social Media/Internet	
Schools and Education	
Influential Individuals (Authors, Lecturers, etc.)	

 Reading

What Difference Can a Word Make?

What encourages people to act on behalf of others? Do words have the power to influence the choices people make?

Raphael Lemkin witnessed a "crime without a name" in the early twentieth century and believed that giving that crime a name, *genocide,* was an essential step toward preventing it from occurring again in the future. In 2014, two New Jersey high-school students began a campaign to promote a word, *upstander,* that gave a name to a behavior that is crucial for building stronger communities and a more humane world. The students, Monica Mahal and Sarah Decker, explain:

> Students can easily recognize the bully, the "bad guy," the one throwing the punches . . . and most can point out the bystanders, the individuals in the shadows, watching and doing nothing . . . so who are the upstanders?
>
> An upstander is an individual who sees wrong and acts, and the most important part is that anyone can become one. Many . . . call the act of standing up "positive bystander intervention," but this misses the point. A person who takes a stand against an act of injustice or intolerance is not a "positive bystander," they are an UPstander. The word itself has the ability to empower students to make an active change in their schools, in an effort to build communities that support difference and unify against intolerance.
>
> The concept of an upstander is critical to the well-being of our society. During bullying prevention movements in our school, the term upstander was used on a casual basis. While we were typing up a speech, huddled in a coffee shop on a cold winter day, the word upstander continued to appear on the screen with the distinct red squiggly line beneath it. The message was clear: there is an error.
>
> We both double checked our spelling, still to no avail of eliminating the spell check notification. At that moment we realized that this groundbreaking term, one that has inspired our own local community to eschew intolerance, is technically not an official English word. Since then, we have been determined to give upstander its deserved spot in the dictionary.
>
> Getting a word in the dictionary involves two key steps: increasing its usage and proving its prevalence in publications. The term upstander is used in diplomacy, particularly by UN Ambassador Samantha Power; in non-profit organizations, such as Facing History & Ourselves; and especially in tolerance movements. We seek to form a united front to bring awareness of this cause to the Oxford and Webster dictionaries. To do so, we have created a Change.org petition to gather support for the upstander movement. . . .
>
> Each one of us has the power and courage to rise as upstanders, to stand up against injustice. To change our communities, our countries, and even our world. Defining the term up-

stander will add legitimacy to this role, and serve as a concept that our society should strive to embrace. Together as upstanders, we can change the course of human history towards a future of mindful, active global citizens.[1]

Mahal and Decker's petition gathered hundreds of signatures online, and their campaign caught the attention of several New Jersey lawmakers. In June 2015, the New Jersey legislature approved a resolution that declared the state's support for the campaign to include *upstander* in both the *Oxford* and the *Merriam-Webster* dictionaries. Soon the dictionary publishers responded in a blog post:

> Oxford University Press frequently receives requests from members of the public to add a particular word to our dictionaries, but an official legislative resolution supporting a word's inclusion may be unprecedented. Nonetheless, that is what happened on June 29, 2015, when the New Jersey State Senate approved a resolution "urging Merriam-Webster, Inc. and the Oxford University Press to include the word *upstander* in their dictionaries." The resolution was the culmination of a years-long effort which arose from an anti-bullying campaign by New Jersey high school students . . .
>
> The New Jersey Senate resolution traces this usage to Samantha Power, current US Ambassador to the United Nations and author of the book *A Problem from Hell: America & the Age of Genocide*, which won the Pulitzer Prize in 2003. In discussing the topic of her book, Power used the term *upstander* to describe individuals who spoke out against genocide, like Henry Morgenthau, the American ambassador to the Ottoman Empire during the Armenian genocide, and Raphael Lemkin, who coined the term *genocide* after World War II. It wasn't long before this strand of meaning was adopted by others and extended from the specific context of genocide to those who stand up for others in the face of any type of prejudice or injustice, including bullying in schools. In 2004, for example, a Holocaust survivor named Lisl Bogart used the term in a presentation to Florida schoolchildren about her experiences during the war:
>
> "I want to ask you today to be upstanders and not bystanders. When you see another student being picked on for being different, stand up for him. When you hear a student being called names, stand up for her. Don't be a silent bystander. Be an upstander." (2004 Palm Beach Post 19 December)[2]

The Oxford University Press added *upstander* to its list of words for potential inclusion in February 2014 and began to monitor how frequently the word was used in publications and public speeches. In December 2016, *upstander* was added to the *Oxford English Dictionary* as a result of the campaign begun by Mahal and Decker.

---

1 Sarah Decker and Monica Mahal, "Define Upstander," *Not in Our Town* blog, entry posted October 22, 2014, accessed October 16, 2015, https://www.niot.org/blog/define-upstander.

2 Oxford Dictionaries, "Legislation meets lexicography: the campaign for dictionary recognition of the word 'upstander,'" *OxfordWords* (blog), entry posted July 24, 2015, accessed October 16, 2015, http://blog.oxforddictionaries.com/2015/07/legislation-lexicography-campaign-upstander/.

Reading

Bullying at School

A bullying incident in school is often the first time a teenager is confronted with the decision of whether to be an upstander or a bystander. In a world full of injustice, suffering, and other social problems, the choice to participate can actually originate very close to home.

The following stories highlight the power of students to make positive change by taking seemingly small actions in response to bullying in their own school communities.

In Canada, two students responded this way when a classmate was taunted because of what he wore:

> Two Nova Scotia students are being praised across North America for the way they turned the tide against the bullies who picked on a fellow student for wearing pink.
>
> The victim — a Grade 9 boy at Central Kings Rural High School in the small community of Cambridge — wore a pink polo shirt on his first day of school.
>
> Bullies harassed the boy, called him a homosexual for wearing pink and threatened to beat him up, students said.
>
> Two Grade 12 students — David Shepherd and Travis Price — heard the news and decided to take action.
>
> "I just figured enough was enough," said Shepherd.
>
> They went to a nearby discount store and bought 50 pink shirts, including tank tops, to wear to school the next day.
>
> Then the two went online to e-mail classmates to get them on board with their anti-bullying cause that they dubbed a "sea of pink."
>
> But a tsunami of support poured in the next day.
>
> Not only were dozens of students outfitted with the discount tees, but hundreds of students showed up wearing their own pink clothes, some head-to-toe.
>
> When the bullied student, who has never been identified, walked into school to see his fellow students decked out in pink, some of his classmates said it was a powerful moment. He may have even blushed a little.
>
> "Definitely it looked like there was a big weight lifted off his shoulders. He went from looking right depressed to being as happy as can be," said Shepherd.
>
> And there's been nary a peep from the bullies since, which Shepherd says just goes to show what a little activism will do.

"If you can get more people against them . . . to show that we're not going to put up with it and support each other, then they're not as big as a group as they think they are," he says.[1]

At Orange High School in Pepper Pike, Ohio, students responded in a different way when they witnessed bullying in their school. They began by trying to learn more about where bullying was happening. After surveying classmates about where they had witnessed bullying, students created maps that showed where bullying incidents commonly took place. "Bully hotspots" included the cafeteria, media lab, and locker rooms.

Explaining the motivation for the project, one student said, "We wanted to spread awareness because people need to know what bullying is. People need to know that it exists in our school. I think addressing it and defining it and spreading awareness that it exists is the first step in preventing and combating it."[2]

Because some of the acts of bullying had been rather subtle, some students either did not recognize them or felt unsure about naming them as bullying. To address this problem, student leaders created a "flash freeze" demonstration to dramatize what bullying looks like so that other students could recognize it and call it out more easily. The demonstration showed students frozen in mid-action, portraying an incident of bullying. Other students in the demonstration would then name the actions, using words like *physical*, *verbal*, *exclusion*, and *cyber-bullying*. The map of bullying "hotspots" and the demonstrations opened up a larger conversation about how to create a safer school and made it more difficult for some students to ignore bullying when they saw it happening.

One student talked about how the project affected his future choices:

> I got made fun of for my name because it didn't sound American, so I was really quiet. I never really talked in school 'cause I was scared of being made fun of. And when you don't talk, you don't make friends. It's a chain reaction. It just gets worse and worse. You lose your confidence. You don't want to speak to anyone. So, I guess doing this project really helps. Whenever I see someone getting bullied, I step in. No matter what age they are, if I know them or not, it doesn't matter. Because I just think about how much I would have loved for someone to step in when I was getting bullied.[3]

---

1 "Bullied student tickled pink by schoolmates' T-shirt campaign," *CBC News Canada,* last modified September 18, 2007, accessed July 12, 2016, http://www.cbc.ca/news/canada/bullied-student-tickled-pink-by-schoolmates-t-shirt-campaign-1.682221.

2 Transcribed from "Students Map Bully Zones to Create a Safer School" (video), *Not in Our Town* website, accessed July 12, 2016, https://www.niot.org/nios-video/students-map-bully-zones-create-safer-school.

3 Transcribed from "Students Map Bully Zones to Create a Safer School" (video), *Not in Our Town* website.

Reading

The Voices of Millions

On March 25, 2013, the Human Rights Campaign (HRC)—an organization that supports lesbian, gay, bisexual, and transgender rights—urged people to change their Facebook profile pictures to a pink-on-red equals sign to show support for marriage equality. That week, the Supreme Court of the United States was debating a case that involved gay marriage. One day later, hundreds of thousands of people had changed their profile pictures to the HRC symbol.

Critics of the campaign worried that too many of those who changed their profile pictures felt satisfied that by taking this relatively easy action, they had "done their part" to support marriage equality. Some critics of online activism have coined terms like "hashtag activism" and "slacktivism" to describe efforts such as the HRC profile-picture campaign that require little real participation. Scott Gilmore, a former Canadian diplomat, writes:

> A slacktivist is someone who believes it is more important to be seen to help than to actually help. She will wear a wristband to demonstrate support, sign a petition to add her voice, share a video to spread the message, even pour a bucket of ice over her head. The one thing slacktivists don't do is help by, for example, giving money or time to those who are truly making the world a better place . . .[1]

Many experts disagree with the skeptics. They argue that the collective voices of groups of internet users can make a real difference. Discussing the HRC campaign, Matt Stempeck, a researcher at the MIT Center for Civic Media, writes:

> No one taking these actions is expecting a direct response from the Supreme Court. . . . Yet this action, taken by many, can matter. We know that support for gay marriage is linked with how likely it is we know someone who is openly gay. And we know that people care deeply about societal norms [social standards]. Ever-increasing support for gay equality, generated at the interpersonal level, is only strengthened by a mass outpouring of support on social networks. . . .[2]

In 2014, another online campaign suggested that the collective voice of a group of social media users can influence not just individual attitudes but also the behavior of institutions, such as the print and broadcast media. After an African American teenager was shot to death by a police officer in Ferguson, Missouri, in summer 2014, thousands of people used Twitter to protest the photograph of the teenager, taken from his Facebook page, that was published by many television networks, newspapers, and websites. Journalist James Poniewozik analyzed the online protest:

---

1 Scott Gilmore, "The problem with #slacktivism," *Maclean's*, last modified November 11, 2014, accessed September 2, 2015, http://www.macleans.ca/society/the-real-problem-with-slacktivism/.

2 J. Nathan Matias, Matt Stempeck, and Molly Sauter, "Green vs. Pink: Change Your Picture, Change the World," MIT Center for Civic Media, blog entry, posted March 28, 2013, accessed July 26, 2016, https://civic.mit.edu/blog/natematias/green-vs-pink-change-your-picture-change-the-world.

On August 10, 2014, teenager Tyler Atkins posted these images on Twitter accompanied by the following tweet: "#IfTheyGunnedMeDown which picture would they use."

The injury, a deadly one, came first. Unarmed 18-year-old Michael Brown was shot to death by police in Ferguson, Mo. Then came the insult: many news accounts used a photo of Brown that showed him, unsmiling, gesturing at the camera in a way that led to unsubstantiated claims that he was "flashing gang signs" . . .

So as people protested in the streets of Ferguson, a meta-protest began on social media. Twitter users, especially African Americans, began a meta-protest, posting pairs of photos with the hashtag #IfTheyGunnedMeDown: a young man in a military dress uniform, say, and the same poster flipping off the camera. If I got shot down, each post asked, which version of me would the media show you?

The term "hashtag activism" has become a kind of putdown lately, with the connotation that it's substituting gestures for action, as if getting something trending is a substitute for actually going out and engaging with the world . . .

But #IfTheyGunnedMeDown was a simple, ingenious DIY [do-it-yourself] form of media criticism: direct, powerful, and meaningful on many levels. It made the blunt point that every time a media outlet chooses a picture of someone like Brown, it makes a statement. It created identification: so many ordinary people—students, servicemen and women, community volunteers—could be made to look like a public menace with one photo dropped in a particular context. And it made a particular racial point: that it's so much easier, given our culture's racial baggage, for a teenager of color to be made to look like a "thug" than [a] white teen showing off for a camera the exact same way.

#IfTheyGunnedMeDown is not going to stop anyone from being gunned down, but it most likely lodged in the memory of editors and producers who make judgments every day. Sure, many of them are already aware of the power of image choices, but #IfTheyGunnedMeDown chose its own images to make a powerful statement—one that people are likely to remember the next time "if" becomes "when."[3]

---

3 James Poniewozik, "#IfTheyGunnedMeDown and What Hashtag Activism Does Right," TIMEonline, last modified August 11, 2014, accessed September 2, 2015, http://time.com/3101550/iftheygunnedmedown-hashtag-activism-michael-brown-twitter/.

 Reading

Acknowledging the Past to Shape the Present

How we think about the past can play a powerful role in shaping the present. In 2013, Bryan Stevenson, a lawyer who started the Equal Justice Initiative to challenge bias and inequity in the US justice system, launched a campaign to memorialize historical sites of racist violence across the American South. He began leading a project to identify, record, and mark places where lynchings occurred, both to accurately report the number of people killed and also to teach the public about the roots of twenty-first-century racial injustice. Between 1877 and 1950, at least 3,950 African Americans were lynched (executed by a mob, without a trial, usually by hanging) after being accused of "crimes" such as knocking on a white woman's door, wearing an army uniform in public after World War II, or bumping into a white girl while running for a train.

Often, Stevenson says, the hangings became public carnivals designed to instill fear. He calls them incidents of domestic terrorism, purposefully used to enforce racial subordination and segregation.[1] "We cannot heal the deep wounds inflicted during the era of racial terrorism until we tell the truth about it," writes Stevenson. "The geographic, political, economic, and social consequences of decades of terror lynchings can still be seen in many communities today and the damage created by lynching needs to be confronted and discussed. Only then can we meaningfully address the contemporary problems that are lynching's legacy."[2]

Students at Overton High School in Memphis, Tennessee, came to a similar conclusion in 2016 after learning about the lynching of Ell Persons. Zoey Parker, a senior, encountered the Persons case while doing a research assignment and shared the story with her classmates. Persons was an African American woodcutter who was burned alive in 1917 after being accused of murder. About 5,000 people from the Memphis community came to watch the event, which was prominently covered by the local newspaper, and gruesome postcards were made showing photos of his head; his murderers had decapitated his body after they had burned him to death.

When Parker's teacher, Dr. Marilyn Taylor, informed her students that the lynching had occurred close to their school, near a present-day drive-in movie theater, students were stunned that something so brutal could have taken place in their own backyard. They were also shocked to realize that an incident that had been widely known about when it happened was almost completely lost to memory a century later. Dr. Taylor reflected, "They have

---

[1] John M. Glionna, "Civil rights lawyer seeks to commemorate another side of Southern heritage: Lynchings," *Los Angeles Times*, July 5, 2015, accessed July 13, 2016, http://www.latimes.com/nation/la-na-alabama-lynchings-20150705-story.html.

[2] "Lynching in America: Confronting the Legacy of Racial Terror," Equal Justice Initiative website, accessed July 13, 2016, http://eji.org/reports/lynching-in-america.

all been to this drive-in. They had a multitude of questions the following day so we put our scheduled lesson aside and they began their investigation."[3]

The students felt they needed to do more than investigate the history, so Dr. Taylor asked them, "What are we going to do about it?"[4]

They decided to turn research into action and form a nonprofit organization called Students Uniting Memphis. This group launched a project to create a memorial garden at the site of Ell Persons's lynching, which in 2016 contained an abandoned bridge support surrounded by river overflow and dense foliage. Students also began to educate their community about Ell Persons. They reached out to a nearby high school where, in 1917, students had been released from classes to attend Persons's lynching, and they partnered with another nonprofit, The Lynching Sites Project of Memphis, which was formed after its founders heard Bryan Stevenson speak about the importance of facing the past.

In 2016, 99 years after Persons's death, more than 100 people gathered at the site of his lynching for an interfaith prayer service. The Lynching Sites Project, Students Uniting Memphis, the Memphis chapter of the NAACP—which was formed in 1917 in response to the Persons lynching—and other student groups then began working together to involve 5,000 people in a commemoration of the 100th anniversary of the lynching in 2017. Students from a Facing History & Ourselves student leadership group based in Memphis were among those who became involved.

"Young people today have to take action in order for history not to repeat itself," said Zoey Parker, the student who first researched Persons's case for Dr. Taylor's class. "We have to be mindful enough to understand we cannot continue to make the same mistakes as those before us."[5]

---

[3] Quoted in Marti Tippens Murphy, "Students Memorialize a Past Tragedy to Create a More Hopeful Future," *Facing Today* (Facing History & Ourselves blog), entry posted May 23, 2016, http://facingtoday.facinghistory.org/students-memorialize-a-past-tragedy-to-create-a-more-hopeful-future.

[4] Quoted in Murphy, "Students Memorialize a Past Tragedy to Create a More Hopeful Future."

[5] Quoted in Murphy, "Students Memorialize a Past Tragedy to Create a More Hopeful Future."

 Reading

Seeking a Strategy that Works

Khalida Brohi was born in a rural village in Pakistan. When she was a young girl, her father and her 14-year-old mother decided to leave their rural village and move to a town where their children could attend school. Even as Brohi attended school in larger Pakistani towns and cities, her father kept a house in their rural homeland in order to keep the family connected to their roots. As she grew older, Brohi realized that she had opportunities denied to peers in her rural homeland. Brohi was troubled and began to look for ways to improve the lives of women and girls in Pakistan—a journey that has had many twists and turns. In a talk presented at a 2014 TED conference, she said,

> I come from an indigenous tribe in the mountains of Balochistan called Brahui. Brahui, or Brohi, means mountain dweller, and it is also my language. Thanks to my father's very strict rules about connecting to our customs, I had to live a beautiful life of songs, cultures, traditions, stories, mountains, and a lot of sheep. But then, living in two extremes between the traditions of my culture, of my village, and then modern education in my school wasn't easy. I was aware that I was the only girl who got to have such freedom, and I was guilty of it. While going to school in Karachi and Hyderabad, a lot of my cousins and childhood friends were getting married off, some to older men, some in exchange, some even as second wives. I got to see the beautiful tradition and its magic fade in front of me when I saw that the birth of a girl child was celebrated with sadness, when women were told to have patience as their main virtue.

These realizations pained Brohi, but she was first moved to act when she learned that a friend had been the victim of an "honor killing." Brohi explains: "Honor killing is a custom where men and women are suspected of having relationships before or outside of the marriage, and they're killed by their family for it. Usually the killer is the brother or father or the uncle in the family." Those who practice honor killing believe that when a woman has a forbidden relationship with a man, she brings shame to her family, and the family's honor can be restored only by killing her. The United Nations believes that there are at least 1,000 such "honor" murders in Pakistan every year, but many more probably go unreported.

After her friend's death, Brohi started trying to raise awareness about the practice of honor killing. When her family got a computer, Brohi found a way to amplify her voice. As one of eight children, she could use the computer for only a few minutes a day, but it opened up a new world for her. She created an online campaign called the WAKE UP Campaign against Honor Killing and connected with supporters in Britain, the United States, and Australia. Members of the news media paid attention to Brohi's movement, and she organized rallies and strikes to speak out for women's rights. But she soon learned that people in her community in Balochistan were insulted by her efforts to challenge centuries-old customs. Her father received anonymous letters, the family's car was stoned, and Brohi received a death threat. She eventually stayed in Karachi for her safety, and she began to think differently about how to protect and empower women in her homeland. In her talk, she went on to explain:

Back in Karachi, as an 18-year-old, I thought this was the biggest failure of my entire life. I was devastated. As a teenager, I was blaming myself for everything that happened. And it turns out, when we started reflecting, we did realize that it was actually me and my team's fault.

There were two big reasons why our campaign had failed big time. One of those, the first reason, is we were standing against core values of people. We were saying no to something that was very important to them, challenging their code of honor, and hurting them deeply in the process. And number two, which was very important for me to learn . . . was that we were not including the true heroes who should be fighting for themselves. The women in the villages had no idea we were fighting for them in the streets. Every time I would go back, I would find my cousins and friends with scarves on their faces, and I would ask, "What happened?" And they'd be like, "Our husbands beat us." But we are working in the streets for you! We are changing the policies. How is that not impacting their life?

. . . The policies of a country do not necessarily always affect the tribal and rural communities. It was devastating—like, oh, we can't actually do something about this? And we found out there's a huge gap when it comes to official policies and the real truth on the ground.

So this time, we were like, we are going to do something different. We are going to use strategy, and we are going to go back and apologize. Yes, apologize. We went back to the communities and we said we are very ashamed of what we did. We are here to apologize, and in fact, we are here to make it up to you. How do we do that? We are going to promote three of your main cultures. We know that it's music, language, and embroidery.

Nobody believed us. Nobody wanted to work with us. It took a lot of convincing and discussions with these communities until they agreed that we are going to promote their language by making a booklet of their stories, fables and old tales in the tribe, and we would promote their music by making a CD of the songs from the tribe, and some drumbeating. And the third, which was my favorite, was we would promote their embroidery by making a center in the village where women would come every day to make embroidery . . .

So this was the model which actually came out—very amazing. Through embroidery we were promoting their traditions. We went into the village. We would mobilize the community. We would make a center inside where 30 women will come for six months to learn about value addition of traditional embroidery, enterprise development, life skills and basic education, and about their rights and how to say no to those customs and how to stand as leaders for themselves and the society. After six months, we would connect these women to loans and to markets where they can become local entrepreneurs in their communities.

We soon called this project Sughar. Sughar is a local word used in many, many languages in Pakistan. It means skilled and confident women. I truly believe, to create women leaders, there's only one thing you have to do: Just let them know that they have what it takes to be a leader. These women you see here, they have strong skills and potential to be leaders. All we had to do was remove the barriers that surrounded them, and that's what we decided to do.

But then while we were thinking everything was going well, once again everything was fantastic, we found our next setback: A lot of men started seeing the visible changes in their wife. She's speaking more, she's making decisions—oh my gosh, she's handling everything in the house. They stopped them from coming to the centers, and this time, we were like, okay, time for strategy two. We went to the fashion industry in Pakistan and decided to do research about what happens there. Turns out the fashion industry in Pakistan is very strong and growing day by day, but there is less contribution from the tribal areas and to the tribal areas, especially women.

So we decided to launch our first ever tribal women's very own fashion brand, which is now called Nomads. And so women started earning more, they started contributing more financially to the house, and men had to think again before saying no to them when they were coming to the centers.[1]

In 2013, Sughar began to build cement halls in Pakistani villages, with the help of the travel website TripAdvisor. They invite other nonprofit organizations to share the spaces for training and education.

---

[1] Khalida Brohi, "How I work to protect women from honor killings," speech presented at TEDGlobal 2014, October 2014, TED website, last modified 2014, accessed August 25, 2015, https://www.ted.com/talks/khalida_brohi_how_i_work_to_protect_women_from_honor_killings.

 Reading

Believing in Others

Jessica Jackley became interested in the problem of poverty as a young girl and went on to found Kiva, an organization that has helped millions of people all over the world by providing small but transformative loans to finance education, businesses, and farms. Jackley's journey to making a difference wasn't always easy, and she often felt powerless and discouraged. Changing how she thought about poor people was a crucial inspiration for her work with Kiva. In a 2010 TED conference talk, Jackley described how stories are the key element that sustains her work and moves others to become involved:

> The stories we tell about each other matter very much. The stories we tell ourselves about our own lives matter. And most of all, I think the way that we participate in each other's stories is of deep importance. I was six years old when I first heard stories about the poor. Now I didn't hear those stories from the poor themselves, I heard them from my Sunday school teacher . . . I remember learning that people who were poor needed something material—food, clothing, shelter—that they didn't have. And I also was taught, coupled with that, that it was my job—this classroom full of five- and six-year-old children—it was our job, apparently, to help. This is what Jesus asked of us. And then he said, "What you do for the least of these, you do for me." Now I was pretty psyched. I was very eager to be useful in the world—I think we all have that feeling. And also, it was kind of interesting that God needed help. That was news to me, and it felt like it was a very important thing to get to participate in.[1]

But Jackley said that as she grew older, she became discouraged by the fact that no matter how hard she worked, the problem of poverty persisted. She continued:

> I felt like I had been just given a homework assignment that I had to do, and I was excited to do, but no matter what I would do, I would fail. So I felt confused, a little bit frustrated and angry, like maybe I'd misunderstood something here. And I felt overwhelmed. And for the first time, I began to fear this group of people and to feel negative emotion towards a whole group of people. I imagined in my head, a kind of long line of individuals that were never going away, that would always be with us. They were always going to ask me to help them and give them things, which I was excited to do, but I didn't know how it was going to work. And I didn't know what would happen when I ran out of things to give, especially if the problem was never going away. In the years following, the other stories I heard about the poor growing up were no more positive. For example, I saw pictures and images frequently of sadness and suffering. I heard about things that were going wrong in the lives of the poor. I heard about disease, I heard about war—they always seemed to be kind of related. And in general, I got this sort of idea that the poor in the world lived lives that were wrought with suffering and sadness, devastation, hopelessness.

---

1 Jessica Jackley, "Poverty, money — and love," speech presented at TEDGlobal 2010, July 2010, TED website, accessed August 25, 2015, https://www.ted.com/talks/jessica_jackley_poverty_money_and_love.

> And after a while . . . I started to feel bad every time I heard about them. I started to feel guilty for my own relative wealth, because I wasn't doing more, apparently, to make things better. And I even felt a sense of shame because of that. And so naturally, I started to distance myself. I stopped listening to their stories quite as closely as I had before. And I stopped expecting things to really change. Now I still gave—on the outside it looked like I was still quite involved. I gave of my time and my money . . . I gave when I was cornered, when it was difficult to avoid and I gave, in general, when the negative emotions built up enough that I gave to relieve my own suffering, not someone else's . . .[2]

Jackley's perspective changed, however, when she heard Dr. Muhammad Yunus speak. Yunus won the 2006 Nobel Peace Prize for his pioneering work in microfinance. Through his organization, the Grameen Bank, Yunus provided "microloans" to the poor. A microloan is a very small, short-term loan that helps provide a poor person with just what they need to make a business or farm profitable and self-sufficient. But it wasn't just hearing about how microfinance works that changed Jackley's perspective. She went on to explain:

> [M]ore importantly, [Yunus] told stories about the poor that were different than any stories I had heard before. In fact, for those individuals he talked about, [being] poor was sort of a side note. He was talking about strong, smart, hardworking entrepreneurs who woke up every day and were doing things to make their lives and their family's lives better. All they needed to do that more quickly and to do it better was a little bit of capital [money]. It was an amazing sort of insight for me.
>
> And I, in fact, was so deeply moved by this . . . that I actually quit my job a few weeks later, and I moved to East Africa to try to see for myself what this was about. For the first time, actually, in a long time I wanted to meet those individuals, I wanted to meet these entrepreneurs, and see for myself what their lives were actually about. So I spent three months in Kenya, Uganda and Tanzania interviewing entrepreneurs that had received 100 dollars to start or grow a business. And in fact, through those interactions, for the first time, I was starting to get to be friends with some of those people in that big amorphous group out there that was supposed to be far away. I was starting to be friends and get to know their personal stories. And over and over again, as I interviewed them and spent my days with them, I did hear stories of life change . . .
>
> So I would hear from goat herders who had used that money that they had received to buy a few more goats. Their business trajectory would change. They would make a little bit more money; their standard of living would shift and would get better. And they would make really interesting little adjustments in their lives, like they would start to send their children to school. They might be able to buy mosquito nets. Maybe they could afford a lock for the door and feel secure. Maybe it was just that they could put sugar in their tea and offer that to me when I came as their guest and that made them feel proud. But there were these beautiful details, even if I talked to 20 goat herders in a row, and some days that's what happened—these beautiful details of life change that were meaningful to them. That was another thing that really touched me. It was really humbling to see for the first time, to really understand that even if I could have taken a magic wand and fixed everything, I probably would have gotten a lot wrong. Because the best way for people to change their

2 Jackley, "Poverty, money — and love."

lives is for them to have control and to do that in a way that they believe is best for them. So I saw that and it was very humbling.[3]

Jackley decided she wanted to help the people she met in East Africa get the loans they needed. She took a crash course in business and finance. She returned to Uganda with a digital camera, took pictures of seven of her friends there who wanted loans, posted their stories on a website, and asked friends and family to help. She explains: "The money came in basically overnight. We sent it over to Uganda. And over the next six months, a beautiful thing happened; the entrepreneurs received the money, they were paid, and their businesses, in fact, grew, and they were able to support themselves and change the trajectory of their lives."

After their initial success, Jackley and a partner expanded the website. Potential donors would now visit the site, read the stories of individuals in need of microloans, and choose the people whose projects they would like to support with their donation. In less than five years, the online platform, called Kiva, was arranging more than $150 million in loans each year to entrepreneurs, farmers, and students in need from over 200 countries. Jackley concluded:

> And while those numbers and those statistics are really fun to talk about and they're interesting, to me, Kiva's really about stories. It's about retelling the story of the poor, and it's about giving ourselves an opportunity to engage that validates their dignity, validates a partnership relationship, not a relationship that's based on the traditional sort of donor-beneficiary weirdness that can happen. But instead a relationship that can promote respect and hope and this optimism that together we can move forward. So what I hope is that, not only can the money keep flowing forth through Kiva—that's a very positive and meaningful thing—but I hope Kiva can blur those lines, like I said, between the traditional rich and poor categories that we're taught to see in the world, this false dichotomy of us and them, have and have not. I hope that Kiva can blur those lines. Because as that happens, I think we can feel free to interact in a way that's more open, more just and more creative, to engage with each other and to help each other . . .
>
> For me, the best way to be inspired is to stop and to listen to someone else's story . . . Whenever I do that, guaranteed, I am inspired . . . And I believe more and more every time I listen in that person's potential to do great things in the world and in my own potential to maybe help. . . . Forget the tools, forget the moving around of resources—that stuff's easy. Believing in each other, really being sure when push comes to shove that each one of us can do amazing things in the world, that is what can make our stories into love stories and our collective story into one that continually perpetuates hope and good things for all of us. So that, this belief in each other, knowing that without a doubt and practicing that every day in whatever you do, that's what I believe will change the world and make tomorrow better than today.[4]

---

3 Jackley, "Poverty, money — and love."

4 Jackley, "Poverty, money — and love."

 Reading

Walking with the Wind

As a young student, John Lewis worked with Dr. Martin Luther King Jr. and became a key leader of the civil rights movement in the United States. He later became a US congressman and a prominent voice for human rights and justice around the world. In the prologue to his memoir, Lewis tells a story from his childhood to describe his vision of how we can face profound challenges and make a better world.

> [A]bout fifteen of us children were outside my aunt Seneva's house, playing in her dirt yard. The sky began clouding over, the wind started picking up, lightning flashed far off in the distance, and suddenly I wasn't thinking about playing anymore; I was terrified . . .
>
> Aunt Seneva was the only adult around, and as the sky blackened and the wind grew stronger, she herded us all inside.
>
> Her house was not the biggest place around, and it seemed even smaller with so many children squeezed inside. Small and surprisingly quiet. All of the shouting and laughter that had been going on earlier, outside, had stopped. The wind was howling now, and the house was starting to shake. We were scared. Even Aunt Seneva was scared.
>
> And then it got worse. Now the house was beginning to sway. The wood plank flooring beneath us began to bend. And then, a corner of the room started lifting up.
>
> I couldn't believe what I was seeing. None of us could. This storm was actually pulling the house toward the sky. With us inside it.
>
> That was when Aunt Seneva told us to clasp hands. Line up and hold hands, she said, and we did as we were told. Then she had us walk as a group toward the corner of the room that was rising. From the kitchen to the front of the house we walked, the wind screaming outside, sheets of rain beating on the tin roof. Then we walked back in the other direction, as another end of the house began to lift.
>
> And so it went, back and forth, fifteen children walking with the wind, holding that trembling house down with the weight of our small bodies. More than half a century has passed since that day, and it has struck me more than once over those many years that our society is not unlike the children in that house, rocked again and again by the winds of one storm or another, the walls around us seeming at times as if they might fly apart.
>
> It seemed that way in the 1960s, at the height of the civil rights movement, when America itself felt as if it might burst at the seams—so much tension, so many storms. But the people of conscience never left the house. They never ran away. They stayed, they came together and they did the best they could, clasping hands and moving toward the corner of the house that was the weakest.
>
> And then another corner would lift, and we would go there.
>
> And eventually, inevitably, the storm would settle, and the house would still stand.

But we knew another storm would come, and we would have to do it all over again.

And we did.

And we still do, all of us. You and I.

Children holding hands, walking with the wind. . . .[1]

---

[1] John Lewis, *Walking with the Wind: A Memoir of the Movement* (New York: Simon & Schuster, 1998), xvi–xvii.

STEP 6

Refining the Thesis and Finalizing Evidence Logs

After finishing this unit, students will need time to complete their evidence logs, develop and refine their thesis statements, organize their evidence into an outline, and draft, revise, and edit their essays. The suggested activities that are presented below will help your students think about the unit as a whole as they answer the writing prompt, as well as start to prepare them to write a strong thesis statement for their essay. For ideas and resources for teaching the remaining steps of the writing process from outlining to publishing, we encourage you to consult the *Common Core Writing Prompts and Strategies* supplement and the online "Teaching Strategies" collection for activities and graphic organizers to support your teaching.

Suggested Activities

Visit **facinghistory.org/thhb** to access all materials referenced in these activities.

1. **Rapid Writing Journal Reflection**

    Now that students have completed all of the lessons for this unit, ask them to complete a Rapid Writing entry in response to the writing prompt:

    > What does learning about the choices people made during the Weimar Republic, the rise of the Nazi Party, and the Holocaust teach us about the power and impact of our choices today?

    Have students debrief their writing with a partner, in a small group, or in a class discussion.

2. **Evidence Logs and Fishbowl Discussion**

    Students should add to their evidence logs events any information from Lessons 22 and 23 that helps them answer the essay question.

    Now that students have gathered their evidence and written numerous journal entries, use the Fishbowl strategy to discuss the following questions, and encourage students to pose their own unanswered questions about the unit and writing prompt:

    > Which choices made by individuals, groups, and nations in the history that you have learned about so far in this unit seemed most significant? How do those choices seem similar to or different from the important choices facing people in the world today?

    How does the evidence you gathered today confirm or challenge your thinking about the writing prompt?

What have you learned over the course of this unit about the relationship between choices people made in the past and the power and impact of your choices today? Which text (reading, video, image), lesson, or activity was most significant in helping your understand this relationship?

3. Thesis Sorting

Depending on what sort of instruction and practice your students have had with thesis statements, you may want to give them an opportunity to practice evaluating the strengths and weaknesses of sample thesis statements before refining their own. You can learn more through Strategy 17: Thesis Sorting in the Common Core Writing Prompts and Strategies supplement.

4. Final Reflection

On exit tickets, ask students to respond to the writing prompt in a statement that takes a clear stance, addresses all elements of the prompt, and can be defended with evidence from the unit.

You can give students written or oral feedback on their working thesis statements in the next lesson and use the information from the exit tickets to determine what skills you may need to (re)teach so that students are equipped to write strong thesis statements.